DESIGNING APPAREL THROUGH THE FLAT PATTERN

OTHER BOOKS BY THE AUTHORS

How to Draft Basic Patterns includes:
- Measurement Charts, Sizes 5 to 15, 6 to 18
- How to Take Body Measurements
- Drafting of Basic Slopers: waist, sleeve,
     skirts, pants, long torso with and without darts
- Converting Dress Slopers into Coat and Suit Slopers
- Designer's Neckline Curve

**New Fashion Areas for Designing Apparel through the
Flat Pattern** includes:
- Oriental Kimonos
- Caftans
- Capes, Hoods
- Shifts
- Cowls, Twists
- Jumpsuits
- Pleats
- Garment Interpretations

DESIGNING APPAREL THROUGH THE FLAT PATTERN

Revised Fifth Edition

Ernestine Kopp, Professor Emeritus of Apparel Design
Former Chairman: Apparel Design Department
Fashion Institute of Technology

Vittorina Rolfo, Professor Emeritus of Apparel Design
Former Chairman: Apparel Design Department
Fashion Institute of Technology

Beatrice Zelin, Professor Emeritus of Apparel Design
Former Assistant Director of Placement
Fashion Institute of Technology

Lee Gross
Former Instructor: Art Department
Fashion Institute of Technology

FAIRCHILD PUBLICATIONS, NEW YORK

Barbara Scholey, book designer
Jessica Zalkind and Elaine Golt Gongora,
sketch illustrators

FOREWORD

In the early 1960's three members of the faculty at the Fashion Institute of Technology—Ernestine Kopp, Vittorina Rolfo and Beatrice Zelin—completed their first edition of *Designing Apparel through the Flat Pattern*. The authors at that time acknowledged their appreciation to the members of the faculty who contributed to the experimental development of the projects included in the book and gave particular thanks to the then President of the Fashion Institute of Technology, Dr. Lawrence L. Bethel, to Founder Dean Emeritus Rosalind Snyder and Technical Consultant and to Dean Emeritus Molly Slonin.

Now in 1981, a fifth edition of the publication is available. Updated procedures to prepare students in the use of the flat pattern as a means to develop original ideas effectively and efficiently are presented. Various approaches to make learning most meaningful and productive have been reevaluated and, after many years of experimentation, newer methods have been collated which achieve excellent results in the understanding of basic principles and their applications. The authors realize these are not the only approaches. However, they do recommend these methods as practical, scientific and accurate in translating ideas into outcomes within a limited period of time with professional results.

Having carried out experiments with beginners, more experienced designers and designers of stature, the authors present this fifth edition of *Designing Apparel through the Flat Pattern* with materials and instructions arranged to facilitate development. I know this edition will serve a valuable purpose for both students and professionals and I commend the authors for their continued efforts.

Shirley Goodman
Executive Director
Educational Foundation for
the Fashion Industries

PREFACE

The trend of the fashion industry is such that a rapid output of new designs is imperative. With the pressure for new lines, manufacturers are using a combination of draping and patternmaking rather than limiting themselves to one method of expression for their designs. Certain style features within a silhouette are better developed through draping, others through patternmaking. Patternmaking, however, offers the designer shortcuts in executing basic parts of a garment within a design, whether the design is original, copied, or mass produced.

The device which facilitates the rapid development of patterns is the *sloper.*

Manufacturers have their own set of slopers, developed from their own specific measurements or from a model form. Slopers must also be changed to conform to the fashion silhouette of the season. Thus, one may encounter a wide variety of basic slopers. The development of the patterns within *Designing Apparel through the Flat Pattern* is such that the principles and instructions may be applied to any variation.

Our objective is to instruct an individual in the use of the flat pattern as a means of developing original ideas effectively and efficiently. We present thoroughly the utilization of the three basic slopers — waist, sleeve and skirt — and some popular variations of these such as the kimono waist, raglan sleeve and pants. An employee in the garment industry using this book should avail himself of the firm's basic patterns. An individual using this book should draft slopers from measurements.

We suggest using the companion text, *How to Draft Basic Patterns,* for instructions on how to develop a scientific basic pattern. A sloper may also be developed through draping muslin on the model form and then converting the muslin pattern into a paper sloper. Miniature slopers in one-quarter scale have been included for experimental use. We suggest that you cut out these slopers and paste them onto a stiff piece of cardboard. It is, however, preferable to develop all problems on the full scale sloper. All results should be tested in muslin for line, proportion and fit before they are used for cutting and construction of garments.

This book attempts to assist individuals on all levels of accomplishment. From the student with no experience to designers who have had many years of experience. Each will select those areas and problems that can best serve his needs. It is advisable that all individuals, no matter how advanced, read this book in sequential order and study the illustrations to gain an awareness of the dependency of one pattern on another.

To understand fully the principles involved in developing slopers and patterns and to obtain accurate results, the tyro in the field must develop the problem, starting with the basic fundamentals of dart manipulation. The individual, depending on his background and ability, should select a sufficient number of applications to master the principle within each unit. A number of applications are provided for each project to supply variety and sufficient practice, if needed. Very few definite or specific measurements have been given. This has been done intentionally to allow for complete freedom of design.

The organization of the material in this book is aimed to promote a scientific approach in the utilization of the basic sloper. This revision includes a unit on basic information needed to develop slopers and patterns. The material covered in this unit, if carefully applied when developing any of the projects in this book, will result in the accurate and professional production of slopers and patterns. New subjects covered in this revised edition include vests, halters, facings, pockets and tabs. All measurements are given in metrics and imperial measurements. For your convenience a Metric Conversion Chart is also included.

We wish to acknowledge the many members of the faculty of the Fashion Institute of Technology who provided inspiration, encouragement and educational leadership in the formation of the first edition many years ago and particular thanks to the late Dr. Lawrence L. Bethel, former President of the Fashion Institute of Technology, Founder Dean Emeritus Rosalind Snyder and to the late Dean Emeritus Molly Slonin.

We wish to extend our gratitude to Professors Ann Cahill, Jeanne Price and Bernard Zamkoff from the Fashion Design Department at the Fashion Institute of Technology for their time and assistance in the formation and development of this revised edition.

1981

Ernestine Kopp
Vittorina Rolfo
Beatrice Zelin

CONTENTS

This unit covers the terminology, identification and proper usage of tools and basic principles applicable to the development of slopers and patterns regardless of size, shape or design. The material covered, if carefully applied to any of the projects in this text, will result in the accurate and professional production of slopers and patterns. It is advisable to study this unit before developing the projects in this text.

A sloper is the popular term used for the basic waist, skirt and sleeve patterns from which all designs are developed in flat patternmaking. Slopers are also called master patterns, block patterns or foundation patterns. They are developed usually without seams, since seam allowances can sometimes interfere with the proportioning and developing of design variations.

Slopers may also be used as patterns. If so, seam allowances must be added.

A pattern represents a piece of a garment developed in sections. All patterns within their shapes include seam and hem allowances, grainline, size, notches, placement for buttons, buttonholes, pockets, etc.

The rules and principles covered and illustrated in this unit and the patterns developed in this text have been worked from various dress slopers. However, the rules and principles and projects may be applied to coat and suit designs as illustrated by some of the sketches. To develop patterns for coats and suits or sub-slopers substitute the basic coat or suit sloper for the dress sloper. Refer to *How to Draft Basic Patterns.*

PROCEDURES USED IN THE DEVELOPMENT OF SLOPERS & PATTERNS

BALANCING

Balancing is the process of matching the two sides of a seam for position of grainline, length of seam and amount of flare or fullness introduced.

CLOSE & CUP

Close and cup is a term used when trueing darts. It means to crease one dartline and match creased fold to opposite dartline and pin dart closed. Fold pattern under at apex or dart point and true seamline crossing dart.

COPY

A thin patternpaper is placed over sections of draft, pinned to prevent shifting and copied using proper tools, lines, crossmarks, etc.

CROSSMARK

A short line which crosses a seamline, dartline, tuck line, etc. Used to indicate seam joining, matching points or stitching points.

CUT

Cut on inside of pencil line. This refers only to cutting finished outside lines on slopers and patterns to retain the original fit when copying and outlining.

DART UNDERLAY

A dart is a ''V'' shaped stitched fold starting at a certain width at one end and tapering to a point at the other end. The material between the stitched lines is called underlay or pick up.

DOT

A small round mark used to denote a specific point on a sloper or pattern, often indicated with an awl.

NOTCHES

Notches are crossmarks transferred from seamline to edge of seam allowance, indicated by a notcher. Notches are used on finished patterns.

OUTLINE

The process of drawing a line along edge of sloper or draft without seam allowance.

TRACING

A tracing wheel is used to transfer pattern lines onto another sheet or sheets of paper or to opposite side of a folded sheet of paper. Folded draft is opened or sheets are separated and traced lines are penciled in with the proper tools.

TRUEING

Trueing is the process of connecting all points on a pattern and checking for accuracy of measurement, dartlines, seamlines, crossmarks, shape of seamlines, etc.

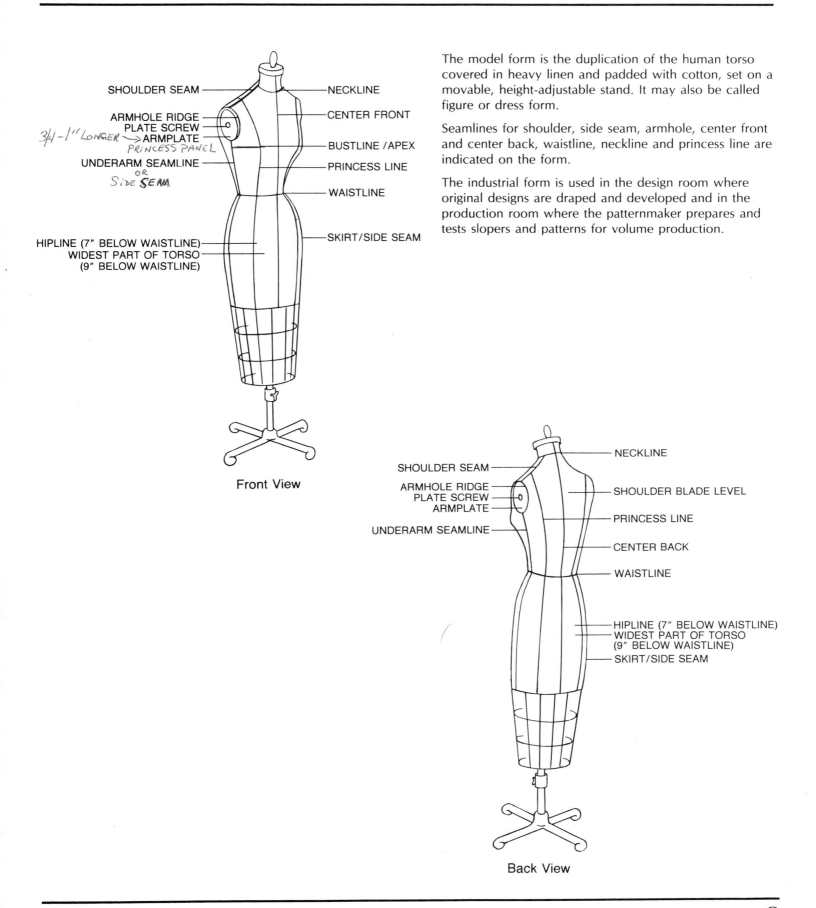

The model form is the duplication of the human torso covered in heavy linen and padded with cotton, set on a movable, height-adjustable stand. It may also be called figure or dress form.

Seamlines for shoulder, side seam, armhole, center front and center back, waistline, neckline and princess line are indicated on the form.

The industrial form is used in the design room where original designs are draped and developed and in the production room where the patternmaker prepares and tests slopers and patterns for volume production.

Front View

SHOULDER SEAM
ARMHOLE RIDGE
PLATE SCREW
3/4 - 1" LONGER → ARMPLATE
PRINCESS PANEL
UNDERARM SEAMLINE
OR
SIDE SEAM

NECKLINE
CENTER FRONT
BUSTLINE / APEX
PRINCESS LINE
WAISTLINE
SKIRT/SIDE SEAM

HIPLINE (7" BELOW WAISTLINE)
WIDEST PART OF TORSO
(9" BELOW WAISTLINE)

Back View

SHOULDER SEAM
ARMHOLE RIDGE
PLATE SCREW
ARMPLATE
UNDERARM SEAMLINE

NECKLINE
SHOULDER BLADE LEVEL
PRINCESS LINE
CENTER BACK
WAISTLINE
HIPLINE (7" BELOW WAISTLINE)
WIDEST PART OF TORSO
(9" BELOW WAISTLINE)
SKIRT/SIDE SEAM

TOOLS & MATERIALS NEEDED TO DEVELOP SLOPERS & PATTERNS

The following list defines the tools and materials needed to develop slopers and patterns discussed in this text. The uses refer specifically to the development of slopers and patterns.

AWL

A pointed tool with a wooden handle. Used to pierce small holes such as to indicate apex.

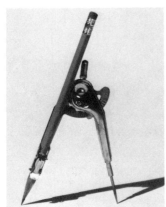

COMPASS

A tool consisting of two rods, one sharply pointed and the other equipped with a drawing end; joined at the top with a hinge to provide an adjustable movement. Compasses are available in various sizes to draw circles of different measurements. Used to make curved or circular lines such as for circular skirts and ruffles.

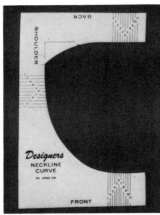

DESIGNER'S NECKLINE CURVE

A clear plastic measuring tool of two curves delineating front and back necklines. Each curve is marked in specific segments corresponding to garment sizes. Used to draft accurately the shape and fit of a neckline.

FRENCH CURVE

A plastic tool shaped into a curve at one end. Used to mark armholes and necklines.

HIP CURVE RULER

A wooden or metal 24-inch (61-cm) ruler that is shaped into a curve at one end. Used to curve hiplines on skirts and pants.

L SQUARE

A wooden, metal or plastic ruler with one side longer than the other. Sides form an "L" as the name implies. Used (1) to draft slopers and patterns; (2) to establish length and grainlines on patterns and slopers.

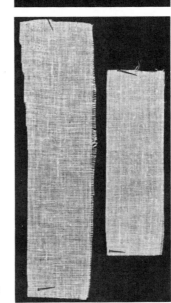

MUSLIN

A plain weave fabric made from bleached or unbleached carded yarns in a variety of weights. The following weights are important to the patternmaker:

1. A coarse weave not highly sized—used to test a basic sloper in fabric.

2. A lightweight muslin— used to test softly draped garments.

3. A heavyweight, firmly woven muslin—used to test tailored garments such as coats and suits.

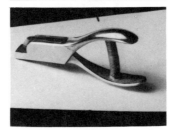

NOTCHER

A hand punching tool which produces a ¹/₁₆" (0.2 cm) nick in paper or Oaktag. Used to establish notches at the outer edge of seam when pattern is completed.

OAKTAG

A heavyweight paper, usually beige in color. Used to make basic slopers.

PATTERNMAKING PAPER

A strong, white paper in a variety of widths and weights, available in rolls. Paper must be soft enough to fold at dartlines or seams and able to remain flat when opened. Do not use tissue paper as it will tear easily. A paper with a grid pattern of dots is also available. This type of patternmaking paper is used for markers in the garment industry.

PENCILS

Red, blue and numbers 2 and 3 lead pencils. Used to mark paper or muslin slopers and patterns.

PINS

A size 17 steel satin straight pin. Used to fasten parts and pieces together.

PUSH PINS

A pin approximately ½″ (1.3 cm) long with a plastic or metal shaped head. Used to secure sloper or pattern pieces to paper.

RULER

A clear plastic, metal or wooden straight edge with clearly marked measurements. It is advisable to have 6″, 8″, 18″ (15, 30 and 46 cm) rulers.

SCISSORS

A cutting instrument at least 9″ in length. Since paper will dull scissors, it is preferable to have two pairs, one for cutting paper and one for cutting fabric.

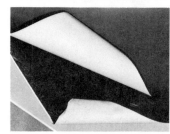

TAPE MEASURE

A narrow, firmly woven 60″ tape with metal tips on each end. Measurements should appear on both sides with number 1 at alternate ends. This will facilitate working with tape since it can be picked up at either end.

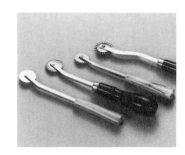

DRESSMAKER'S TRACING PAPER

Paper coated on one side with wax or chalk. It is carbon paper made for the garment industry. Red and blue colors are used for patternmaking to transfer pattern lines onto muslin. White carbon is used to transfer pattern lines onto garment fabric.

TRACING WHEEL

A small hand tool with a serrated or pointed wheel at one end. Used to transfer (1) one side of the pattern to the other and (2) pattern lines to muslin or fabric. There are two types of wheels.

> 1. Dull point—used on fabric (will not damage fabric).
>
> 2. Sharp point—used on paper (will not cut paper).

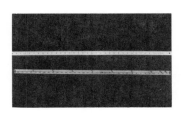

YARDSTICK

A 36″ or 45″ (91 or 115 cm) wooden or metal straight edge. Measurements are clearly marked.

PREPARATION OF MUSLIN FOR TESTING OF SLOPERS & PATTERNS

When testing slopers in muslin, it is important to block and press properly the muslin used, so that lengthwise (selvage) and crosswise grains are at right angles to each other.

FIGURE 1

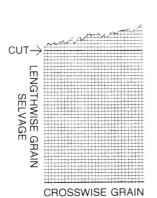

If upper edge of muslin is not cut on grain, adjust by tearing or pulling one of the woven threads. Cut on the pulled thread line.

FIGURE 2

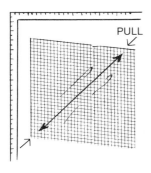

On this piece of muslin grains are true on all sides. Muslin must be blocked so that lengthwise and crosswise grains are at *perfect* right angles to each other. Pull muslin in the direction illustrated by arrows.

FIGURE 3

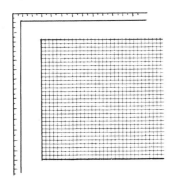

Muslin is block and pressed and ready for cutting.

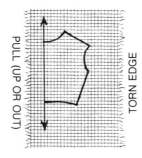

FIGURE 4

Muslin illustrated has tightly woven selvage. Use any of the following methods to adjust:

1.   cut into selvage every ½" (1.3 cm) to release tension;

2.   cut away selvage;

3.   place sloper or pattern for testing 2" or 3" (5.1 to 7.6 cm) in from selvage.

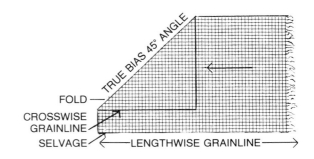

FIGURE 5

To obtain true bias (45° angle) fold muslin matching crosswise to lengthwise grain.

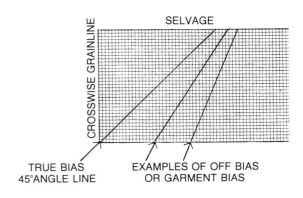

FIGURE 6

Muslin illustrates two lines not on true bias. They are referred to as off bias or garment bias.

IDENTIFICATION OF SEAMS & DARTS ON BASIC SLOPERS

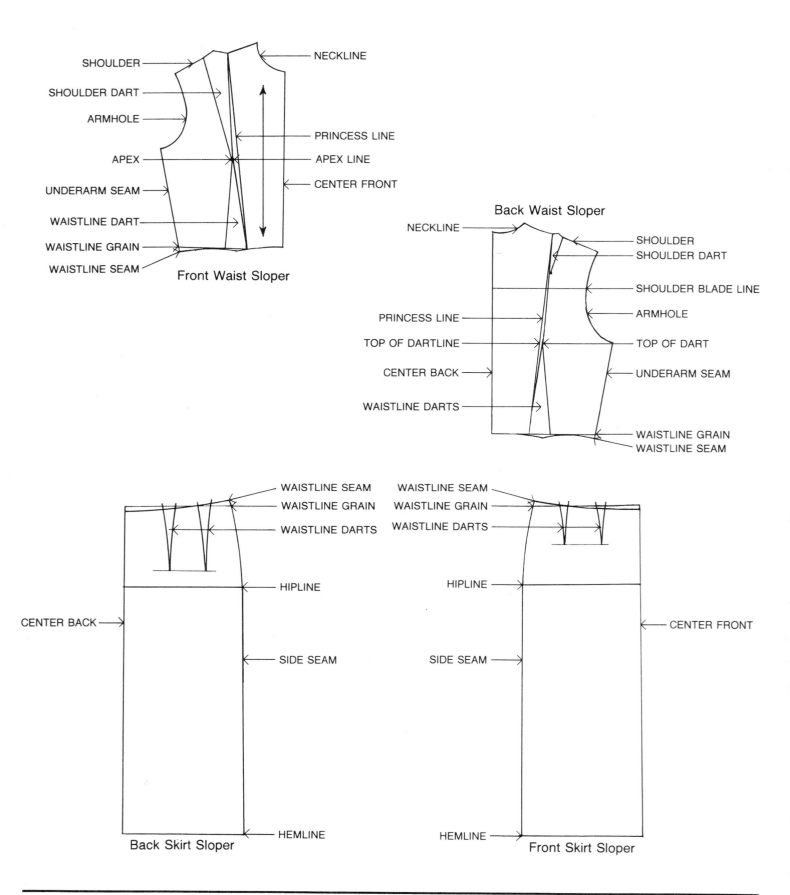

SHOULDER

SHOULDER DART

ARMHOLE

APEX

UNDERARM SEAM

WAISTLINE DART

WAISTLINE GRAIN

WAISTLINE SEAM

NECKLINE

PRINCESS LINE

APEX LINE

CENTER FRONT

Front Waist Sloper

Back Waist Sloper

NECKLINE

SHOULDER

SHOULDER DART

SHOULDER BLADE LINE

ARMHOLE

PRINCESS LINE

TOP OF DARTLINE

CENTER BACK

WAISTLINE DARTS

TOP OF DART

UNDERARM SEAM

WAISTLINE GRAIN

WAISTLINE SEAM

WAISTLINE SEAM

WAISTLINE GRAIN

WAISTLINE DARTS

HIPLINE

CENTER BACK

SIDE SEAM

HEMLINE

Back Skirt Sloper

WAISTLINE SEAM

WAISTLINE GRAIN

WAISTLINE DARTS

HIPLINE

CENTER FRONT

SIDE SEAM

HEMLINE

Front Skirt Sloper

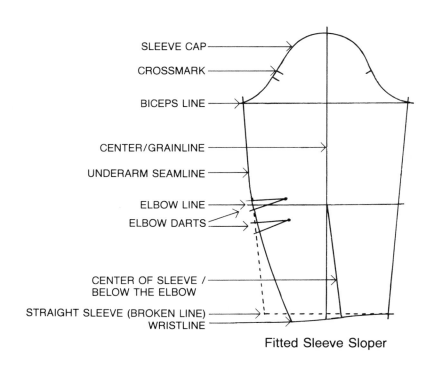

SLEEVE CAP

CROSSMARK

BICEPS LINE

CENTER/GRAINLINE

UNDERARM SEAMLINE

ELBOW LINE

ELBOW DARTS

CENTER OF SLEEVE /
BELOW THE ELBOW

STRAIGHT SLEEVE (BROKEN LINE)

WRISTLINE

Fitted Sleeve Sloper

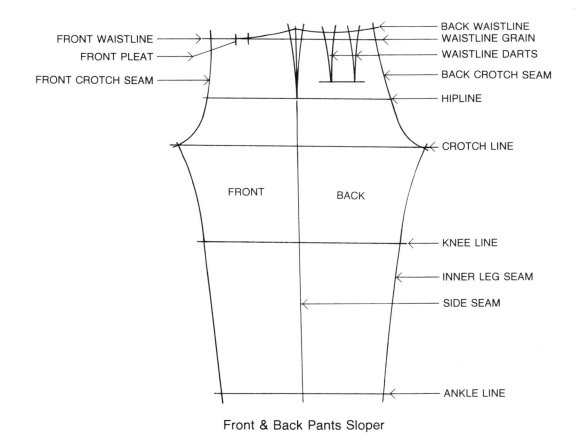

FRONT WAISTLINE

FRONT PLEAT

FRONT CROTCH SEAM

BACK WAISTLINE

WAISTLINE GRAIN

WAISTLINE DARTS

BACK CROTCH SEAM

HIPLINE

CROTCH LINE

FRONT   BACK

KNEE LINE

INNER LEG SEAM

SIDE SEAM

ANKLE LINE

Front & Back Pants Sloper

To true darts on waists, skirts, sleeves, and pants, regardless of length or depth, follow the same procedures. The principles are the same, the position of the dart is different.

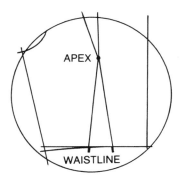

FIGURE 1

To form darts draw lines between crossmarks and dots. This diagram illustrates waistline dartlines to apex.

Note: To true accurately a seam which is intersected by a dart, close, cup and pin dart before trueing as length is lost on the folded dart seamline. Amount to be added when blending depends upon the angle caused by the depth of the dart underlay.

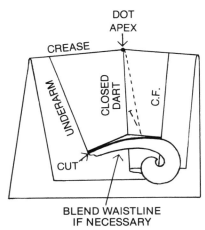

FIGURE 2

A.　To true front waistline dart crease dartline nearest center front from waistline to apex.

B.　Cup at apex. Close and pin dart. Continue to crease paper from apex towards center front and underarm seam.

C.　To true waistline place French curve on paper (as illustrated). Trace dart underlay on trued waistline to opposite side.

D.　Open draft. Pencil in traced lines.

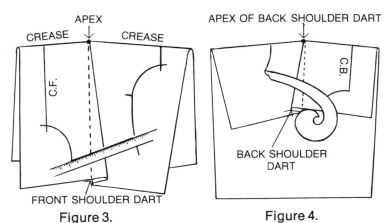

Figure 3.　　　　Figure 4.

FIGURES 3 & 4

These diagrams illustrate trueing front and back shoulder darts.

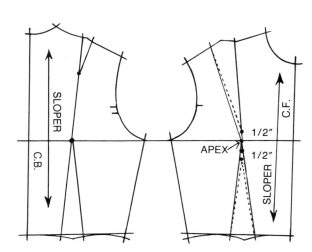

FIGURE 5

When the *two-dart front waist sloper* is used as a *dress pattern,* the shoulder dart must be shortened across the bustline for ease. If more ease is desired, waistline dart may also be shortened.

A.　To shorten shoulder dart from apex on *dartline nearest neckline* measure up ½" (1.3 cm). Dot. Draw a line from dot to dartline nearest armhole for new dartline (broken line).

B.　To shorten waistline dart, from top and at *center of dart* measure down ½" (1.3 cm). Dot. Draw two dartlines from dot to waistline for new dart (broken line).

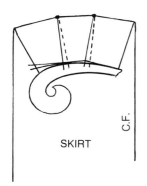

FIGURE 6

This diagram illustrates trueing skirt waistline darts.

SKIRT

C.F.

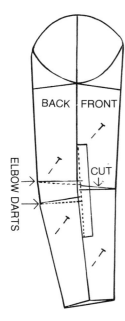

Figure 7.

BACK FRONT

ELBOW DARTS

CUT

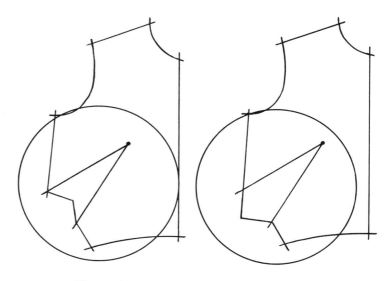

Figure 8.

Figure 9.

FIGURES 7, 8, 9

This diagram illustrates trueing sleeve elbow darts and underarm seam (broken lines). For more information refer to drafting shaped sleeve sloper in *How to Draft Basic Patterns.* Note: 1. To true basic darts crease as indicated. However, these darts, as well as darts covered in Dart Manipulation unit may be creased on either dartline to obtain different effects or to incorporate the dart into the design of the garment. 2. Some darts throughout this text are trued to save material in mass production cutting layouts. For example in Figure 8 upper dartline is creased and saves material as dart underlay is shortened, but in Figure 9 lower dartline is creased and uses more material as dart underlay is longer. 3. When center of dart is on the straight grain, the problem in #2 does not exist. Principle only applies when darts are placed on an angle.

TRUEING WAIST SEAMLINES FOR SLOPERS & PATTERNS (BEFORE ALLOWING SEAMS)

Traced & Trued Slopers

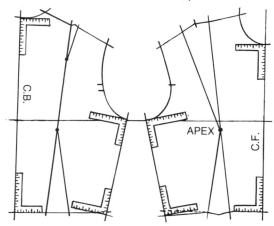

FIGURE 1

A.   Cross all intersections.

B.   Use an L-square to check all intersections. Intersections must be at right angles to each other with allowance of approximately $1/16''$ to $1/8''$ (0.2 to 0.3 cm) depending upon how acute the angle. See placement of L-squares.

C.   When completing slopers, cut away paper on seamlines and notch dartlines. With awl indicate end of each dart.

D.   When developing patterns allow seams; cut and notch seams.
Note: For accurate fit of sloper or pattern, it is important to cut directly next to pencil line inside of seamline or seam allowance.

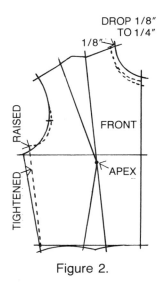

Figure 2.

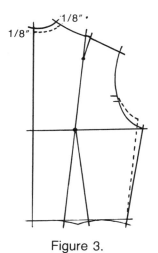

Figure 3.

FIGURES 2 & 3

A.   When working on slopers that will be used in volume production, the back and front necklines of the basic slopers should always be lowered to allow for variations of individual figure types and for bulk of fabric.

B.   On front neckline lower $1/8''$ to $1/4''$ (0.3 to 0.6 cm) at center front and $1/8''$ (0.3 cm) at shoulder. Blend new neckline.

C.   On back neckline lower $1/8''$ (0.3 cm) at center back and at shoulder. Blend new neckline.

D.   If a dress sloper is to be used for a sleeveless garment make the following adjustments:

1.   On front and back slopers adjust underarm seam so that ease will be approximately $1/4''$ (0.6 cm) at armhole. Dot. Draw a line to waistline and underarm intersection (broken line).

2.   Raise armhole so that drop at armhole will be approximately $1/2''$ (1.3 cm) below armhole plate on model form or armpit. This is an armhole on a basic sleeveless garment and not a stylized sleeveless armhole.

3.   Front of armhole should be curved inward slightly to release tightness (broken line in Figure 2).

4.   Repeat same for back armhole with the exception that armhole is blended differently than front armhole (follow broken line).

Note: To true all seamlines on skirts, sleeve and pants follow the same procedure as for trueing seamlines on waist.

TRUEING & BALANCING UNDERARM SEAMS ON WAISTS & STRAIGHT SLEEVES

A rule to follow for final trueing of all vertical seamlines on slopers and when allowing seams to complete patterns is: all balanced seams that are to be seamed together should be pinned and seamlines trued, seam allowances added, cut and crossmarks notched in pinned position.

FRONT & BACK WAIST

FIGURE 1

A. To true underarm seam on waist place back waist over front waist matching waistline crosswise grainlines at underarm seam and waistline intersections. See dot at intersection (pivoting point).

B. With pencil hold back waist at pivoting point and pivot back waist until center back is parallel to center front on front waist. *Note:* 1. The width between center back and center front varies due to the size of the bust measurement. The larger the bust measurement the greater the space between the center front and center back.
2. Before pinning at underarm recheck that crosswise grains match at underarm and center back is parallel to center front.
3. If one armhole is higher adjust by compromising and blending at line between upper and lower armhole. Repeat at waistline. Trace adjusted lines to opposite side (darker lines).

C. Add a seam allowance at underarm seam. Cut as illustrated. Separate patterns. Pencil in traced lines. Add seam allowance to remainder of front and back patterns.

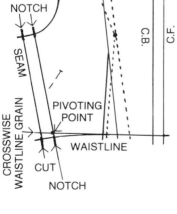

STRAIGHT SLEEVES

FIGURE 2

Fold sleeve draft matching front and back seamlines and elbow grainline. If armhole and/or wristline do not match, adjust as stated in Figure 1. With sleeve folded allow seams; cut and notch seams.
Note: This procedure applies only to straight sleeves without elbow darts. For information on how to true fitted sleeves, refer to the text *How to Draft Basic Patterns.*

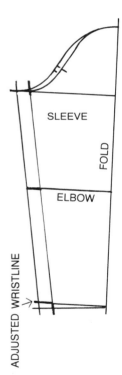

The following principles may be used to:

1.   True balanced seamlines with or without flares

2.   True unbalanced seamlines with flares

3.   True bias or off bias seamlines joined to straight grain seamline

4.   True and balance seamlines on a one-piece garment (shift, tent, etc.).

5.   True and balance side and crotch seams on pants

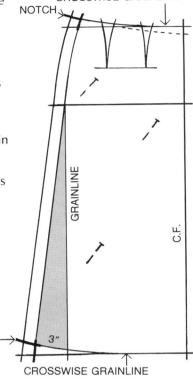

TRUEING BALANCED SEAMLINES WITH OR WITHOUT FLARES

FIGURE 1

This diagram illustrates a straight skirt with side seams on grainlines and 3" (7.6 cm) flare added to each side seam (shaded area).

BALANCED SIDE SEAM FLARES

FIGURE 2

A.   To true side seam place front over back skirt draft matching hiplines and crosswise grain at waistline. Pin. Center front and center back must be parallel to each other.

B.   If one waistline at side seam extends above the other, compromise by drawing a line between the two.

C.   If hemlines at side seams do not match, correct by measuring from hipline to hemline same amount as at center front on both front and back side seams. The front and back length must be the same. *Note:* The wider the flare the greater the shaping at side seam. See adjusted hemline in relation to crosswise grainline at hemline.

D.   Trace *only* adjusted hemline and waistline (darker lines). Add side seam; cut and notch at waistline, hipline and hemline.

E.   Separate patterns. Pencil in adjusted traced lines. Add seams and hem to remainder of pattern.

FIGURE 3

On gored skirts all seamlines are trued by matching hiplines and straight grainlines near flare line (broken line). If any corrections are needed, follow the procedure discussed in Figure 2.

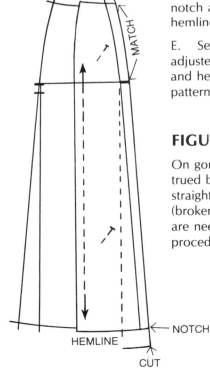

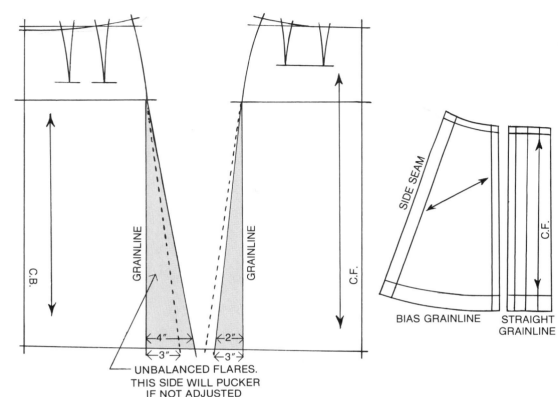

UNBALANCED FLARES.
THIS SIDE WILL PUCKER
IF NOT ADJUSTED

TRUEING BIAS OR OFF BIAS SEAMLINES JOINED TO STRAIGHT GRAIN SEAMLINE

FIGURE 5

Because of the extreme difference in the grainlines of each piece to be joined, a great deal of puckering will occur on the bias side and distort the hang of the skirt. To make adjustments cut skirt in fabric to be used with regular seamline and hem allowance with the following exception:

At both bias seamlines on side gore allow twice the seam allowance. As bias stretches in length seam allowance decreases. Amount of stretch depends upon fabric used.

BIAS GRAINLINE   STRAIGHT GRAINLINE

TRUEING UNBALANCED SEAMLINES WITH FLARES

FIGURE 4

This diagram illustrates a skirt with different amounts of flare added to front and back side seams. Illustrated: skirt front with 2" (5.1 cm) flare; skirt back with 4" (10.2 cm) flare.

Note: Depending upon the type of fabric used, the seam may distort the "hang" of the skirt. The side seam with the most flare will pucker. To make this adjustment, balance seam by compromising. Take 1" (2.5 cm) off the back and add it to the front. Both flares will be 3" (7.6 cm).

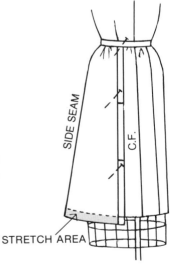

STRETCH AREA

FIGURE 6

A.   Pin skirt sections to model form at *waistline only* with bias seams overlapping straight grain seamlines. This will allow the bias gore the freedom to hang and stretch.
Note: Manufacturers will often let the skirt hang for twenty-four hours before correcting pattern.

B.   Before removing the skirt from the form pin seam and place two crossmarks with pins or tailor's chalk (as illustrated). Measure a new hemline.
Note: Shaded area indicates the amount stretched. If seam has changed due to stretching, re-mark side seam.

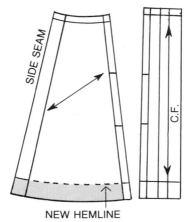

NEW HEMLINE

FIGURE 7

With seams in pinned position remove skirt from model form. Trace through crossmarks, seam and hem. Separate sections. Adjust seam and hem allowance and cut.

Note: When the sections are stitched together, the bias seam is stretched over the straight grainline between the notches.

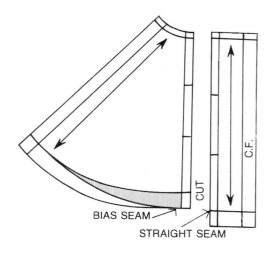

BIAS SEAM
STRAIGHT SEAM

FIGURE 8

This diagram illustrates a skirt developed with a bias seam joined to a straight grain seam. See bias adjustment at hem (shaded area).

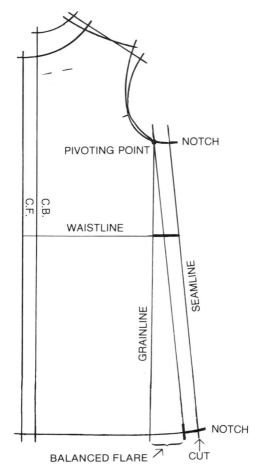

NOTCH
PIVOTING POINT
WAISTLINE
SEAMLINE
GRAINLINE
NOTCH
BALANCED FLARE
CUT

TRUEING & BALANCING SEAMLINES ON A ONE-PIECE GARMENT (SHIFT, TENT, ETC.)

FIGURE 9

A.   With back section face up, place back on front matching side seam/armhole intersections.

B.   Pivoting point is side seam/armhole intersection. With pencil hold back in place and pivot back until center back is parallel to center front. If waistline and/or hemline do not match, adjust waistline crossmark and hemline by compromising.

FIGURE 10

Balance flare, if necessary.

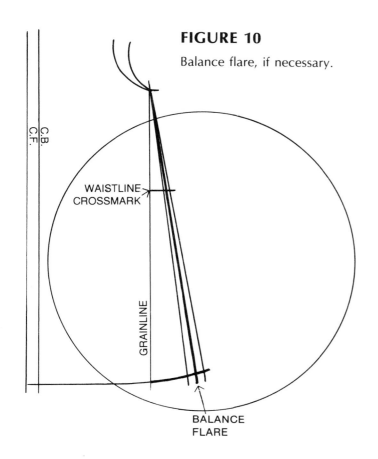

WAISTLINE CROSSMARK

C.B.
C.F.

GRAINLINE

BALANCE FLARE

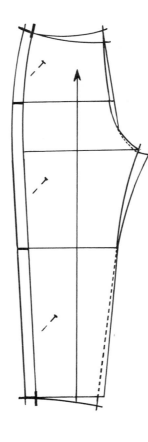

TRUEING & BALANCING SIDE & CROTCH SEAMS ON PANTS

FIGURE 11

A. Place front of pants on back matching hiplines on side seams. If waistline, knee line and/or hemline do not match, adjust by compromising.

B. The inner leg seam is trued in two steps:

> 1. match seam at knee line to hemline;
>
> 2. match seam at knee line to crotch.

Adjust by compromising.

CURVED, DIAGONAL & HORIZONTAL SEAMS

Curved, diagonal and horizontal seams should be checked and matched for accuracy of shape of seamlines and notches. Differences should be corrected by compromising.

ESTABLISHING CROSSMARKS ON SLEEVE & WAIST ARMHOLES

FIGURE 1

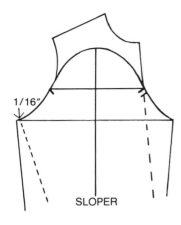

A.   Place sleeve sloper over front waist sloper matching front armholes. Extend sleeve armhole ¹⁄₁₆″ (0.2 cm) beyond waist armhole for a smoother fit at underarm.

B.   Pivot rest of sleeve up to crossmark. Curve of sleeve armhole and waist armhole should match at least halfway up towards crossmark. Blend armhole within this area, if necessary. If crossmarks do not match, trace sleeve crossmark to waist.

C.   Repeat with back of sleeve and waist.

FIGURE 2

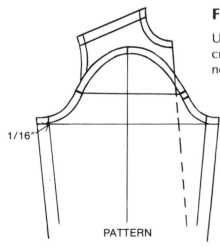

Use method of checking crossmarks in Figure 1 to check notches on finished patterns.

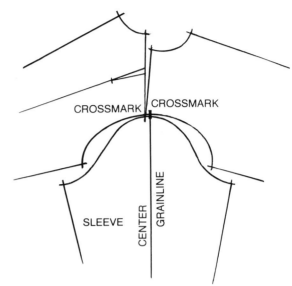

FIGURE 3

A.   When draping or testing muslin for fit of sleeve, center of sleeve (grainline) may not match shoulderline on form. This is due to the placement of the shoulderline on the form.

B.   If it is desirable to leave shoulderline as is, crossmark the sleeve to match shoulderline.

C.   If desired, shoulder seam may be changed to match center of sleeve. This is often done to facilitate production.

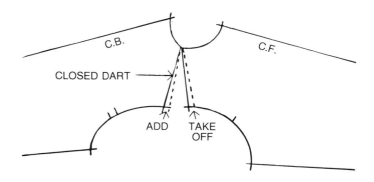

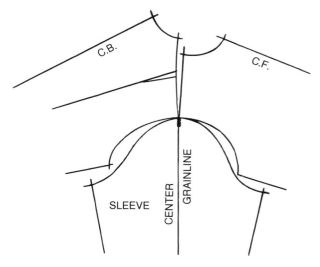

FIGURE 4

A.   To change shoulderline crossmark the waist to match center of sleeve.

B.   Draw a line from neck/shoulderline intersection on front waist to crossmark at armhole (broken line). Amount eliminated on one side of shoulderline must be added to other side (broken line).

FIGURE 5

This diagram illustrates center of sleeve crossmark matching adjusted shoulderline.

CROSSMARKS & NOTCHES

The placement and the number of crossmarks or notches used vary from one design to another and from one manufacturer to another, but the principles needed to establish crossmarks or notches are always the same and are applied to all seams on waists, skirts, sleeves, pants, etc.

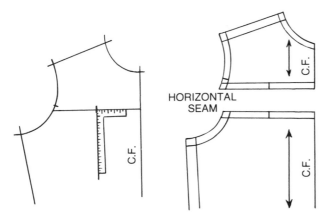

Figure 1.

HORIZONTAL SEAM

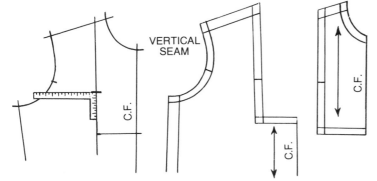

VERTICAL SEAM

Figure 2.

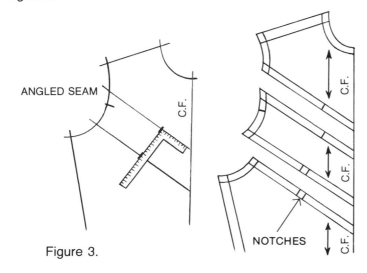

ANGLED SEAM

NOTCHES

Figure 3.

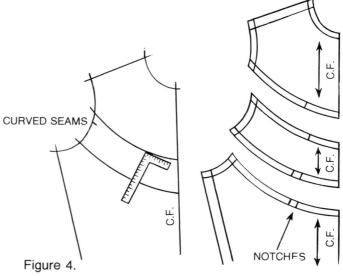

CURVED SEAMS

NOTCHES

Figure 4.

FIGURES 1, 2, 3, 4

A.   All crossmarks placed on a seam must be squared at right angles from the seamlines regardless of whether the seam is vertical, horizontal, diagonal, curved or shaped.

B.   To establish notches on pattern extend crossmarks from seamline to seam allowance.

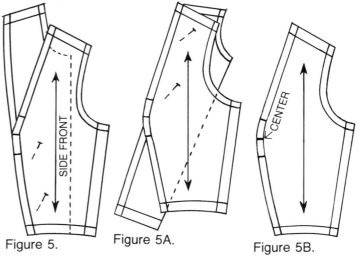

SIDE FRONT

CENTER

Figure 5.   Figure 5A.   Figure 5B.

FIGURES 5, 5A, 5B

To insure the accurate matching of princess line seams and retain the ease at the bustline:

A.   Match princess line seam from waistline up to lower crossmark. Pin and notch together.

B.   Unpin. Repeat matching princess line seam from shoulder down to upper crossmark. Pin and notch together. See Figure 5A.

C.   Unpin. Check center between crossmarks for accuracy and notch separately. See Figure 5B.

SEAM ALLOWANCES

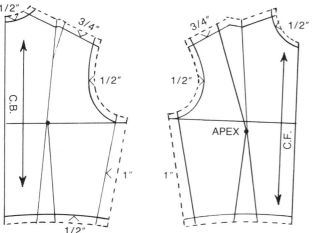

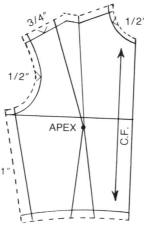

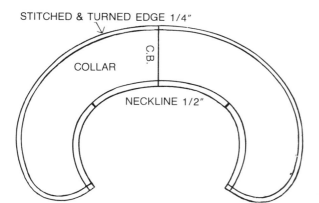

A *seam allowance* is that portion of the muslin or paper pattern extending a determined amount from the seamline to the pattern edge. Seam allowances vary from one manufacturer to another and will vary depending upon the type of fabric used. In this text, the following seam allowances are used and are based on the seam allowances used on higher priced garments.

Shoulder Seams ¾" (1.9 cm)

Underarm Seams, Side Seams, Waistlines 1" (2.5 cm)

Armholes, Necklines, Pants Crotch and Inner Leg Seams, all detailed and curved seams such as gored, yoke and princess line ½" (1.3 cm)

Stitched and Turned Under Seams such as edge of collar and belts if fabric tends to fray ¼"–⅜" (0.6–1 cm)

Underlay of a deep dart (may be cut away allowing seam) ½" (1.3 cm)

When cutting seam allowances, seams intersecting sharp angled seams *must* be turned back before cutting angled seam (as illustrated). However, all seams may be turned back if desired.

MASS PRODUCTION

Before grading an original pattern for mass production, duplicates are made. This is a process of testing the fit of an original pattern and production procedures of the garment. Once adjustments are made, the original pattern is then graded into various sizes. The seam allowance lines on the original pattern are used as guidelines when grading (see Original Princess Line Pattern). The seam allowances on the graded patterns are indicated only by notches (see Mass Production Pattern).

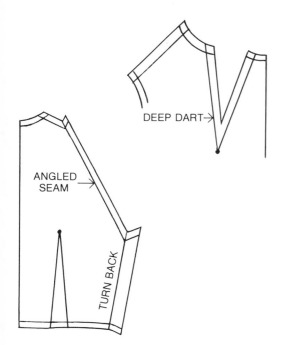

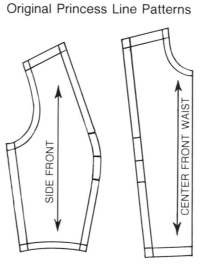

Original Princess Line Patterns

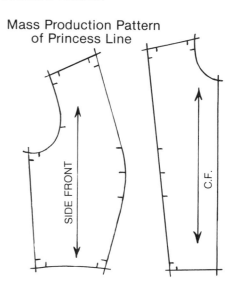

Mass Production Pattern of Princess Line

HEM ALLOWANCES

A *hem allowance* is that portion of the muslin or paper pattern extending a determined amount from the hemline to the pattern edge. Hem allowances vary from one manufacturer to another and from one design or cut of garment; they also vary on type of fabric used and price of garment. The following suggested hem allowances can be classified as average allowances used by the industry.

Blouses

    Overblouse ½"–2" (⅓–5.1 cm)
    Tuck-in Blouse ¼–1" (0.6–2.5 cm)

Coats 2–2½" (5.1–6.4 cm)

Jackets

    Lined 1½–2" (3.8–5.1 cm)
    Unlined 2–2½" (5.1–6.4 cm)

Shorts 1" (2.5 cm)

Skirts

    Straight, with one or more pleats, slightly shaped, flared, wrap-around, dirndl 1–2½" (2.5–5.1 cm)

Dirndl made of chiffon or other sheer fabrics* 2–12" (5.1–30.5 cm)

Bias, full-flared** 1–1½" (2.5–3.8 cm)

Circular*** 1" (2.5 cm)

Commercially pleated**** 1–1½" (2.5–3.8 cm)

Pants 1" (2.5 cm)

Sleeves

    Straight Sleeves. Use facings on shaped sleeves ½–2" (1.3–5.1 cm)

*A wide hem gives body to a lightweight fabric and produces a border effect which is especially effective on evening dresses.

**Wider hems pucker and stretch as bias hangs.

***Skirt gets wider as it gets longer, therefore, when hem is turned up it is too full for skirt.

****Hem is sewn before fabric is pleated.

IDENTIFICATION OF FINISHED PATTERNS

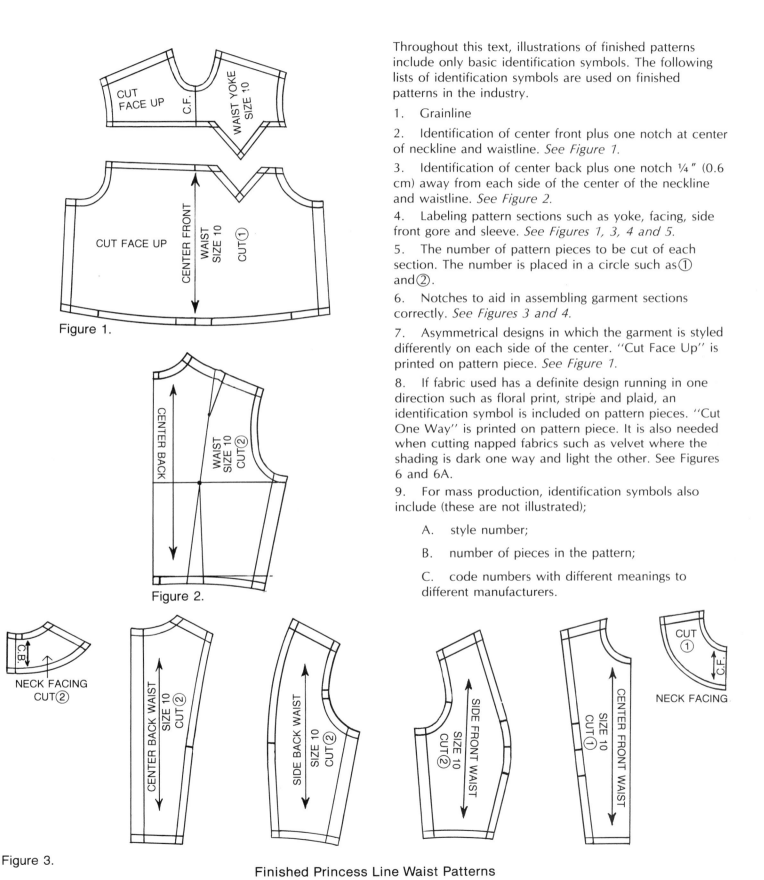

Throughout this text, illustrations of finished patterns include only basic identification symbols. The following lists of identification symbols are used on finished patterns in the industry.

1.   Grainline

2.   Identification of center front plus one notch at center of neckline and waistline. *See Figure 1.*

3.   Identification of center back plus one notch ¼" (0.6 cm) away from each side of the center of the neckline and waistline. *See Figure 2.*

4.   Labeling pattern sections such as yoke, facing, side front gore and sleeve. *See Figures 1, 3, 4 and 5.*

5.   The number of pattern pieces to be cut of each section. The number is placed in a circle such as ① and ②.

6.   Notches to aid in assembling garment sections correctly. *See Figures 3 and 4.*

7.   Asymmetrical designs in which the garment is styled differently on each side of the center. "Cut Face Up" is printed on pattern piece. *See Figure 1.*

8.   If fabric used has a definite design running in one direction such as floral print, stripe and plaid, an identification symbol is included on pattern pieces. "Cut One Way" is printed on pattern piece. It is also needed when cutting napped fabrics such as velvet where the shading is dark one way and light the other. See Figures 6 and 6A.

9.   For mass production, identification symbols also include (these are not illustrated);

    A.   style number;

    B.   number of pieces in the pattern;

    C.   code numbers with different meanings to different manufacturers.

Figure 1.

Figure 2.

Figure 3.   Finished Princess Line Waist Patterns

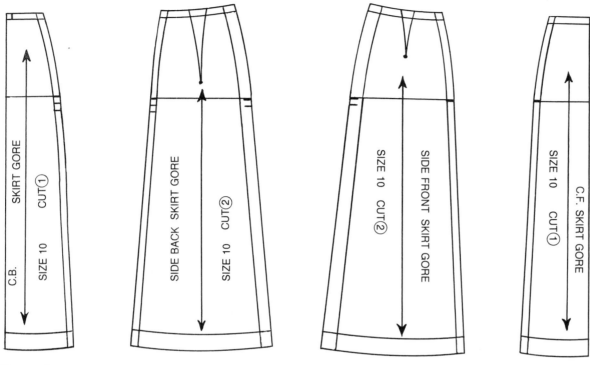

Figure 4.

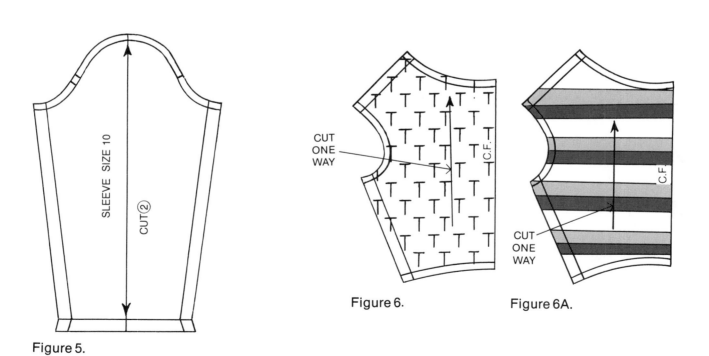

Figure 5.

Figure 6.

Figure 6A.

SLOPERS IN ONE-QUARTER SCALE
introduction

The *sloper* is the device from which other slopers, patterns and designs may be developed. It is also known within the apparel industry as a foundation, master, block or basic pattern.

Slopers differ from one firm to another and often within a firm. The differences occur because all firms do not use the same measurements for a given size, and firms that do adhere to the same measurements for a given size differ because of the sculpturing of the form within the measurements. Regardless of the method of development, all slopers should be checked for accuracy, fit and balance of seamlines. The principles for developing and trueing patterns are not affected by the differences found in the slopers.

The following slopers are needed to develop various designs and patterns:

1. sleeve slopers

    A. fitted sleeve sloper
    B. straight sleeve sloper

2. front waist slopers

    A. front waist sloper with waistline dart
    B. front waist sloper with shoulder and waistline darts

3. back waist slopers

    A. back waist sloper with shoulder and waistline darts

B. back waist sloper with neckline and waistline darts

4. front and back torso length slopers
5. front and back kimono/dolman sleeve slopers
6. front and back skirt slopers with waistline dart(s)
7. front and back pants slopers with waistline dart(s)

For your convenience, we have included one-quarter scaled miniature slopers for experimental use. It is desirable, however, to develop all problems on a full scale.

The *kimono or dolman sleeve sloper* may be used as a one-piece kimono sloper by matching overarm seamline and darting shoulderline from neckline to crossmark.

KEY TO SLOPERS
Necklines

1. Solid lines = Figure Neckline

2. Broken lines = Lowered Neckline. Lower neckline ⅛" to ¼" (0.3 to 0.6 cm) for mass production to allow for variations in figure types and bulk of fabric used.

Waistlines

Broken lines indicate shirring adjustments.

Front Waist
Muslin Pattern
on Model Form

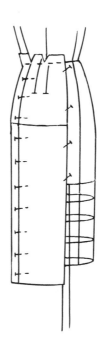

Skirt Muslin
Pattern on
Model Form

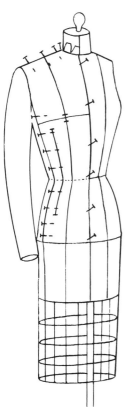

Fitted Sleeve & Front Torso
Muslin Patterns on Model Form

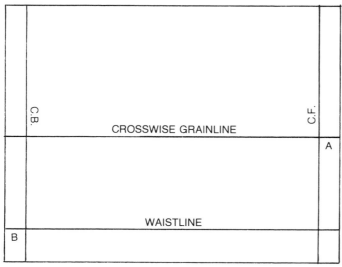

Figure 1.

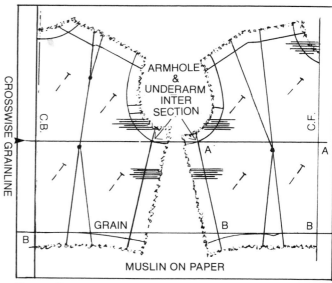

Figure 2.

PREPARATION OF MUSLIN PATTERN

1.   To duplicate accurately a draped muslin pattern into a paper sloper, the muslin should be *pressed* carefully in harmony with the grainline and *trued* before transferring to paper.

2.   On front waist muslin draw a line on the crosswise grainline from the center front through the armhole/underarm intersection and center front from waistline to side seam. Label *A* and *B* (as illustrated).

3.   Repeat on back waist muslin.

Note: If necessary pull thread to obtain grainline.

FRONT & BACK WAIST SLOPERS

FIGURE 1

A.   Cut paper approximately 26″ (66 cm) square.

B.   Measure widest part of front and back muslin waists (armhole/undearm intersections to center front and center back).

C.   On paper draw two parallel vertical lines the width of front and back measurement plus 4″ (10.2 cm).
Note: Check that lines are the same width at the top and bottom.

D.   Label *center front* and *center back* (as illustrated).

E.   Draw a horizontal line at right angles to vertical lines halfway down. Label *A* at each end and *crosswise grainline* (as illustrated).

F.   On muslin measure distance between A and B at center front.

G.   On paper use measurement from A at each end. Dot. Draw line between dots. Label *B* and *waistline.*

FIGURE 2

A.   Place front waist muslin on paper matching center front and crosswise grainlines at A and waistline at B. Pin. Smooth remainder of pattern into position. Pin.

B.   Repeat on back waist muslin.
Note: Be careful not to stretch muslin grainwise or at cut edges. When entire muslin pattern is secured, check to see that all grainlines are at right angles to each other. See illustration for direction of grainline at armholes and underarm.

C.   With tracing wheel trace finished seamlines, darts and crossmarks onto paper.

D.   Remove muslin. Pencil in all traced lines. True darts and seams. Refer to trueing instructions in Basic Information Needed to Develop Slopers & Patterns.

E.   After trueing cut away excess paper from sloper seamlines.
Note: Pencil lines should be removed. Cut next to line inside of sloper.

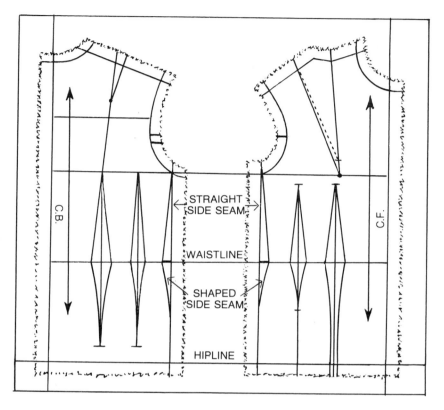

TORSO, FITTED SLEEVE & SKIRT SLOPERS

1.   The principles for transferring and trueing muslin patterns into paper slopers for a fitted sleeve, skirt or torso sloper are the same as for front and back waist slopers. For instructions on drafting all basic slopers refer to *How to Draft Basic Patterns.*

2.   If the torso muslin pattern was developed on a figure with a flat bustline, the front waistline dart will end in a point at the hipline.

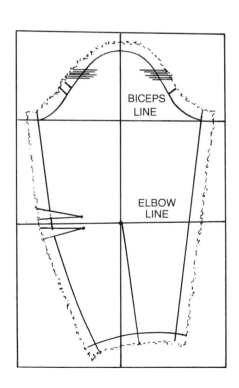

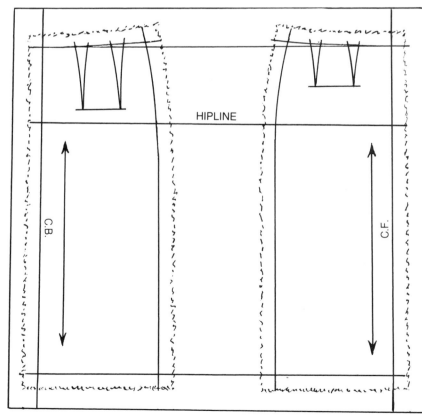

DART MANIPULATION
introduction

Darts are V-shaped stitched folds formed when material is picked up at a given depth and which taper to a point. They are structural lines needed to shape and fit a flat piece of material to a three-dimensional form. Darts may be applied to many sections and types of garments such as waists, sleeves, skirts, and slacks. They are decorative and functional as well as structural.

Double-pointed darts are formed when material is picked up at a given depth and taper to nothing at *each end.* They are used to fit the center front of a waist from apex to apex or the waistline of a torso-length garment.

The *decorative dart* holds fullness where it will contribute to the design. This dart may be stitched on the outside or inside of a garment. The direction in which it is pressed depends on the effect desired on the individual garment.

Dart fullness may be broken into several smaller darts, converted into tucks, dart tucks, pleats or shirring; or may be concealed cleverly in design features or seam lines.

Darts may be placed at the neckline, shoulder, armhole, underarm seam line, waistline, and center front of the bodice without sacrificing original fit. Regardless of their position, all darts must converge at the apex of the bust. The apex or bust point is the pivoting point on a front waist sloper for waist dart manipulation.

Dart manipulation can be accomplished through the *pivot* or *slash methods.* The *pivot method* is recommended where single darts are to be repositioned. This method may appear more intricate to the beginner, but when the principle is understood it is faster and results in greater accuracy. However, where more than one dart is desired, as in the unit on *Division of Basic Front Waist Darts,* the *slash method* is recommended. In this case, the slash method is faster and more accurate. The principle of dart manipulation may be used on other sections of a garment.

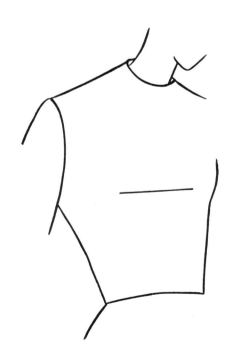 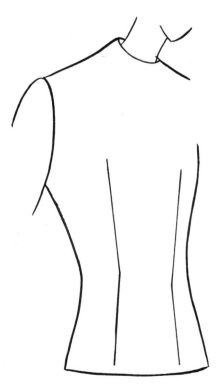

Double-pointed Darts

To develop the many different designs of back waists, it is important that a back waist with neckline dart sloper be developed.

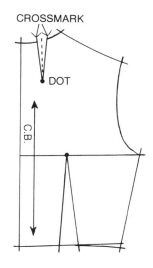

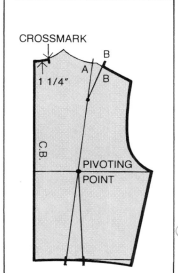

FIGURE 1

A. Use *back waist sloper with shoulder and waistline darts.*

B. To prepare sloper:

1. Establish position of neckline dart desired. Crossmark. Illustrated: 1¼" (3.2 cm) from center back.

2. Label shoulder dartlines *A* and *B* (as illustrated).

C. Cut paper approximately 15" × 25" (38.1 × 63.5 cm).

D. Place sloper on paper. Crossmark on paper waist dartlines and neckline crossmark. Outline sloper from shoulder at dartline B to armhole, armhole, underarm, waistline, center back and neckline to crossmark.

E. With awl indicate top of waistline dart.

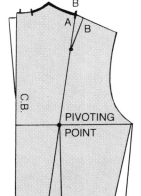

FIGURE 2

A. Pivoting point is at top of waistline dart.

B. Hold sloper at pivoting point and pivot sloper until dartline A meets crossmark B.

C. On paper crossmark at neckline crossmark. Outline sloper from neckline crossmark to shoulder and shoulder to A. Dot end of dart.

D. Remove sloper. True all lines crossing all intersections.

FIGURE 3

A. Establish the center grainline between neckline crossmarks parallel to center back (broken line).

B. Length of neckline dart should equal length of shoulder dart. Establish length of dart on broken line. Dot.

C. To form neckline dart draw a straight line from neckline crossmarks to dot.

D. True all lines crossing all intersections.

E. Establish grainline parallel to center back.

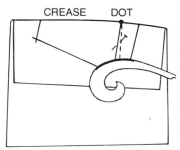

FIGURE 4

A. To true neckline dart crease dartline nearest center back. Close, cup and pin dart. True neckline with French curve. Trace dart underlay on trued neckline to opposite side.

B. With dart closed cut excess paper from neckline. Open draft. Cut on remaining seamlines and notch dartlines.

Note: 1. Since this is a sloper and not a pattern, seam allowance is not necessary.

2. *Neckline Variations*—The neckline dart may be placed anywhere from 1" (2.5 cm) from center back to shoulder/neckline intersection. The dart may be divided into multiple darts in the form of a sunburst design if the dart underlay is considerably larger than average. If the dart is divided, new darts may be shorter.

FIGURE 5

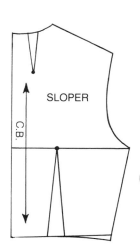

This diagram illustrates *Finished Back Sloper.*

UNDERARM & WAISTLINE DARTS
sketch 2

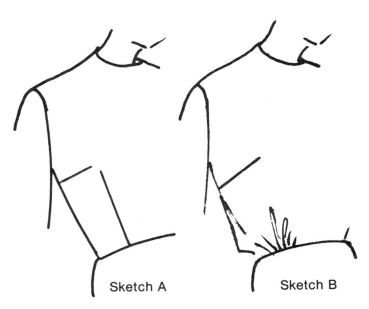

Sketch A   Sketch B

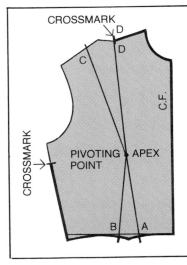

FIGURE 2

A. Cut paper approximately 15″ × 25″ (38.1 × 63.5 cm).

B. Place sloper on paper. Crossmark on paper dartline D and waist dartlines and underarm crossmark. Outline sloper from shoulder at dartline D to neckline, neckline, center front, waistline, and underarm to crossmark.

C. With awl indicate apex.

FIGURE 1

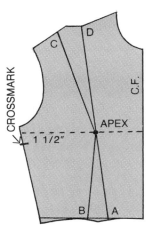

A. Use *two-dart front waist sloper.*

B. To prepare sloper:

1. Establish position of underarm dart. Using an L-square, square a line from center front through apex to underarm seam. Crossmark on underarm seamline. If crossmark is less than 1½″ (3.8 cm) below armhole, measure 1½″ (3.8 cm) below armhole.

Note: When apex line is less than 1½″ (3.8 cm) from armhole, it is too close to accommodate dart properly. By lowering apex line, dart will be on a slight slant and give a more pleasing effect to garment.

2. Label shoulder and waistline dartlines *A, B, C, D* (as illustrated).

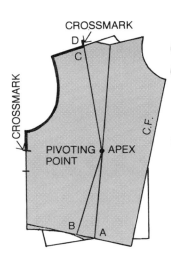

FIGURE 3

A. Pivoting point is at apex.

B. Hold sloper at pivoting point and pivot sloper until dartline C touches shoulder crossmark D.

C. On paper crossmark on underarm seam. Outline sloper from shoulder at dartline C to armhole, armhole and underarm crossmark.

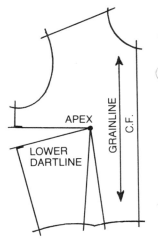

FIGURE 4

A. Remove sloper. Pencil in apex dot.

B. To form underarm dart draw a straight line from underarm seam crossmarks to apex, extending dartlines at underarm seam.

C. True all lines crossing intersections *except* at underarm dart.

D. Establish grainline parallel to center front.

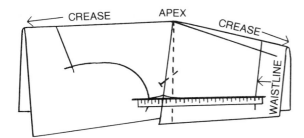

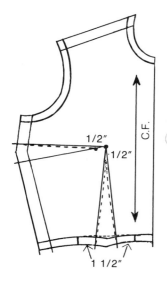

FIGURE 5

A.   To true underarm dart crease lower dartline. Close, cup and pin dart. True underarm seams (as illustrated). Trace dart underlay on trued underarm seam to opposite side.

B.   With dart closed allow seam and cut.

FIGURE 6

A.   Open paper. Pencil in traced dart underlay.

B.   To complete pattern allow seams on remaining seamlines; cut and notch seams.

C.   Dart may be shortened ½" (1.3 cm) for ease (as illustrated).

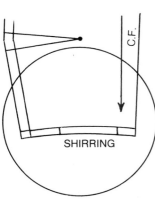

FIGURE 6A

To develop shirred waistline blend dart area and establish crossmarks as illustrated in Figure 6.

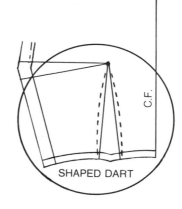

FIGURE 6B

To develop form-fitting waist shape waistline dart (as illustrated).

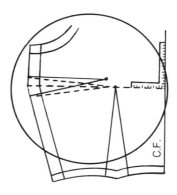

FIGURE 7

When pivoting a shoulder dart to the underarm using the 1½" (3.8 cm) drop, the center of the dart underlay is off grain due to the slant of the dart. When a stripe or plaid fabric is used the dart can be adjusted so that the center of the dart underlay is on grain. Therefore the stripe or plaid fabric will match and form a chevron effect.

A.   Square a line from center front across to center of dart underlay at underarm seam line.

B.   Draw dartlines to new apex.

C.   True new dart.

ARMHOLE & WAISTLINE DARTS
sketch 3

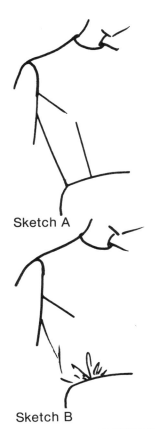

Sketch A

Sketch B

The armhole dart may be placed wherever desired for styling. However, if it is placed at the position of the armhole muscle it will give a better fit. The muscle line is located approximately one-third up on the front armhole of the sloper. (This refers to a natural shoulder armhole and not a padded shoulder.)

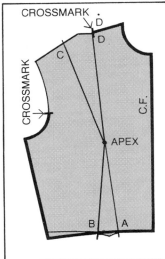

FIGURE 1

A. Use *two-dart front waist sloper.*

B. To prepare sloper:

   1. Establish position of armhole dart desired. Crossmark on armhole seamline.

   2. Label shoulder and waistline dartlines *A, B, C, D* (as illustrated).

C. Cut paper approximately 15" × 25" (38.1 × 63.5 cm).

D. Place sloper on paper. Crossmark on paper dartlines A, B and D and armhole crossmark. Outline sloper from shoulder at dartline D to neckline, neckline, center front, waistline, underarm and armhole to crossmark.

E. With awl indicate apex.

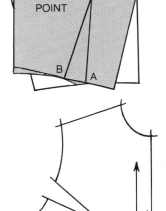

FIGURE 2

A. Pivoting point is at apex.

B. Hold sloper securely at pivoting point and pivot sloper until dartline C touches shoulder crossmark D.

C. On paper crossmark on armhole. Outline sloper from shoulder at dartline C to armhole and armhole to crossmark.

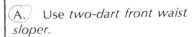

FIGURE 3

A. Remove sloper. Pencil in apex dot.

B. To form armhole dart draw a straight line from armhole crossmark to apex extending dartlines at armhole.

C. True all lines crossing intersections *except* at armhole dart.

D. Establish grainline parallel to center front.

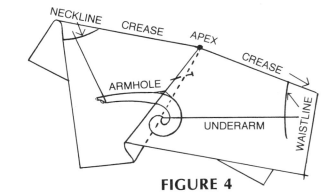

FIGURE 4

A. To true armhole dart crease either dartline depending upon desired effect. Close, cup and pin dart. True armhole with French curve. Trace dart underlay on trued armhole to opposite side.

B. With dart closed allow seam and cut.

FIGURE 5B

To develop form-fitting waist shape waistline dart (as illustrated).

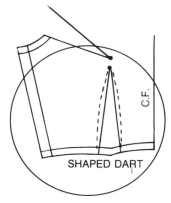

SHAPED DART

FIGURE 5

A.   Open paper. Pencil in traced dart underlay.

B.   To complete pattern allow seams on remaining seamlines; cut and notch seams.

C.   Darts may be shortened ½" (1.3 cm) for ease (as illustrated).

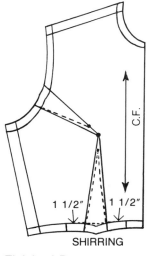

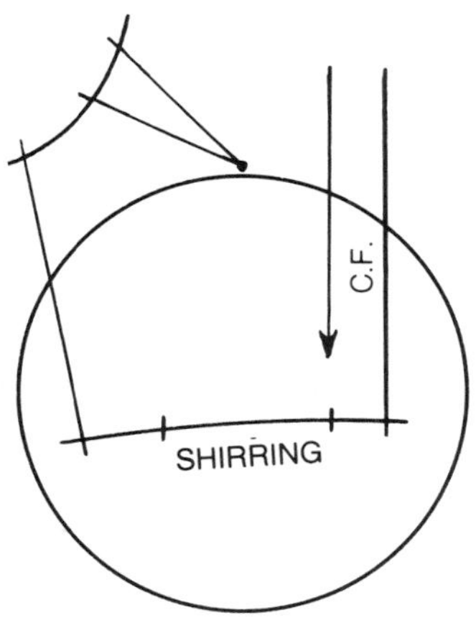

SHIRRING

Finished Pattern

FIGURE 5A

To develop shirred waistline blend dart area and establish crossmarks as illustrated in Figure 5.

SHIRRING

Sketch A

Sketch B

Sketch C

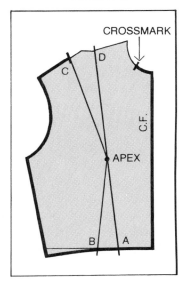

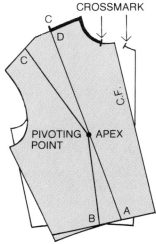

FIGURE 2

A.   Pivoting point is at apex.

B.   Hold sloper securely at pivoting point and pivot sloper until dartline D touches shoulder crossmark C.

C.   On paper crossmark at neckline. Outline sloper from shoulder at dartline C to neckline crossmark.

The neckline dart may be stitched or unstitched, used as a dart tuck, caught only at neckline seam or shirred. It may be made in combination with a waistline dart. For greater ease at neckline, the waistline dart may be pivoted into neckline dart (see Neckline Dart, sketch 8). This dart may be placed at any position on the neckline.

SKETCH A

FIGURE 1

A.   Use *two-dart front waist sloper.*

B.   To prepare sloper.

    1.   Establish position of neckline dart desired. Crossmark on neckline.

    2.   Label shoulder and waistline dartlines *A, B, C, D* (as illustrated).

C.   Cut paper approximately 15″ × 25″ (38.1 × 63.5 cm).

D.   Place sloper on paper. Crossmark on paper dartlines A, B, C and neckline crossmark. Outline sloper from shoulder at dartline C to armhole, armhole, underarm, waistline, center front and neckline to crossmark.

E.   With awl indicate apex.

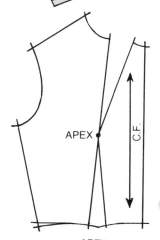

FIGURE 3

A.   Remove sloper. Pencil in apex dot.

B.   To form neckline dart draw a straight line from neckline crossmarks to apex extending dartlines at neckline.

C.   True all lines, crossing intersections *except* at neckline dart.

D.   Establish grainline parallel to center front.

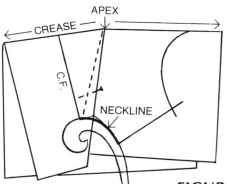

FIGURE 4

A.   To true neckline dart crease either dartline depending upon effect desired. Close, cup and pin dart. True neckline with French curve. Trace dart underlay on trued neckline seam to opposite side.

B.   With dart closed allow seam and cut.

SKETCHES B, C

FIGURE 7

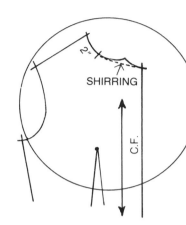

A.   To develop shirred *neckline:*

①   Blend neckline (broken line).

②   Place a crossmark for shirring approximately 1½" to 2" (3.8 to 5.1 cm) down from shoulder seam.

B.   To develop shirred *waistline* (sketch C):

1.   Measure 1½" (3.8 cm) on each side of dartlines. Crossmark.

2.   Blend dart point at waistline (broken line in Figure 5).

FIGURE 5

A.   Open paper. Pencil in traced dart underlay.

B.   To complete pattern allow seams to remaining seams; cut and notch seams.

ⓒ   Darts may be shortened ½" (1.3 cm) for ease (as illustrated).

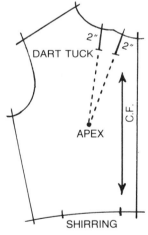

Finished Pattern

FIGURE 6

To develop dart tuck extend dartlines down to desired length. Crossmark. Illustrated: 2" (5.1 cm).

CENTER FRONT & WAISTLINE DARTS
sketch 5

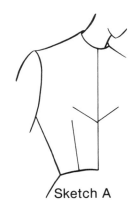

/ Sketch A

The center front dart may be planned at any point on the center front, at right angles to the apex, or on a slant above or below the apex depending on the effect desired. In sketch 5A, the direction of the dart slants from the apex *down* towards the waistline.

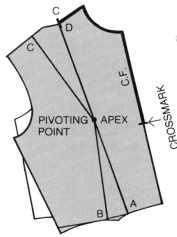

FIGURE 2

A. Pivoting point is at apex.

B. Hold sloper at pivoting point and pivot sloper until dartline D touches shoulder crossmark C.

C. On paper crossmark at center front. Outline sloper from shoulder at dartline C to neckline, neckline and center front to crossmark.

/ Sketch B

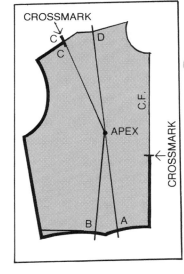

SKETCH A

FIGURE 1

A. Use *two-dart front waist sloper.*

B. To prepare sloper:

1. Establish position for center front dart desired. Crossmark on center front seamline.

2. Label shoulder and waistline dartlines *A, B, C, D* (as illustrated).

C. Cut paper approximately 15″ × 25″ (38.1 × 63.5 cm).

D. Place sloper on paper. Crossmark on paper dartlines A, B, C and center front crossmark. Outline sloper from shoulder at dartline C to armhole, armhole, underarm, waistline, and center front to crossmark.

E. With awl indicate apex.

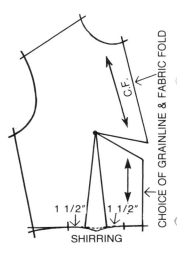

1 1/2″   1 1/2″

SHIRRING

FIGURE 3

A. Remove sloper. Pencil in apex dot.

B. To form center front dart draw a straight line from center front crossmarks to apex extending dartlines at center front.

C. True all lines crossing intersections *except* at center front dart.

D. Establish grainline parallel to center front (as illustrated). *Note:* Center front may also be cut with center front grainline from dart to waistline or with a center front seamline from neckline to waistline.

E. To establish crossmarks for a shirred waistline see illustration.

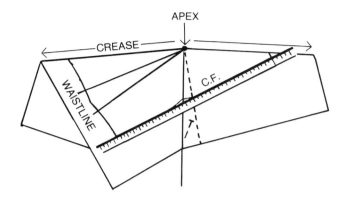

FIGURE 6

To develop shirred waistline see Figure 3.

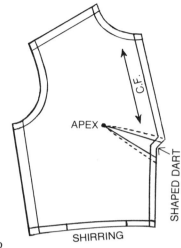

FIGURE 4

A.   To true center front dart crease upper dartline. Close, cup and pin dart. True center front line. Trace dart underlay on trued line to opposite side.

B.   With dart closed allow seam and cut.

FIGURE 5

A.   Open paper. Pencil in traced dart underlay.

B.   To complete pattern allow seams on remaining seamlines; cut and notch seams.
Note: 1.   *Waistline dart* may be shortened ½" (1.3 cm).
2.   Center front dart may not be shortened. It ends at the apex. In fact, the dart is often shaped for a better fit (broken line in Figure 6).

SKETCH B
FIGURE 7

A.   To develop pattern for this sketch, follow procedure as for sketch A with the following exception: true dart, crease and close lower dartline.

B.   For principles on how to establish extension, facing and buttonholes refer to Buttons & Buttonholes.

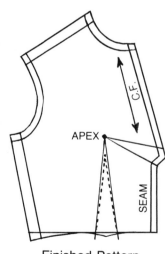

Finished Pattern

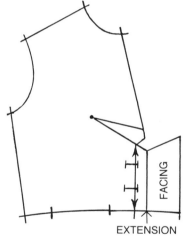

Sketch A

A one-dart front sloper is necessary in the development of the many different front waist designs.

Sketch B

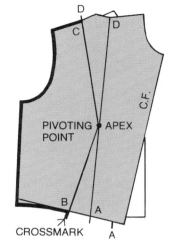

FIGURE 2

A. Pivoting point is at apex.

B. Hold sloper securely at pivoting point and pivot sloper until dartline C touches crossmark D.

C. On paper crossmark dartline B. Outline sloper from shoulder at dartline D to armhole, armhole, underarm, waistline to dartline B.

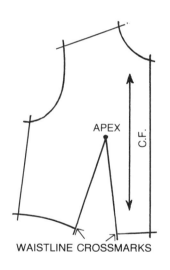

WAISTLINE CROSSMARKS

FIGURE 3

A. Remove sloper. Pencil in apex dot.

B. To form waistline dart draw a straight line from waistline crossmarks to apex extending dartlines at waistline.

C. True all lines crossing intersections *except* waistline dart.

D. Establish grainline parallel to center front.

FIGURE 1

A. Use *two-dart front waist sloper*.

B. On sloper label shoulder and waistline dartlines *A, B, C, D* (as illustrated).

C. Cut paper approximately 15″ × 25″ (38.1 × 63.5 cm).

D. Place sloper on paper. Crossmark on paper dartlines A and D. Outline sloper from shoulder at dartline D to neckline, neckline, center front, waistline to dartline A.

E. With awl indicate apex.

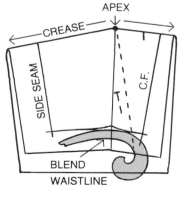

FIGURE 4

A. To true waistline dart crease dartline nearest center front. Close, cup and pin dart. True waistline with French curve. Trace dart underlay on trued waistline to opposite side.

B. With dart closed cut on seamline.

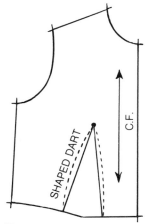

Finished Sloper

FIGURE 5

A.   Open paper. Pencil in traced dart underlay.

B.   For a finished sloper cut on remaining seamlines and notch dartlines.

C.   For a shaped dart see illustration.

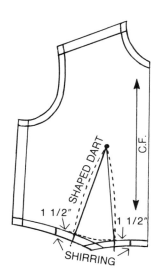

Finished Pattern

FIGURE 6

A.   If sloper is to be used as a pattern, allow seams; cut and notch seams.

B.   To develop shirred waistline follow illustration.

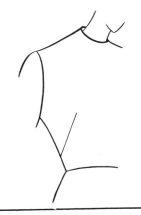

A French dart is an underarm dart placed at an angle and pointed towards the apex of the bust. This dart may be placed anywhere between the waistline and underarm intersection and up to one-third of the underarm seam.

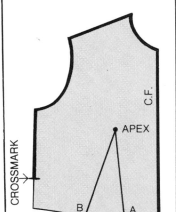

FIGURE 1

A. Use *one-dart front waist sloper.*

B. To prepare sloper:

    1. Establish position of French dart desired. Crossmark on underarm seamline.

    2. Label waistline dartlines *A* and *B* (as illustrated).

C. Cut paper approximately 15" × 25" (38.1 × 63.5 cm).

D. Place sloper on paper. Crossmark on paper at dartline A and underarm seam crossmark. Outline sloper from waistline at dartline A to center front, center front, neckline, shoulder seam, armhole and underarm seam to crossmark.

E. With awl indicate apex.

FIGURE 2

A. Pivoting point is at apex.

B. Hold sloper at pivoting point and pivot sloper until dartline B touches crossmark A.

C. On paper crossmark at underarm seam. Outline sloper from waistline at dartline B to underarm seam crossmark.

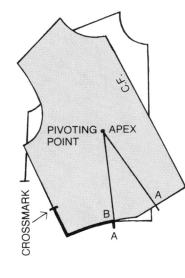

FIGURE 3

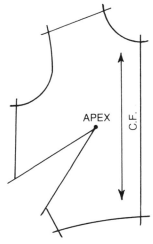

A. Remove sloper. Pencil in apex dot.

B. To form French dart draw a straight line from underarm seam crossmarks to apex extending dartlines at underarm seam.

C. True all lines crossing intersections *except* at underarm seam dart.

D. Establish grainline parallel to center front.

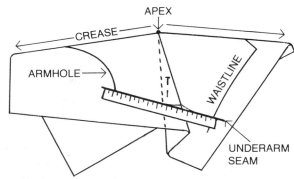

FIGURE 4

A. To true French dart crease either dartline depending on desired effect. Close, cup and pin dart. True underarm seam. Trace dart underlay on trued underarm to opposite side.

B. With dart closed allow seam and cut.

FIGURE 5

A. Open paper. Pencil in traced dart underlay.

B. To complete pattern allow seams on remaining seamlines; cut and notch seams.

C. To develop tight fit between apex and underarm seam see broken line. The amount to be curved depends upon the shape of the individual figure type or model form.

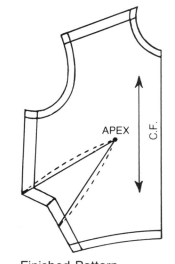

Finished Pattern

Sketch A

Sketch B

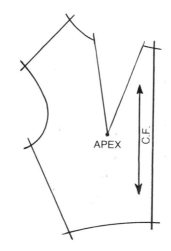

FIGURE 3

A.   Remove sloper. Pencil in apex dot.

B.   To form neckline dart draw a straight line from neckline crossmarks to apex extending dartlines at neckline.

C.   True all lines crossing intersections *except* at neckline dart.

D.   Establish grainline parallel to center front.

SKETCHES A & B

FIGURE 1

A.   Use *one-dart front waist sloper.*

B.   To prepare sloper:

1.   Establish position of neckline dart desired. Crossmark on neckline.

2.   Label waistline dartlines *A* and *B* (as illustrated).

C.   Cut paper approximately 15″ × 25″ (38.1 × 63.5 cm).

D.   Place sloper on paper. Crossmark on paper dartline A and neckline crossmark. Outline sloper from waistline at dartline A to center front, center front and neckline to crossmark.

E.   With awl indicate apex.

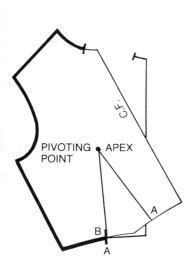

FIGURE 2

A.   Pivoting point is at apex.

B.   Hold sloper at pivoting point and pivot sloper until dartline B touches crossmark A.

C.   On paper crossmark neckline crossmark. Outline sloper from waistline at dartline B to underarm, underarm, armhole, shoulder and neckline to crossmark.

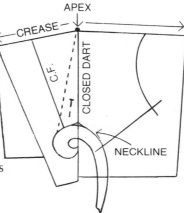

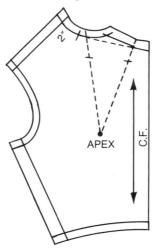

Finished Pattern

FIGURE 4

A.   To true neckline dart crease either dartline depending upon effect desired. Close, cup and pin dart. True neckline with French curve. Trace dart underlay on trued neckline to opposite side.

B.   With dart closed allow seam and cut.

FIGURE 5

A.   Open paper. Pencil in traced dart underlay.

B.   To complete pattern allow seams on remaining seamlines; cut and notch seams.

C.   To develop dart tuck follow dartlines down to desired length and crossmark.

D.   To develop shirred neckline (sketch B):

1.   Blend neckline (broken line).

2.   Crossmark for shirring approximately 2″ (5.1 cm) down from shoulder.

SHOULDER/NECKLINE DART
sketch 9

Sketch A

Sketch B

The shoulder/neckline dart may be used as a stitched dart, a dart tuck, or left unstitched caught only at the seam. This dart may be combined with a waistline dart. If so desired, work with the two-dart front sloper.

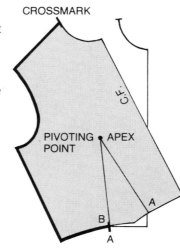

CROSSMARK

FIGURE 2

A.   Pivoting point is at apex.

B.   Hold sloper at pivoting point and pivot sloper until dartline B touches crossmark A.

C.   Crossmark shoulder/neckline intersection. Outline sloper from waistline at dartline B to underarm, underarm, armhole and shoulder.

SKETCH A

FIGURE 1

A.   Use *one-dart front waist sloper.*

B.   To prepare sloper:

    1.   Establish position of shoulder/neckline dart at shoulder/neckline intersection. Crossmark.

    2.   Label waistline dartlines *A* and *B* (as illustrated).

C.   Cut paper approximately 15″ × 25″ (38.1 × 63.5 cm).

D.   Place sloper on paper. Crossmark on paper dartline A and crossmark at shoulder/neckline intersection. Outline sloper from waistline at dartline A to center front, center front to shoulder/neckline crossmark.

E.   With awl indicate apex.

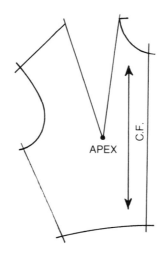

FIGURE 3

A.   Remove sloper. Pencil in apex dot.

B.   To form shoulder/neckline dart draw a straight line from shoulder/neckline crossmarks to apex extending dartline at shoulder/neckline crossmarks.

C.   True all lines crossing intersections *except* at shoulder/neckline dart.

D.   Establish grainline parallel to center front.

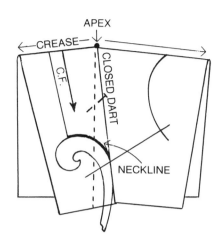

SKETCH B

A.   This sketch illustrates darts on reverse with tie end and bow inserted under dart.

B.   To develop pattern for this sketch follow procedure as for sketch A with the following exception: To true dart crease *dartline nearest armhole.*

FIGURE 4

A.   To true shoulder/neckline dart crease either dartline depending upon effect desired. Close, cup and pin dart. True dart with French curve. Trace dart underlay on trued shoulder/neckline to opposite side.

B.   With dart closed allow seam and cut.

FIGURE 5

A.   Open paper. Pencil in traced dart underlay.

B.   To complete pattern allow seams on remaining seamlines; cut and notch seams.

C.   To develop dart tuck follow dartline down to desired length and crossmark.

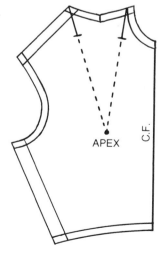

Finished Pattern

CENTER FRONT DART
sketch 10

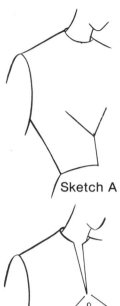

Sketch A

Sketch B

This project is similar to Center Front & Waistline Darts, sketch 5, with one exception. In sketch 5, the shoulder dart has been pivoted to the center front and the waistline dart has been retained. In this sketch all the dart fullness is absorbed into the center front.

SKETCH A

FIGURE 1

A.   Use *one-dart front waist sloper.*

B.   To prepare sloper:

1.   Establish position of diagonal center front dart. Crossmark on center front.

2.   Label waistline dartlines *A* and *B* (as illustrated).

C.   Cut paper approximately 15″ × 25″ (38.1 × 63.5 cm).

D.   Place sloper on paper. Crossmark on paper dartline B and center front crossmark. Outline sloper from waistline at dartline B to underarm, underarm, armhole, shoulder, neckline and center front to crossmark.

E.   With awl indicate apex.

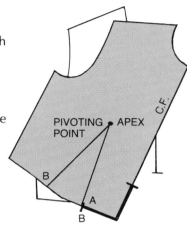

FIGURE 2

A.   Pivoting point is at apex.

B.   Hold sloper securely at pivoting point and pivot sloper until dartline A touches crossmark B.

C.   On paper crossmark center front crossmark. Outline sloper from waistline at dartline A to center front crossmark.

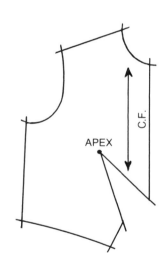

FIGURE 3

A.   Remove sloper. Pencil in apex dot.

B.   To form diagonal center front dart draw a straight line from center front crossmarks to apex extending dartlines at center front.

C.   True all lines crossing intersections *except* at center front dart.

D.   Establish grainline parallel to upper section of center front (as illustrated).
Note: Center front may also be cut with center front grainline from dart to waistline or with a center front seamline from neckline to waistline.

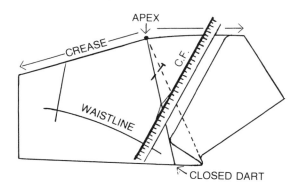

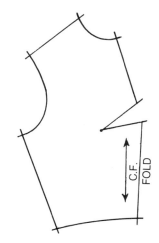

SKETCH B

FIGURE 6

A. Plan dartline from apex up towards neckline.

B. To true dart for this sketch crease lower dartline.

C. Cut section below dart on grainline and fold of fabric.

FIGURE 4

A. To true diagonal center front dart crease either dartline depending upon effect desired. Close, cup and pin dart. True center front line. Trace dart underlay on trued center front line to opposite side.

B. With dart closed allow seam and cut.

FIGURE 5

A. Open paper. Pencil in traced dart underlay.

B. To complete pattern allow seams on remaining seamlines; cut and notch seams.

C. To develop tight fit through center front midriff area see broken line. The amount to be curved depends upon the shape of the individual figure type or model form.

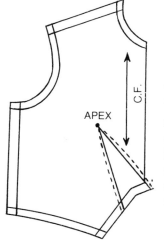

Finished Pattern

HORIZONTAL CENTER FRONT BUSTLINE DART
sketch 11

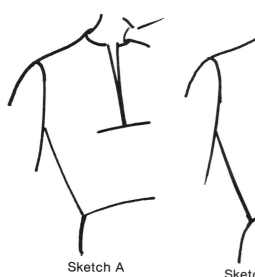

Sketch A

Sketch B

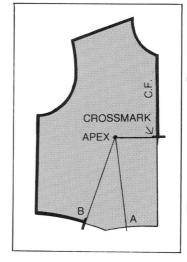

FIGURE 2

A.   Cut paper approximately 15″ × 25″ (38.1 × 63.5 cm).

B.   Place sloper on paper. Crossmark on paper dartline B and center front crossmark. Outline sloper from waistline at dartline B to underarm, underarm, armhole, shoulder, neckline and center front to crossmark.

C.   With awl indicate apex.

SKETCH A

FIGURE 1

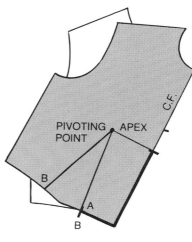

A.   Use *one-dart front waist sloper.*

B.   To prepare sloper:

1.   Establish position of horizontal center front bust dart. Using an L-square, square a line from center front to apex. Crossmark on center front.

2.   Label waistline dartlines *A* and *B* (as illustrated).

FIGURE 3

A.   Pivoting point is at apex.

B.   Hold sloper securely at pivoting point and pivot sloper until dartline A touches crossmark B.

C.   On paper crossmark at center front. Outline sloper from waistline at dartline A to center front crossmark.

FIGURE 4

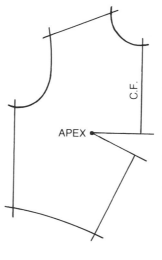

A.   Remove sloper. Pencil in apex dot.

B.   To form horizontal center front bust dart draw a straight line from center front crossmarks to apex extending dartlines at center front.

C.   True all lines crossing intersections *except* at center front dart.

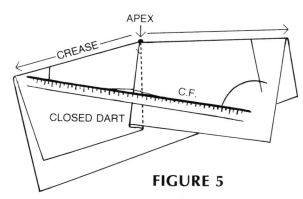

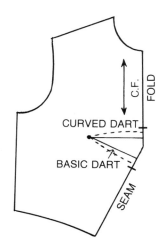

SKETCH B
FIGURE 7

Establish crossmarks for shirring 1″ (2.5 cm) above and below dartlines. Cut waist on grain and fold from neckline to dartline.

FIGURE 5

A. To true horizontal center front bust dart crease either dartline depending upon effect desired. Close, cup and pin dart. True center front. Trace dart underlay on trued center front line to opposite side.

B. With dart closed allow seam and cut.

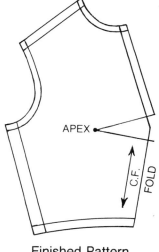

Finished Pattern

FIGURE 6

A. Open paper. Pencil in traced dart underlay.

B. To complete pattern allow seams on remaining seamlines; cut and notch seams.

C. To develop different design effects, the garment may be cut:

  1. With seam down the center front and the straight grain either above or below apex (sketches A and B).

  2. With upper or lower section on the fold.

D. To develop tight fit through the center of the waist this dart may be curved (broken line). The amount to be curved depends upon the shape of the individual figure type or model form.

DIVISION OF BASIC FRONT WAIST DARTS
introduction

Basic darts may be divided into two or more darts at
various positions on a waist with an understanding of the
principles discussed in this unit.

To develop multiple darts, the new dartlines must always
touch the side of the dart to be absorbed. In order to
accomplish this, it may be necessary to pivot a basic dart
to a new position on the waist. The proper selection of
basic waist slopers to be used in the division of darts will
be discussed in this unit.

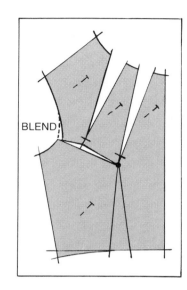

FIGURE 2

A.   Place draft on another sheet of paper. Pin lower section.

B.   Close armhole dart. Distribute spaces *evenly* between cut lines at neckline. Pin sections in place.

C.   Draw new dartlines. Blend armhole.

Note: For shorter darts from lower dartline measure up 1" (2.5 cm) and crossmark. Dot center of darts at crossmark. Draw a line from dots to dartlines at neckline.

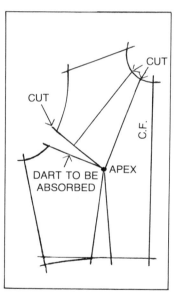

FIGURE 1

A.   Use *two-dart front waist sloper.*

B.   Cut paper approximately 15" × 25" (38.1 × 63.5 cm).

C.   Place sloper on paper and outline pivoting shoulder dart to armhole.

D.   Remove sloper. True all lines crossing all intersections.

E.   Establish cut lines for new darts from neckline to apex and to upper dartlines as desired. For a graceful effect, space darts so that they fan out slightly towards upper dartline.

F.   Cut on lines from neckline to upper dartline.

G.   Cut from armhole on upper dartline to apex.

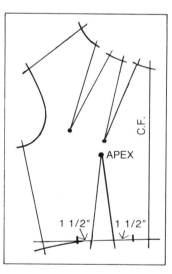

FIGURE 3

A.   Outline draft and remove.

B.   True all lines crossing intersections *except* at new dart.

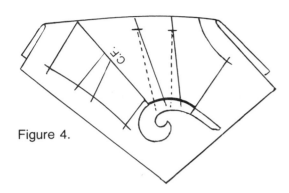

Figure 4.

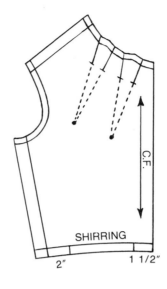

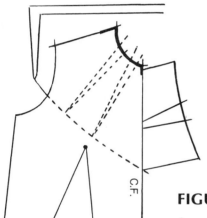

Figure 4A.

FIGURE 5

A.   Open darts. Pencil in traced dart underlay.

B.   To complete pattern allow seam on remaining seamlines; cut and notch seams.

C.   Establish grainline parallel to center front.

D.   To develop dart tucks see illustration.

E.   To develop shirred waistline see illustration.

FIGURES 4 & 4A

A.   Close and cup darts with fold of darts facing away from center front. Pin.

B.   With darts closed true neckline using front sloper (see Figure 4A).
Note: If draft neckline is smaller or larger than sloper neckline, increase or decrease darts until sloper fits at center front, neckline, shoulder and armhole (if instructions are followed accurately, adjustment should be very slight).

C.   Outline neckline and retrue with French curve.

D.   Remove sloper. Trace adjusted neckline to opposite side.

E.   With darts closed allow seam at neckline and cut.

Sketch 2

To develop pattern for this sketch follow procedures discussed in sketch 1. The only difference is in the position of the dart on the waist. Use *one-dart front waist sloper.* Pivot dart to underarm seam. Underarm seam dartline may be extended beyond apex ½″ (1.3 cm) if needed for better distribution of darts.

Sketch 3

To develop pattern for this sketch follow procedures discussed in sketch 1. The only difference is in the position of the dart on the waist. Use *one-dart front waist sloper.* Pivot dart to armhole.

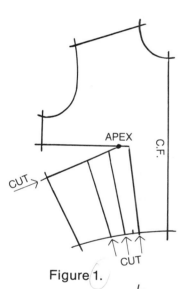

Figure 1.

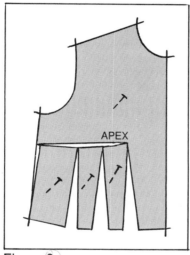

Figure 2.

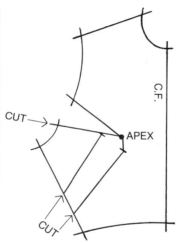

Figure 1.

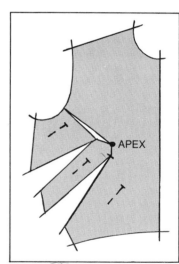

Figure 2.

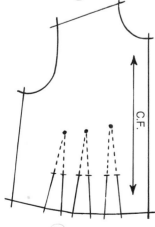

Figure 3.

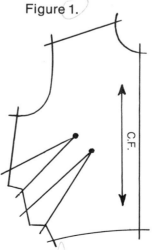

Figure 3.

DIVISION OF BASIC FRONT WAIST DARTS
sketches 4, 5

Sketch 4

To develop pattern for this sketch follow procedures discussed in sketch 1. The only difference is in the position of the dart on the waist. Use *one-dart front waist sloper.* Pivot dart to center front bustline.

Sketch 5

To develop pattern for this sketch follow procedures discussed in sketch 1. The only difference is in the position of the dart on the waist. Use *two-dart front waist sloper.* Pivot shoulder dart to armhole.

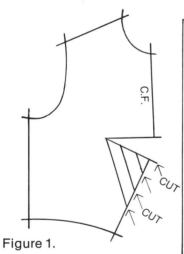

Figure 1.

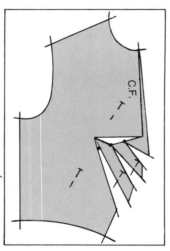

Figure 2.

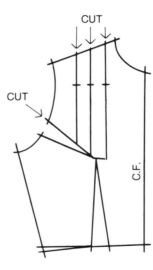

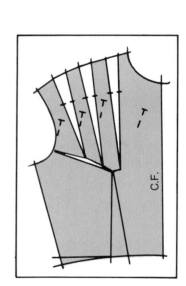

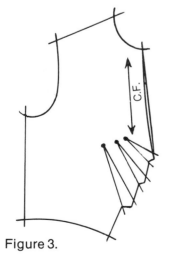

Figure 3.

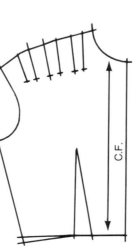

Sketch 6

To develop pattern for this sketch follow procedures discussed in sketch 1. The only difference is in the position of the dart on the waist. Use *two-dart front waist sloper. No pivoting* of dart is required. Establish grainline on any of the three positions illustrated.

Sketch 7

To develop pattern for this sketch follow procedures discussed in sketch 1. The only difference is in the position of the dart on the waist. Use *two-dart front waist sloper.* Pivot shoulder dart to neckline. This sketch illustrates that dartlines need not always be straight lines. Stylized darts may be shortened more than 1″ (2.5 cm) away from the apex. When dartlines are shortened, the shoulder dart cannot be absorbed completely by the new darts. Half of the shoulder is pivoted into the waistline dart and the other half is divided equally between the new dartlines.

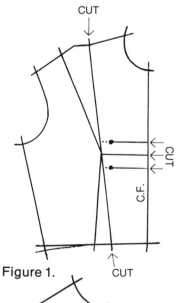

Figure 1.

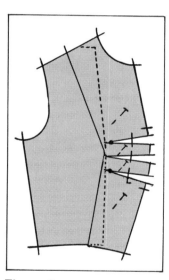

Figure 2.

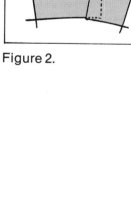

Figure 3.

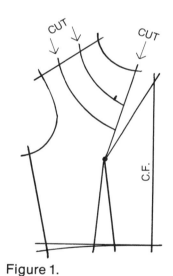

Figure 1.

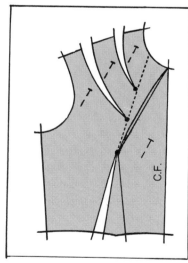

Figure 2.

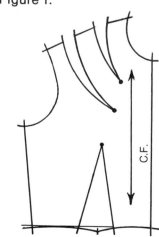

Figure 3.

The major function of darts is to control the fit of a waist or garment to the curves or contour of the human body.

In this unit, the original fit of the waist is retained, but the darts are eliminated by introducing yokes, decorative seamlines, bands, shirring or other variations.

Shaded areas represent dart or darts to be eliminated.

Use *two-dart front waist sloper.* In sketches 1, 2 and 3 waistlines may be darted or shirred.

Sketch 1

Sketch 2

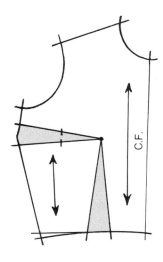

C.F.

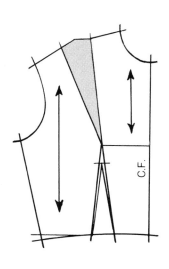

C.F.

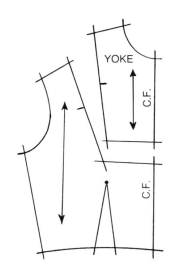

YOKE

C.F.

C.F.

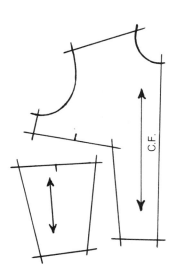

C.F.

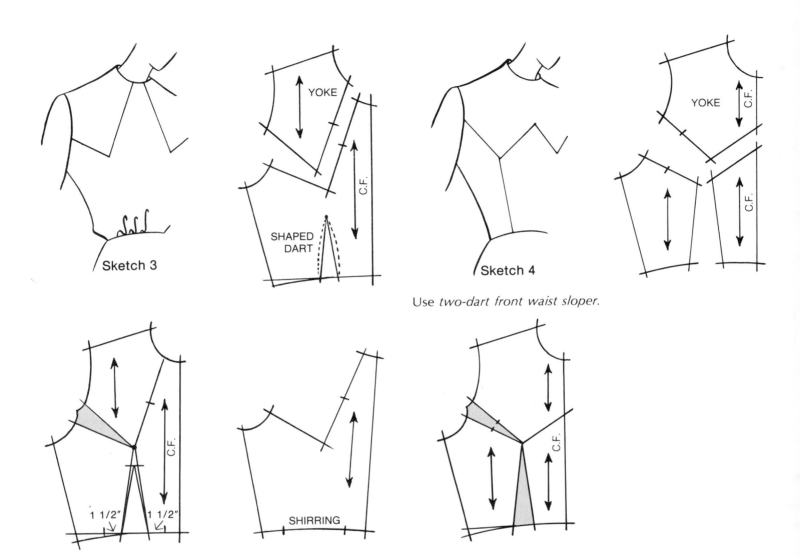

Sketch 3

YOKE

C.F.

SHAPED DART

Sketch 4

YOKE

C.F.

C.F.

Use two-dart front waist sloper.

C.F.

1 1/2"   1 1/2"

SHIRRING

C.F.

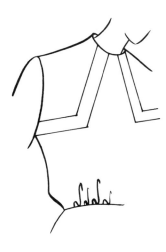

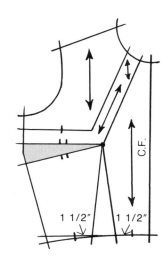

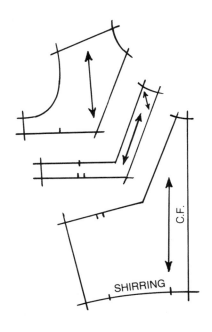

Use *two-dart front waist sloper.*

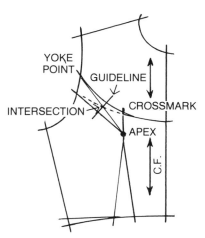

FIGURE 2

From lower dartline draw a new curved dartline crossing guideline/dartline intersection (broken line). Blend at yoke crossmark.

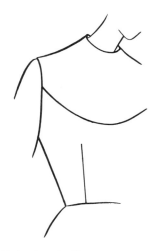

This sketch illustrates curved dart on shaped yokeline.

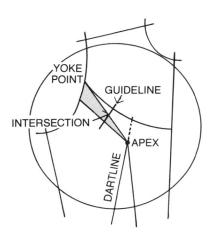

FIGURE 1

A.   Use *two-dart front waist sloper.*

B.   Establish yoke point at armhole. Pivot shoulder dart to yoke point (shaded area).

C.   Draw desired curved yokeline from armhole yoke point across to center front (as illustrated).

D.   Draw a guideline from yokeline through dart at the point where the space between dart and yokeline is equal to depth of dart underlay.

E.   Establish crossmark on yokeline above apex.

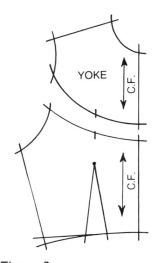

Figure 3.

Use *one-dart front waist sloper.*

Refer to Facings and Buttons & Buttonholes.

Sketch 7

Sketch 8

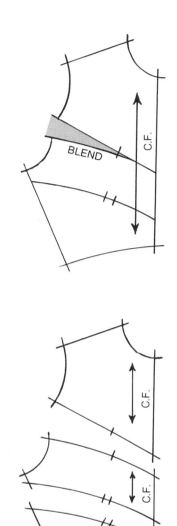

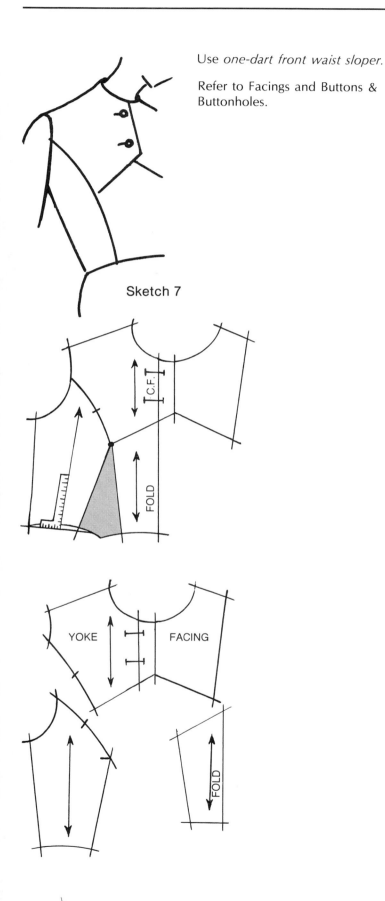

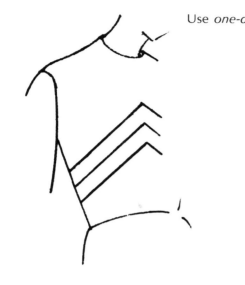

Use *one-dart front waist sloper.*

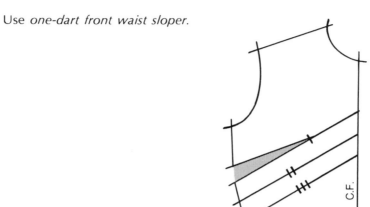

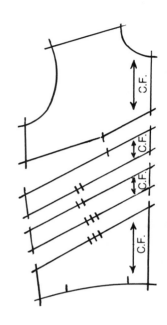

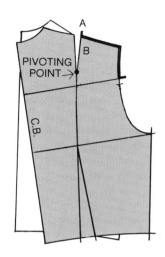

FIGURE 2

A.   Pivoting point is bottom of shoulder dart.

B.   Hold sloper securely at pivoting point and pivot sloper until dartline B meets dartline A. On paper crossmark new position of yokeline at armhole.

C.   Outline sloper from shoulder at dartline B to new position of yokeline at armhole.

D.   Remove sloper. Pencil in shoulder dart dot.

FIGURE 3

A.   Measure distance between C and new position of yokeline at armhole. Measure down from C this same amount. Label *D*.

B.   Dot on yokeline directly under shoulder dart dot.

C.   Draw a slightly curved line from A to dot on yokeline.

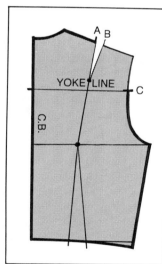

FIGURE 1

A.   Use *back waist sloper with shoulder and waistline darts*.

B.   On sloper square yokeline from center back as desired.

C.   Label shoulder dartlines *A* and *B* (as illustrated).

D.   Cut paper 16" × 25" (40.6 × 63.5 cm).

E.   Place sloper on paper. Crossmark on paper dartline A. Outline sloper from shoulder at dartline A to neckline, neckline, center back, waistline, underarm, armhole to yokeline crossmark.

F.   At armhole label yokeline C.

G.   With awl indicate bottom of shoulder dart.

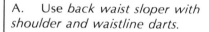

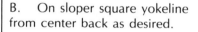

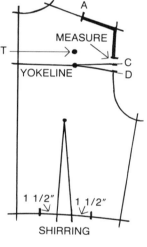

FIGURE 4

A.   Copy yokeline following yokeline to C.

B.   Copy bottom waist section following yokeline to D.

C.   True all lines crossing all intersections.

D.   On bottom waist section establish crossmarks at waistline for shirring if desired.

E.   Establish grainline parallel to center back on both sections.

F.   To complete pattern allow seams; cut and notch seams. *Note:* If fullness is desired with straight yoke add amount desired at center back.

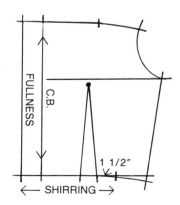

To develop the pattern for this sketch follow procedure discussed in sketch 10.

Note: To achieve desired fullness with a shaped yoke, the waist section must be slashed and spread.

Sketch A

Sketch B

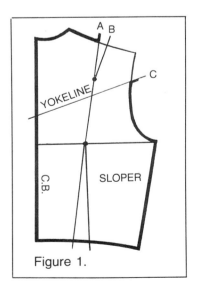

Figure 1.

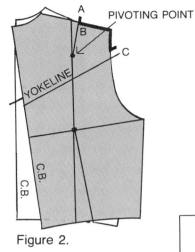

Figure 2.

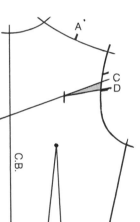

Figure 3.

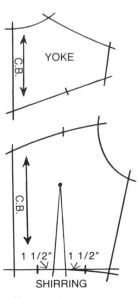

Figure 4.

Figure 5.

Figure 5 A.

STYLIZED WAISTS WITH SHIRRING
introduction

Shirring is a means of introducing fullness into a waist, skirt, sleeve, etc. It can be functional, as it can provide more freedom of movement, or it can be purely decorative, adding an interesting feature to a garment. The waists discussed in this unit are examples of decorative shirring details and, in some cases, the dart has been eliminated or absorbed into the shirring detail.

STYLIZED WAISTS WITH SHIRRING
sketches 1, 2

Sketch 1

To select slopers and develop stylized waists with shirring follow principles discussed in Division of Basic Front Waist Darts, sketch 1, with the following exception:

Do not mark darts as dart fullness will be shirred.

To introduce fullness in addition to the basic dart fullness, extra slash lines may be added (sketch 2). Slash lines indicate the direction in which the fullness will drape. Slash lines may radiate in any direction, but they must always end at a seamline or dartline.

Darts may be substituted for shirring if desired in any one of the following styles illustrated.

Establish crossmarks on original drafts to control distribution of fullness.

Sketch 2

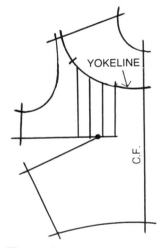

Figure 1.

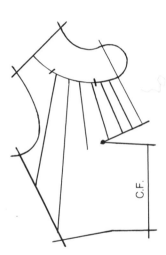

Figure 1.

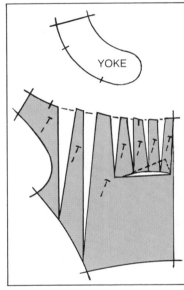

Figure 2.

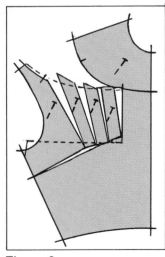

Figure 2.

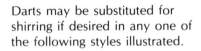
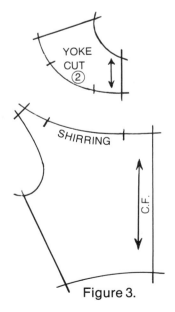

Figure 3.

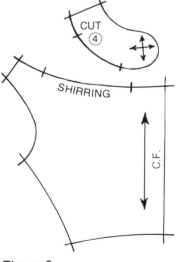

Figure 3.

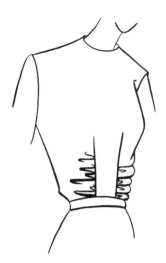

The shirring details in these sketches do not depend upon the use of basic darts. Slash lines are introduced wherever fullness is desired. However, these slash lines must always be placed between two seams. The amount of spread between slash lines depends upon the type of fabric used and the amount of fullness desired.

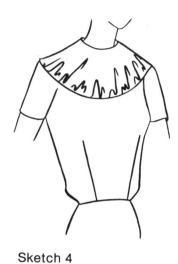

Sketch 3

Sketch 4

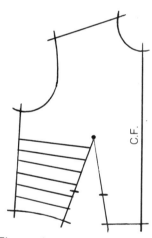

Figure 1.

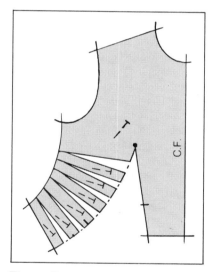

Figure 2.

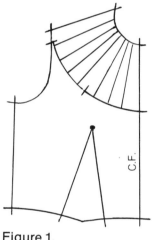

Figure 1.

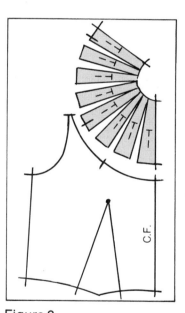

Figure 2.

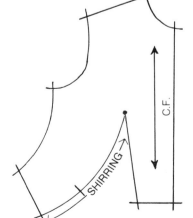

Figure 3.

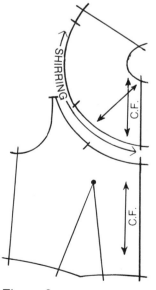

Figure 3.

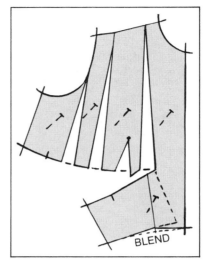

Figure 2.

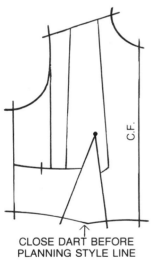

CLOSE DART BEFORE
PLANNING STYLE LINE

Figure 1.

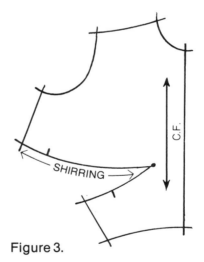

Figure 3.

A flange is a partially stitched dart, tuck, or fold placed at the end of a shoulder, at the back and/or at the front of a waist. It is a decorative use of the basic dart and facilitates the introduction of added fullness whenever desired.

A flange softens the effect in the garment design and helps the fit of garment. It is sometimes used to hide defects of the body such as hollow areas above the bustline. When a flange is introduced into the design on the back of a garment, it is often for the purpose of adding fullness to a basic back waist. Tennis players, golfers, skiers, or orchestra conductors find this extra width advantageous.

The effects obtained through the use of flanges are:

1.   A diagonal fold running from the end of the shoulder to the apex of the bust;

2.   A lengthwise fold starting at the end of the shoulder and finishing at the side of the bustline;

3.   A lengthwise fold extending from the end of the shoulder into the waistline.

Flanges may be used on all types of apparel such as dresses, coats, suits, sportswear, active sportswear, rainwear, children's wear, loungewear and work clothes.

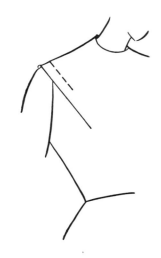

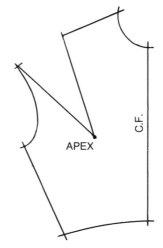

FIGURE 3

A.   Remove sloper. True all lines crossing all intersections.

B.   To form flange dart draw lines from shoulder crossmarks to apex.

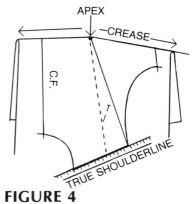

FIGURE 1

A.   Use *one-dart front waist sloper.*

B.   On sloper label waistline dartlines *A* and *B* (as illustrated).

C.   Cut paper approximately 15″ × 25″ (38.1 × 63.5 cm).

D.   Place sloper on paper. Crossmark on paper dartline A and shoulder/armhole intersection. Outline sloper from shoulder to neckline, neckline, center front and waistline to dartline A.

E.   With awl indicate apex.

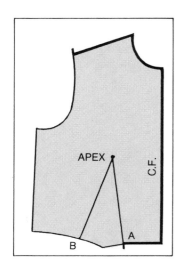

FIGURE 2

A.   Pivoting point is at apex.

B.   Hold sloper securely at pivoting point and pivot sloper until B touches A.

C.   On paper crossmark armhole/shoulder intersection. Outline sloper from crossmark at armhole/shoulder intersection to underarm, underarm and waistline to dartline B.

FIGURE 4

A.   To true shoulder flange crease dartline nearest center front. Close, cup and pin flange. True shoulderline. Trace flange underlay on trued shoulderline to opposite side.

B.   With flange closed allow seam and cut.

FIGURE 5

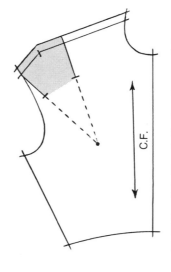

A.   Open flange. Pencil in traced flange lines.

B.   Establish grainline parallel to center front.

C.   To complete pattern allow seams on remaining seamlines; cut and notch seams.

D.   This flange may be stitched as a dart or tuck (as illustrated). To develop flange tuck refold dart and measure down desired length of tuck. Crossmark. Illustrated: 3″ (7.6 cm).

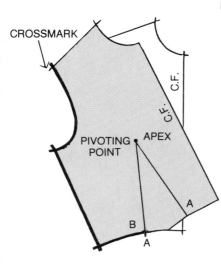

Sketch A

Sketch B

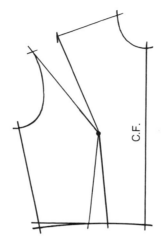

C.F.

FIGURE 3

A. Remove sloper. True all lines crossing all intersections.

B. To develop flange dart draw lines from shoulder crossmarks to apex.

C. To true shoulder flange crease dartline nearest center front. Close, cup and pin flange. True shoulderline. Trace flange underlay on trued shoulderline to opposite side.

D. With flange closed allow seam and cut.

E. Open flange. Pencil in traced flange underlay.

FIGURE 4

A. Establish grainline parallel to center front.

B. To complete pattern allow seams on remaining seamlines; cut and notch seams.

C. This flange may be stitched as a dart or tuck (as illustrated). To develop flange tuck refold dart and measure down desired length of tuck. Illustrated: 3" (7.6 cm).

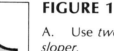

APEX

C.F.

FIGURE 1

A. Use *two-dart front waist sloper.*

B. On sloper label shoulder dartlines *A* and *B* (as illustrated).

C. Cut paper approximately 15" × 25" (38.1 × 63.5 cm).

D. Place sloper on paper. Crossmark on paper dartline B, armhole/shoulder intersection and waist dartlines. Outline sloper from armhole/underarm intersection, underarm seam, waistline, center front, neckline, and shoulder to B.

E. With awl indicated apex.

FIGURE 2

A. Pivoting point is at apex.

B. Hold sloper securely at pivoting point and pivot sloper until dartline A touches crossmark B.

C. Crossmark armhole/shoulderline intersection. Outline remainder of sloper.

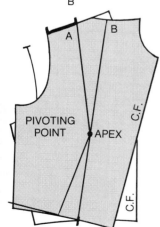

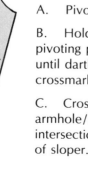

PIVOTING POINT

APEX

C.F.

C.F.

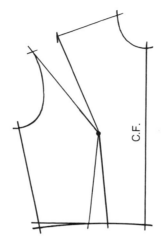

C.F.

1 1/2"   1 1/2"

‹SHIRRING›

PARALLEL TO ARMHOLE FRONT FLANGE
sketch 3

Sketch A

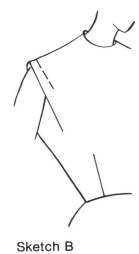

Sketch B

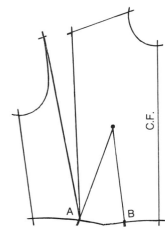

FIGURE 3

A.   Remove sloper. True all lines crossing all intersections.

B.   Draw a line from shoulder crossmarks to A.

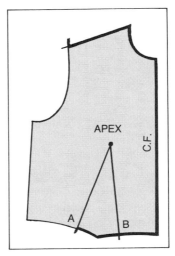

FIGURE 1

A.   Use *one-dart front waist sloper.*

B.   On sloper label waist dartlines *A* and *B* (as illustrated).

C.   Cut paper approximately 15″ × 25″ (38.1 × 63.5 cm).

D.   Place sloper on paper. On paper crossmark dartlines A and B and shoulder/armhole intersection. Outline sloper from waistline at dartline A to center front, center front, neckline and shoulder.

E.   With awl indicated apex.

FIGURE 2

A.   Pivoting point is at A.

B.   Hold sloper securely at pivoting point and pivot sloper until shoulder/armhole intersection has been moved from original position to desired depth of flange. Average flange: 2″ (5.1 cm).

C.   Crossmark shoulder/armhole intersection at new position. Outline sloper from waistline at dartline A to underarm, underarm seam and armhole.

FIGURE 4

A.   To true flange crease dartline nearest center front. Close, cup and pin flange.

B.   Measure down 3″ (7.6 cm) for flange tuck. Crossmark.

C.   Trace crossmark and shoulder through flange underlay.

D.   With flange closed allow seam and cut.

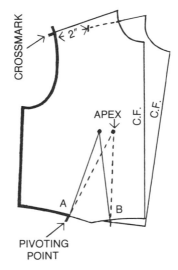

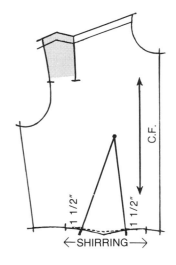

FIGURE 5

A.   Open flange. Pencil in traced flange underlay.

B.   Establish grainline parallel to center front.

C.   To complete pattern allow seams on remaining seamlines; cut and notch seams.

PARALLEL TO ARMHOLE BACK FLANGE
sketch 4

This back flange may be used alone or with front flange parallel to armhole (sketch 3). When used with the front flange, they must be developed as in sketch 5.

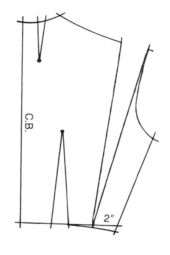

FIGURE 3

A. Remove sloper. True all lines crossing all intersections.

B. Draw lines from shoulder crossmarks to waistline crossmarks.

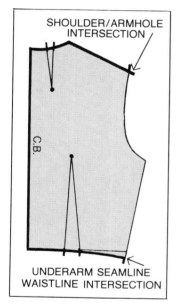

SHOULDER/ARMHOLE INTERSECTION

C.B.

UNDERARM SEAMLINE WAISTLINE INTERSECTION

FIGURE 1

A. Use *back waist sloper with neckline and waistline darts.*

B. Cut paper approximately 15″ × 25″ (38.1 × 63.5 cm).

C. Place sloper on paper. On paper crossmark shoulder/armhole and waistline/underarm seam intersections.

D. Outline shoulder to neckline, neckline, neckline dart, center back, waistline and waistline dart.

D. With awl indicate ends of darts.

FIGURE 2

A. To establish *pivoting point* at waistline measure in from underarm seam 2″ (5.1 cm). Crossmark. Pivoting point is this waistline crossmark.

B. Hold sloper at pivoting point and pivot sloper until shoulder/armhole intersection has been moved from original position to desired depth of flange. Average flange: 2″ (5.1 cm).

C. Crossmark shoulder/armhole intersection at new position. Outline sloper armhole and underarm seam.

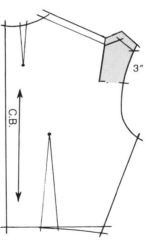

FIGURE 4

To true flange refer to Parallel to Armhole Front Flange, Figures 4 and 5.

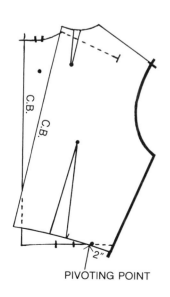

PIVOTING POINT

This front and back flange waist can be used to develop a garment of any length, from bolero to evening wear length, as waistline ends on a straight grain. To achieve the straight grain, part of the sloper dart pick-up is eliminated without loss of fit across the bustline (fullness lost is regained through the flange folds).

Sketch A   Front View   Back View

Sketch B   Front View   Back View

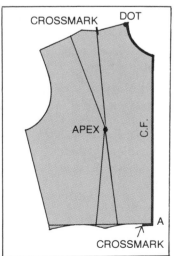

Sketch D

Sketch C

SKETCHES A & B PREPARATION OF FRONT SLOPER

FIGURE 1

A.   Use *two-dart front waist sloper*.

B.   Cut paper approximately 15″ × 25″ (38.1 × 63.5 cm).

C.   Place sloper on paper. Outline neckline and center front. Crossmark waistline/centerfront intersection. Label *A*. Crossmark shoulder dartline nearest center front. Dot neck/shoulderline intersection.

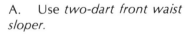

CROSSMARK   DOT

APEX   C.F.

A

CROSSMARK

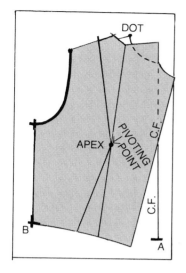

FIGURE 2

A.   Pivoting point is at apex.

B.   To eliminate shoulder dart, hold sloper at pivoting point and pivot sloper until shoulder dart is closed. Outline armhole. Dot shoulder/armhole intersection and crossmark waistline/underarm intersection. Label *B*. Crossmark underarm/armhole intersection.

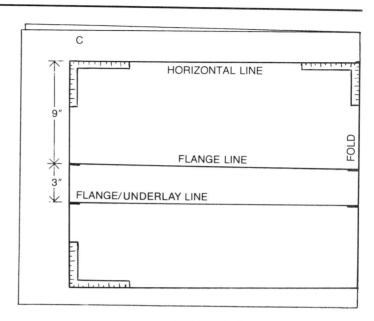

FIGURE 4

A.   Cut paper approximately 24" × 48" (61 × 121.9 cm). It is very important that this piece of paper is cut accurately.

B.   Fold paper in half. Pin. With fold of paper to your right-hand, square a line from fold across top edge, down left-hand side and across bottom edge to fold. Label top line *horizontal line;* left-hand intersection *C*.

C.   Recheck rectangle for accuracy. Cut away excess paper on all three edges to fold.

D.   To establish flange underlay from C and from fold measure down 9" (22.9 cm). Crossmark. Draw a line between crossmarks. Label *flange line.*

E.   To establish flange underlay from flange line at edge and fold measure down 3" (7.6 cm). Crossmark. Draw a line between crossmarks. Label *flange underlay.*

F.   Trace all crossmarks to opposite side.

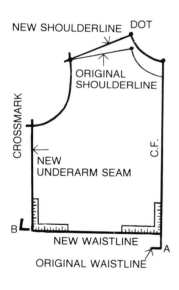

FIGURE 3

A.   Remove sloper.

B.   Draw a line, very lightly, joining dots on shoulderline. Label *original shoulder.*

C.   Square a line across from waistline/center front to B. Label *new waistline.* Square a line up from new waistline to crossmark at underarm/armhole intersection.
Note: To retain the fit and straight grain at the waistline, the difference lost on the center front between A and new waistline must be added to the front neckline.

D.   Place front sloper over draft matching centers. Sloper waistline should touch *new waistline.* Outline neckline. Dot neck/shoulderline intersection.

E.   Remove sloper. Draw a line from dot to end of original shoulder. Label *new shoulder.*

F.   Cut away excess paper at new waistline, neckline and shoulder and from remaining draft. Follow darker lines.

HORIZONTAL LINE

VERTICAL LINE

FLANGE LINE

FLANGE UNDERLAY LINE

FIGURE 5

A.   Open paper. Continue flange line and flange underlay to traced crossmarks.

B.   Draw a line over crease. Label *vertical line*.

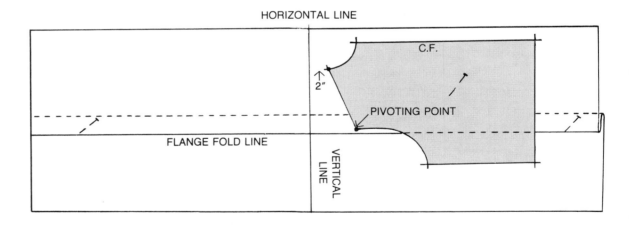

HORIZONTAL LINE

C.F.

2″

PIVOTING POINT

FLANGE FOLD LINE

VERTICAL LINE

FIGURE 6

A.   Crease flange line. Match fold of flange line to flange underlay. Pin.

B.   Place front waist draft on paper with shoulder/armhole intersection ⅛″ (0.3 cm) from flange line and with shoulder/neckline intersection approximately 2″ (5.1 cm) from vertical line.

C.   Hold draft at shoulder/armhole intersection and pivot draft until center front is parallel to horizontal line. Pin.

D.   Outline waist. Dot shoulder/neckline and shoulder/armhole intersections.

E.   Remove draft. True all lines crossing all intersections.

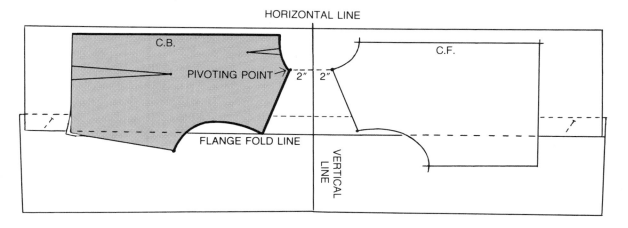

PREPARATION OF BACK SLOPER

FIGURE 7

A.   Use *back waist sloper with neckline and waistline darts.*

B.   On front waist draw a short, broken line parallel to horizontal line from dot at shoulder/neckline intersection. This will serve as a guideline for placement of back waist sloper.

C.   Place back waist sloper 2" (5.1 cm) away from vertical line with shoulder/neckline intersection of sloper touching broken guideline. Hold sloper at shoulder/neckline intersection and pivot sloper until center back is parallel to horizontal line.

Note: 1. Center back extends beyond center front due to back neckline dart. 2. The shoulder may touch or may extend beyond flange line due to ease. 3. If sloper was developed with shoulder dart, shoulder will extend beyond fold of flange line. In either case, flange line is used for end of shoulder.

D.   Outline center back, neckline, neckline dart, shoulderline and armhole. Dot neckline/shoulder and shoulder/armhole intersection. Crossmark waistline/underarm intersection.

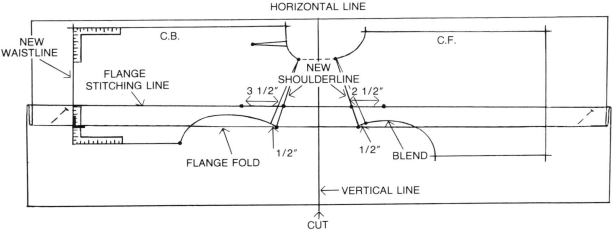

FIGURE 8

A. Remove sloper. Square a line from center back through crossmark at waistline/underarm intersection for new waistline. Square a line up from waistline to dot at underarm/armhole intersection.
Note: Front and back underarm seam lengths should be equal. If not adjust at back waistline.

B. On front waist draft from shoulder/armhole intersection measure up ½" (1.3 cm). Dot on flange fold line. Blend a line from fold into armhole. Draw a line from shoulder dot to neckline dot. Label *new shoulderline.*

C. Repeat on back waist draft. *Note:* The additional height is added to the shoulderlines to allow for the double thickness of the flange and seam allowances.

The amount to add is determined by the bulkiness of the fabric used and the number of flanges added. Final adjustment must be made when testing pattern in fabric.

D. To establish flange stitching line on flange underlay dot new shoulderline of front and back waist drafts. On front waist draft from dot measure down 2½" (6.4 cm). Dot. On back waist draft measure down 3½" (8.9 cm). Dot. See enlarged area in Figure 8A.

E. On front and back waist drafts trace new shoulderline, flange stitching line and armhole to opposite side. With awl indicate ends of flange stitching lines.

F. Cut on vertical line to separate front and back waist drafts.

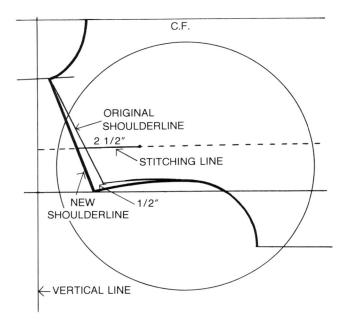

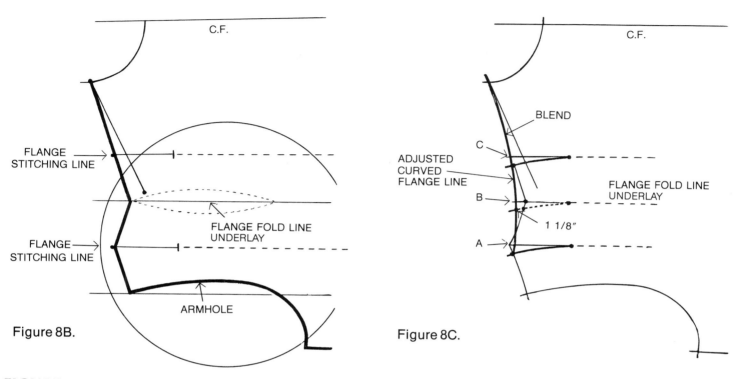

Figure 8B.

Figure 8C.

FIGURE 8B

A.   Open front waist draft.

B.   Draw a solid line between dots on flange stitching lines (as illustrated). Crossmark ends of lines.

C.   Pencil in traced armhole. *Do not* pencil traced armhole lines near flange fold line.

FIGURE 8C

A.   To curve flange lines at shoulderline label original straight lines *A, B, C* (as illustrated).

B.   From A measure ¼" (0.6 cm) towards armhole. Dot. Blend a curved line down length of straight stitching line (heavier line). Repeat at B and C.

C.   To add height to shoulder at flange fold line, from broken curved line opposite B measure up from original shoulder dot ⅛" (0.3 cm). Dot

D.   Draw a line from adjusted curved flange lines A to dot at B to B to C. Blend C towards neckline if necessary (heavier line)

BACK WAIST

FIGURE 9

A.   Open back waist draft. To adjust back shoulderline, with front face up match front and back waist drafts at shoulderline matching neckline and armhole intersections. Pin. Trace front adjusted shoulderline and flange dots on shoulderline to back.

B.   With front and back waist drafts in pinned position, allow seam on shoulder; cut and notch seam on adjusted curved flange lines.

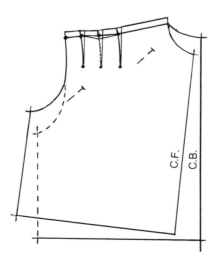

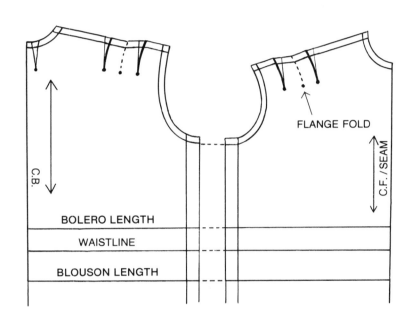

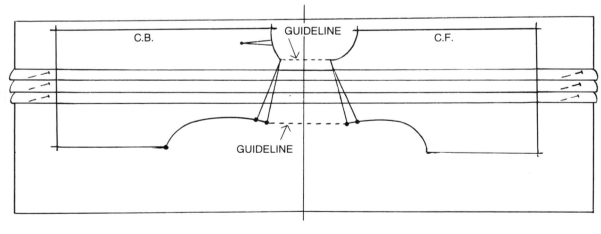

FIGURE 10

A. Separate front and back waist drafts. On back waist draft, curve in stitching lines to dots (heavier lines) and flange fold line to dot (broken line).

B. Establish grainlines parallel to centers.

C. Allow seams on remaining seamlines; cut and notch seams.

D. Adjust length desired.

SKETCHES C & D

Sketch C illustrates two flanges. Sketch D illustrates a coat with three flanges starting 1" (2.5 cm) in from the edge. If a slight side seam is desired, add when draft is completed.

FIGURE 11

A. To introduce two or more flanges prepare paper the same as for sketches A and B increasing width of paper amount needed for additional flanges. When cutting paper as in Figure 4, cut paper wider for the additional flanges and longer for desired length of garment. Plan, mark and fold paper into number of flanges desired.

B. To complete pattern follow procedure as for sketches A and B.

A princess line waist is a waist with vertical seams, which can be applied to both front and back. The most popular or basic princess line starts at the center of the shoulder and extends into the waistline, eliminating the need for basic darts. Princess line seams, however, may start at any position on the shoulder or at the armhole and may take on various shapes as illustrated in sketches 4, 5 and 6 in this unit.

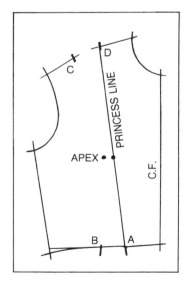

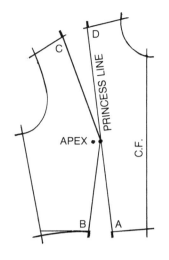

FIGURE 2

Draw dartlines from B and C to adjusted apex (as illustrated).

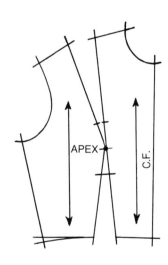

FIGURE 3

A.   On both sections establish grainline parallel to center front.

B.   Crossmark apex and 2″ (5.1 cm) above and below apex. All crossmarks should be at right angles to seams.
Note: These crossmarks are needed to control ease at the bust area.

FIGURE 1

A.   Use *two-dart front waist sloper.*

B.   Cut paper approximately 15″ × 25″ (38.1 × 63.5 cm).

C.   Place sloper on paper and outline.

D.   On paper crossmark waistline and shoulder dartlines. With awl indicate apex.

E.   Remove sloper. Label dartlines *A, B, C, D* (as illustrated).

F.   True all lines crossing all intersections.

G.   Draw a straight line from A to D. Label *princess line.*
Note: Occasionally, the princess line will not touch apex. This is caused by the different positions of the apex on the different figure types. If this occurs, on the princess line dot another apex opposite the original apex.

FIGURE 4

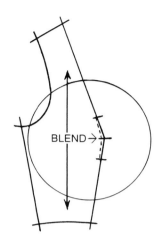

A.   Copy each section with grainlines and crossmarks.

B.   True all lines crossing all intersections.

C.   Blend at apex.
Note: If a stretch or knit fabric is used blend as illustrated.

D.   To complete pattern allow seams; cut and notch seams.
Note: Check crossmarks for accuracy before notching seams. Refer to Crossmarks & Notches.

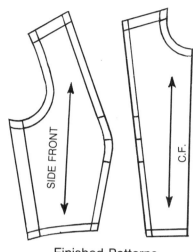

Finished Patterns

FIGURE 5

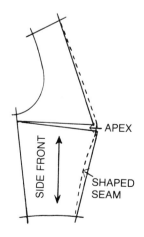

A.   *For woven fabric that will shrink easily*—Side front of waist should be slashed from apex to underarm and spread ⅛" (0.3 cm) for ease and for a better fit at the bustline area.

B.   *For a tighter fit at the midriff area*—Seam may be shaped on the side front section (broken line). Repeat on center front section by pinning together the seams to be joined from the apex down to the waistline seam and tracing the shaped seam to the other side. Adjust seam allowance.

PRINCESS LINE BACK WAISTS
sketch 2

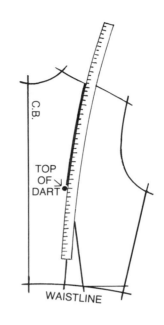

FIGURE 2

A. Place curved ruler on A through top of waistline dart to approximately 2″ to 3″ (5.1 to 7.6 cm) above waistline. See position of curved ruler.

B. Draw a slightly curved line from A to top of waistline dart (heavier line). Label *princess line*.

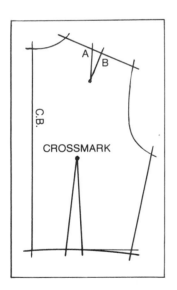

FIGURE 1

A. Use *back waist sloper with shoulder and waistline darts*.

B. Cut paper approximately 15″ × 25″ (38.1 × 63.5 cm).

C. Place sloper on paper and outline.

D. On paper crossmark shoulder and waistline dartlines. With awl indicate top of shoulder and waistline darts.

E. Remove sloper. Draw lines from crossmarks to top of darts. Label shoulder dartlines *A* and *B* (as illustrated).

F. True all lines crossing all intersections.

G. Pencil top of waistline dart.

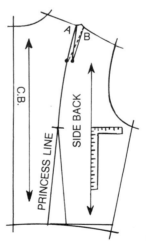

FIGURE 3

A. On both sections establish grainline parallel to center back.

B. Crossmark top of waistline dart.

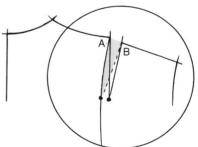

FIGURE 3A

The princess line may not touch the bottom of the shoulder dart. If this occurs, draw a new dartline the same length as the original dart from B to princess line.

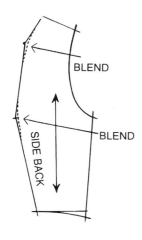

FIGURE 4

A.   Copy each section with grainlines and crossmarks.

B.   True all lines crossing all intersections.

C.   Blend side back princess line (broken line).

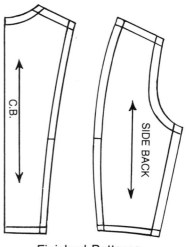

Finished Patterns

FIGURE 5

To complete pattern allow seams; cut and notch seams. *Note:* Check crossmarks for accuracy before notching seams. Refer to Crossmarks & Notches.

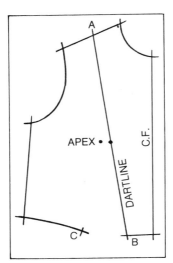

FIGURE 3

A.   Establish grainline parallel to center front.

B.   Crossmark apex and 2″ (5.1 cm) above and below apex. All crossmarks should be at right angles to seams.
Note: These crossmarks are needed to control ease at the bust area.

C.   To establish grainline on side front section place ruler at waistline. Draw a broken line from underarm to C to serve as guideline.

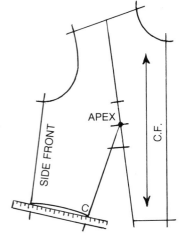

FIGURE 1

A.   Use *one-dart front waist sloper.*

B.   Cut paper approximately 15″ × 25″ (38.1 × 63.5 cm).

C.   Place sloper on paper and outline.

D.   On paper crossmark waistline dartlines. With awl indicate apex.

E.   Remove sloper. Label dartlines *B* and *C* (as illustrated).

F.   True all lines crossing all intersections.

G.   Divide shoulderline in half. Crossmark and label *A*.

FIGURE 3A

To establish grainline at center of section square a line up from guideline.

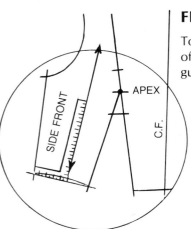

H.   Draw a straight line from A to B. Label *princess line.*
Note: Occasionally, the princess line will not touch the apex. This is caused by the different positions of the apex on the different figure types. If this occurs, on the princess line dot another apex opposite the original apex dot.

FIGURE 2

Draw dartline from C to adjusted apex.

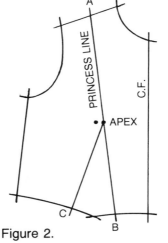

Figure 2.

FIGURE 4

A.   Copy each section with grainlines and crossmarks.

B.   True all lines crossing all intersections.

C.   To complete pattern allow seams; cut and notch seams.
Note: Check crossmarks for accuracy before notching seams. Refer to Crossmarks & Notches.

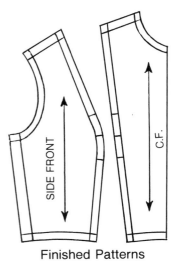

Finished Patterns

Sketch 4

1. Use *one-dart front waist sloper.*

2. To develop patterns for these sketches follow the same procedure as for Princess Line Front Waist *from One-dart Sloper,* sketch 3.

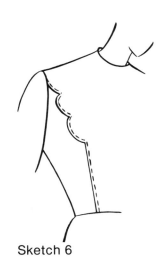

Sketch 6

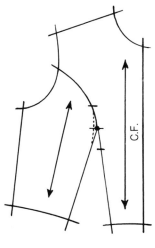

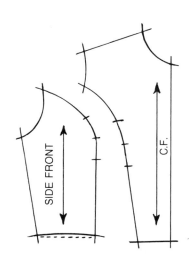

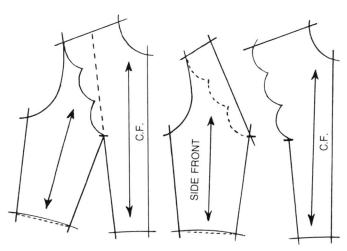

Sketch 5

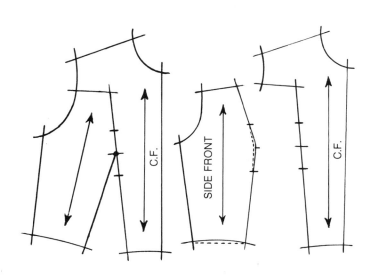

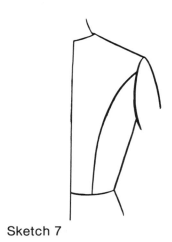

Sketch 7

FIGURE 1

A. Use *back waist sloper with shoulder and waistline darts.*

B. Cut paper approximately 15″ × 25″ (38.1 × 63.5 cm).

C. On sloper dot armhole to indicate desired position of curved princess line.
Note: Shoulder dart will be eliminated by pivoting dart to princess line dot.

D. Place sloper on paper. On paper copy dot on armhole. Outline sloper from dot on armhole to underarm, underarm, waistline, center back, neckline and shoulder to first neck dartline. Crossmark and label *A*.

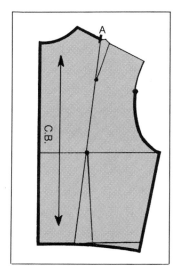

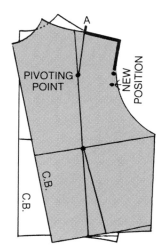

FIGURE 2

A. Pivoting point is end of shoulder dart.

B. Hold sloper securely at pivoting point and pivot sloper until dartline closest to armhole touches crossmark A. Outline remainder of sloper.

C. Dot armhole at new position.

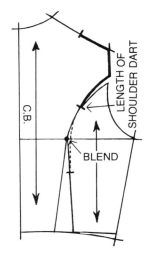

FIGURE 3

A. Draw a curved line from upper dot to top of waistline dart for princess line. Blend lower dot towards princess line the length of original shoulder dart. Illustrated: 3″ (7.6 cm).

B. Crossmark top of waistline dart and 2″ (5.1 cm) above and below waistline dart. Blend a slightly curved line between crossmarks (broken line).

C. On center back and side back sections establish grainlines parallel to center back.

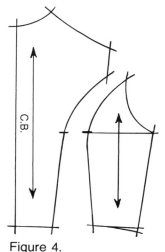

Figure 4.

FIGURES 4 & 4A

A. Copy center back and side back sections with crossmarks between upper and lower crossmarks.

B. True all lines crossing all intersections.

C. To true armhole place center back section over side back section matching princess line at top of dart to armhole. Blend a new armhole (broken line in Figure 4A).

D. To complete pattern allow seams; cut and notch seams.

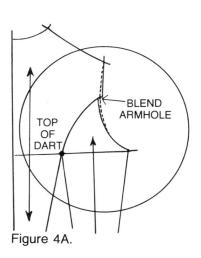

Figure 4A.

Sketch 8

In the previous sketches, the princess line was always aimed at the apex and the sloper darts were absorbed in the seam. In the following variations, the princess line falls to the right or left of the apex and the sloper darts are absorbed by introducing a dart across the princess line thereby retaining the original fit of the garment.

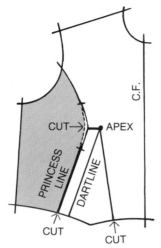

FIGURE 2

A.   Crossmark bust dartline and 2″ (5.1 cm) above and below bust dartline. All crossmarks should be at right angles to seams. Blend line between crossmarks (broken line).

B.   Cut princess line seam from waistline to bust dartline and across dartline to apex.

C.   Cut waistline dartline closest to center front from waistline to apex.

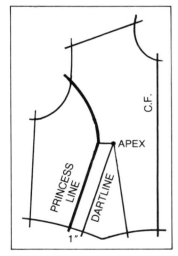

Figure 1.

FIGURES 1 & 1A

A.   Use *one-dart front waist sloper.*

B.   Cut paper approximately 15″ × 25″ (38.1 × 63.5 cm).

C.   Place sloper on paper and outline. Crossmark waistline dartlines. With awl indicate apex.

D.   Remove sloper. True all lines and darts crossing all intersections.

E.   Draw a line at least 1″ (2.5 cm) away from the apex towards underarm and down parallel to dartline. Label *princess line.*

F.   To complete princess line draw a slightly curved line from end of dartline at apex up to armhole.

G.   Draw a line from apex at right angle to center front. This will be position of bust dart. *Note:* The bust dartline may also slant upwards from princess line to apex (broken line in Figure 1A).

FIGURE 3

A.   Close waistline dart and pin (as illustrated).

B.   Establish grainlines on center front and side front sections (as illustrated). *Note:* To establish grainline on side front section refer to Princess Line Front Waist, sketch 3, Figures 3 and 3A.

C.   Copy each section with grainlines and crossmarks.

D.   True all lines crossing all intersections.

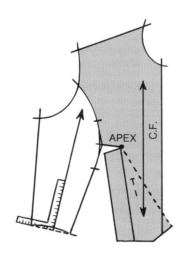

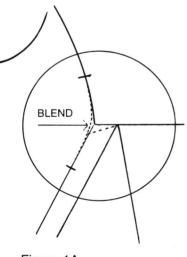

Figure 1A.

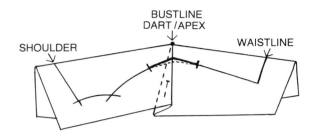

FIGURE 4

A.   Close, cup and pin short bustline dart. Blend line (broken line).

B.   Trace blended line to opposite side. Open draft. Pencil in traced lines.

C.   To complete patterns allow seams; cut and notch seams. *Note:* Check crossmarks at bustline area for accuracy before notching seams.

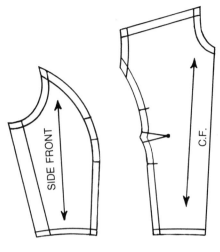

Finished Patterns

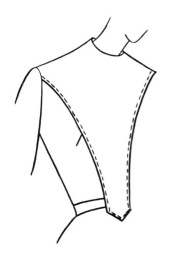

To develop pattern for this sketch follow the same procedure as for Princess Line Front Waist with Bustline Dart on Center Section, with the following exception:

Develop the bustline dart on the side section

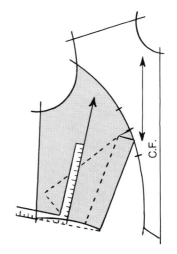

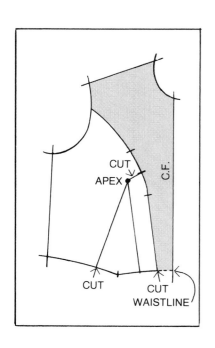

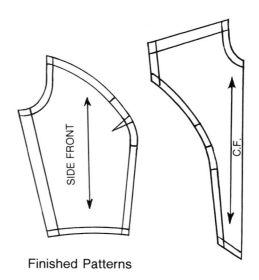

Finished Patterns

BLOUSES
introduction

Blouses are garments that cover the body from the shoulder to below the waistline. Styles and details for blouses are in accordance with the current fashion picture. They may be fitted, straight and boxy or loose and baggy. The importance of blouses varies from one fashion season to another, but it is a garment that is always present in fashion and used in all categories of dress such as active sportswear, daytime and evening wear.

Blouse openings may be located on the center front, center back, shoulder and/or underarm. Blouses made of stretch fabrics may not include openings as it is possible to slip the garment over the head easily without the need of a placket.

Blouses fall into two categories: (1) *tuck-in* and (2) *overblouse.* The length of a *tuck-in* blouse averages 4 to 7 inches (10.2 to 17.8 cm) below the waistline depending upon the manufacturer or price of the garment. The overblouse may start at the waistline and extend down to the thigh depending upon the style of a current fashion trend.

Blouses may be worn with skirts, suits, pants, shorts, culottes and jumpers.

Sketch A Tuck-in Blouse

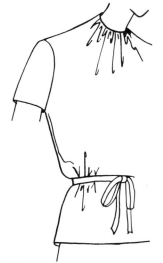

Sketch B Overblouse

Sketch C Blouson

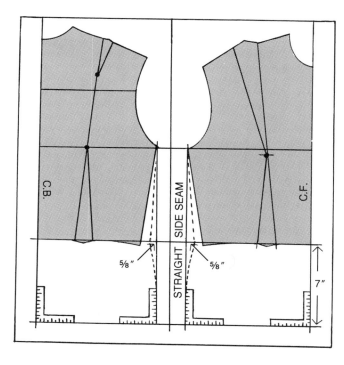

SKETCH A

FIGURE 1

If a torso sloper is not available, a blouse sloper can be developed from a two-dart front and back waist sloper. Place the front and back slopers on paper (shaded area). To adjust underarm seam, square a line from hipline up to underarm/armhole intersection on front and back. If a shaped seam is desired, at waistline measure in ⅝" (1.6 cm), dot and draw lines from dot to armhole and curve hip side seam (broken lines).

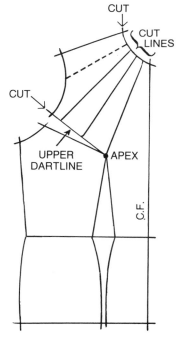

FIGURE 2

A.   Use *two-dart front torso sloper.*

B.   Cut paper approximately 15" × 30" (38.1 × 76.2 cm).

C.   Place sloper on paper and outline pivoting shoulder dart to armhole (as illustrated).

D.   Remove sloper. True all lines crossing all intersections.

E.   To develop neckline for shirring draw radiating lines from neckline to upper dartline and apex (as illustrated).
Note: If additional fullness is desired, draw an additional line from neckline to armhole (broken line).

F.   Cut draft on all finished lines.

G.   Cut on lines from neckline to upper dartline, apex and armhole.

H.   Cut on upper dartline from armhole to apex.

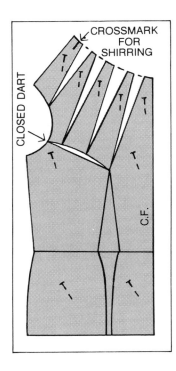

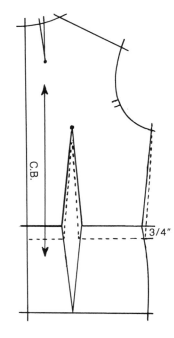

FIGURE 3

A.   Pin draft to another sheet of paper closing underarm dart.

B.   Cut lines will spread at neck. Spread cut sections evenly and pin.

C.   Blend new neckline. To establish end of neckline shirring, from shoulder/neckline intersection measure down 1" to 2" (2.5 to 5.1 cm). Crossmark.

D.   Accurately outline all finished lines of draft onto paper.

FIGURE 5

A.   Use *back torso length sloper.*

B.   Cut paper approximately 15" × 30" (38.1 × 76.2 cm).

C.   Place sloper on paper and outline. Length should be the same as front.

D.   Remove sloper. True all lines crossing all intersections.

E.   Establish grainline parallel to center back.

F.   To true side seam with front draft face up pin front and back drafts together matching seamlines.

G.   Trace adjusted front side seam to back.

H.   With drafts in pinned position allow seam; cut and notch waistline at underarm seam.

I.   Separate back and front drafts. Add seams to remainder of pattern.

J.   Use sleeve sloper to establish armhole crossmarks.

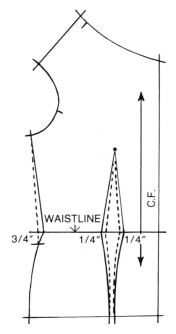

FIGURE 4

A.   Remove draft. Retrue all lines crossing all intersections.

B.   Establish grainline parallel to center front.

C.   A tuck-in blouse has a tendency to ride up. It is necessary, therefore, to establish a new waistline at side seams on front and back blouse drafts. On front draft, from waistline measure down ¾" (1.9 cm). Crossmark.

D.   To readjust underarm seam, draw a straight line from lowered waistline crossmark to armhole (broken lines).

E.   Shape waistline dart to give blouse slightly more ease (broken line). Illustrated: ¼" (0.6 cm).

F.   Use sleeve sloper to establish armhole crossmarks.

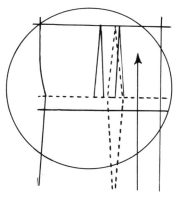

FIGURE 5A

Front and back darts may be stitched from waistline to hipline or may be divided into smaller darts (as illustrated).
Note: For a fitted overblouse retain original shape of underarm seam. Additional shaping depends upon the stretchability of fabric used.

SKETCHES B & C

For straight hanging blouses, eliminate waistline darts. Draw a straight line parallel to center front from underarm to hipline or to desired length.

Sketch A

Sketch B

1. Any waist or torso sloper may be used to develop the dropped shoulder cap.

2. Darts on slopers may be moved by pivoting to desired position or may be eliminated by introducing detailed seams.

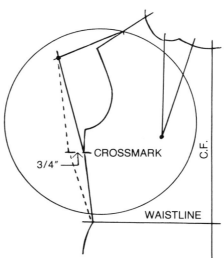

FIGURE 2

If the finished garment is to be worn as a jumper, from crossmark on underarm seamline measure out ¾" to 1" (1.9 to 2.5 cm). Crossmark. Draw a line from dot on new shoulderline to crossmark to waistline (broken line).

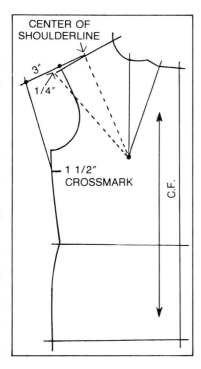

SKETCH A

FIGURE 1

A. Cut paper approximately 15" × 30" (38.1 × 76.2 cm).

B. Place sloper on paper and outline pivoting dart to desired position on neckline.

C. Remove sloper. True all lines crossing all intersections.

D. To establish new shoulder measure ¼" (0.6 cm) above shoulder/armhole intersection. Dot.

E. Draw a straight line from center of shoulder to dot extending line 3" (7.6 cm) beyond dot. Label *new shoulderline*. Dot.

F. On underarm seamline from armhole/underarm intersection measure down 1½" (3.8 cm). Crossmark.

G. To form cap sleeve draw a line from dot on new shoulderline to crossmark.

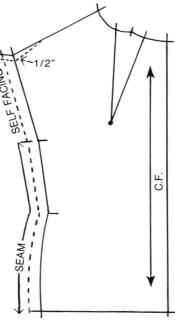

FIGURE 3

A. To develop a more form-fitting shoulder cap shape as illustrated with broken line.

B. Cap sleeve may be finished with:

    1. A self facing by extending the underarm seam up to shoulderline. Turn paper under on this line and trace shoulder seam to opposite side.

    2. A separate facing; refer to Facings.

C. Establish grainline parallel to center front.

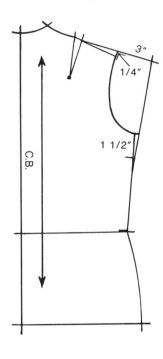

FIGURE 4

A. To develop cap sleeve on back follow same procedure as for front.

B. To complete pattern with front face up pin front and back together matching underarm seams. In pinned position:

    1. true seam;

    2. trace to opposite side;

    3. allow seam; cut and notch seams.

C. Separate front and back patterns and allow seams to remainder of pattern; cut and notch seam.

SKETCH B

A. To develop cap sleeve follow instructions as for sketch A.

B. To introduce princess line seam refer to Princess Line Front Waist from One-dart Sloper.

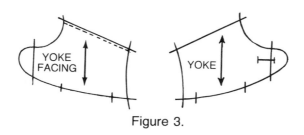

Figure 3.

FIGURE 3

A.   Copy yoke, crossmarks, buttonhole and grainline.

B.   For yoke facing pin yoke draft onto another sheet of paper. Carefully trace yoke crossmarks, grainline to opposite side.

C.   Separate sections and place opposite to each other. Label: *yoke* and *yoke facing*.

D.   On yoke facing pencil in all traced lines. For a better fit of facing at shoulderline measure in 1/16" (0.2 cm). Refer to Facings.

FIGURE 4

Open waist draft. Blend shirring line between crossmarks.

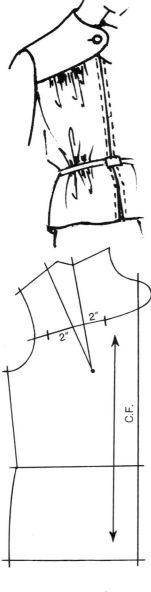

FIGURE 1

A.   Cut paper approximately 15" × 30" (38.1 × 76.2 cm).

B.   Use *front torso length sloper*.

C.   Place sloper on paper and outline. Remove sloper. True all lines crossing all intersections.

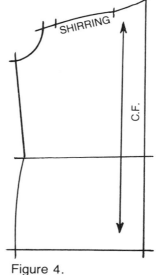

Figure 4.

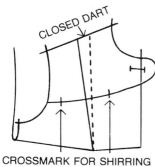

CROSSMARK FOR SHIRRING

FIGURE 2

A.   Close front shoulder dart.

B.   Plan and draw yokeline desired.

C.   Indicate crossmarks for shirring and plan yoke buttonhole.

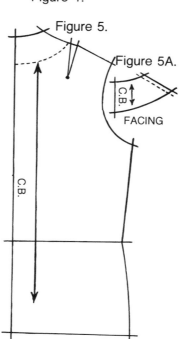

Figure 5.

Figure 5A.

FIGURES 5 & 5A

A.   Copy back and develop back neck facing.

B.   To complete patterns with front face up pin front and back together matching underarm seams. In pinned position:

1.   true seam;

2.   trace to opposite side;

3.   allow seams; cut and notch seams.

C.   Separate and allow seams to remainder of patterns; cut and notch seams.

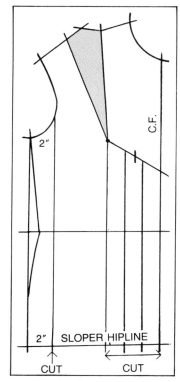

Figure 1.

FIGURES 1 & 1A

A.   Use *front torso length sloper.*

B.   Cut paper approximately 15″ × 30″ (38.1 × 76.2 cm).

C.   Place sloper on paper and outline. Remove sloper. True all lines crossing all intersections. *Note:* 1.   For yoke variations see broken lines in Figures 1A. 2.   If curved yokeline is desired refer to Elimination of Darts into Yokes or Decorative Seams, sketch 6, Figures 1 and 2, to direct and blend lower end of dart into yokeline.

D.   Draw yokeline as desired and crossmark for control of shirring.

E.   To develop front fullness draw cut lines parallel to center front (as illustrated).

F.   To develop a side seam flare from underarm seam at hipline measure in 2″ (5.1 cm). Square a line up to armhole parallel to center front.

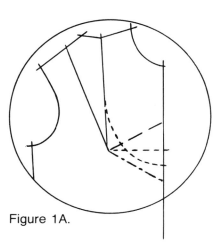

Figure 1A.

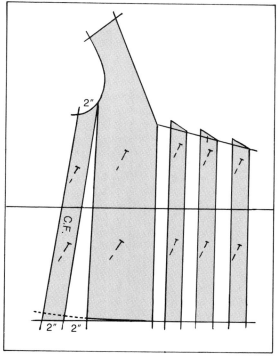

FIGURE 2

To develop flare and shirring lines at side seam and front of blouse follow illustration and spread desired amount.

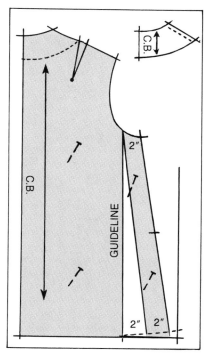

FIGURE 4

Illustrates the development of back overblouse with neck facing.

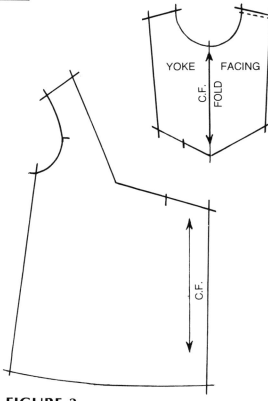

FIGURE 3

Illustrates completed front waist.

WAISTS WITH MIDRIFFS
introduction

A midriff is the part of a garment that covers the middle part of the body and, usually, fits snugly around the rib cage without the use of darts.

A midriff may also extend down over the hips and into the skirt area (see sketch 3) and, if it is not too wide, this type of midriff also may be developed without darts

Front View

Back View

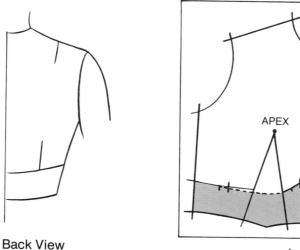

FIGURE 2

A.   Open waistline dart. Blend a line between crossmarks for shirring (broken line).

B.   Establish grainline parallel to center front.

C.   True all lines crossing all intersections.

D.   To complete waist pattern allow seams (using midriff line for finished line instead of waistline); cut and notch seams.

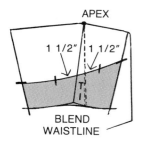

BLEND
WAISTLINE

FIGURE 1

A.   Use *one-dart front waist sloper.*

B.   Cut paper approximately 15″ × 25″ (38.1 × 63.5 cm).

C.   Place sloper on paper and outline. With awl indicate apex.

D.   Remove sloper. True all lines crossing all intersections.

E.   Close, cup and pin dart. Outline desired midriff line. Blend waistline.

F.   On midriff line crossmark both sides of dart for shirring. Illustrated: 1½″ (3.8 cm).

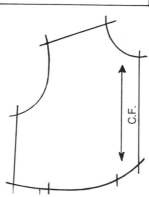

FIGURE 3

To develop a back midriff pattern follow same procedure as for front.

FIGURE 1A

A.   With waistline dart closed, copy midriff section with crossmarks.

B.   Establish grainline parallel to center front.

C.   True all lines crossing all intersections.

D.   To complete midriff pattern allow seams; cut and notch seams.

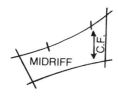

MIDRIFF

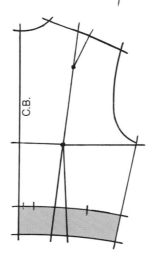

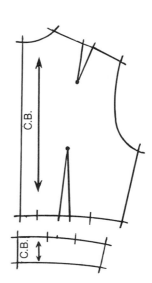

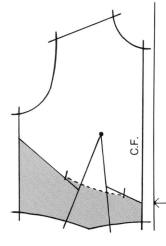

FIGURE 2

A.   Open waistline dart. Blend a line between crossmarks for shirring (broken line).

B.   To develop extension for buttonhole measure out from center front 1″ (2.5 cm). Draw a line parallel to center front.

FIGURE 1

A.   Use *one-dart front waist sloper.*

B.   Cut paper approximately 24″ (61 cm) square.

C.   Place sloper on paper near left-hand side allowing space for extension and facing on right-hand side (see Figure 2) and outline.

D.   Remove sloper. True all lines crossing all intersections.

E.   Close and cup dart. Outline desired midriff line. Blend waistline.

F.   On midriff line crossmark both sides of dart for shirring. Illustrated: 1½″ (3.8 cm).

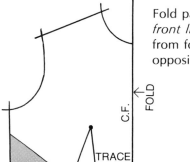

FIGURE 3

Fold paper under on *center front line.* Trace midriff line from fold to crossmark to opposite side.

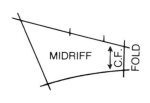

FIGURE 1A

A.   With waistline dart closed, copy midriff section with crossmarks.

B.   Establish grainline parallel to center front.

C.   True all lines crossing all intersections.

D.   To complete midriff pattern allow seams; cut and notch seams.

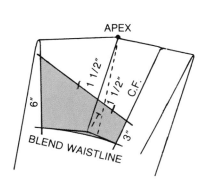

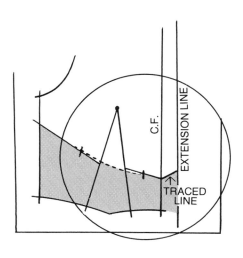

FIGURE 4

Open paper. Pencil in traced line.

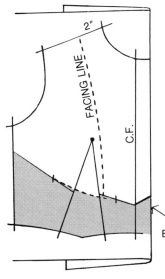

FIGURE 5

A.   Establish facing line on shoulder and midriff lines (broken line).

B.   Fold paper under on *extension line.* Trace to opposite side neckline, shoulderline, facing and midriff lines to extension fold.

C.   Open paper. Pencil in all traced lines.

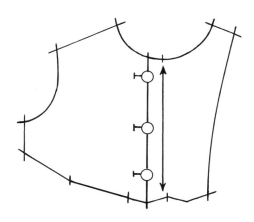

FIGURE 6

A.   Plan and mark buttonholes as desired. Refer to Buttons & Buttonholes.

B.   Establish grainline parallel to center front.

C.   To complete waist pattern, allow seams (using midriff line instead of waistline); cut and notch seams.

Front View

Back View

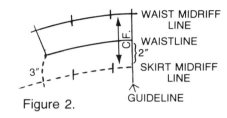

Figure 2.

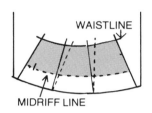

Figure 2A.

SKIRT MIDRIFF SECTION

FIGURES 2 & 2A

A. On midriff draft measure 2″ (5.1 cm) below waistline. Draw a curved midriff line parallel to waistline extending line 3″ (7.6 cm) at side seam (broken line).

B. To develop front skirt and midriff line on skirt outline basic front skirt sloper (Figure 4).

C. Close darts (as illustrated in Figure 2A). Retrue waistline, if necessary.

D. Measure 2″ (5.1 cm) below skirt waistline. Draw a curved line parallel to waistline (broken line).

E. With skirt darts closed, measure broken line minus ⅜″ (1 cm) ease allowed in the development of the skirt sloper. Crossmark.

F. On midriff draft, measure across skirt midriff line the measurement obtained from skirt draft. Dot and draw a curved hipline from dot up to waistline (broken line).

G. To establish crossmarks on skirt midriff line copy waist midriff crossmarks.

H. True all lines crossing all intersections.

I. Establish grainline parallel to center front.

J. To complete front midriff pattern allow seams; cut and notch seams.

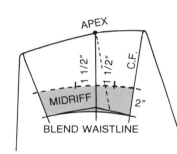

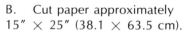

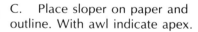

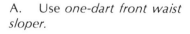

SHAPED MIDRIFF

FIGURE 1

A. Use *one-dart front waist sloper.*

B. Cut paper approximately 15″ × 25″ (38.1 × 63.5 cm).

C. Place sloper on paper and outline. With awl indicate apex.

D. Remove sloper. True all lines crossing all intersections.

E. Close and cup dart. Blend waistline.

F. Measure 2″ (5.1 cm) above waistline. Draw a curved midriff line parallel to waistline.

G. On midriff line crossmark both sides of dart for shirring. Illustrated: 1½″ (3.8 cm).

H. With waistline dart closed, trace off midriff section with crossmarks extending center front line from waistline down 3″ (7.6 cm) (Figure 2). Label *guideline.*

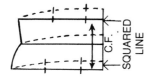

STRAIGHT MIDRIFF

FIGURE 3

If straight midriff is desired (depending upon stretchability of fabric used), adjust as illustrated by solid lines.

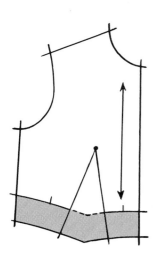

FIGURE 4

A.   Open waist draft. Blend a line between crossmarks for shirring (broken line).

B.   Establish grainline parallel to center front.

C.   True all lines crossing all intersections.

D.   Allow seams (using midriff for finished line). Cut and notch seams.

COMPLETING SKIRT

FIGURE 5

A.   Open skirt draft. Blend skirt midriff line (broken line).

B.   True all lines crossing all intersections.

C.   To establish shirring crossmarks measure distance from side seam and center front on lower midriff line. Repeat measurement on skirt.

D.   Establish grainline parallel to center front.
Note: For a fuller skirt with fullness evenly distributed on skirt midriff line, add amount desired at center front (broken line).

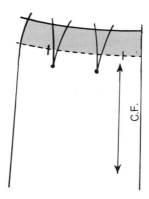

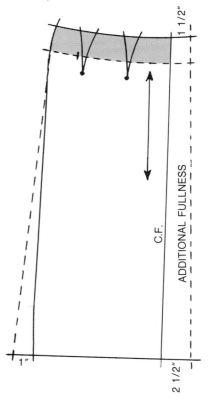

BACK MIDRIFF

To develop back midriff pattern follow same procedure as for front midriff.

HALTERS
introduction

A halter is a type of garment encircling the waist and neck leaving the arms and shoulders bare. The back may be cut high or low. With a low-cut back, the front of the garment is supported by a band, strap or necklace fastened around the neck or crisscrossed across the back.

Front View

Back View

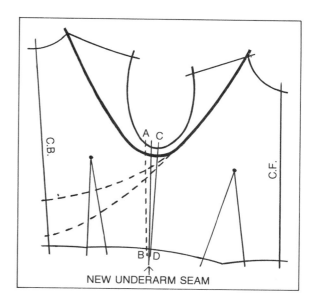

NEW UNDERARM SEAM

FIGURE 2

A. Use *back waist sloper.*

B. Place underarm of back sloper to guideline of front draft matching armholes and waistline. Outline sloper.

C. Remove sloper. True all lines crossing all intersections.

D. To establish new underarm seam place a dot between A and C at armhole and B and D at waistline.

E. Draw a line between dots. Label *new underarm seam.*

F. Draw desired halter line (heavier line). Broken lines illustrate back variations.

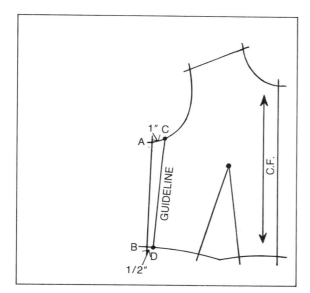

FIGURE 1

A. Use *one-dart front sloper.*

B. Cut paper approximately 25″ (63.5 cm) square.

C. Place sloper towards right-hand edge of paper and outline.

D. Remove sloper. True all lines crossing all intersections. Label underarm *A* and *B* (as illustrated).

E. To tighten waist eliminate ½″ (1.3 cm) fullness allowed on front and back armhole [total 1″ (2.5 cm)] and on armhole measure 1″ (2.5 cm) from A. Dot. Label *C.*

F. To eliminate ¼″ (0.6 cm) fullness allowed on front and back waistline [total ½″ (1.3 cm)], on waistline measure ½″ (1.3 cm) from B. Dot. Label *D.*

G. Draw a straight line from C to D. Label *guideline.*

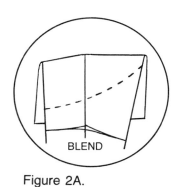

Figure 2A.

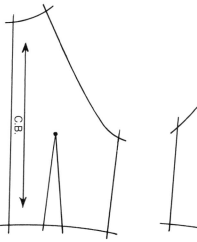
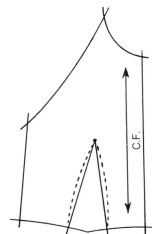

FIGURE 2A

With a low-cut back cup, close and pin dart. Blend waistline and copy.

FIGURE 3

A.   Copy front and back drafts onto other sheets of paper.

B.   True all lines crossing all intersections.

C.   Establish grainlines parallel to centers.

D.   To develop a fitted dart curve waist dartline (broken line).

E.   To complete patterns allow seams; cut and notch seams.

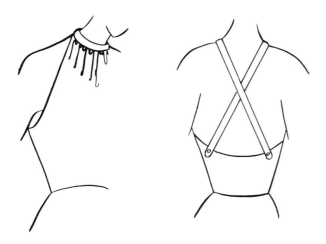

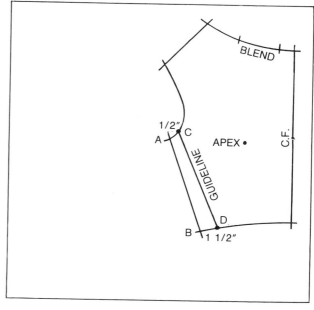

Sketch A Front & Back View

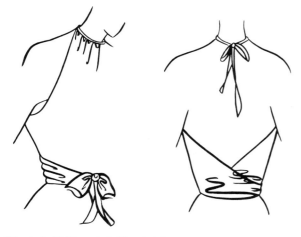

Sketch B Front & Back View

SKETCH A

FIGURE 1

A.   Use *one-dart front waist sloper.*

B.   Cut paper approximately 25″ (63.5 cm) square.

C.   Place sloper towards right-hand edge of paper. Outline sloper pivoting waistline dart to neckline.

D.   Remove sloper. True all lines crossing all intersections.

E.   Blend neckline. Label underarm *A* and *B* and *apex* (as illustrated).

F.   To tighten waist eliminate ½″ (1.3 cm) fullness allowed on front and back armholes [total 1″ (2.5 cm)] and on armhole measure 1″ (2.5 cm) from A. Dot. Label *C*.

G.   To eliminate back waistline dart measure depth of dart underlay on back sloper plus ¼″ (0.6 cm) ease allowed on waistline. 1¼″ (3.2 cm) plus ¼″ (0.6 cm) = 1½″ (3.8 cm). Measure this amount from B. Label *D*.

H.   Draw a straight line from C to D. Dot. Label *guideline.*

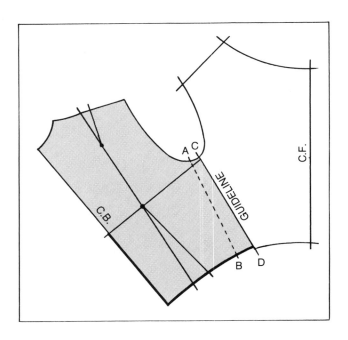

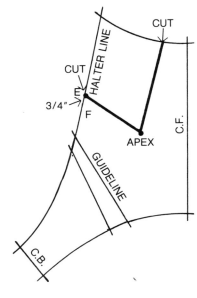

FIGURE 4

A. To tighten halter line for a better fit measure approximately one-third of the way down on the halter line from neckline. Dot. Label *E.*

B. Draw a line from E to apex.

C. On neckline measure one-third from center front. Dot.

D. Draw a line from apex to dot.

E. From E measure down ¾″ (1.9 cm). Label *F.*

FIGURE 2

A. Use *back waist sloper.*

B. Place underarm of back sloper to guideline of front draft matching armholes.

C. Outline sloper from halfway down center back to waistline (heavier lines).

FIGURE 5

Cut both lines to apex. Overlap E to F. Pin.
Note: Neckline fullness is increased automatically.

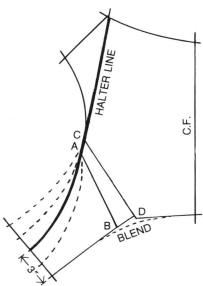

FIGURE 3

A. Remove sloper. Draw desired halter line (heavier line). Illustrated: 3″ (7.6 cm) above waistline at center back. Broken lines illustrate back variations.

B. Blend waistline at underarm (broken line).

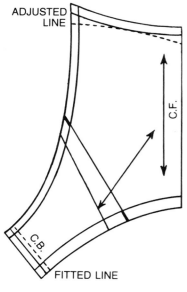

ADJUSTED LINE

C.F.

C.B.

FITTED LINE

FIGURE 6

A.   Pin draft onto another sheet of paper and outline.

B.   Remove draft. True all lines crossing all intersections. Indicate underarm seams with crossmarks (as illustrated).

C.   Establish grainline as desired (straight or bias at center front).

D.   To complete pattern allow seams; cut and notch seams.

E.   Neckline may be finished with a binding or band with tie ends that will secure halter at center back neck or crisscross back. Cut band on lengthwise grain. Double the desired finished width and length.

F.   After testing in muslin or fabric, the following adjustments may be needed:

   1.   If halter line and center front stretch, decrease measurement at neckline (broken line) and adjust seam allowance.

   2.   If fit of waistline is too loose or too tight, decrease or increase measurement at center back (broken line).

FIGURE 7

If a side seam is desired, measure halfway between guideline and underarm. Establish a new underarm seam (as illustrated).

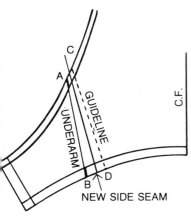

C.F.

C

A

GUIDELINE

UNDERARM

B   D

NEW SIDE SEAM

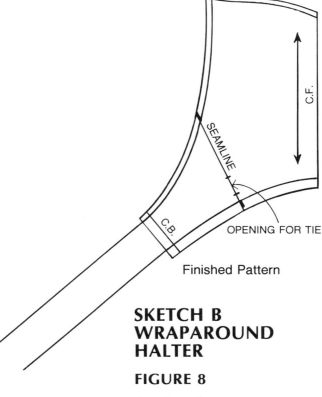

SHIRRING

C.F.

SEAMLINE

C.B.

OPENING FOR TIE

Finished Pattern

SKETCH B WRAPAROUND HALTER

FIGURE 8

A.   Extend pattern at center back for tie ends. Length and width depends upon the size of bow and type of finish.

B.   Plan opening for tie end (as illustrated). Size of opening depends upon thickness of fabric.

TWO-PIECE HALTER WITH LOW BACK
sketch 3

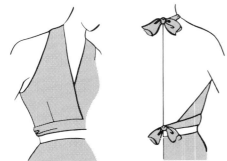

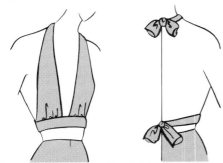

Sketch A Front & Back View

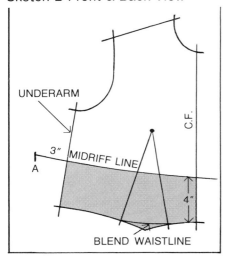

Sketch B Front & Back View

The *neckline* of this two-piece halter may be planned at the center front, away from the center front to achieve a space between bustline, or overlapped into a surplice.

The *underarm* may end at the underarm/waistline intersection or extend anywhere towards the center back.

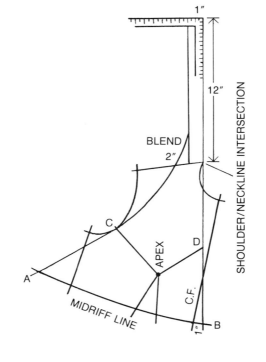

FIGURE 1

A. Use *one-dart front waist sloper.*

B. Cut paper approximately 15″ × 30″ (38.1 × 76.2 cm).

C. Place center front of sloper towards bottom and near the right-hand edge of paper. Outline sloper.

D. Remove sloper. True all lines crossing all intersections.

E. Blend waistline at bottom of waistline dart (as illustrated).

F. On center front measure up 4″ (10.2 cm) from waistline. Draw a line parallel to waistline extending line at underarm seam 3″ (7.6 cm). Crossmark and label A. Label *midriff line* and *underarm.*

G. At center front extend midriff line to edge of paper.

H. Cut excess paper from midriff line.

FIGURE 2

A. On midriff line at center front measure out 1″ (2.5 cm) for surplice line. Label *B.* Note: The more this line extends, the higher the neckline overlaps. The less this line extends, the deeper and more plunging the neckline. Broken lines in Figure 9 illustrate variations.

B. Draw a straight line from B to shoulder/neckline intersection extending the line 12″ (30.5 cm). This line can be longer or shorter depending upon the size of the bow for neck ties desired.

C. Square a line 1″ (2.5 cm) at this point. Draw a line parallel to surplice line to complete neck tie.

D. Crossmark at deepest point of armhole. Label *C.*

E. Draw a straight line from A to C.

F. Draw a curved line upwards from C to neck tie about 2″ (5.1 cm) above shoulderline blending into tie end.

G. To tighten surplice and halter lines for better fit:

    1. Place a crossmark on surplice line halfway between B and shoulderline. Label *D.*

    2. Draw a line from D to apex and from apex to C.

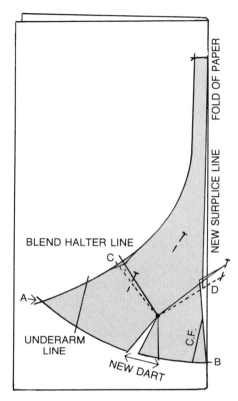

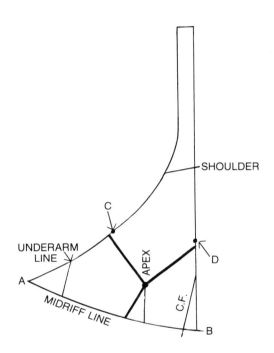

FIGURE 3

A.   Cut paper away from draft at A, around tie end down to B.

3.   From D measure up ½" to ¾" (1.3 to 1.9 cm). Dot.

C.   From C measure up same amount. Dot.
Note: The measurement used depends upon bust size, fit desired and fabric type used.

D.   Cut draft from D to apex and from C to apex.

E.   Cut dartline nearest underarm seam from midriff line to apex.

FIGURE 4

A.   Overlap draft at D and C to dots. Pin.
Note: This will increase depth of midriff dart.

B.   Cut another sheet of paper 30" (76.2 cm) square. Fold paper in half for a self-lined halter pattern.
Note: Halter can be cut double only if a lightweight fabric is used.

C.   Place draft on paper matching surplice line to fold. Pin.
Note: D will not touch fold.

D.   True halter line if necessary by blending overlapped area.

E.   Trace all finished lines, underarm seam and new midriff line dart to opposite side.

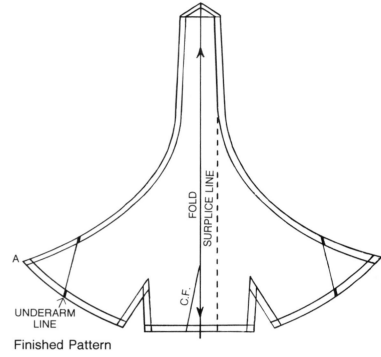

Finished Pattern

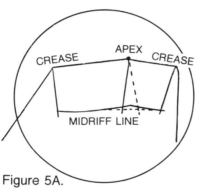

Figure 5A.

FIGURES 5 & 5A

A.   Remove draft. Open paper.

B.   Fold, cup and true dart on draft (Figure 5A). Refold draft and pin. Trace trued dart underlay to opposite side.

C.   With draft pinned allow seams on midriff line; cut and notch seams.

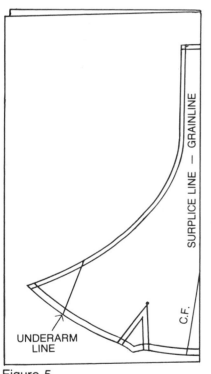

Figure 5.

FIGURE 6

A.   Open draft. Pencil in all traced lines.

B.   Establish grainline over surplice line.
Note: Halter facing can be seamed if it is a separate piece and cut in a thinner fabric. The broken line is for seaming.

C.   If dart is too bulky, it may be cut with seam allowance (as illustrated).
Note: If shirring or pleats are used instead of a dart, the facing of the surplice should always retain the dart for a smoother fit.

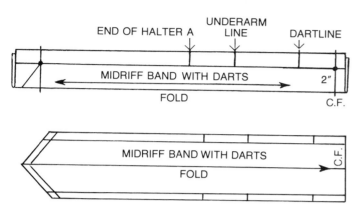

Finished Pattern

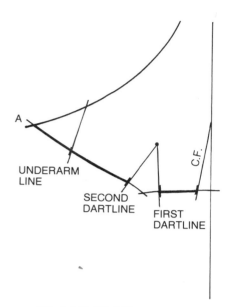

PREPARATION OF MIDRIFF BAND

FIGURE 7

A. Measure midriff line with dart closed and add length desired for ties.

B. Cut paper 6" (15.2 cm) wide and desired length determined in B.

C. Fold paper in half lengthwise. On right-hand side of paper square a line up from fold. Label *center front.*

D. Measure width of band desired from fold at center front and at other end of tie. Dot. Illustrated: 2" (5.1 cm). Draw a straight line between dots.

PLANNING CROSSMARKS ON BAND FOR MIDRIFF WITH DART

FIGURE 8

A. Measure halter pattern from center front to first dartline, from second dartline to underarm line, from underarm line to A (heavier line).

B. Using these measurements, establish crossmarks on midriff band starting from center front.

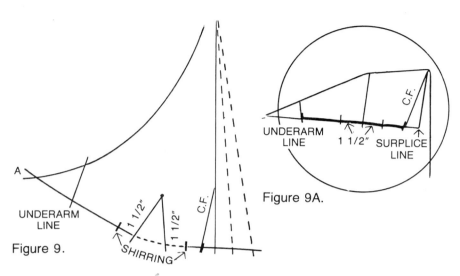

Figure 9A.

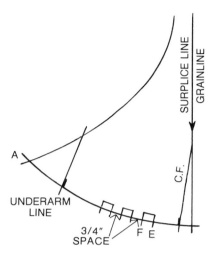

Figure 9.

PLANNING MIDRIFF SHIRRING & CROSSMARKS ON BAND

FIGURES 9 & 9A

A.   Measure 1½" (3.8 cm) on either side of dartlines. Crossmark. Blend waistline in dart area (broken line).

B.   To establish band crossmarks close dart (Figure 9A) and measure from center front to first crossmark, from first crossmark to second crossmark and from second crossmark to underarm.

C.   Open dart and measure from underarm to A at end of halter.

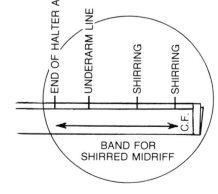

FIGURE 10

Using these measurements establish crossmarks band (as illustrated).

PLANNING MIDRIFF SIDE PLEATS & CROSSMARKS ON BAND

FIGURE 11

A.   To establish position for front pleat measure in from center front. Illustrated: 2" (5.1 cm). Label *E*.

B.   Measure depth of new dart (Figure 4).

C.   Divide this measurement into three equal parts for three pleats.

D.   From E measure over one-third of dart for first pleat. Label *F*.

E.   From F measure over ¾" (1.9 cm) for space between pleats.

F.   Repeat for two more pleats.

G.   Establish lines for tucks parallel to surplice line.

H.   To establish crossmarks on band close pleats and follow instructions as for other band.

SURPLICE WAISTS
introduction

A surplice is a garment that overlaps in front to form a high or low V-neckline. The position of the neckline depends upon how far the diagonal line extends beyond the center front at the waistline and where neckline ends on the shoulder. Broken lines in sketch 1, Figure 1, illustrate variations.

A surplice garment may have a surplice line in front, back or both front and back.

SURPLICE WAIST WITH FRENCH DART
sketch 1

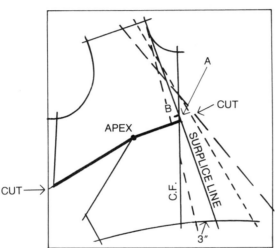

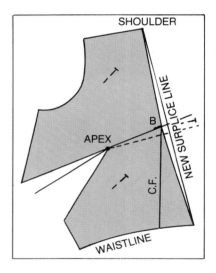

FIGURE 1

A.   Use *one-dart front waist sloper.*

B.   Cut paper approximately 25" (63.5 cm) square.

C.   Place sloper on paper. Outline sloper pivoting dart into French dart.

D.   Remove sloper. True all lines crossing intersections *except* at French dart.
Note: If surplice is to be developed as a sleeveless garment, adjust underarm and armhole as in One Shoulder Décolletage, Figure 1, G.

E.   Extend waistline at center front amount desired. Illustrated: 3" (7.6 cm). Broken lines illustrate variations.
Note: The more the line is extended at waistline, the higher the neckline.

F.   To establish surplice line draw a straight line from extended waistline to neckline/shoulder intersection or to any point on shoulder. Label *surplice line.* Broken lines illustrate various positions for surplice lines.

G.   To tighten surplice line for better fit draw a line from apex to center of surplice line. Label *A.*

H.   On surplice line from A measure up ½" to ¾" (1.3 to 1.9 cm) depending on fabric and fit. Crossmark and label *B.*

I.   Cut on line from A to apex and along upper dartline from underarm to apex.

FIGURE 2

A.   Pin draft to another sheet of paper overlapping A and B. *Note:* This will increase depth of French dart.

B.   To establish new surplice line draw a straight line from shoulder to waistline. Label *new surplice line.*

C.   Trace all lines onto attached paper.

D.   Remove draft. Pencil in all traced lines.

E.   Retrue all lines crossing all intersections.

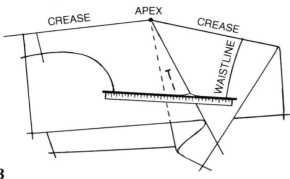

FIGURE 3

Close, cup and true French dart. Trace underarm seam through dart underlay. Open draft. Pencil in traced lines.

Finished Patterns

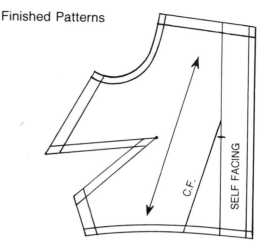

Figure 5.

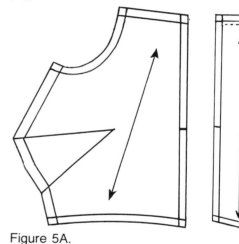

Figure 5A.

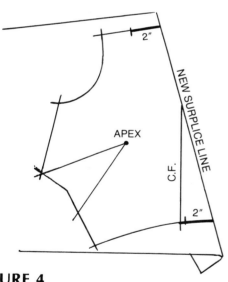

FIGURE 4

A.   To develop a self facing on surplice line fold paper under along new surplice line.

B.   On shoulder and waistline from fold measure in 2" (5.1 cm). Crossmark.

C.   Trace shoulder, waistline and crossmarks to opposite side (heavier line).

FIGURE 5

A.   Open paper. Pencil in shoulder and waistline. Draw a straight line between crossmarks.

B.   To complete pattern allow seams and cut. If dart underlay is exceptionally deep, it is often eliminated by allowing seams (Figure 5). If dart is retained, fold, cup and true dart underlay (Figure 5A).
Note: To prevent the bias surplice line from stretching on a self facing, place a tape in fold of surplice facing line.

FIGURE 5A

Facing for surplice may be cut as a separate piece.

A.   Crossmark center of surplice line to match seam (Figure 5).

B.   Copy facing and allow seams.

C.   Use waist draft as pattern. Allow seam at surplice line; cut and notch seam.

D.   To prevent surplice line from stretching, grainline on facing should be placed parallel to facing edge.

ONE SHOULDER DÉCOLLETAGE
sketch 2

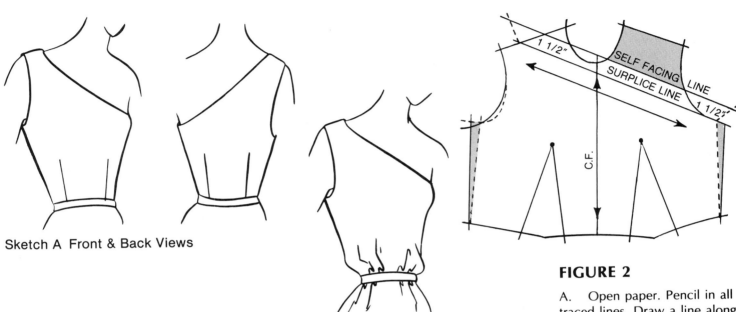

Sketch A Front & Back Views

Sketch B

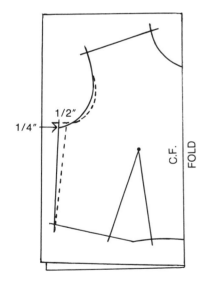

SKETCH A

FIGURE 1

A. Use *one-dart front waist sloper*.

B. Cut paper approximately 25″ (63.5 cm) square. Fold paper in half and crease.

C. With fold of paper to your right hand, place center front of sloper to fold of paper. Outline sloper and remove.

D. True all lines crossing all intersections.

E. To develop tight-fitting, high armhole sleeveless waist, at armhole/underarm intersection measure in ½″ (1.3 cm) and up ¼″ (0.6 cm). Draw a straight line from this point to waistline/underarm intersection. Blend a new armhole (follow broken line accurately).

F. Trace all lines to opposite side.

FIGURE 2

A. Open paper. Pencil in all traced lines. Draw a line along crease of paper. Label *center front*.

B. Crossmark position for desired surplice line on right and left side of sloper.
Note: Surplice line may be placed higher or lower than illustrated, but line should not fall more than ½″ (1.3 cm) above normal neckline at center front.

C. Draw a straight line between crossmarks. Label *surplice line*.

D. To develop self facing from surplice line measure up approximately 1½″ (3.8 cm). Dot. Draw a line parallel to surplice line. Label *self facing line*.

E. Fold paper under on surplice line. Trace shoulder and underarm seams to opposite side.

F. Open paper. Pencil in all traced lines (broken line).

G. Establish grainline at either center front or parallel surplice line.

FIGURE 3

A. To develop back surplice waist use *back waist sloper with neckline and waistline darts.*

B. Follow procedure as for front. Tighten underarm and armhole same amount.

C. Blend armhole into original armhole. *Do not* scoop out as in front armhole.

D. To check for accuracy of seamlines match front and back drafts at surplice line, shoulder and underarm seams.

E. To complete pattern allow seams; cut and notch seams.

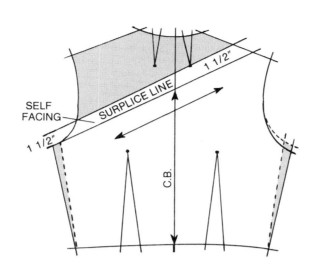

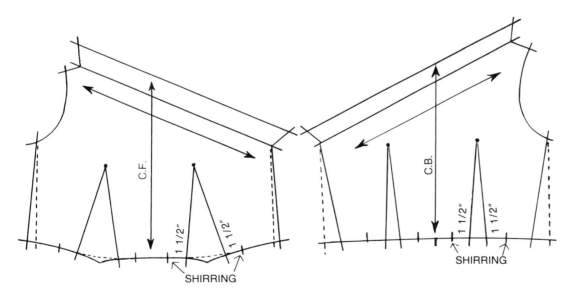

SKETCH B

FIGURE 4

A. If shirred waistline is desired establish crossmarks on front and back 1½" (3.8 cm) on each side of dartlines. Blend dartline at front waistline seam (broken line).

B. If additional shirring is desired on back draft, draw underarm seams parallel to center back (broken line). To balance underarm seams on front, draw underarm parallel to center front (broken line). Establish new shirring crossmarks distributing fullness as desired.

C. To plan armhole facings refer to Facings.

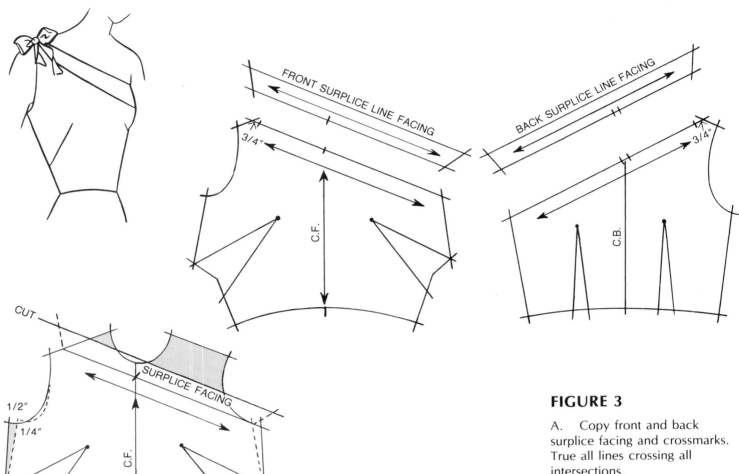

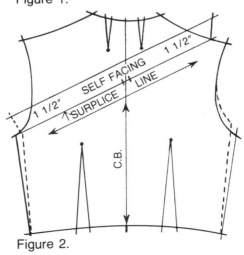

Figure 1.

Figure 2.

FIGURE 3

A.   Copy front and back surplice facing and crossmarks. True all lines crossing all intersections.

B.   Allow seams around facings; cut and notch seams.

C.   Allow seam on waist surplice line; cut off excess of self facing.

D.   To complete patterns allow seams on remaining seamlines; cut and notch seams.

E.   On surplice lines of completed front and back patterns, from shoulder seam measure in ¾" (1.9 cm). Crossmark. This is the amount of space needed for tieing bow (unless a separate bow is to be attached).

F.   Measure from crossmark to underarm seam plus desired amount for bow.

FIGURES 1 & 2

A.   To develop front and back waist patterns for this surplice waist variation, follow same procedure as for sketch 2. The procedure is the same regardless of the position of darts. For this sketch, however pivot front waistline dart into a French dart.

B.   Place one crossmark on surplice line on front waist.

C.   Place two crossmarks on surplice line on back waist. *Note:* Both crossmarks should be at right angles to surplice line.

SURPLICE NECK FINISHED WITH ROLLED BAND & BOW

FIGURE 4

A.   Cut paper 7″ (17.8 cm) wide and approximate length needed for band and bow.

B.   Fold paper in half lengthwise.

C.   From fold at both ends measure 2″ (5.1 cm). Draw a straight line length of paper. Label *seamline.*

D.   At right-hand end of paper, measure in 3″ (7.6 cm). Square a line from fold to seamline. Dot. Label *A.*

E.   Place seamline of band over surplice line on front waist pattern with A at underarm seam. On band crossmark center front and ¾″ (1.9 cm) crossmark near shoulder.

F.   On band from ¾″ (1.9 cm) crossmark measure length desired for bow and tie ends. Illustrated: 18″ (45.7 cm). Dot. Square a line from dot to fold.

G.   For point at tie end measure from line on fold 1½″ (3.8 cm). Dot. Draw a line from seamline dot to dot on fold.

H.   To complete pattern allow seams; cut and notch seams. Establish grainline (as illustrated). Trace finished lines and crossmarks to opposite side.

I.   Open and pencil in traced lines.

J.   Repeat for back band and bow.

K.   To plan armhole facings refer to Facings.

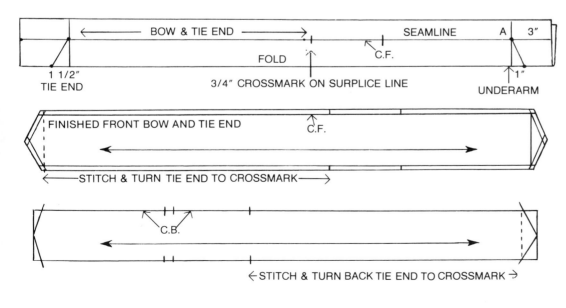

Front View

This surplice waist is not attached to a skirt. It is wrapped around the body or draped to the side. Ties may be used to fasten surplice waists in front, back or at the underarm seam with a bow, buckle, buttons or hooks. For economical cutting layouts, ties may be seamed to the underarm seam. A slit in the underarm seam is needed to pull ties through and around garment. Size of slit opening will vary depending upon the width and thickness of ties.

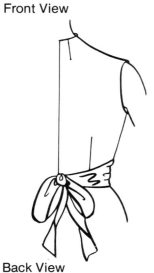

Back View

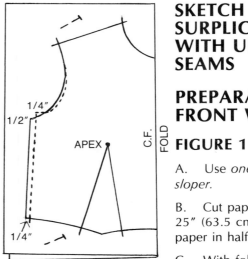

SKETCH A
SURPLICE WAIST WITH UNDERARM SEAMS

PREPARATION OF FRONT WAIST

FIGURE 1

A.   Use *one-dart front waist sloper.*

B.   Cut paper approximately 25" (63.5 cm) square. Fold paper in half and crease.

C.   With fold of paper to your right hand, place center front of sloper to fold of paper. Outline sloper and remove.

D.   True all lines crossing all intersections.

E.   To develop tight-fitting, high armhole sleeveless waist, measure in ½" (1.3 cm) and up ¼" (0.6 cm) at armhole/ underarm intersection and ¼" (0.6 cm) at waistline.

F.   Draw a new underarm seam. Blend new armhole. Follow broken lines accurately.

G.   Cut along all finished lines, new underarm seam and armhole. Trace dart to opposite side.

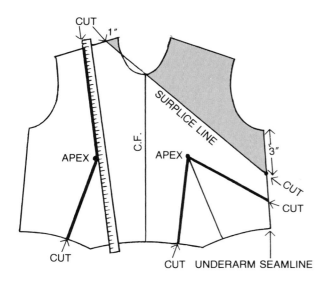

FIGURE 2

A.   Open draft. Pencil in traced dartlines. Draw a line over crease. Label *center front.*

B.   To establish surplice line, on right-hand side of draft from armhole/underarm intersection, measure down desired amount. Dot. Illustrated: 3" (7.6 cm).

C.   Draw a line from dot through center front/neckline intersection up to shoulder and away from neckline desired amount. Illustrated: 1" (2.5 cm). Label *surplice line.* Cut on surplice line.

D.   On left-hand side of draft, place ruler on waist dartline nearest center front. Draw a line from dartline to shoulder (heavier line).

E.   On right-hand side of draft draw a line from apex to center of new underarm seam (heavier line).

F.   Cut on heavier lines (as illustrated).

FIGURE 3

A.   Close waistline darts and pin.

B.   Pin front waist draft onto a large sheet of paper (position as illustrated).

C.   Blend shoulder and add crossmarks for shirring

D.   To establish new underarm seam draw a line from waistline to surplice line (heavier line).

E.   Outline all finished lines and crossmarks lightly. Trace center front to paper.

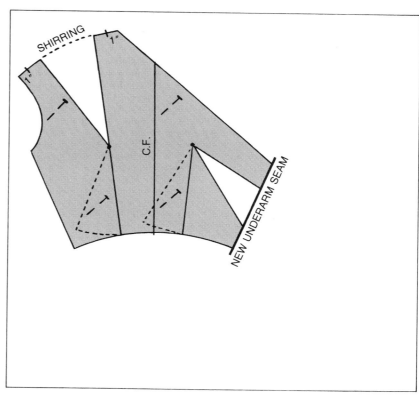

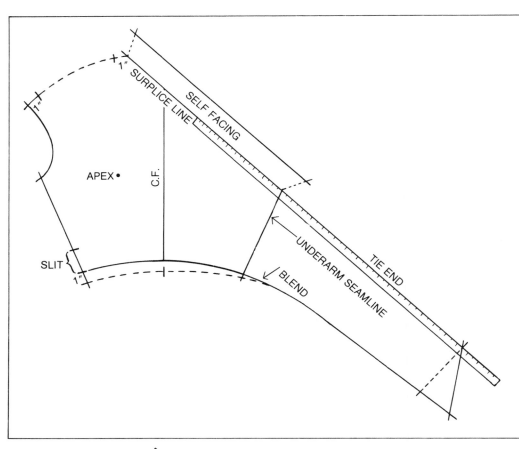

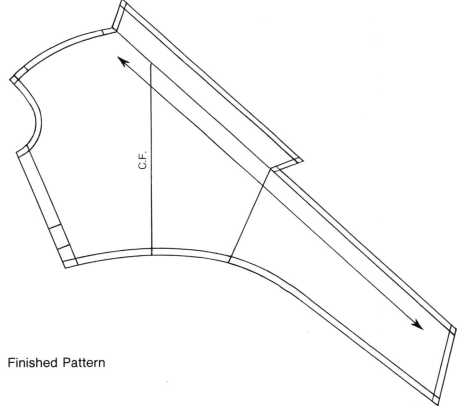

Finished Pattern

FIGURE 4

A. Remove draft. Pencil in center front. True all lines crossing all intersections.

B. To develop self facing from surplice line measure up 2" (5.1 cm).

C. Draw a line parallel to surplice line and cut.

D. To shape end of facing fold paper under on surplice line. Trace part of shoulder and underarm seams to opposite side. Open draft. Pencil in traced lines.

E. To develop tie ends place yardstick on surplice line. Draw a line from shoulder extending length desired.

F. Blend a line from waistline/underarm intersection to desired width and length of tie end.

G. Since a separate surplice has a tendency to ride up, it is advisable to lengthen the surplice 1" to 2" (2.5 to 5.1 cm) at waistline. Add amount desired at underarm seam. Blend into tie end (broken line).

H. Establish position of slit on underarm seam (as illustrated). Crossmark.

FIGURE 5

A. Establish grainline parallel to surplice line.

B. To complete pattern allow seams; cut and notch seams.

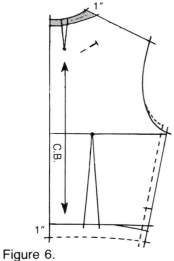

1"

C.B.

1"

Figure 6.

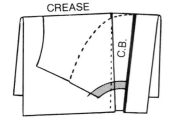

CREASE

C.B.

Figure 6A.

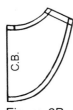

C.B.

Figure 6B.

PREPARATION OF BACK WAIST

FIGURES 6, 6A, 6B

A.   Use *back waist sloper with waistline and neckline darts.*

B.   Cut paper approximately 15" × 20" (38.1 × 50.8 cm).

C.   Place sloper on paper and outline. Remove sloper.

D.   True all lines crossing all intersections.

E.   To adjust back neckline at shoulder/neckline intersection measure in same amount as on front shoulder. Crossmark. Blend new neckline (solid area).

F.   To develop a back neck facing close dart (Figure 6A). Place draft onto another sheet of paper. Trace adjusted neckline, shoulder and depth of facing desired. Depth of back facing should equal front facing at shoulder. Illustrated (broken line): 2" and 6" (5.1 and 15.2 cm).

G.   Remove facing draft. True all lines on facing crossing intersections and notch neckline (Figure 6B).

H.   To adjust armhole and underarm seams of back refer to Figure 1, E, however, blend armhole as illustrated on back.

I.   Add 1" (2.5 cm) to back waistline to match front waistline (broken line).

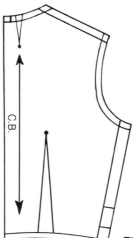

C.B.

Finished Pattern

FIGURE 7

A.   Retrue all adjusted lines crossing all intersections.

B.   To complete pattern allow seams on back and neck facing; cut and notch seams.

C.   To plan armhole facings refer to Facings.

SURPLICE WAIST WITHOUT UNDERARM SEAMS & WITH BACK DARTS

FIGURE 8

A.   Use adjusted back developed in Figures 6, 7 and 8. Cut on all finished seams.

B.   Match back and front drafts at underarm seams.

C.   Pin and outline back. Remove drafts.

D.   True all lines crossing all intersections.

E.   To complete pattern allow seams; cut and notch seams.

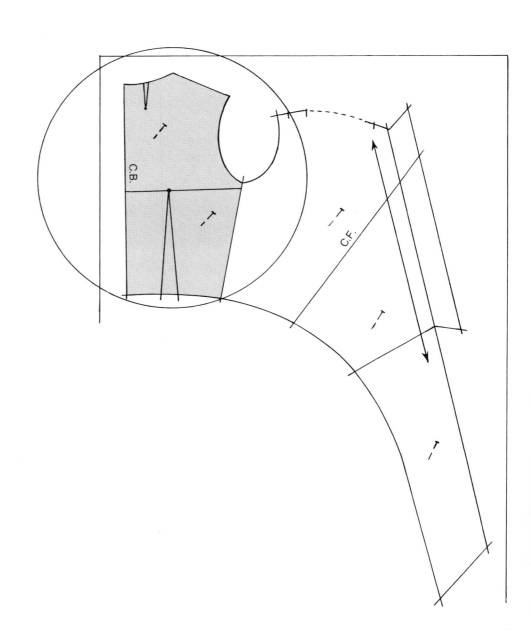

Figure 8. Back View

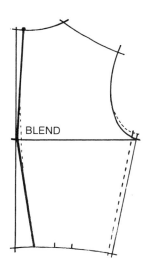

BLEND

SURPLICE WAIST WITHOUT UNDERARM SEAMS & BACK DARTS

FIGURE 9

A. Use adjusted back developed in Figures 6, 7 and 8.

B. On neckline from center back measure in depth of neckline dart underlay. Dot.

C. On waistline from center back, measure in depth of waistline dart underlay. Dot.

D. Place a crossmark on line across back.

E. Draw a line from neckline dot to crossmark on center back and waistline dot. Blend (as illustrated).

F. Cut along adjusted center back seam, underarm seam (broken line) and remaining pattern.

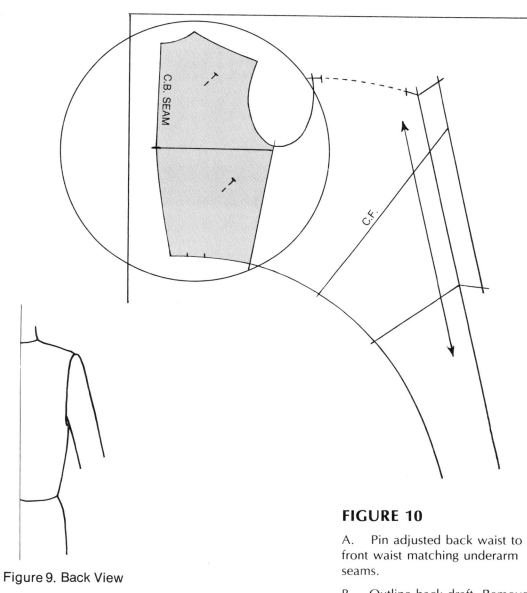

C.B. SEAM

C.F.

Figure 9. Back View

FIGURE 10

A. Pin adjusted back waist to front waist matching underarm seams.

B. Outline back draft. Remove draft. True all lines crossing all intersections.

C. To complete pattern allow seams; cut and notch seams.

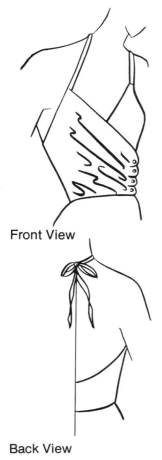

Front View

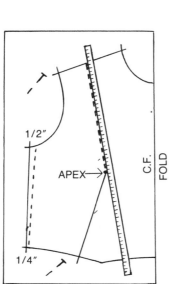

Back View

This surplice waist is not attached to a skirt. It is wrapped around the body or draped to the side. Ties may be used to fasten surplice waists in front, back or at the underarm seam with a bow, buckle, buttons or hooks. For economical cutting layouts, ties may be seamed to the underarm seam. A slit in the underarm seam is needed to pull ties through and around garment. Size of slit opening will vary depending upon the width and thickness of ties.

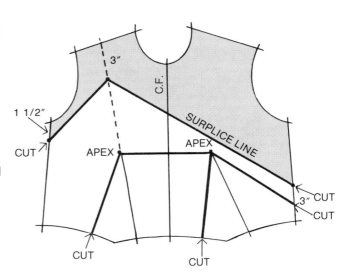

PREPARATION OF FRONT WAIST

FIGURE 1

A.   Cut paper approximately 25" (63.5 cm) square.

B.   Fold paper in half and crease.

C.   Use *one-dart front waist sloper.*

D.   Place center front of sloper to fold of paper and outline.

E.   Remove sloper. True all lines, crossing all intersections.

F.   To develop tight-fitting waist, measure in ½" (1.3 cm) at armhole/underarm intersection and ¼" (0.6 cm) at waistline. Draw a new underarm seam (broken line).

G.   Place a ruler on dartline nearest center front. Extend dartline through shoulderline (broken line).

H.   Cut along all finished lines and new underarm seam. Trace dart to opposite side.

FIGURE 2

A.   Open draft. Pencil in traced dartlines. Draw a line over crease. Label *center front.*

B.   To establish surplice line and new armhole:

   1.   Measure down 3" (7.6 cm) from shoulder.

   2.   On left-hand side of draft at armhole/underarm intersection measure down 1½" (3.8 cm). Dot.

   3.   On right-hand side of draft at waistline/underarm intersection measure up 3" (7.6 cm). Dot.

Draw a line between dots (heavier line).

C.   Draw a line from apex to apex and from apex to center of new underarm seam (heavier line).

D.   Cut away excess paper from surplice line and new armhole (shaded area).

E.   Cut along line from underarm to apex across to apex and down along dartlines.

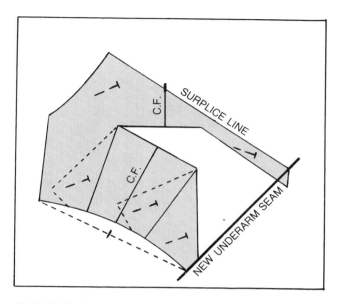

FIGURE 3

A.   Close darts. Pin draft onto another sheet of paper.

B.   Draw a line from waistline to top of surplice line (heavier line). Label *new underarm seam*. Seam will be shirred or pleated approximately 3″ to 4″ (7.6 to 10.2 cm) depending upon effect desired.

C.   To complete pattern, outline draft lightly. Straighten waistline (broken line). Crossmark center of waistline and surplice line.

D.   Remove draft. True all lines, crossing all intersections.

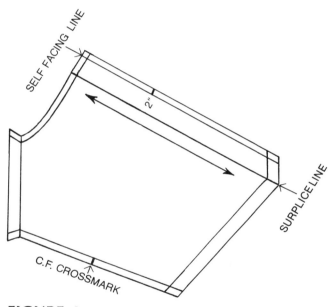

FIGURE 4

A.   To develop self facing from surplice line measure up 2″ (5.1 cm). Draw a line parallel to surplice line.

B.   Fold paper under on surplice line. Trace part of underarm seam and armhole to opposite side. Open paper. Pencil in traced lines.

C.   Allow seams; cut and notch seams.
Note: When testing pattern in fabric, some adjustment will be necessary at draped underarm seam depending upon the stretchability of the fabric used.

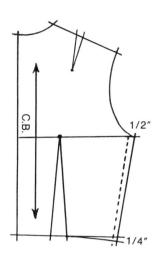

PREPARATION OF BACK WAIST

FIGURE 5

A. Cut paper approximately 15" × 20" (38.1 × 50.8 cm).

B. Copy and outline back waist sloper.

C. Remove sloper. True all lines crossing all intersections.

D. At armhole/underarm intersection, measure in ½" (1.3 cm). At waistline/ underarm intersection, measure in ¼" (0.6 cm). Draw a new underarm seam.

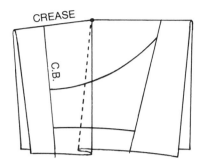

FIGURE 6

Cup and close waistline dart and plan style line. Underarm seam must be the same length as the front underarm seam on the left-hand side of draft.

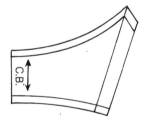

FIGURE 7

A. Copy back section. True, add seams and cut.

B. To plan back and armhole facings refer to Facings.

A vest is a sleeveless garment opened in front and worn over a blouse, dress or as part of a suit. The classic vest is fitted with a "V" neckline, drops one to two inches below the waistline with points in front, and has a button and buttonhole closing.

Vests vary in:

1. Fit—fitted, semi-fitted, loose;

2. Length—bolero to torso;

3. Shape—scooped necklines, square armholes and necklines, cutaway hemlines, etc.

Vests are often embellished with collars, pockets, braid, embroidery, lacing, etc.

BOLERO-TYPE UNFITTED VEST
sketch 1

Sketch A

Sketch B

Sketch C

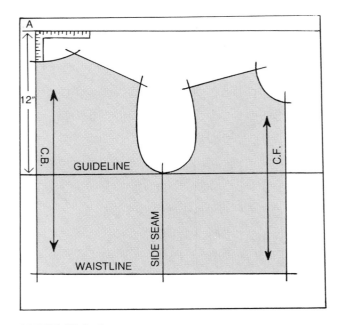

SKETCH A

FIGURE 1

A. Cut paper approximately 27" (68.6 cm) square.

B. Square a line across top and down left-hand side of paper. Label horizontal line, *A* and vertical line, *center back* (as illustrated).

C. From A measure down 12" (30.5 cm). Square a line across paper. Label *guideline*.

D. Use *front and back dartless slopers*. On slopers square a line from center front and center back to armhole/underarm intersection. Label *guideline*.

E. Place back sloper on paper matching center backs and guidelines.

F. Outline sloper and remove. True all lines crossing all intersections.

G. Place front sloper on paper matching underarm seams.

H. Outline sloper and remove. True all lines crossing all intersections.

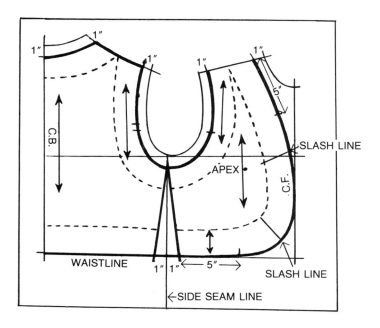

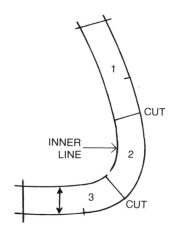

FIGURE 2

A. To develop semi-fitted look, at waistline measure in 1" (2.5 cm) on each underarm seam. Dot. Connect dots to armholes.

B. On front neckline measure in 1" (2.5 cm). Dot. Draw a style line to underarm seam (as illustrated).

C. On front and back shoulderlines measure in 1" (2.5 cm). Draw curved armholes ending 1½" (3.8 cm) below original armhole at underarm.

D. Draw back neckline (as illustrated).

E. Plan and indicate desired width of facings for center front, armholes, back neckline and back hemline (broken lines). Illustrated: 2" (5.1 cm).

F. Establish facing crossmarks:

  1. one crossmark on front armhole and two on back armhole;

  2. one crossmark 5" (12.7 cm) down from front shoulder;

  3. one crossmark 5" (12.7 cm) in from underarm seam on style line.

G. Establish slash lines for adjusting facing. Slant slash lines from crossmarks towards apex (as illustrated).

H. Establish grainlines parallel to center front and center back (as illustrated).

FIGURE 3

A. Copy front facing, grainline, crossmarks and slash lines.

B. Number sections and cut out facing (as illustrated).

C. To adjust facing cut slash lines towards, but not through, facing inner line.

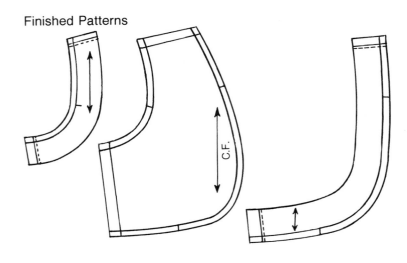

Finished Patterns

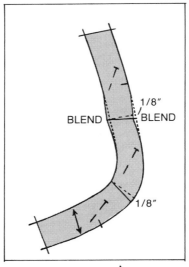

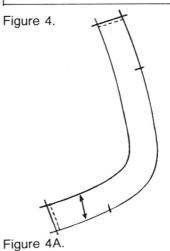

Figure 4.

Figure 4A.

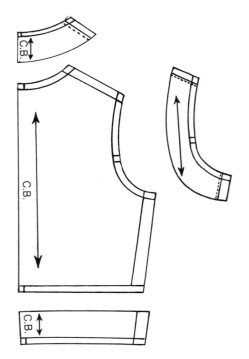

FIGURES 4 & 4A

A.   Pin sections onto another sheet of paper overlapping cut lines ⅛" (0.3 cm).
Note: The amount overlapped may be less or more depending upon the stretchability of the fabric used and the fit desired.

B.   Outline facing. Copy crossmarks and grainline. Blend lines, if necessary (broken lines).

C.   To tighten facing from shoulder and underarm seam measure in ¹⁄₁₆" (0.2 cm) (broken lines in Figure 4A).
Note: To plan facings refer to Facings.

FIGURE 5

A.   Copy all remaining facings with grainlines and crossmarks.

B.   Copy front and back of vest.

C.   True all lines crossing all intersections.

D.   To complete pattern allow seams; cut and notch seams.

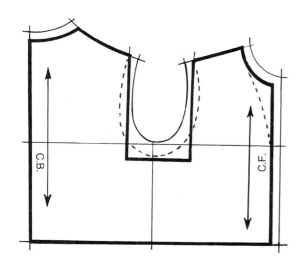

SKETCHES B & C

FIGURE 6

Style lines are illustrated by broken lines for sketch B and solid lines for sketch C.

A. Add facings, grainline and hem allowance.

B. Copy pattern and complete as for sketch A.

Note: If width of fabric permits, vest may be cut in one piece.

BOLERO-TYPE VEST WITH SHAWL COLLAR
sketch 2

Sketch A

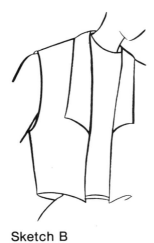

Sketch B

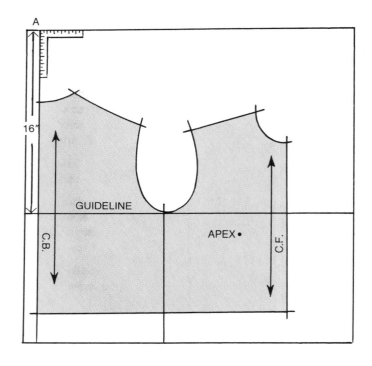

SKETCH A

FIGURE 1

To develop pattern for this sketch follow the same procedure discussed in sketch 1, Figure 1 with the following exception:

From A measure down 16″ (40.6 cm). Crossmark. Square a line across paper. Label *guideline*.

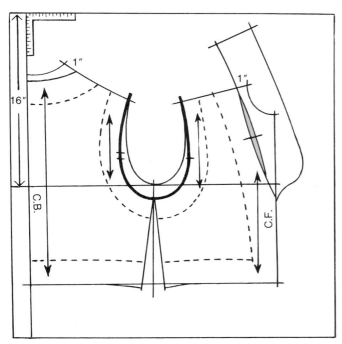

Figure 2.

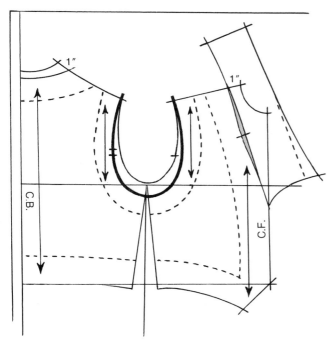

Sketch B Figure 3.

FIGURES 2 & 3

A.   Establish new neckline on front by measuring in 1″ (2.5 cm) from original neckline. Crossmark.

B.   Repeat at back blending neckline to center back.

C.   *Note:* When developing collar away from the original neckline, length of back collar must equal new back neckline. To develop collar refer to Shawl Collar—Narrow Variations. Plan collar style lines as illustrated on drafts.

D.   Plan and indicate front facing to underarm seam, armhole, back neckline and back hemline (broken lines).
Note: Allow ease on top shawl collar.

E.   Establish grainlines and crossmarks.

F.   Copy pattern. True all lines crossing all intersections.

G.   To complete pattern allow seams; cut and notch seams. Refer to sketch 1, Figure 6.

Sketch A Front & Back View

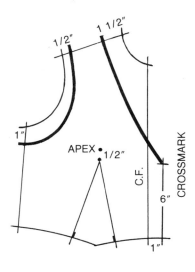

Sketch B

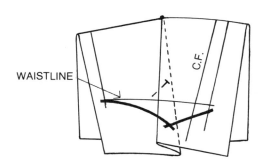

FIGURE 2

A. To plan stylized point crease dartline nearest center front. Cup at apex. Fold and close dart. Pin.

B. Draw style line below waistline desired.
Note: Point does not touch dartline so as to facilitate construction at the point.

C. Trace style line over dart underlay to opposite side.

SKETCH A

FIGURE 1

A. Use *one-dart front waist sloper.*

B. Cut paper approximately 15" × 25" (38.1 × 63.5 cm).

C. Outline sloper. Dot apex. Crossmark waist dartlines. Remove sloper.

D. From apex measure down ½" (1.3 cm). Dot. Draw a line from dot to dartline crossmarks.

E. True all lines crossing all intersections.

F. To plan front extension from center front measure out desired amount based on size of buttonhole. Illustrated: 1" (2.5 cm). Draw a line parallel to center front from waistline to depth desired for neckline. Illustrated: 6" (15.2 cm). Crossmark.

G. On shoulder measure in 1½" (3.8 cm) from neckline. Crossmark.

H. Draw a slightly curved neckline from shoulder to top of extension line. Crossmark (heavier line).

I. On shoulder measure in ½" (1.3 cm) from armhole and 1" (2.5 cm) down from armhole/underarm intersection. Crossmark. Draw new armhole.

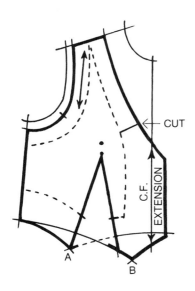

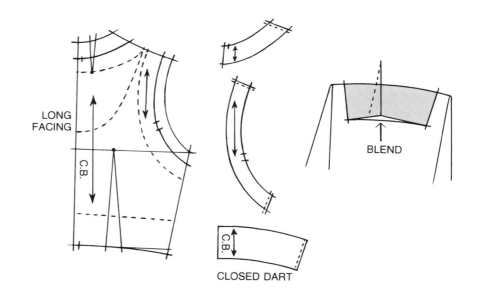

FIGURE 3

A. Open draft. Pencil in a short line on each side of dartline A and B.

B. Refer to Bolero-type Unfitted Vest to:

    1. Develop back.

    2. Plan and finish facings with these exceptions:

        a. cut line on facing in line with apex;

        b. close dart on facing.

C. Establish grainlines and crossmarks.

D. Copy pattern. True all lines crossing all intersections.

E. To complete patterns allow seams; cut and notch seams.

F. To plan buttonholes refer to Buttons & Buttonholes.

SKETCH B

FIGURE 4

To develop pattern for this sketch follow the same procedure as in sketch A with the following exceptions:

A. Plan extension 2″ to 3″ (5.1 to 7.6 cm) wide;

B. *Do not* shape waistline.

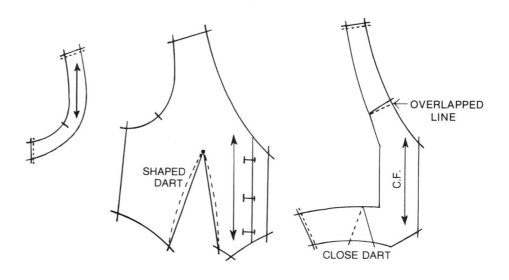

Finished Patterns

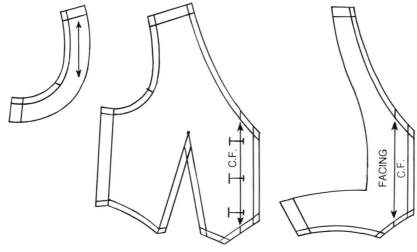

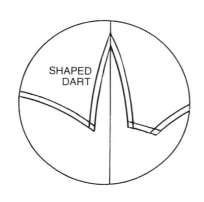

SHAPED
DART

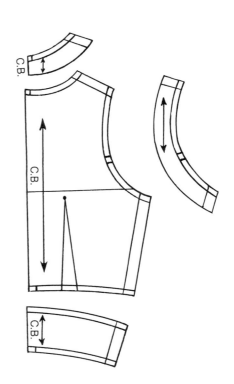

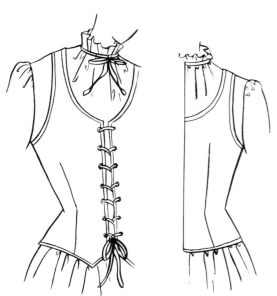

Sketch A Front & Back View

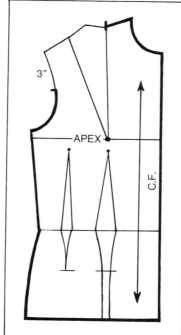

Figure 1.

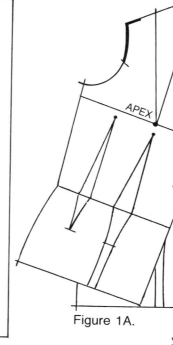

Figure 1A.

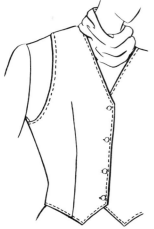

Sketch B

SKETCH A

FIGURES 1 & 1A

A.   Use *front torso length sloper.*

B.   Cut paper approximately 15″ × 25″ (38.1 × 63.5 cm).

C.   Outline sloper pivoting shoulder dart to armhole. Illustrated: 3″ (7.6 cm) down from shoulder.
Note: 1.   Side dart is not necessary. 2. For principles on pivoting refer to Dart Manipulation unit, Armhole & Waistline Darts, sketch 3.

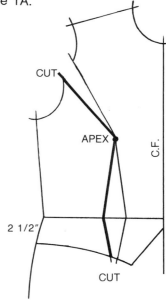

FIGURE 2

A.   Remove sloper. True all lines crossing all intersections.

B.   Draw armhole dart to apex.

C.   Draw style line desired below waistline. Illustrated: 2″ (5.1 cm).

D.   Cut dartlines to apex (as illustrated).

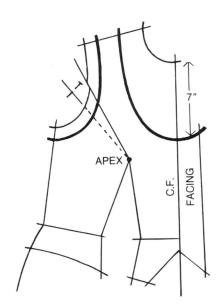

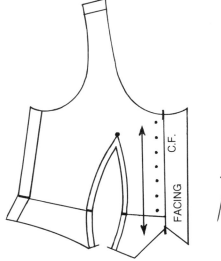

Figure 4.   Figure 4A.

FIGURE 3

A.   Close armhole dart and pin. Waistline dart will open automatically.

B.   Draw neckline. Illustrated: 7" (17.8 cm). Draw armhole desired.

C.   To plan self front facing, from center front measure out 2" (5.1 cm). Draw a line parallel to center front.

D.   To obtain shape of facing from neckline to hem of facing, fold paper under at center front. Trace neckline and hemline to opposite side.

E.   Open draft. Pencil in traced lines.

FIGURE 4

A.   Copy front. True all lines crossing all intersections.

B.   Establish grainline parallel to center front.

C.   Plan position of eyelets.

D.   To complete pattern allow seams at shoulder, underarm and waistline dart.
Note: Since this vest will be finished with a bound edge at the neckline, armhole and hemline, no seam allowance is necessary as the stitching line must be within the finished line. Example: For a ⅜" (1 cm) binding, stitching line will be ⅜" (1 cm) in from finished seamline.

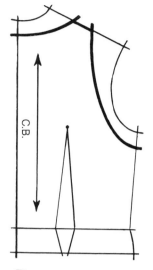

Figure 5.

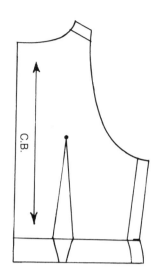

Figure 5A.

FIGURE 5

Develop back as illustrated.

FIGURE 5A

Complete back pattern as illustrated.

Note: If space between darts at hemline is wide enough for seam allowance, allow seam as in front dart. If not, stitch as a dart.

SKETCH B

To develop the pattern for this sketch follow the same procedure as for sketch A with the following exceptions:

A.   Plan extension for size of buttonholes used (diameter of button).

B.   Prepare a straight neckline style line.

C.   Plan facings.

D.   Allow seams on all seamlines.

Sketch A Front & Back View

Sketch B Front & Back View

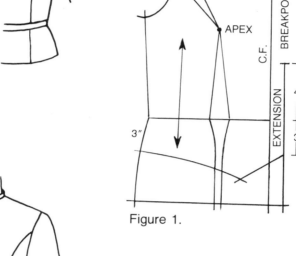

Figure 1.

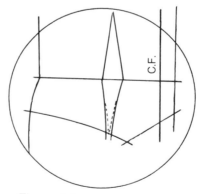

Figure 1A.

SKETCH A

FIGURE 1

A.   Use *front torso length sloper.*

B.   Cut paper approximately 18″ × 27″ (45.7 × 68.6 cm).

C.   Outline sloper pivoting shoulder dart to armhole. Illustrated: 3″ (7.6 cm) down from shoulder.
Note: 1.   Side dart is not necessary. 2. For principles on pivoting refer to Dart Manipulation unit, Armhole & Waistline Darts, sketch 3.

D.   Remove sloper. True all lines crossing all intersections.

E.   Draw armhole dart to apex.

F.   On side front waist section, establish grainline parallel to center front.

G.   To plan extension draw a line parallel to center front, width desired, up to breakpoint desired. Illustrated: width, 1″ (2.5 cm) for 1″ (2.5 cm) buttonhole; breakpoint, 4″ (10.1 cm). Crossmark and label *breakpoint.*

H.   Draw style line desired below waistline. Illustrated: 3″ (7.6 cm) at underarm seam and 3″ (7.6 cm) at center front.

FIGURE 1A

Taper hipline dart to nothing (broken lines).
Note: This additional ease is needed for a smoother fit over the skirt.

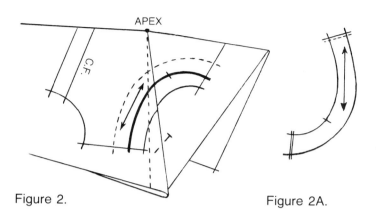

Figure 2. Figure 2A.

FIGURES 2 & 2A

A. Crease upper armhole dartline. Close, cup and pin dart.

B. With dart closed:

1. Outline armhole desired (heavier line). Trace armhole to opposite side.

2. From new armhole measure in depth of facing. Illustrated (broken line): 1" (2.5 cm). Crossmark at deepest part of armhole.

3. On facing establish grainline parallel to center front.

4. Copy armhole facing, grainline and crossmark.

C. Remove facing draft. True all lines crossing all intersections and adjusted shoulder (broken line in Figure 2A).

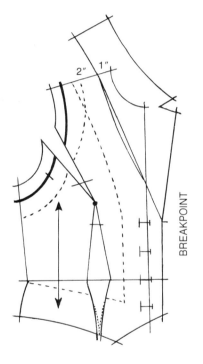

FIGURE 3

A. Open draft. Pencil in traced line.

B. To develop collar refer to Shawl Collar—Narrow Variations.
Note: Front neckline is 1" (2.5 cm) in from original neckline. Adjust back neckline to match front. Length of back collar must equal new back neckline.

C. Plan collar and hemline facing (broken line).

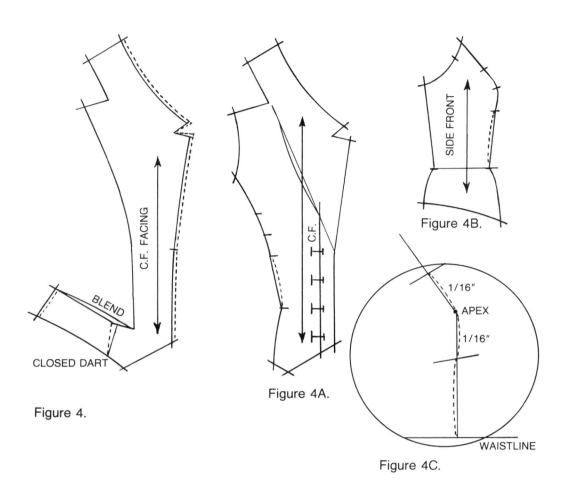

Figure 4.

Figure 4A.

Figure 4B.

Figure 4C.

FIGURES 4, 4A, 4B, 4C

A. ' Copy front facing. Close waistline dart. Blend line and add ease to conceal seam. Illustrated (broken line): $\frac{1}{16}$" (0.2 cm).

B. Copy center front and side sections (Figure 4A and 4B). Establish grainlines. True all lines crossing all intersections.

C. Blend princess line (broken line in Figure 4C).

D. To plan buttonholes refer to Buttons & Buttonholes.

E. To complete pattern allow seams; cut and notch seams.

Finished Patterns

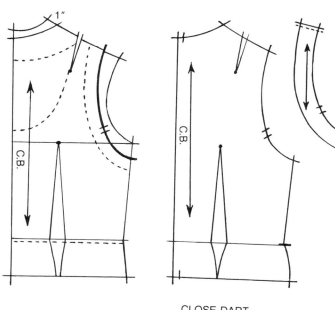

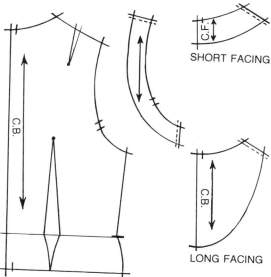

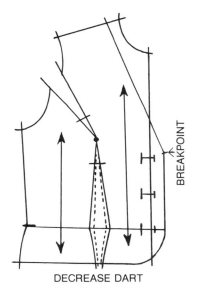

SHORT FACING

LONG FACING

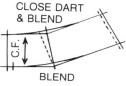

CLOSE DART & BLEND

C.F.

BLEND

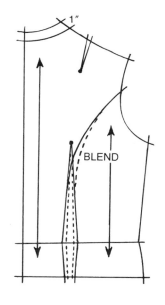

1"

BLEND

DECREASE DART

BREAKPOINT

FIGURE 5

A. Develop back as illustrated.
Note: Shoulder and underarm seams must equal those on front.

B. Copy front and back patterns (as illustrated).
Note: Choose either short or long neck facing.

C. To complete pattern allow seams; cut and notch seams.

SKETCH B

FIGURE 6

To develop pattern for this sketch follow the same procedure as for sketch A with this additional instruction:

Adjust back waistline dart and blend into princess line (broken line).

FACINGS
introduction

Facings are used to finish any shaped or curved edge where a self hem is difficult to apply such as on necklines, front openings, collars, hemlines, yokes, pockets and shaped welt or slot seams. Facings play an important role in the fit and finish of garments as a decorative or functional part of the garment.

The following principles can be applied to *all* garment areas that require facings.

1.   When facings are finished and applied to the wrong side of a garment, they should be cut smaller than the right side of the garment due to the curved contour of the body. How much smaller and where on the facing this adjustment should be made depends upon the shape of the area to be faced and the thickness of the fabric used.

2.   When facings are used as trimmings, they must be cut larger as they become the outer part of the finished garment.

All facings in this unit are developed without seams. To complete each project true all lines crossing all intersections. Allow seams; cut and notch seams.

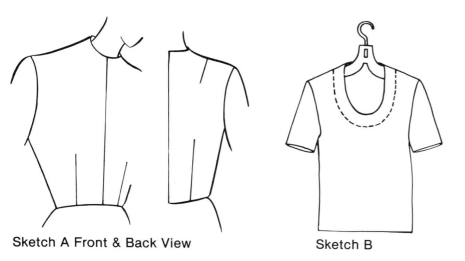

Sketch A Front & Back View

Sketch B

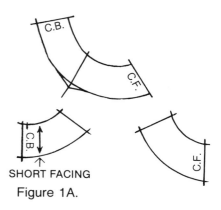

SHORT FACING

Figure 1A.

FIGURE 1A

A.   To blend front and back facings at neckline and outer shoulder edge, match shoulder seamlines at neckline and pin. Blend if necessary (as illustrated).

B.   Separate sections. True all lines crossing all intersections. Allow seams; cut and notch seams.

SKETCH B

FIGURES 2 & 2A

Some firms use a deep back facing for "hanger appeal" of garment. It is generally used when the front neckline is cut low as in sketch B. Plan desired depth of facing and follow same procedures as for sketch A.

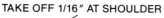

TAKE OFF 1/16" AT SHOULDER   TAKE OFF 1/16" AT SHOULDER

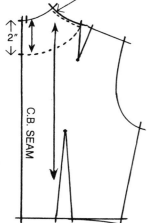

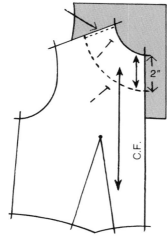

SKETCH A

FIGURE 1

A.   On front waist draft, plan and draw shape of facing desired parallel to neckline curve (broken line). Illustrated: 2" (5.1 cm).

B.   From shoulderline of facing measure down 1/16" (0.2 cm). Draw a broken line parallel to shoulderline.

C.   Pin front waist draft at upper part onto another sheet of paper. Trace facing lines, neckline, center front and grainline parallel to center front to opposite side.

D.   Separate sections. Pencil in all traced lines. Label *center front*.

E.   Repeat for back. Label *center back*. Crossmark ¼" (0.6 cm) from center back.

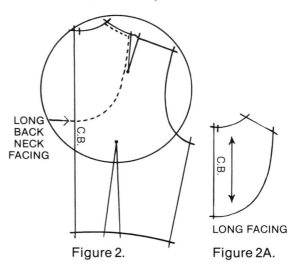

LONG BACK NECK FACING

Figure 2.   Figure 2A.

LONG FACING

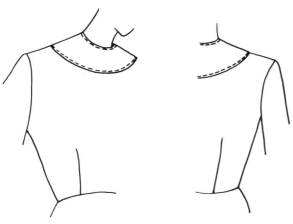

Front & Back View

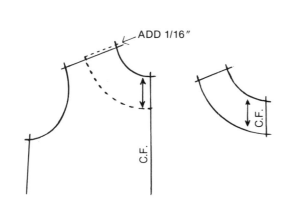

DECORATIVE NECKLINE FINISH

FIGURE 1

Plan front neckline facing (broken line).

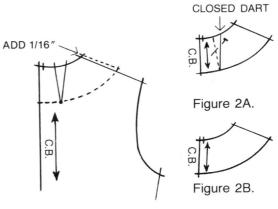

Figure 2.

FIGURES 2, 2A, 2B

On a back waist with a neckline dart, plan, draw and copy facing (broken line in Figure 1). Close dart, pin and blend neckline and outer edge of facing (Figure 2A). Recopy facing with dart closed (Figure 2B).

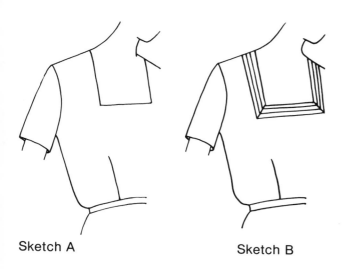

Sketch A

Sketch B

SKETCH B
TOP DECORATIVE
NECKLINE FINISH

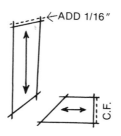

←ADD 1/16″

C.F.

FIGURE 2

To use facing as a top decorative finish follow same procedure as for sketch A with the following exception: add 1/16″ (0.6 cm) at shoulder.
Note: Decorative facing may be cut in one with lengthwise, crosswise grain or bias at center front or cut with mitered corners depending upon fabric used and effect desired.

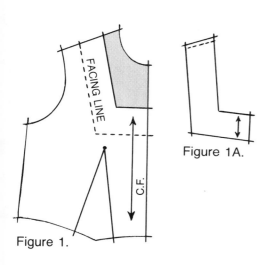

FACING LINE

C.F.

Figure 1.

Figure 1A.

SKETCH A

FIGURES 1 & 1A

Plan and copy squared neckline desired and facing (broken line).

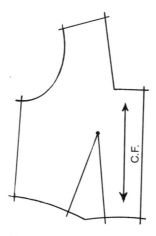

C.F.

FIGURE 3

This diagram illustrates front waist pattern without seams.

FACINGS FOR SCOOPED LOW-CUT NECKLINES
sketch 4

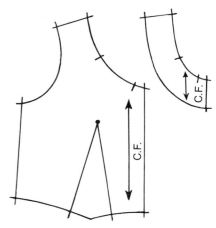

FIGURE 2

This diagram illustrates pattern sections without seams.

FIGURES 1, 1A, 1B

It is necessary to tighten facing around apex area as well as at the shoulder for scooped and low-cut necklines. This insures a close fitting neckline above the bustline (Figures 1A and 1B).

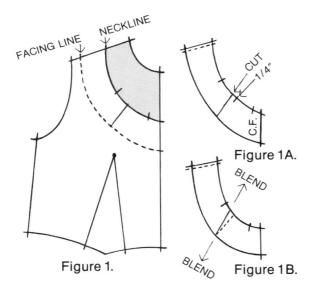

Figure 1.

Figure 1A.

Figure 1B.

BACK NECK FACING

FIGURE 3

A. Use *back waist sloper with neckline dart.* Dart will be eliminated automatically when lowering neckline.

B. To develop back facing follow same procedures as for front with the following exception: tighten at shoulder and, if necessary, $1/16''$ (0.6 cm) at center back.

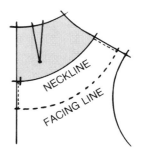

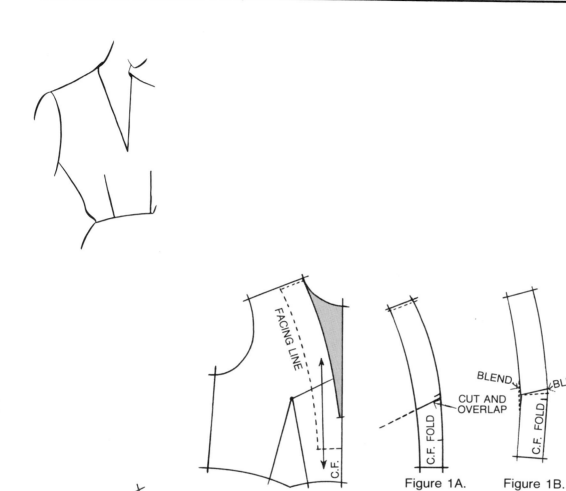

Figure 1.

Figure 1A.   Figure 1B.

Figure 2.

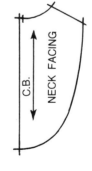

FIGURE 3

A.   A long back facing is necessary for ''hanger appeal'' with this plunging front V-neckline.

B.   To develop back facing use *back waist with shoulder dart.*

FIGURES 1, 1A, 1B, 2

A.   Plan plunging neckline and facing.

B.   To tighten facing, draw line from apex to neckline (Figures 1A and 1B) and cut and overlap (as illustrated).

FACINGS FOR SLEEVELESS GARMENTS
sketches 6, 7, 8

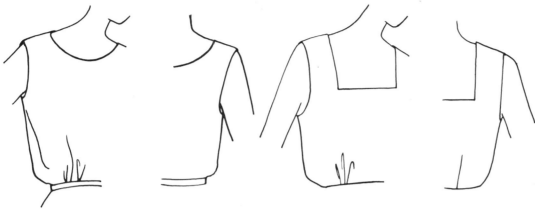

Sketch 6 Front & Back View   Sketch 7 Front & Back View

Facings for necklines and armholes on sleeveless garments with low-cut necklines and narrow shoulders are generally cut in one piece. However, the shoulder should not be planned less than ½″ (1.3 cm) wide as it becomes difficult to stitch and turn facing at the shoulder. *Note:* When shoulder is the width illustrated in sketch 8, facing may be cut in two pieces (broken line). Outer edge of facing may be shaped following broken line. Copy and complete facings.

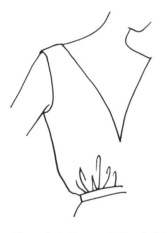

Sketch 8 Front & Back View

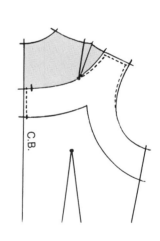

Sketch 6

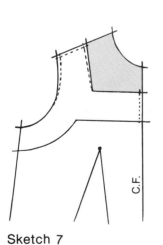

Sketch 7

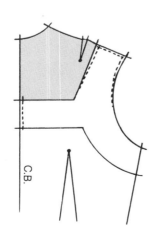

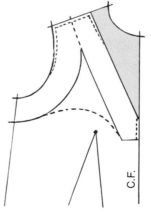

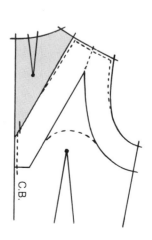

Sketch 8

Front & Back View

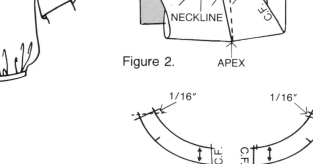

Figure 2.

Figure 2A.

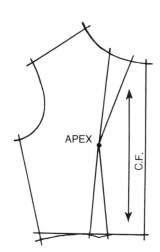

FIGURE 1

A.   Cut paper approximately 18″ × 24″ (45.7 × 61 cm).

B.   Use *two-dart front waist sloper*. Place sloper on paper and outline pivoting shoulder dart to neckline.

C.   Remove sloper. True all lines crossing all intersections.

FIGURES 2, 2A

1.   Close and cup neckline dart. Plan neckline and shaped neckband.

B.   To control neckline shirring, on lower edge of neckband measure from shoulderline 2½″ (6.4 cm). Crossmark.

C.   With neckline dart in closed position, place two sheets of paper between folded waist draft. Pin.

D.   Trace neckband (shaded area) and crossmark. Remove band drafts (Figures 2A and 2B). Separate sections. Label *neckband* and *facing band* (as illustrated). Pencil in all traced lines. True all lines crossing all intersections. Establish grainline parallel to center front. (Note difference between neckband and facing as illustrated by broken lines).
Note: The neckband and facing may have to be adjusted to insure a proper fit depending on the amount of shirring and the thickness of the fabric used.

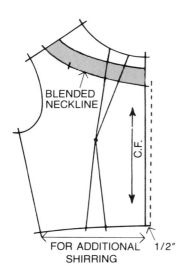

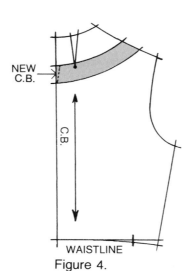

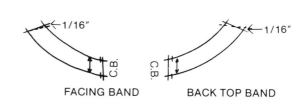

FACING BAND   BACK TOP BAND

Figure 4.

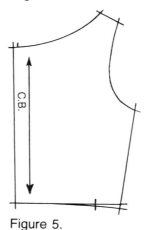

Figure 5.

FIGURE 3

A.   Open waist draft. Blend neckline.

B.   On waist draft, establish grainline parallel to center front. *Note:* If additional fullness is desired, add ½" to 1" (1.3 to 2.5 cm) at center front (broken line).

FIGURES 4 & 5

A.   To develop facing for back waist follow same procedure as for front.
Note: If back neckline dart intersects neckband, on top line of neckband measure in from center back the depth of the dart in neckband. Draw a line down to bottom line of neckband. Label *new center back.*

B.   On waist, neckband and facing drafts, establish grainline parallel to center back.

C.   To complete pattern sections allow seams; cut and notch seams.

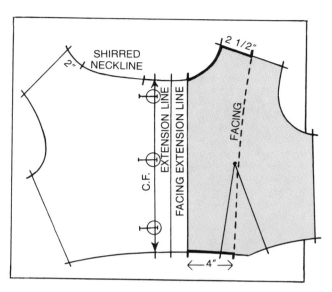

FIGURE 2

A. Open draft. Pencil in traced lines. Draw a line between traced crossmarks. Label *facing extension.*

B. For a self facing, place center front of sloper to facing extension. Outline sloper from neckline to shoulder for 2½″ (6.4 cm) and crossmark; outline waistline for 4″ (10.2 cm) and crossmark.

C. Remove sloper. Draw a slightly curved line between crossmarks (broken line).

Note: 1.   Shirred neckline is held to original neckline measurement by facing neckline.
2.   To mark buttonholes refer to Buttons & Buttonholes.
3.   To develop collar refer to Mandarin Collar.

D. Establish grainline on center front.

E. To complete pattern allow seams; cut and notch seams.

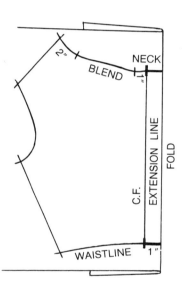

FIGURE 1

A. Use *one-dart front waist sloper.*

B. Outline sloper pivoting waistline dart to neckline.

C. Remove sloper. Indicate crossmarks for shirring 2″ (5.1 cm) in from shoulder and 1″ (2.5 cm) in from center front. Blend neckline.

D. Establish extension line.

E. Fold paper under on extension line. Trace neckline, waistline from fold to center front and crossmarks to indicate center front at neck and waistline (darker lines).

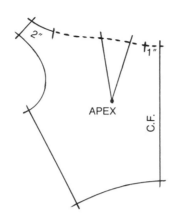

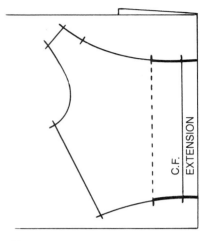

Figure 3.

FIGURE 2

A.   Using this draft as a sloper, outline and pivot waistline dart to new neckline. Remove sloper.

B.   Establish crossmarks for shirring 2" (5.1 cm) in from shoulder and 1" (2.5 cm) in from center front. Blend neckline.
Note: Since this scooped neckline is finished usually with a binding or narrow hem for a drawstring insertion, the facing at the front waist does not need to reach the shoulder.

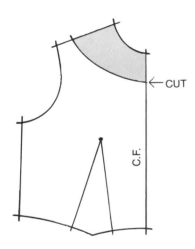

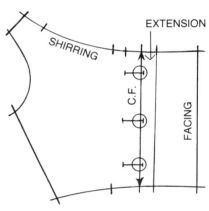

Figure 4.

FIGURE 1

A.   Use *one-dart front waist sloper.*

B.   Outline sloper. Establish neckline as desired.

C.   Cut along all finished lines and new neckline.

FIGURES 3 & 4

A.   For a self facing establish extension line. Fold paper under on extension line. Trace neckline and waistline for 1" (2.5 cm) beyond length of desired buttonhole (darker lines in Figure 4). Open paper. Draw a straight line between traced waistline and neckline crossmarks. Label *facing.* To mark buttonholes refer to Buttons & Buttonholes.

B.   Establish grainline on center front.

C.   To complete pattern allow seams; cut and notch seams.

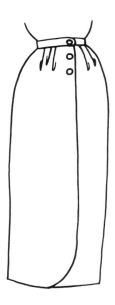

Sketches 12 and 13 are examples of areas of a garment that require a facing. Regardless of where a facing is used, the facing takes the shape and grainline of what is being faced. To insure a smooth and flat fit the facing is cut smaller if finished to the wrong side of the garment and larger if finished to the right side of the garment.

To complete asymmetrical skirt facing place pattern opposite to area to be faced and label *face up*.

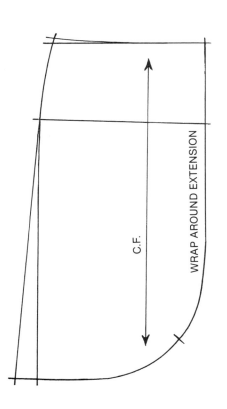

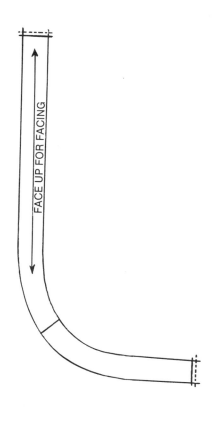

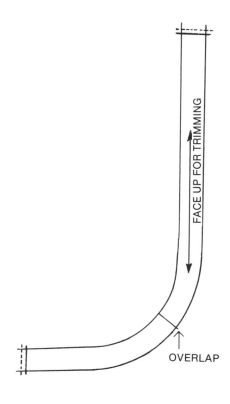

FACINGS FOR DECORATIVE SLEEVES
sketch 13

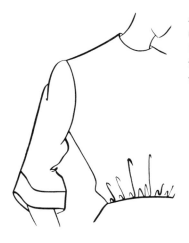

Asymmetrical sleeve facing is used as a decorative finish. Label *face up* (as illustrated) if fabric used has a right and wrong side.

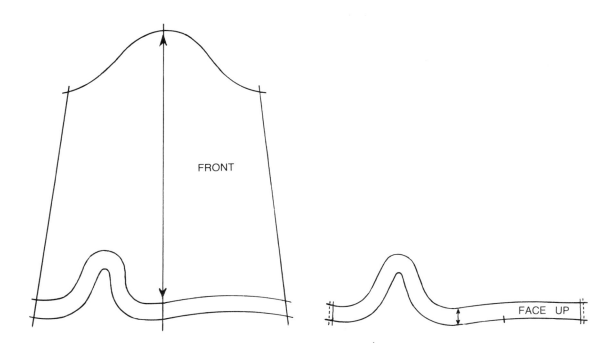

FRONT

FACE UP

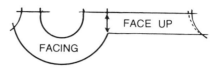

FIGURE 2

Facing for waist section.

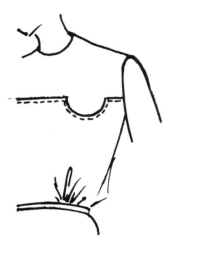

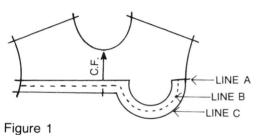

Figure 1

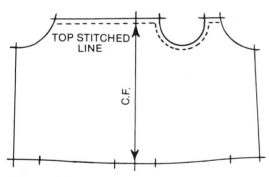

Figure 1A.

FIGURES 1 & 1A

Line A indicates finished edge for welt. Line B indicates stitching line for joining of lower waist faced edge to yoke for welt finish (Figure 1A). Line C is seam allowance below stitching line (broken line).

Note: The seam allowed on the lower edge of the yoke and the width of the facing are determined by the size of the welt seam.

FACINGS FOR YOKES
sketch 15

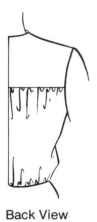

Back View

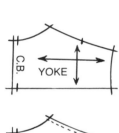

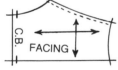

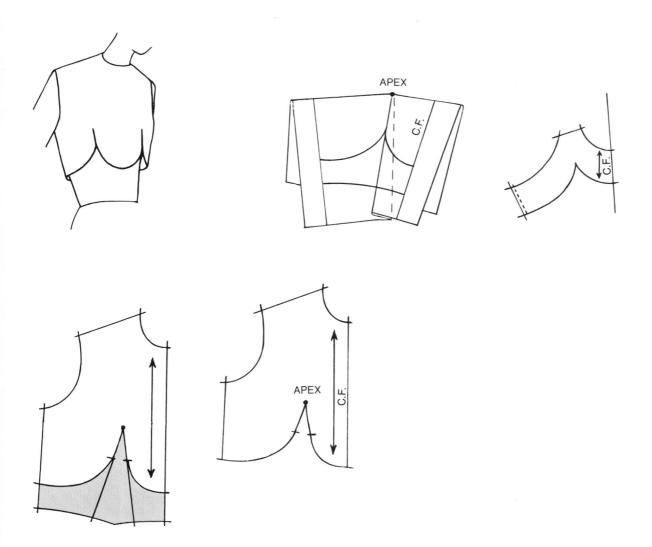

BUTTONS & BUTTONHOLES
introduction

Buttons have and always will play a major function in fastening and decorating a garment in all categories. A button is a three-dimensional form attached to different parts of a garment. Buttons are available in a wide range of sizes and are designated by line (ligne), inches or centimeters, indicating the diameter of the button.

Buttons are made in a variety of materials, shapes and contours. They vary in shape from flat, half-ball to ball. The novelty shapes include square, rectangle, triangle and log shape. The most popular finish is a smooth surface. The decorative buttons are carved designs, jeweled, nailheads, and stitched.

There are two types of buttons:

1. The sew-through button with two or four holes for attaching to the garment.

2. A button with a metal, fabric, plastic or thread shank providing concealed attachment to the garment. The width of the shank also varies and determines the placement of the buttonhole on a garment.

A buttonhole is an opening in a garment large enough to accommodate a button. Buttonholes are made on the overlap of the garment. Women's garments button right over left. Garments may be planned for vertical or horizontal buttonhole placement. On designs with a tab closure, lengthwise placement is preferred.

The principles for planning and marking buttonholes are always the same regardless of position.

BUTTON SIZES

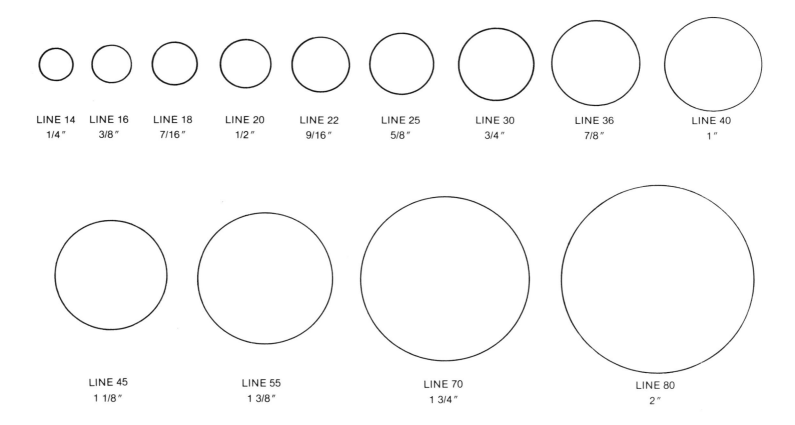

| LINE 14 | LINE 16 | LINE 18 | LINE 20 | LINE 22 | LINE 25 | LINE 30 | LINE 36 | LINE 40 |
| 1/4" | 3/8" | 7/16" | 1/2" | 9/16" | 5/8" | 3/4" | 7/8" | 1" |

| LINE 45 | LINE 55 | LINE 70 | LINE 80 |
| 1 1/8" | 1 3/8" | 1 3/4" | 2" |

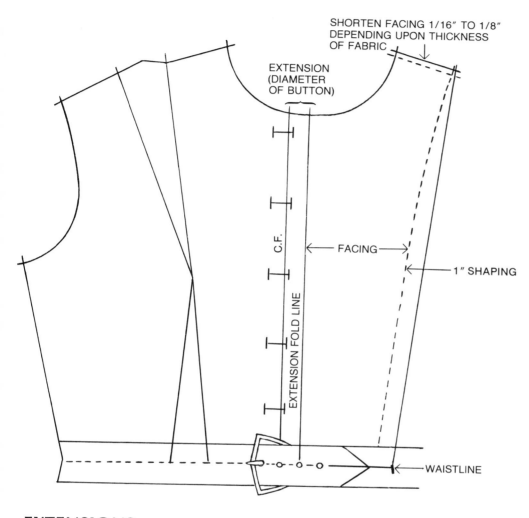

SHORTEN FACING 1/16" TO 1/8"
DEPENDING UPON THICKNESS
OF FABRIC

EXTENSION
(DIAMETER
OF BUTTON)

C.F.

FACING

1" SHAPING

EXTENSION FOLD LINE

WAISTLINE

1 1/8"
LENGTH OF
BUTTONHOLE

SHANK

1/16" SHANK
ALLOWANCE

C.F.

FOLD

1"
EXTENSION

FOLD

EXTENSIONS

FIGURE 1

A.   Diagram illustrates complete pattern.

B.   When the center of a button is placed on the center of a garment, half of the button will extend to the right and half to the left of the center. This makes allowance for an extension necessary.

C.   Width of extension equals diameter of button.

FIGURE 2

Diagram illustrates buttons, buttonholes and extension in relation to center front line.

LENGTH OF BUTTONHOLE

The length of a buttonhole is determined by the diameter of the button plus ⅛″ (0.3 cm). For ball, jeweled or odd-shaped buttons, it may be necessary to allow more than ⅛″ (0.3 cm). To determine the allowance needed, test buttonhole size by cutting a slit in a scrap of fabric and slipping button through.

PLACEMENT OF BUTTONHOLE FOR NECKLINE WITH OR WITHOUT SET-IN COLLAR

On a neckline with or without set-in collar the buttonhole is placed one-half the diameter of the button plus ¼″ (0.6 cm) away from the neckline. Refer to Figure 1.

PLACEMENT OF BUTTONHOLE FOR REVERE NECKLINE

On a revere neckline the buttonhole must be placed at breakpoint of revere. Buttonhole controls the breakpoint of revere (see Buttonholes Planned for Double-Breasted Garments, Figure 1).

GARMENT WITH A BELT

To plan and mark buttonholes above and below the waistline on garments worn with a belt, space buttonholes so that belt or buckle is at least 1½″ (3.8 cm) away from buttons. Refer to Figure 1.

GARMENT WITHOUT A BELT

On a garment without a belt place a buttonhole exactly on waistline regardless of whether garment has or has not a waistline seam. This will maintain the snug fit at the waistline. On coats and suits it is sometimes desirable to place buttonholes ⅛″ to ½″ (0.3 to 1.3 cm) above or below the waistline to achieve certain effects.

PLANNING SPACE BETWEEN BUTTONHOLES

After determining the position of neckline and waistline buttonhole, divide the remaining space by the number of buttonholes desired. Whenever possible place a buttonhole at bust level to prevent garment from gapping.

FINAL MARKING OF BUTTONHOLE FOR CENTER OF GARMENT

Buttonhole extends at least ¹⁄₁₆″ (0.2 cm) to the left of the center of a garment (right side of illustration) to allow for shank of button. Some novelty buttons have very wide shanks. When this occurs, measure the shank and extend buttonhole to the left of the center half the measurement of the shank (Figure 2).

Width of shank does not change size of buttonhole. The buttonhole starts ¹⁄₁₆″ (0.2 cm) or more from the right side in illustration.

FACINGS

A.   A facing may be cut in one with the waist as illustrated in Figure 1 or as a separate piece. In either case, the facing must be wide enough to extend at least 1″ (2.5 cm) beyond the end of the buttonhole and should be the same shape as the garment at the neckline, shoulder and waistline.

B.   Fold paper on extension foldline. Trace neckline, shoulder and waistline to first dartline to opposite side. Crossmark shoulder and waistline dartlines.

C.   Draw a straight line between shoulderline and waistline crossmarks. Shape line (as illustrated in Figure 1).

The placement of buttonholes on double-breasted garments is controlled by the finished edge of the garment and not by the center front.

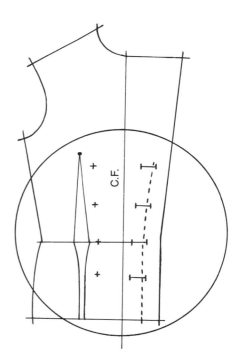

EXTENSION FOLDED UNDER

← WRONG SIDE OF GARMENT

RIGHT SIDE OF GARMENT

RIGHT END OF BUTTONHOLE

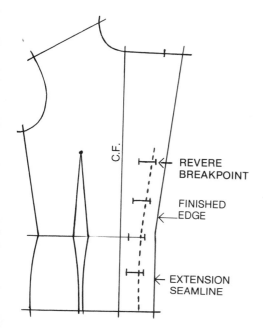

C.F.

← REVERE BREAKPOINT

← FINISHED EDGE

← EXTENSION SEAMLINE

FIGURE 1

A. To establish buttonhole guideline from extension seamline measure in towards center front the diameter of the button used.

B. Draw a line, very lightly, parallel to extension seamline up to revere breakpoint.

C. To plan and mark buttonholes refer to Buttonholes Planned for Center Closing, Figures 1 and 2.

FIGURE 2

A. To mark placement of buttons on the left-hand side of garment, fold draft on center front line with double-breasted extension turned under (shaded area).

B. With awl indicate the right-hand end of the buttonhole.

C. Open draft.

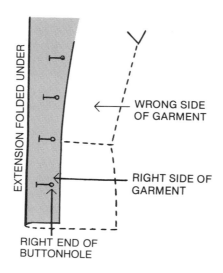

C.F.

FIGURE 3

Mark position of buttons with crosses.

VERTICAL BUTTONHOLES

Vertical buttonholes have a tendency to gap and unbutton easily. It is advisable to use them only on a loose fitting garment or when they enhance the design of a garment such as on tab openings.

To plan and mark vertical buttonholes refer to Buttonholes Planned for Center Closing, Figures 1 and 2.

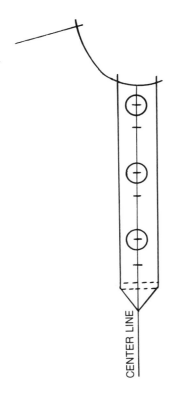

FIGURE 1

Some manufacturers plan vertical buttonholes so that the button rests at the top end of the buttonhole.

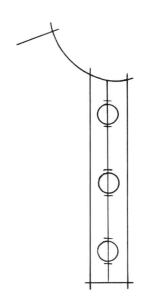

FIGURE 2

Some manufacturers plan vertical buttonholes so that the button rests in the center of the buttonhole.

Diagonal buttonholes may be used as a design feature or when the fabric used on the garment ravels a great deal. They may also be used to follow the straight grain of a bias-cut garment.

To plan and mark diagonal buttonholes refer to Buttonholes Planned for Center Closing, Figures 1 and 2.

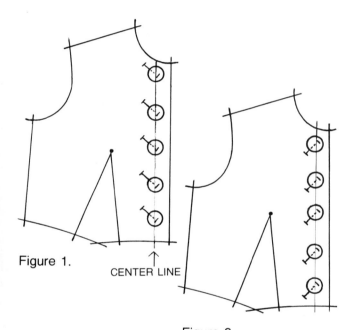

Figure 1.

CENTER LINE

Figure 2.

BUTTONHOLES PLANNED FOR POCKETS

Buttonholes on pockets are placed generally at a right angle to the opening of the pocket.

All buttonholes should be placed so that buttons will be balanced within the finished edge of the pocket.

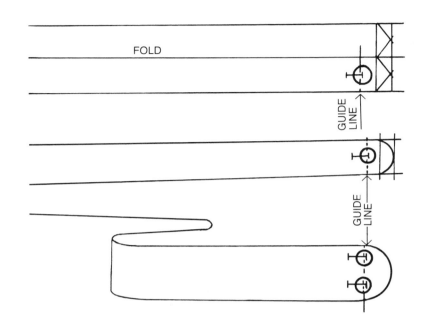

BUTTONHOLES PLANNED FOR BELTS

Buttonholes on belts are placed generally in the direction of the length of the belt.

All buttonholes should be placed so that buttons will be balanced within the finished edge of the belt.

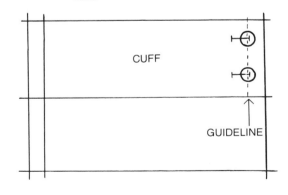

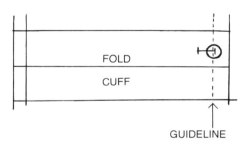

BUTTONHOLES PLANNED FOR CUFFS

All buttonholes should be placed so that buttons will be balanced within the finished edge of the cuff.

Buttonholes on cuffs are placed generally in the direction of the length of the cuff.

A collar is a decorative and functional feature on the neckline of a garment. As a decorative feature, the collar frames the face and enhances both the garment and the wearer. It is both decorative and functional as well as providing warmth to the wearer.

Collars may be attached to a garment or may be finished separately. When finished separately, they are pinned or basted to the neckline and removed for laundering or cleaning.

Collars may be cut on the bias, on the lengthwise or crosswise grain depending upon the pattern or texture of the fabric and the effect desired. In mass production, the grain is often governed by the layout. Usually, collars are made double—a top collar and an under collar—and often include interfacing.

There are three broad classifications of collars:

1. Separate set-in collars such as the Peter Pan and mandarin Collars

2. Collars developed in part or whole in one with the waist such as the shawl collar

3. Two-piece notched collar with a lapel and separate collar

Regardless of the classification, all collars fit into one of the following categories and take on one of three shapes (as illustrated):

1. Flat fitting with a concave shape

2. Rolled with a convex shape

3. Stand-up with a straight line

A *flat-fitting collar,* regardless of width, rolls over from the neckline seam and either ripples or lies flat on the body. The neckline seam should always be concealed by the roll of the collar no matter how flat the collar.

A *rolled collar,* regardless of width, is a collar that has a stand. A stand is the material under the collar at the center back which extends upward from the garment neckline to the point where a collar rolls or folds over. This stand averages ½ to 1½ inches (1.3 to 3.8 cm) high.

A *stand-up collar* is a collar that has no roll back.

A *shirtwaist collar* is a rolled collar attached to a straight or shaped stand-up neckband.

All collars, regardless of the classification, can be developed with any type of sloper, two dart, dartless, kimono, raglan, coat etc. Since the emphasis in this chapter, is on developing collars and not garments, the *one-dart sloper* has been used for developing all the collars.

1

2

3

Flat-fitting Collar

Detachable Collar

Rolled Collar

Stand-up Collar

Shirtwaist Collar

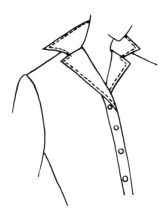

Sketch A

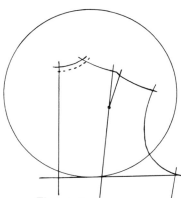

Sketch B

Sketch C

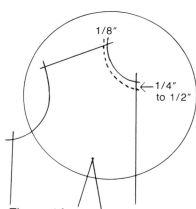

Figure 1.

Figure 1A.

1/8"

← 1/4" to 1/2"

The convertible collar is a rolled collar and, as the name implies, can be worn open or closed. It can be developed as:

1.   A one-piece collar with collar edge on fold of fabric with a slight shaping at the neckline and with a stylized point.

2.   A two-piece collar with a seam at the collar edge with shaping at both collar edge and neckline and with a stylized point.

Both collars are developed in this sketch.

SKETCH A ONE-PIECE CONVERTIBLE COLLAR

FIGURES 1 & 1A

A.   To allow additional ease for neck and attaching collar on back and front sloper neckline adjust as follows:

    1.   lower center back and shoulder ⅛" (0.3 cm);

    2.   lower center front ¼" to ½" (0.6 to 1.3 cm) and shoulder ⅛" (0.3 cm);

    3.   blend new necklines (broken lines).

B.   To develop collar measure:

    1.   new neckline from center back to shoulder;

    2.   new neckline from center back to center front.

The width of an average convertible collar measures 2½" to 3½" (6.4 to 8.9 cm) at center back. A wider collar results in a stand too high for comfort for the average neck.

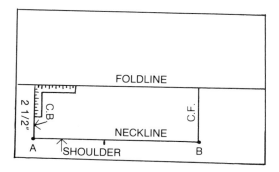

FIGURE 2

A.   Cut paper approximately 12″ × 18″ (30.5 × 45.7 cm).

B.   Fold paper in half and crease. Open paper. Draw a line over crease. Label *fold line* (collar edge).

C.   At left-hand edge of paper, square a line down from fold line equal to the desired width of the collar. Label *center back.* Illustrated: 2½″ (6.4 cm). Dot end of center back. Label *A.*

D.   From A draw a line parallel to fold line to equal the combined length of front and back neckline. Label *neckline.* Dot end of neckline. Label *B.*

E.   From B square a line up to fold line. Label *center front.*

F.   From A measure across on neckline back neckline measurement for position of shoulder. Crossmark. Label *shoulder.*

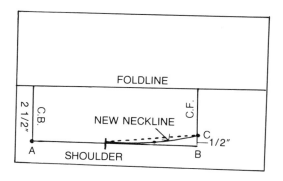

FIGURE 3

A.   From B measure up on center front ½″ (1.3 cm) and dot. Label *C.*

B.   Draw a straight line from C to shoulder crossmark (broken line).

C.   Halfway between C and shoulder crossmark on broken line, measure down ⅛″ (0.3 cm) and dot. Draw a slightly curved line from shoulder crossmark to dot to C to establish a new front collar neckline.

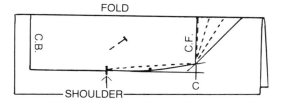

FIGURE 4

A.   Fold paper under on fold line and pin.

B.   Determine collar point as desired. See broken lines for variations.

C.   Trace center back, neckline, shoulder crossmark and collar point to opposite side.

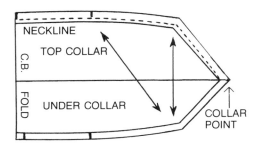

Figure 5.

FIGURE 5

A. Open draft. Pencil in all traced lines and shoulder crossmark.

B. Label draft *top collar* and *under collar* (as illustrated).

C. Starting at center back on neckline of top collar allow $\frac{1}{16}$" to $\frac{1}{8}$" (0.2 to 0.3 cm) depending upon thickness of fabric and taper to nothing at the collar point. Follow illustration accurately.
Note: This additional ease on top collar neckline allows for a smoother roll over the under collar and also conceals seam from collar point to neckline. This principle applies to all collars when collar edge line is cut on fold with the exception of stand-up collars such as a mandarin collar.

D. On neckline of top collar crossmark center back. On neckline of under collar crossmark $\frac{1}{4}$" (0.6 cm) away from center back.
Note: Crossmarks on top collar and under collar are placed in different positions to facilitate the identification of the top and under collars.

E. Establish grainline as desired.

F. To complete pattern allow seams; cut and notch seams.

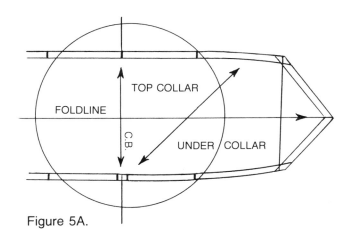

Figure 5A.

FIGURE 5A

This diagram illustrates one-piece collar opened and shows placement of crossmarks on collar in relation to center back.

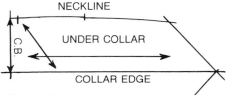

Figure 6.

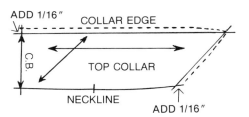

Figure 6A.

FIGURES 6 & 6A

These diagrams illustrate the same collar, but they are seamed at collar edge line. Ease is allowed on top collar edge line instead of neckline for this type of collar. Follow illustration. Taper to nothing at collar point.

SKETCH B
TWO-PIECE
CONVERTIBLE
COLLAR WITH
SHAPED COLLAR
EDGE LINE

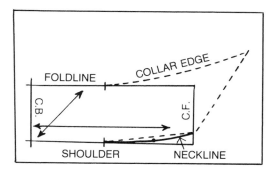

FIGURE 7

Note: This collar cannot be cut in one piece because of the stylized collar edge line.

A.   To develop the pattern for this collar refer to sketch A, Figures 1, 2 and 3.

B.   Establish shoulder crossmark on fold line. This crossmark acts as a guide when shaping desired stylized collar line and point (broken lines).

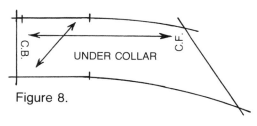

Figure 8.

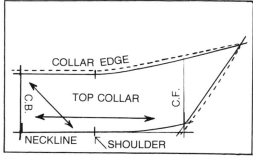

Figure 8A.

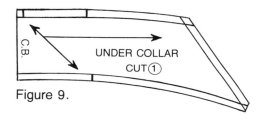

Figure 9.

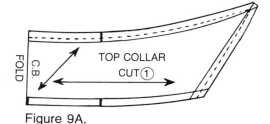

Figure 9A.

FIGURES 8, 8A, 9, 9A

A.   Pin collar draft to another sheet of paper. Trace all lines and both shoulder crossmarks to opposite side.

B.   Separate drafts. Place collar sections opposite to each other. Pencil in all traced lines. True all lines crossing intersections.

C.   Indicate center back. Label drafts *under collar* and *top collar* (Figures 8 and 8A). *Note:* When a collar is seamed on both sides, it has a tendency to curl especially when the angle of the collar point is acute. To correct this, ease is allowed on both sides of the collar point and not on the top collar edge line only.

D.   On top collar from center back on collar edge line measure up ¹/₁₆″ (0.2 cm). Draw a line tapering to nothing starting approximately 1½″ (3.8 cm) away from collar point. Continue from nothing at point to ¹/₁₆″ (0.2 cm) at neckline (follow broken line in Figure 8A carefully).

E.   On top collar neckline crossmark center back. On under collar neckline crossmark ¼″ (0.6 cm) away from center back.

F.   To complete collar patterns allow seams; cut and notch seams and crossmarks (Figure 9)

Sketch A

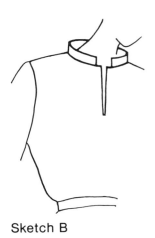

Sketch B

Sketch C

The mandarin collar is a standing band that extends up from the neckline and may be designed to meet at the center front overlap or to end somewhere between the shoulder and center front of the garment (see illustrations). A mandarin collar may be planned to fit at the normal neckline or on a scooped neckline. Also called coolie, Chinese, military, Nehru and stand-up collar.

For design purposes when using a check, plaid or stripe fabric, it is advisable to cut this collar as a straight band of fabric the length and width desired. If not cut on the straight grain, the shape of the neckline will cut into the pattern of the fabric (see Figure 6). A collar cut on the straight grain is also easier to handle and less expensive to produce making it practical for mass production. However, if fit is of the utmost importance, a shaped collar gives a close and smoother fit.

SKETCH A
ONE-PIECE
MANDARIN COLLAR

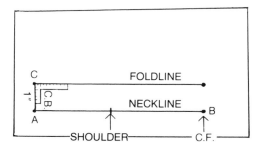

FIGURE 1

A.   On *one-dart sloper* adjust neckline to allow ease for attaching collar as in One-piece Convertible Collar, before taking neckline measurement.

B.   Cut paper approximately 12" × 18" (30.5 × 45.7 cm).

C.   Draw a line near bottom edge of paper equal to the combined length of the front and back neckline. Label *neckline.*

D.   Dot each end of neckline. Label *A* and *B* (as illustrated).

E.   Square a line up to the height of the mandarin collar desired. Dot. Label *C* and *center back.* Illustrated: 1" (2.5 cm).

F.   From C and center back square a line parallel to neckline. Label *fold line* (top edge of collar).

G.   From A at center back measure on neckline for position of shoulder crossmark.

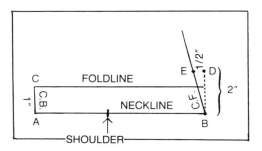

Figure 2.

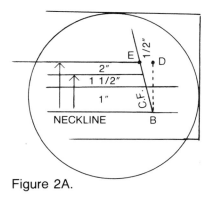

Figure 2A.

FIGURES 2 & 2A

A.   From B square a line up 2" (5.1 cm) and dot. Label *D* (broken line).

B.   From D measure in ½" (1.3 cm) and dot. Label *E.*

C.   Draw a straight line from B to E. Label *center front.*
Note: The line from B to E is a tested guideline. A mandarin collar regardless of its height must end on this line to achieve a proper fit at center front. See Figure 2A for various mandarin collar heights.

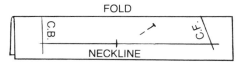

FIGURE 3

A.   Fold paper under on fold line and pin.

B.   Trace center back, neckline, shoulder crossmark and center front to opposite side.

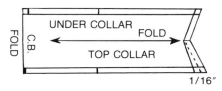

FIGURE 4

A.   Open draft. Pencil in all traced lines and shoulder crossmark.

B.   Label draft *under collar* and *top collar* (as illustrated).

C.   On neckline at center front of top collar allow ¹/₁₆" (0.2 cm). From this point draw a line to fold line tapering to nothing (broken line).
Note: This is to conceal center front collar seam.

D.   On neckline of top collar crossmark center back. On neckline of under collar crossmark ¼" (0.6 cm) away from center back.

E.   To complete pattern allow seams; cut and notch seams.

ONE-PIECE MANDARIN COLLAR WITH SHAPED NECKLINE

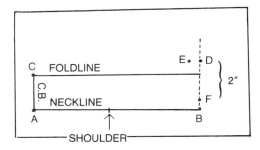

FIGURE 5

A.   To develop pattern for this collar refer to One-piece Mandarin Collar, Figure 1.

B.   From B square a line up 2" (5.1 cm) and dot. Label *D* (broken line).

C.   From D measure in ½" (1.3 cm) and dot. Label *E.*

D.   From B measure up ½" (1.3 cm) and dot. Label *F.*

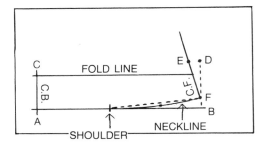

FIGURE 6

A.   Draw a straight line from E to F (solid line). Label *center front.*

B.   Draw a straight line from F to shoulder crossmark (broken line).

C.   Halfway between F and shoulder crossmark on broken line measure down ⅛" (0.3 cm) and dot. Draw a slightly curved line from F to dot to shoulder crossmark to establish a new front collar neckline.

D.   To complete pattern refer to One-piece Mandarin Collar, Figures 3 and 4.

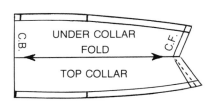

FIGURE 7

This diagram illustrates a finished one-piece mandarin collar with a shaped neckline.

TWO-PIECE MANDARIN COLLAR WITH SHAPED NECKLINE & COLLAR LINE

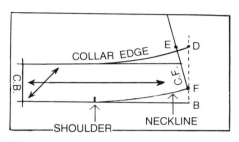

Figure 8.

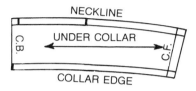

Figure 8A.

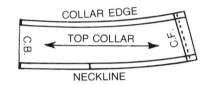

Figure 8B.

FIGURES 8, 8A, 8B

To develop the pattern for this collar refer to One-piece Mandarin Collar with Shaped Neckline with the following exceptions:

A.   Shape the collar line parallel to neckline (Figure 8).

B.   Pin collar draft onto another sheet of paper. Trace all collar lines, shoulder crossmark and grainline desired to opposite side.

C.   Separate drafts. Place collars opposite to each other. Label *under collar* and *top collar*. Pencil in all traced lines.

D.   True all lines crossing all intersections.

E.   Allow $\frac{1}{16}$" (0.2 cm) parallel to center front seam to conceal seam of under collar (broken line).

F.   On top collar crossmark center of collar line and neckline (Figure 8B).

G.   To facilitate identification of under collar crossmark center of collar line and crossmark neckline $\frac{1}{4}$" (0.6 cm) away from center back (Figure 8A).

H.   To complete pattern allow seams; cut and notch seams.

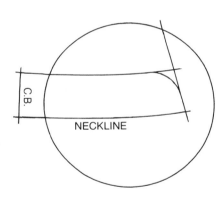

FIGURE 9

This diagram illustrates a mandarin collar with rounded center front.

SKETCH B

This sketch illustrates a mandarin collar away from neck at shoulder and center front.

SKETCH C

This sketch illustrates buttoned mandarin collar.

WING COLLAR
sketch 3

Wing Collar with Tab

A wing collar is a tailored shirt collar with spread points and is stitched on a neckband. It is also called dandy collar.

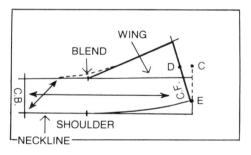

Figure 1.

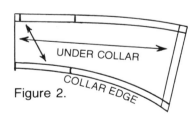

Figure 2.

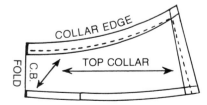

Figure 2A.

FIGURES 1, 2, 2A

A.   To develop the pattern for this sketch refer to One-piece Mandarin Collar with Shaped Neckline, Figures 5 and 6 with the following exception:

> Place a crossmark on collar edge line opposite shoulder crossmark on neckline.

B.   Shape the collar edge line starting from crossmark opposite shoulder crossmark (as illustrated).

C.   Pin draft onto another sheet of paper.

D.   To complete pattern refer to Mandarin Collar, sketch 2, Figure 8, B, C and D.

E.   To conceal seam allow $\frac{1}{16}$" (0.2 cm) from center back at collar edge line and center front neckline. When drawing lines taper to nothing at collar point (broken line in Figure 2A).

F.   Crossmark center of collar edge line on both top and under collars.

G.   Crossmark center of neckline on top collar.

H.   On neckline of under collar crossmark ¼" (0.6 cm) in from center back to facilitate identification of under collar.

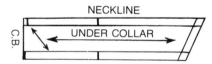

Figure 3.

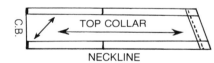

Figure 3A.

FIGURES 3 & 3A

A.   To develop the draft for collar neckband refer to One-piece Mandarin Collar or One-piece Mandarin Collar with Shaped Neckline.

B.   Band should be approximately 1" (2.5 cm) wide. Cut into two pieces.

C.   To complete pattern refer to Two-piece Mandarin Collar with Shaped Neckline.

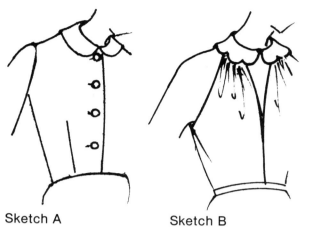

Sketch A   Sketch B

Sketch C

A Peter Pan collar is a one-piece or two-piece flat collar with rounded ends at center front or at both center front and center back. It is also called Buster Brown, Eton or Dutch collar. The Peter Pan collar may have a flat look, just enough stand to conceal the neckline seam or a high stand at center back with stand variations in between depending upon the effect desired.

To obtain the different heights of the stand refer to the following formula. For each additional 1" (2.5 cm) overlap at the shoulder, the collar stand increases ¼" (0.6 cm).

Overlap
1" (2.5 cm)
2" (5.1 cm)
3" (7.6 cm)
4" (10.2 cm)

Stand
¼" (0.6 cm)
½" (1.3 cm)
¾" (1.9 cm)
1" (2.5 cm)

The maximum overlap is 4" (10.2 cm) or neckline will lose its shape. See illustrations of the various shapes of Peter Pan collars.

There are two ways to develop patterns for Peter Pan collars: (1) develop the collar directly over the waist sloper and (2) develop the collar using the sloper neckline measurement. The collar developed from the sloper neckline measurement hugs the neck while the collar developed over the waist sloper stands slightly away from the neck and has a perky look.

SKETCH A
ONE-PIECE PETER PAN COLLAR

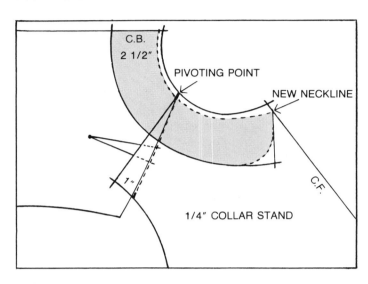

C.B. 2 1/2"

PIVOTING POINT

NEW NECKLINE

C.F.

1"

1/4" COLLAR STAND

FIGURE 1

A. Use *front and back waist slopers with or without shoulder darts.*

B. Cut paper approximately 18″ × 25″ (45.7 × 68.5 cm).

C. Outline upper section of back waist sloper (as illustrated). It is not necessary to include shoulder dart. Remove sloper.

D. On front waist sloper from shoulder/armhole intersection measure down 1″ (2.5 cm). Crossmark.

E. Match front and back slopers at shoulder/neckline intersection. Hold front waist sloper securely at neckline and pivot front sloper until crossmark at armhole touches back sloper at shoulder.

F. With sloper in this position outline upper section of front waist sloper. Remove sloper.

True all lines crossing all intersections.

G. Adjust neckline as in One-piece Convertible Collar, Figure 1.

H. At center back measure desired width of collar. Illustrated: 2½″ (6.4 cm). Continue collar edge line to center front parallel to new neckline (broken line).

I. Crossmark neckline at shoulder intersection. Label *center back* of collar.

J. Establish curve or point of collar at center front as desired (broken line).

K. Pin collar draft to another sheet of paper. Trace collar edge line, adjusted neckline, crossmark and grainline desired to opposite side.

FIGURE 2

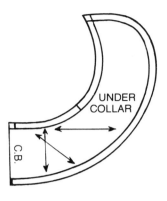

UNDER COLLAR

C.B.

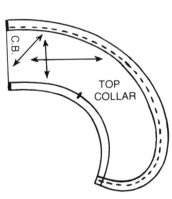

C.B.

TOP COLLAR

A. Separate drafts. Place drafts opposite each other. Label *under collar* and *top collar*. Pencil in all traced lines and crossmark.

B. Indicate center back on both drafts.

C. On neckline and collar edge line of top collar crossmark center back.

D. On under collar crossmark center of collar edge line and crossmark ¼″ (0.6 cm) in from center back to facilitate identification of under collar.

E. On collar edge line of top collar allow $\frac{1}{16}$″ (0.2 cm) ease (broken line).

F. To complete pattern allow seams; cut and notch seams. *Note:* If collar is too tight or too large for the neckline when tested (depending upon thickness of fabric), adjust collar at center back. Adjusted line must be parallel to center back.

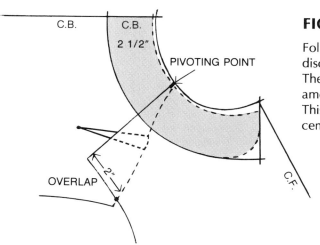

Figure 3. 1/2" Collar Stand

FIGURES 3, 4, 5

Follow same procedure discussed in Figures 1 and 2. The only difference is in the amount overlapped at shoulder. This creates a higher roll in center back.

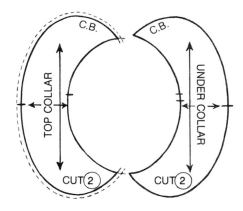

TWO-PIECE PETER PAN COLLAR

To develop pattern for this collar refer to One-piece Peter Pan Collar with the following exceptions:

A. The collar is shaped at both center front and center back;

B. Four collars are cut instead of two: two under collars and two top collars.

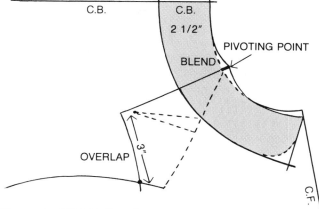

Figure 4. 3/4" Collar Stand

SKETCH B

After shaping collar the desired width, as in sketch A, plan scalloped edge within collar edge line.

SKETCH C

Ruffle added to collar may be cut on the lengthwise or crosswise grain or on the bias. The length of the ruffle should be at least one and a half times circumference of collar depending upon thickness of fabric.

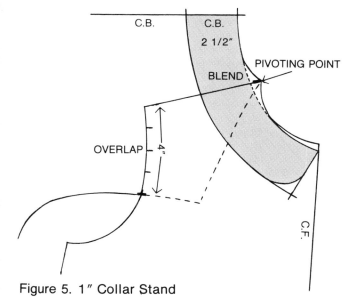

Figure 5. 1" Collar Stand

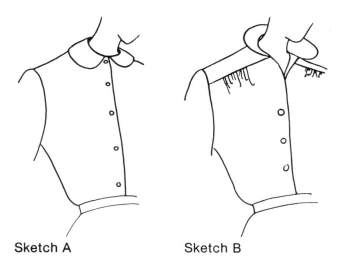

Sketch A   Sketch B

The height of the stand of a Peter Pan collar developed without a sloper is the same as for a Peter Pan collar developed with a sloper. However, the formulas used to obtain the stand at center back for these collars is reversed.

1" (2.5 cm) stand—measure up at center back 1" (2.5 cm)

¾" (1.9 cm) stand—measure up at center back 2" (5.1 cm)

½" (1.3 cm) stand—measure up at center back 3" (7.6 cm)

¼" (0.6 cm) stand—measure up at center back 4" (10.2 cm)

SKETCH A

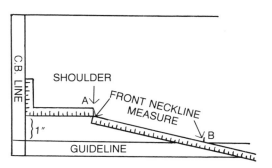

FIGURE 1

A.   Adjust neckline on sloper as in One-piece Convertible Collar, Figure 1, before taking neckline measurements.

B.   Cut paper approximately 15" (38.1 cm) square.

C.   Approximately 1" (2.5 cm) from the bottom edge of paper, square two lines at right angles to each other at the left-hand side of paper. Label *center back* and *guideline* (as illustrated).

D.   At center back and guideline intersection measure up 1" (2.5 cm). Square a line across to equal back neckline measurement. Crossmark. Label *A* (Shoulder).

E.   Place a ruler at A and pivot ruler until front neckline measurement touches guideline. Dot. Label *B*.

F.   Draw a straight line from A to B for front neckline.

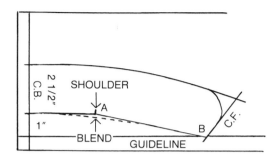

FIGURE 2

A.   Use a French curve to blend neckline at A (broken line).

B.   At B draw a short line at a 45° angle. Label *center front*.

C.   Measure desired width of collar at center back. Illustrated: 2½" (6.4 cm). Draw a line parallel to neckline from center back to center front.

D.   Establish curve or point at front of collar as desired.

E.   To complete pattern refer to Peter Pan Collar Developed from Sloper, Figures 1 and 2.

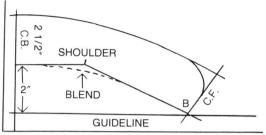

Figure 3.

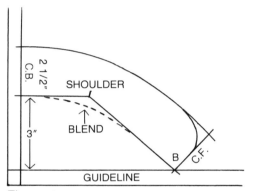

Figure 4.

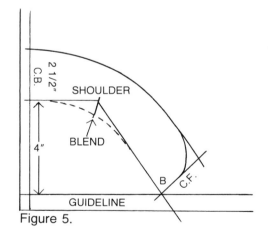

Figure 5.

FIGURES 3, 4, 5

Same procedure applies as discussed in Figures 1 and 2. The only difference is in the amount measured at center back.

SKETCHES B & C

These sketches illustrate use of Peter Pan collars on different styles.

SQUARE & ROUND BERTHA COLLAR
sketch 6

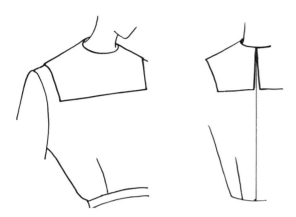

Sketch A Front & Back View

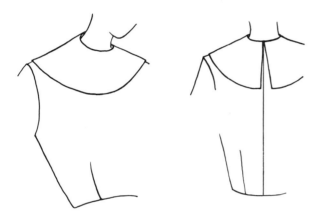

Sketch B Front & Back View

A Bertha collar is a large cape-like collar falling over the shoulders. The procedure for developing the pattern drafts for a Bertha collar is the same as for developing the Peter Pan collar with the following exception— the maximum overlapping at the shoulder is 2″ (5.1 cm) for a 1″ (2.5 cm) stand. Illustrations: 1″ (2.5 cm) overlap for ½″ (1.3 cm) stand.

SKETCH A

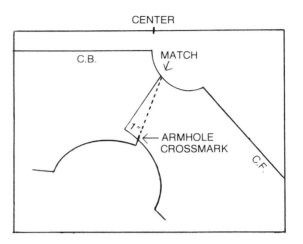

FIGURE 1

To complete this section of the draft refer to Peter Pan Collar Developed without a Sloper, Figures 1 to 6.

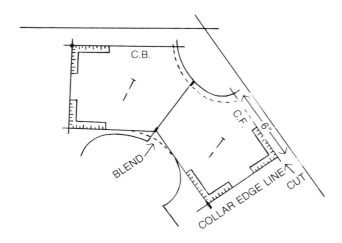

FIGURE 2

A.   At neckline crossmark shoulder (as illustrated).

B.   Adjust neckline as in Peter Pan Collar, sketch 4 (broken line).

C.   From the adjusted center front neckline measure down the desired length of collar. Illustrated: 6" (15.2 cm). Square a line across draft. Label *collar edge line.*

D.   On collar edge line determine width of collar from center front. Crossmark.

E.   Square a line up from crossmark to shoulderline.

F.   Center back depth equals center front depth plus 2¾" (7 cm). From adjusted center back neckline measure down depth for collar. Dot. *Note:* The additional 2¾" (7 cm) includes the 2¼" (5.7 cm) difference between the depth of front and back necklines plus ¼" (0.6 cm) or shoulder pick-up plus stand of collar which in this case is ¼" (0.6 cm).

G.   Square a line indefinitely across from center back dot. Then square a line up to shoulder to meet front collar edge line.

H.   Pin collar draft onto another sheet of paper. Trace all collar edge lines, adjusted neckline, shoulder and neckline crossmarks to opposite side.

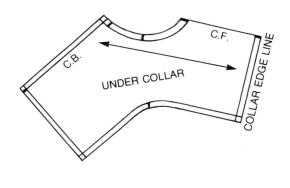

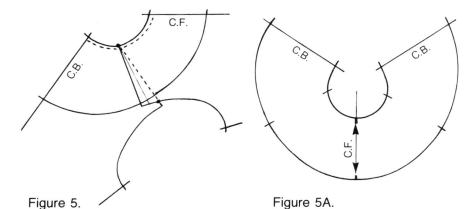

Figure 5.

Figure 5A.

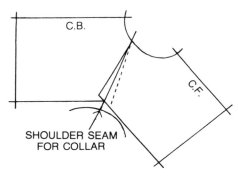

Figure 3. Finished Pattern

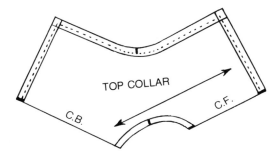

Figure 4.

FIGURES 3, 4, 5, 5A

A.   Separate draft from traced collar. Place collar drafts opposite each other. Label *under collar, top collar, center back* and *center front.*

B.   On under collar crossmark center front neckline, collar edge line and center back collar edge line. Crossmark center back neckline ¼" (0.6 cm) in from center back to facilitate identification of under collar.

C.   On top collar crossmark center front neckline, collar edge line and center back collar edge line.

D.   On both collars establish grainline parallel to center front.

E.   To complete pattern allow seams; cut and notch seams. *Note:* Collar may be planned: 1. With back or front opening (sketch A, Figure 3); 2. Seamed at shoulder (center of overlapped area near armhole, Figure 4); 3. With collar edge line rounded instead of squared (sketch B, Figure 5A).

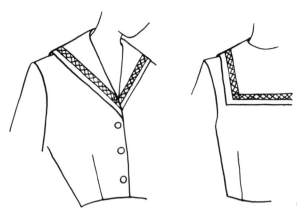

Sketch A Front & Back View

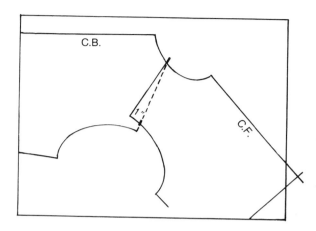

Figure 1.

Sketch B

A sailor collar is a large square collar hanging in back. Front tapers to a "V." It may also be called a Middy collar. The procedure for developing the sailor collar is the same as for developing a Bertha Collar, with the following exceptions:

A.   Collar ends on extension line (see Figure 2);

B.   Adjusted neckline starts at center back and tapers into front neck style line (as illustrated with broken line in Figure 2);

C.   Shape of collar edge line (see Figure 2);

D.   Ease allowed on top collar tapers to nothing at front end (see top collar Figure 3A).

Sketches A, B and C illustrate uses of sailor collar on different styles.

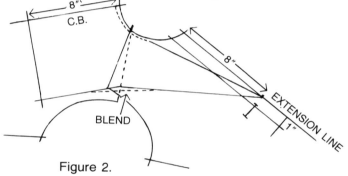

Figure 2.

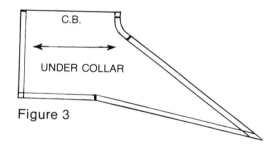

Figure 3

Sketch C

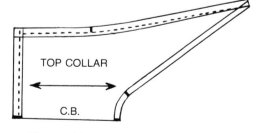

Figure 3A.

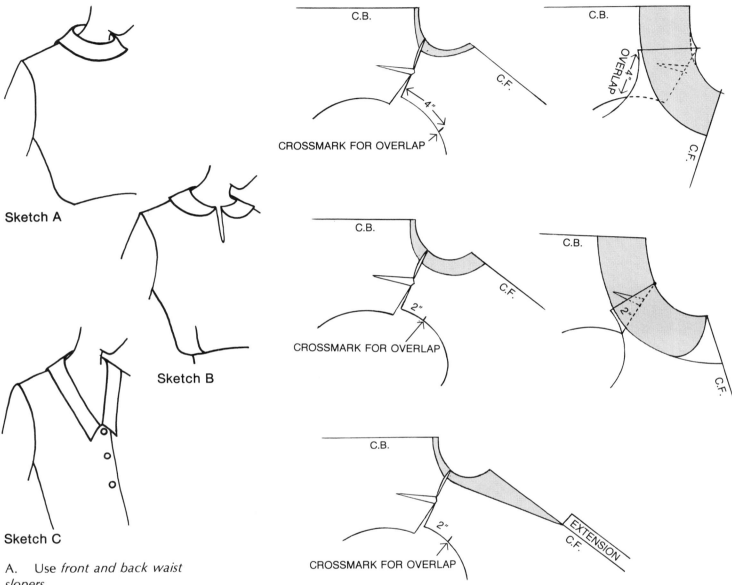

Sketch A

Sketch B

Sketch C

A. Use *front and back waist slopers.*

B. Match back and front necklines at shoulder and armhole. Do not overlap shoulder. Outline upper sections of slopers.

C. Plan neckline desired (as illustrated).

D. Cut away shaded area.

E. To develop and complete pattern refer to One-Piece Peter Pan Collar Developed from a Sloper.

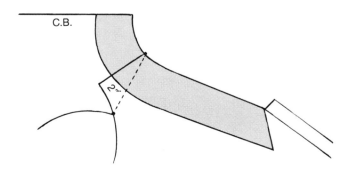

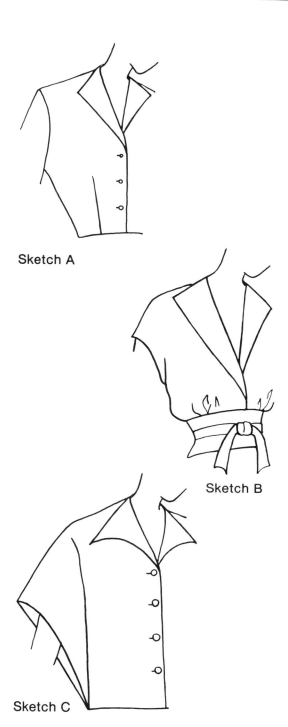

Sketch A

Sketch B

Sketch C

Revere is another name for lapel. It is actually an extension of the front opening of the garment which folds back revealing the facing. It may be developed on any type of waist or torso sloper with or without darts.

SKETCH A

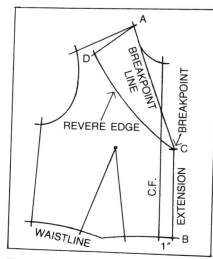

Figure 1.

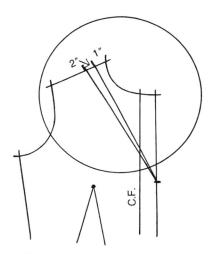

Figure 1A.

FIGURES 1 & 1A

A. Use *front waist sloper.*

B. Cut paper approximately 20″ × 30″ (50.8 × 76.2 cm).

C. Place sloper near left-hand side of paper along bottom edge. Outline sloper.

D. Remove sloper. True all lines crossing all intersections.

E. Label neck/shoulderline intersection *A.*

F. On waistline from center front measure out 1″ (2.5 cm) for extension. Label *B.* Width of extension equals diameter of button.

G. Draw a line parallel to center front from B up to desired breakpoint. Crossmark. Label *C.*

H. Draw a line from C to A. Label: *breakpoint roll line.* *Note:* The neckline on any revere may be planned away from the original neckline (see Figure 1A).

I. Plan desired width of revere starting at A. Label *D.* Draw a straight or curved line from D tapering to nothing at C (as illustrated). Label *revere edge.*

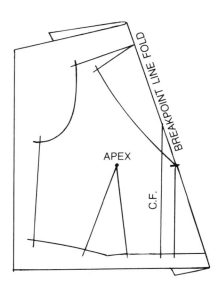

FIGURE 2

A.   Fold paper under on breakpoint roll line.

B.   Trace revere line to opposite side.

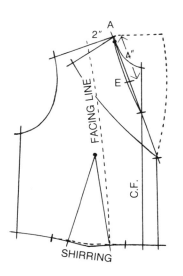

FIGURE 3

A.   Open draft. Pencil in traced revere line (broken line).

B.   To indicate facing, from A on shoulderline measure 2″ (5.1 cm). Crossmark.

C.   Draw a slightly curved line from crossmark to bottom of waistline dartline (broken line).

D.   For better fit of revere, a dart should be planned on breakpoint roll line. On line from A measure down 4″ (10.2 cm). Crossmark.

E.   From crossmark measure out ½″ (1.3 cm). Label E.

F.   From A measure down ¼″ (0.6 cm). Dot. Blend a curved line from dot to E. Then blend from E tapering to nothing towards center front line. Crossmark end of dart.
Note: The function of the dart is to shape and tighten the underside of the revere for a better fit. The dart allows the revere collar facing to roll over to the right side of the garment smoothly.

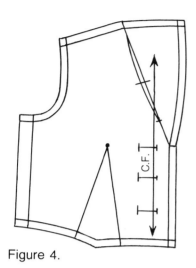

Figure 4.

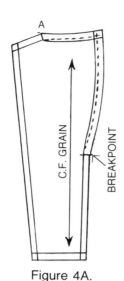

Figure 4A.

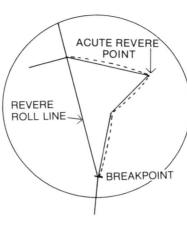

Figure 4B.

FIGURES 4, 4A, 4B

A. Copy front waist draft.

B. Plan and mark buttonholes. First buttonhole starts at breakpoint. Refer to Buttons & Buttonholes.

C. Copy revere facing without roll line dart.

D. To conceal the finished seam on the revere, add $1/16''$ to $1/8''$ (0.2 to 0.3 cm) ease to facing. The amount added depends upon the thickness of the fabric used. Start at A and blend to nothing at breakpoint (broken line in Figure 4A).
Note: On an acute pointed revere, add ease tapering to nothing at point as illustrated in Figure 4B.

E. True all lines crossing all intersections. Establish grainlines parallel to center front.

F. Allow seams; cut and notch seams.

BACK WAIST & BACK NECK FACING

FIGURES 5 & 5A

A. Cut paper approximately $15'' \times 24''$ (38.1 × 61 cm).

B. Outline *back waist sloper*.

C. To plan back neck facing from neck/shoulder intersection measure 2″ (5.1 cm). Crossmark. This crossmark must match the facing crossmark established on the front waist shoulder.

D. On center back measure down 6″ (15.2 cm). Draw in facing line (broken line).
Note: This garment has a low front neck opening which calls for a long back facing. Refer to Facings.

E. Copy back neck facing (Figure 5A).

F. True all lines crossing all intersections. On back waist and neck facing establish grainline parallel to center back.

G. To complete pattern allow seams; cut and notch seams.

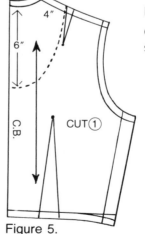

Figure 5.

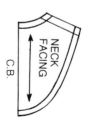

Figure 5A.

SKETCHES B & C

These sketches illustrate revere variations used on different types of garments.

SHAWL COLLAR–NARROW VARIATIONS
sketch 10

Sketch A

Sketch B

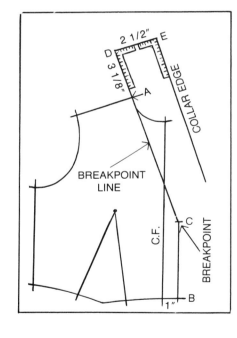

Sketch C

The shawl collar is a collar and revere cut in one piece with the front waist and can *only* be worn open. There are many variations of the shawl collar from narrow to cape and the collar edge may be notched or styled as desired. Collar may be developed on any type of waist or torso sloper with or without darts.

SKETCH A
FIGURE 1

A. Use *front waist sloper.*

B. Cut paper approximately 20″ × 30″ (50.8 × 76.2 cm).

C. Place sloper near left-hand side of paper along bottom edge. Outline sloper.

D. Remove sloper. True all lines crossing all intersections.

E. Label neck/shoulder intersection *A.*

F. From center front on waistline measure out 1″ (2.5 cm) for extension. Label *B.* Width of extension equals diameter of button.

G. Draw a line parallel to center front from B up to desired breakpoint. Crossmark. Label *C.*

H. Draw a line from C through A. Label *breakpoint line.* Extend line beyond A to equal back neck measurement. Label *D.* This measurement may vary depending upon figure. Illustrated: 3⅛″ (7.9 cm) for size 12.

I. From D square a line 2½″ (6.4 cm) for center back of collar. Label *E.*

J. From E square a line down parallel to breakpoint line towards breakpoint. Label *collar edge line.*

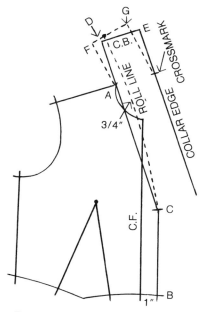

Figure 2.

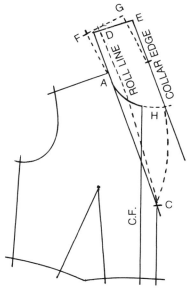

Figure 3.

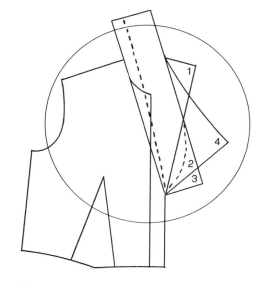

Figure 3A.

FIGURE 2

A.   From D at center back of collar measure out ¼" to ½" (0.6 to 1.3 cm) for additional ease on collar edge. Label *F*. Blend a slightly curved line from F to A (broken line).

B.   From F square a line the length of the original collar width (broken line). Label *G*. Illustrated: 2½" (6.4 cm).

C.   On collar edge place a crossmark opposite shoulderline. Blend a curved line from G down to crossmark parallel to new back neckline (broken line).

D.   To establish collar roll line from F measure 1" (2.5 cm). Dot. Draw a line following curve of back neckline to ¾" (1.9 cm) away from A gradually tapering to nothing at C (broken line). Label *roll line*.

FIGURES 3 & 3A

A.   To develop collar edge style line for sketch B draw a curved line from C to any point on line E (broken line).
Note: See style line variations in Figure 3A.

B.   For placement of shawl notch, as in sketches A and C, square a line from center front/neck intersection towards right-hand side of paper. Label *H* (broken line).
Note: If a lower notch is desired square a line below neckline.

C.   Trace line H, roll line, neck, center back of collar, collar edge and crossmark at C to opposite side.

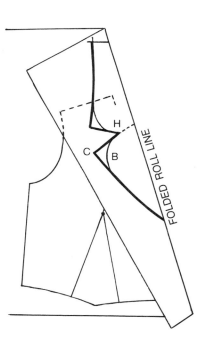

FIGURE 4

A.   With wrong side face up crease on traced roll line and fold paper over to right side.

B.   Draw collar style line desired blending into traced back collar line (heavier lines).

FIGURE 5

Note: Collar for sketch A will be developed into a complete pattern.

A. Open draft. Trace stylized collar to right side. Pencil in traced lines.

B. For a better fit of under collar, a dart should be planned on breakpoint line. From A on breakpoint line measure down 4″ (10.2 cm). Crossmark.

C. From crossmark measure out ½″ (1.3 cm). Label *I*. Blend a curved line starting ¼″ (0.6 cm) below A to crossmark and down to nothing towards center front line (shaded area). Crossmark end of dart.
Note: 1. For a more rounded neckline, dart underlay will be deeper at I. This dart usually ends approximately 2″ to 4″ (5.1 to 10.2 cm) above breakpoint depending upon the depth of dart. The muslin fitting will determine the exact point.
2. The function of the dart is to shape and tighten the underside of the shawl collar for a better fit. The dart also allows the collar facing to roll to the right side of the garment smoothly.

D. To indicate facing from A measure 2″ (5.1 cm) on shoulderline. Crossmark.

E. Draw a slightly curved line from crossmark to bottom of waistline dartline (broken line).

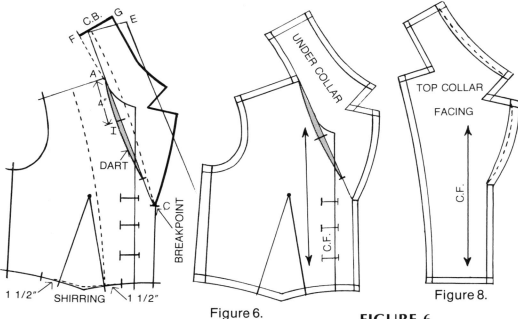

Figure 5.

Figure 6.

Figure 8.

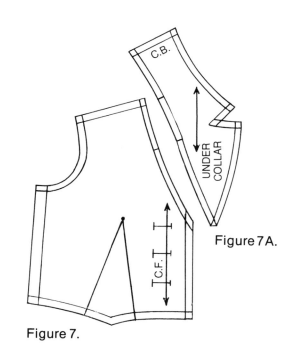

Figure 7.

Figure 7A.

FIGURE 6

Collar may be cut in one with waist.

FIGURE 7

Collar may be cut with front waist and under collar seamed on breakpoint line following curved line on waist and straight line on collar.
Note: Regardless of collar the facings are always cut in one piece (Figure 8).

FIGURE 8

A. To conceal seam of undercollar to top collar add ¹⁄₁₆″ to ⅛″ (0.2 to 0.3 cm), depending upon thickness of fabric, tapering to nothing at breakpoint (broken line).

B. Copy pattern as desired. True all lines crossing all intersections.

C. Establish grainlines parallel to center front.

D. To complete pattern allow seams; cut and notch seams.

E. For back refer to Revere without Collar, Figure 5.

Collar may be developed on any type of waist or torso sloper with or without darts. The following types of collars can be developed from this shawl collar draft:

1. sailor, large shawl, cape:

2. flat to high roll;

3. notched variations.

Sketch A Front & Back View

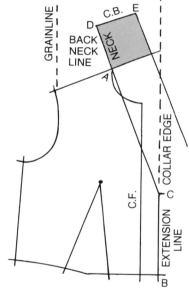
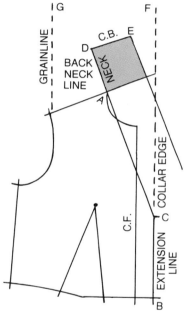

Sketch B

Sketch C Front & Back View

SKETCH A FLAT SAILOR COLLAR

FIGURE 1

A.   To develop the flat sailor collar refer to Shawl Collar—Narrow Variations, Figure 1, A through J.

B.   To establish sailor collar edge line continue extension line parallel to center front from B up full length of paper. Label *F, collar edge line* (broken line).

C.   From shoulder/armhole intersection draw a line parallel to collar edge line. Label *G, grainline.*

D.   Extend shoulderline from A towards collar edge line.

E.   Identify back neckline. Label neck on shaded area.

F.   Copy shaded neck section onto another piece of paper. Label *neckline.* Cut away excess paper.

FIGURE 2

A.   Fold neck section into quarters.

B.   Open section and cut on folded lines *towards but not through* neckline.

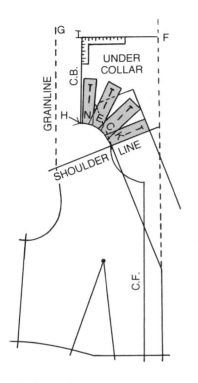

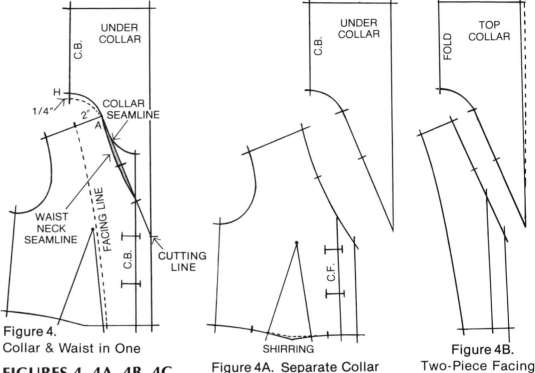

Figure 4.
Collar & Waist in One

Figure 4A. Separate Collar

Figure 4B.
Two-Piece Facing

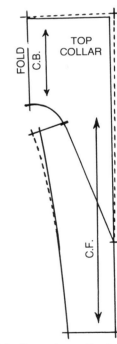

Figure 4C. One-piece Facing

FIGURE 3

A.   Place cut neck sections in original position on draft matching shoulderlines.

B.   Spread cut sections until they are parallel to grainline G. Label *neckline H.*

C.   Draw curved neckline. Draw a line parallel to grainline G from H desired length of sailor collar. Dot. Label *I* and *center back.*

D.   Square a line across from I to extension line F.

FIGURES 4, 4A, 4B, 4C

A.   Remove neck sections. True all lines crossing all intersections.

B.   Add ¼″ (0.6 cm) at H and blend into neckline (broken line). This prevents upward pull of center back of collar. Label *under collar.*

C.   To develop breakpoint line dart and facing line, refer to Shawl Collar—Narrow Variations, Figure 5, B through E.

D.   To complete pattern refer to Shawl Collar—Narrow Variations, Figures 6, 7 and 8. *Note:* 1. For a more economical layout of pattern all collars in this category may be joined at the dartline separating collar from garment (see Figures 4A, 7, 8A). 2. Center back of collars are usually cut on fold. 3. Facing for Figure 4 may be cut in two pieces (Figure 4B) or in one piece (Figure 4C).

SKETCHES B & C
HIGH-ROLL
NOTCHED SHAWL &
CAPE COLLARS

FIGURES 5, 6, 6A, 7

A. To develop collar patterns for these sketches follow same procedure as for sketch A, Figure 1, A through F and Figure 2, A and B.

B. From G square a line across paper.

C. Draw a true bias line down from G (as illustrated).

D. Spread cut sections until they are parallel to bias line. Pin. Label *neckline H.*

E. Draw curved neckline. Draw a line parallel to bias line from H desired length of high roll shawl collar. Illustrated: 7" (17.8 cm). Crossmark. Label *I.*

F. From I curve line for shawl collar edge to breakpoint.

G. Establish stylized notch in collar, if desired. Collar notch should be in line with neckline (see J).

H. For cape collar extend line another 2" (5.1 cm) or more (see cape collar line).

I. To complete pattern for sketches B or C refer to Shawl Collar—Narrow Variations, Figures 6, 7 and 8.
Note: Facing for Figure 7 is cut in one piece as in Figure 6A.

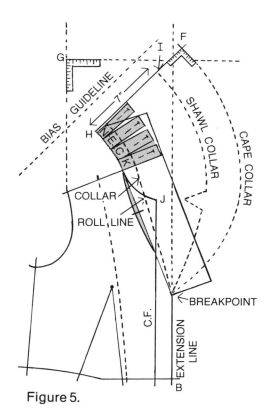

Figure 5.

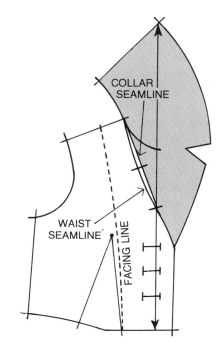

Figure 6. Collar & Waist in One

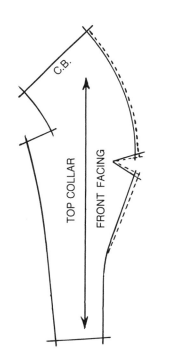

Figure 6A. Facing & Top Collar in One

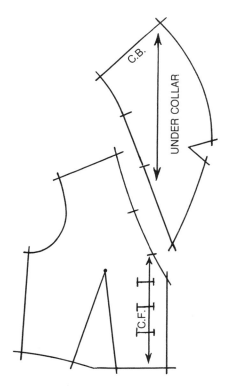

Figure 7. Separate Collar

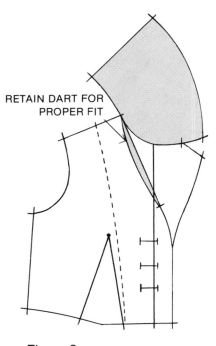

RETAIN DART FOR
PROPER FIT

Figure 8.

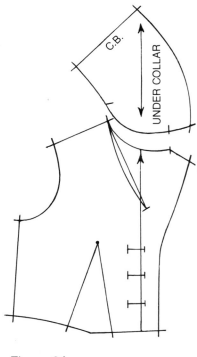

Figure 8A.

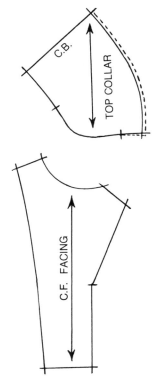

Figure 8B.

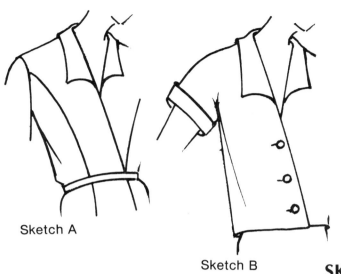

Sketch A

Sketch B

Collar may be developed on any type of waist or torso sloper with or without darts. It may be cut in one piece with waist or seamed to garment on breakpoint line.

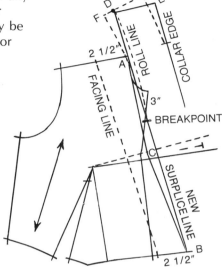

SKETCH A

FIGURE 1

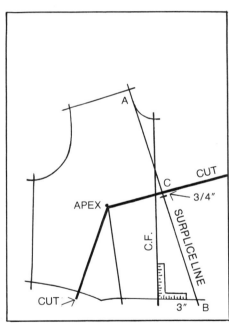

A.   Use *front waist sloper.*

B.   Cut paper approximately 20″ × 30″ (50.8 × 76.2 cm).

C.   Place sloper near left-hand side of paper along bottom edge. Outline sloper.

D.   Remove sloper. True all lines crossing all intersections.

E.   Label neck/shoulderline intersection *A.*

F.   On waistline from center front measure out 3″ (7.6 cm). Label *B.*

G.   Draw a straight line from B to A. Label *surplice line.*

H.   For better fit of surplice line, draw a line from apex to center of surplice line. Label *C.* Continue line to edge of paper.

I.   On surplice line at C measure down ¾″ (1.9 cm). Crossmark.

J.   Cut on line from edge of paper to apex (as illustrated).

K.   Cut on dartline nearest underarm from waistline to apex.

FIGURE 2

A.   Overlap cut area matching C to crossmark. Pin. Waistline dart underlay will automatically increase.

B.   Draw a new surplice line from B to A, extending line for back neck measurement. Label *D.* Illustrated: 3⅛″ (7.9 cm) for size 12.
Note: To develop back neck collar section refer to Shawl Collar—Narrow Variations, Figure 1, I and J and Figure 2, A, B and C.

C.   To establish breakpoint on draft, from original neckline/center front intersection measure down 3″ (7.6 cm). Crossmark. Label *breakpoint.*

D.   To establish collar roll line from F measure in 1″ (2.5 cm). Dot. Draw a line tapering to nothing at breakpoint (broken line).

E.   Trace crossmark at collar breakpoint, roll line, back neckline, center back of collar, collar edge line to crossmark to opposite side.

Finished Patterns

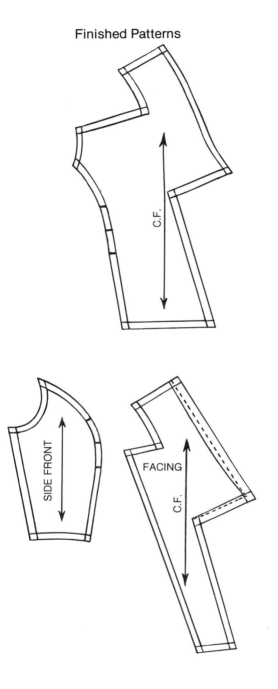

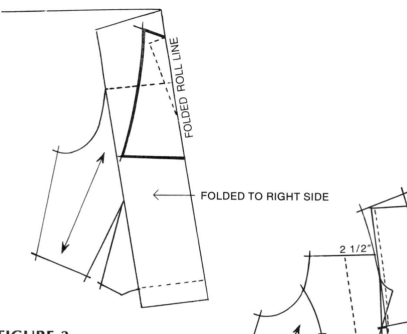

FOLDED ROLL LINE

← FOLDED TO RIGHT SIDE

FIGURE 3

A.   With wrong side face up crease roll line to breakpoint folding paper over to right side.

B.   Draw collar style line desired blending into back collar edge line and breakpoint (darker lines).

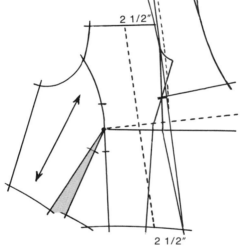

2 1/2"

2 1/2"

FIGURE 4

A.   Open draft. Trace collar edge line to right side. Pencil in all traced lines.

B.   To develop princess line refer to Princess Line Front Waist Variations, sketch 4.

C.   To establish facing line measure 2½" (6.4 cm) from shoulderline and waistline. Draw a line parallel to surplice line.

D.   To complete pattern refer to Revere without Collar, Figures 4 and 5.

SKETCH B

This sketch illustrates collar on a different garment style.

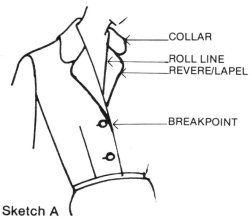

Sketch A

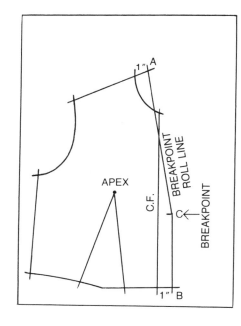

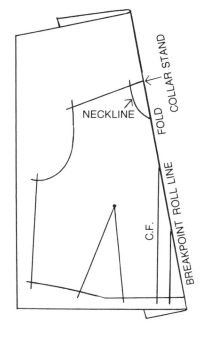

FIGURE 1

A.   Use *one-dart front waist sloper.*

B.   Cut paper approximately 20″ × 30″ (50.8 × 76.2 cm).

C.   Place sloper near left-hand side of paper along bottom edge. Outline sloper.

D.   Remove sloper. True all lines crossing all intersections.

E.   To establish collar stand, at neck/shoulderline intersection extend shoulderline 1″ (2.5 cm). Label *A*.

F.   At waistline/center front intersection measure out 1″ (2.5 cm) for extension. Label *B*. Width of extension equals diameter of button.

G.   Draw a line parallel to center front from B up to desired breakpoint. Label *C*.

H.   Draw a line from C to A for breakpoint roll line.

Sketch B

A notched collar is a two-piece collar that can only be worn open. It consists of a lapel or revere, which is usually cut in one with the garment, and a collar, which meets the lapel resulting in a notch. Notched collars are used in all garment categories from tailored coats and suits to evening wear.

Sketch C

FIGURE 2

A.   Fold paper under on breakpoint roll line.

B.   Trace neckline and collar stand to opposite side.

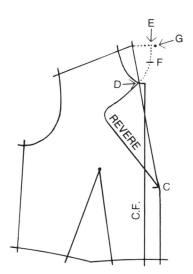

FIGURE 3

A.   Open paper. Pencil in traced lines. Label *D* and *E* (as illustrated).

B.   From neckline intersection D outline desired style of revere ending at C.

C.   Divide neckline between D and E in half. Label *F.*

D.   From E extend line ¼″ (0.6 cm). Dot. Label *G.*

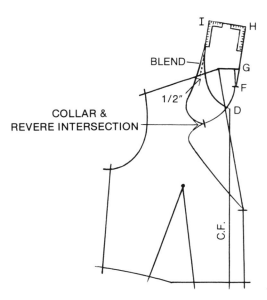

FIGURE 4

A.   Draw a straight line from F through G extending line for back neckline measurement. Label *H*. Illustrated: 3⅛″ (7.9 cm) for size 12. This measurement may vary depending upon figure types.

B.   Square a line from H two times the height of the center back neck stand plus ½″ (1.3 cm). Label *I*. This measurement applies only to high rolled collars where the collar edge line does not extend more than ½″ (1.3 cm) below back neckline seam. Illustrated: 2½″ (6.4 cm).
Note: Example for obtaining this measurement: 1″ for stand, 1″ for collar to roll over stand, ½″ to cover neck seamline equals 2½″.

C.   From I square a guide line to shoulderline (broken line). Blend rest of desired collar style line ending at any point on top revere line.

D.   Crossmark where collar and revere intersect.

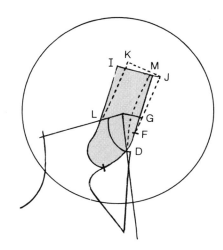

FIGURE 5

A.   For additional ease on back collar edge line (dotted line), from H measure out ¼″ (0.6 cm). Dot. Label *I*.

B.   Blend a slightly curved line from J to G.

C.   From J square a line equal to the original width of collar— 2½″ (6.4 cm). Label *K.*

D.   Blend a curved line from K down to L.

E.   To establish collar roll line, from J on center back neckline measure in 1″ (2.5 cm). Label *M.*

F.   From M square a line down 2″ (5.1 cm). Blend line to D (broken line).

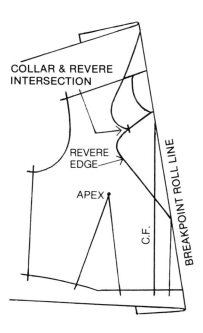

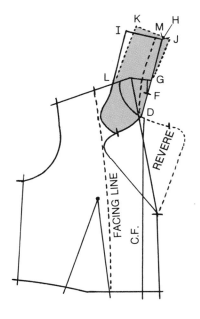

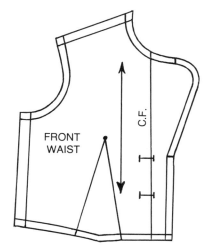

FIGURE 6

A.   Refold paper under at breakpoint roll line.

B.   Trace *only* revere edge line and crossmark where collar and revere intersect to opposite side.

FIGURE 7

A.   Open draft. Pencil in traced revere edge line and crossmark.

B.   On shoulderline from L measure in 2″ (5.1 cm) for facing. Crossmark.

C.   Draw a line from crossmark on shoulderline to end of waist dartline (slightly curved broken line).

FIGURE 8

A.   Copy front waist. Plan and mark buttonholes. Refer to Buttons & Buttonholes.

B.   Establish grainline parallel to center front.

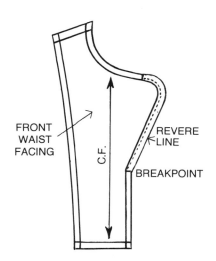

FIGURE 9

A.   Copy front waist facing. Allow 1/16″ to 1/8″ (0.2 to 0.3 cm), depending upon thickness of fabric, for ease on revere facing. Start from nothing at crossmark and blend to nothing at breakpoint (broken line).

B.   Establish grainline parallel to center front.

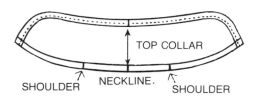

Figure 10.

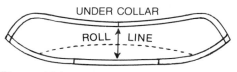

Figure 10A.

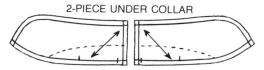

Figure 10B.

FIGURE 10

Copy top collar and indicate crossmarks and grainline. Allow $\frac{1}{16}$" to $\frac{1}{8}$" (0.2 to 0.3 cm) for ease to outer edge of collar (broken line).

FIGURE 10A

Copy under collar.

FIGURE 10B

A. Under collar may be cut with a seam at center back and is often cut on the bias for a smoother roll.

B. True all seams on all pattern sections.

C. To complete patterns allow seams; cut and notch seams.

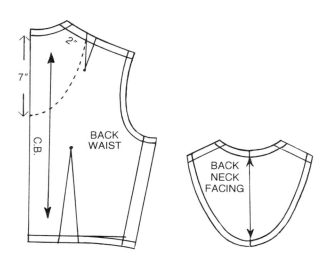

FIGURE 11

To develop back waist outline back waist sloper and complete as illustrated.
Note: For a low cut front neckline, the back neck facing should be longer for "hanger appeal" of garment. Refer to Facings.

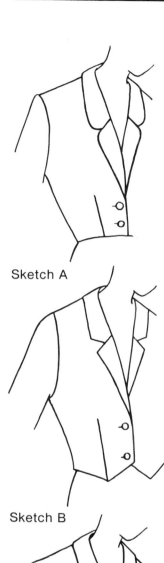

Sketch A

Sketch B

Sketch C

Collar may be developed on any type of waist or torso sloper with or without darts.

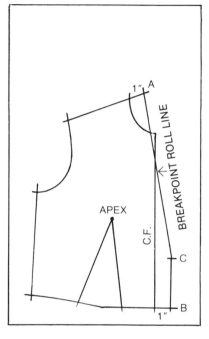

FIGURE 1

A.   Use *one-dart front waist sloper.*

B.   Cut paper approximately 20″ × 30″ (50.8 ″ 76.2 cm).

C.   Place sloper near left-hand side of paper along bottom edge. Outline sloper.

D.   Remove sloper. True all lines crossing all intersections.

E.   To establish collar stand at neck/shoulderline intersection extend line 1″ (2.5 cm). Label *A.*

F.   At waistline/center front intersection measure out 1″ (2.5 cm) for extension. Label *B.* Width of extension equals diameter of button.

G.   Draw a line parallel to center front from B up to desired breakpoint. Label *C.*

H.   Draw a line from C to A for breakpoint roll line.

FIGURES 2 & 2A

A.   Fold paper under on breakpoint roll line.

B.   Plan position of low-notched collar line. From original neckline, measure down 1½″ (3.8 cm). Label *D.* This measurement may vary depending upon position of notch desired and position of breakpoint.
Note: The lower the notched collar line the deeper the neckline. Depth must be indicated on revere roll line before completing the draft. See variations in Figure 2A.

C.   Blend new neckline into original neckline stopping at crossmark which is approximately at the center of the original neckline.

D.   Trace new neckline (broken line) and collar stand to opposite side.

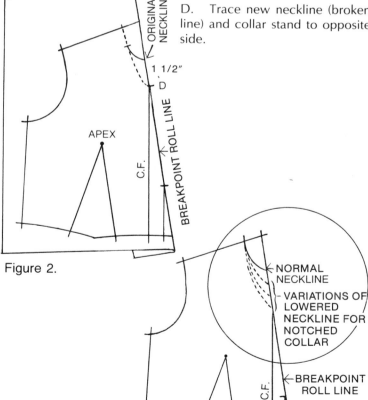

Figure 2.

Figure 2A.

To complete the collar draft and pattern sections refer to Two-piece Notched Collar, Figures 3 through 11.

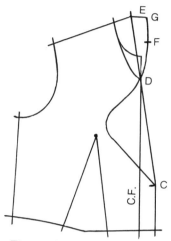

E
G
F
D
C
C.F.

Figure 3.

I
H
G
D
C.F.

Figure 4.

K
M
I
J
H
L
G
D

Figure 5.

C.F.

Figure 6.

K
M
H
I
J
L
G
F
D
C.F.
BLEND

Figure 7.

FRONT
WAIST
C.F.

Figure 8.

FACING
C.F.

Figure 9.

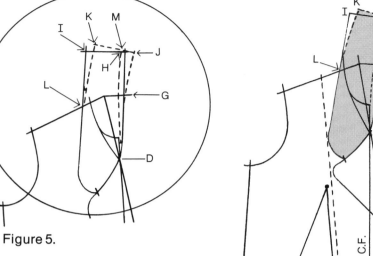

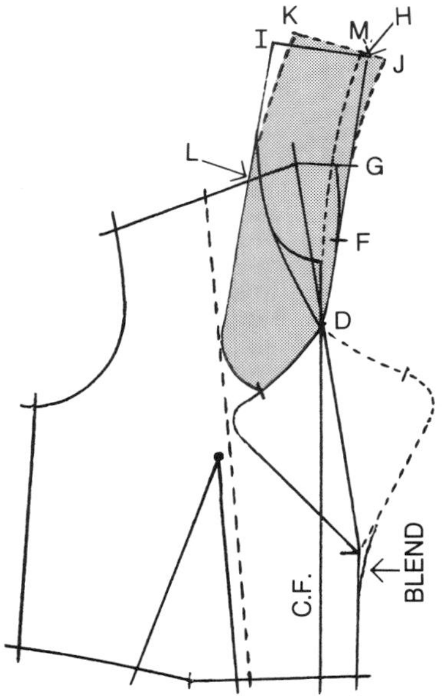

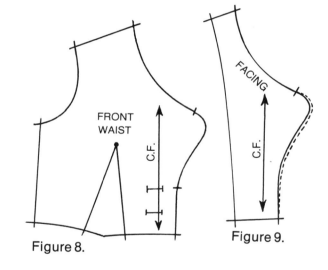

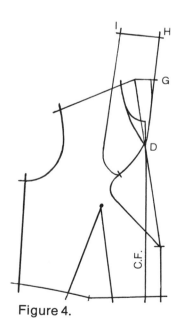

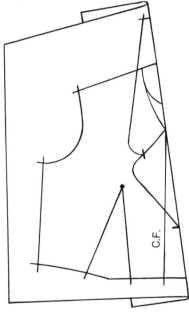

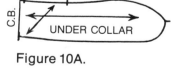

NECKLINE
C.B.
UNDER COLLAR

Figure 10A.

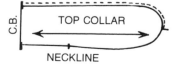

C.B.
TOP COLLAR
NECKLINE

Figure 10B.

Sketch A

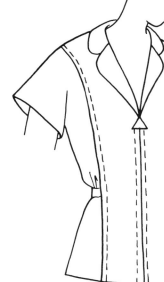

Sketch B

Sketch C

Sketch D

Collar may be developed on any type of waist or torso sloper with or without darts.

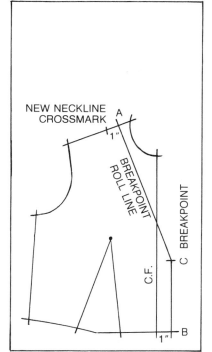

FIGURE 1

A.   Use *one-dart front waist sloper.*

B.   Cut paper approximately 20″ × 30″ (50.8 × 76.2 cm).

C.   Place sloper near left-hand side of paper along bottom edge. Outline sloper.

D.   Remove sloper. True all lines crossing all intersections.

E.   To establish new neckline from neck/shoulderline intersection measure in 2″ (5.1 cm). Crossmark. Label *new neckline.*
Note: This measurement can be more or less depending upon style desired.

F.   To establish collar stand from new neckline crossmark measure 1″ (2.5 cm). Label *A.*

G.   At waistline/center front intersection measure out 1″ (2.5 cm) for extension. Label *B.* Width of extension equals diameter of button.

H.   Draw a line parallel to center front from B up to desired breakpoint. Label *C.*

I.   Draw a line from C to A for breakpoint roll line.

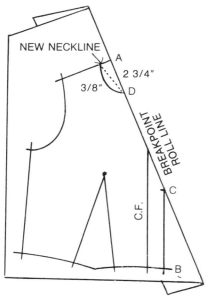

FIGURE 2

A.   Fold paper under on breakpoint roll line.

B.   To develop the new neckline from A measure down 2¾" (7 cm). Label *D*.
Note: The neckline may be lower depending upon style of notched collar.

C.   Draw a straight line from new neckline crossmark to D (broken line).

D.   Draw a curved line for new neckline (see arrow in illustration). The deepest point should not be more than ⅜" (1.0 cm).

E.   Trace new neckline and collar stand to opposite side.

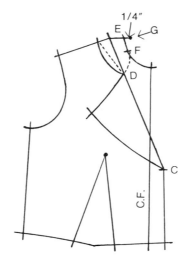

FIGURE 3

A.   Open paper. Pencil in traced lines.

B.   From neckline intersection D outline desired style of revere ending at C.

C.   Divide neckline between D and E in half. Label *F*.

D.   Extend line from E ¼" (0.6 cm). Dot. Label *G*.

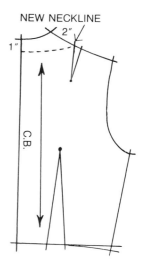

FIGURE 4

Note: Before collar can be completed on front waist draft, back waist neckline must be adjusted before measurement can be obtained.

A.   Outline *back waist sloper.*

B.   Remove sloper. True all lines crossing all intersections.

C.   Measure in from neck/shoulderline intersection same amount establish on front —2" (5.1 cm). Crossmark. Blend in new back waist neckline (broken line).

D.   Measure length of new back neckline. Use this measurement for developing back collar section on front waist draft.

NOTCHED COLLAR–AWAY FROM NECK continued

sketch 15

To complete collar draft and pattern sections refer to Two-piece Notched Collar, Figures 4 through 10 and Note under Figure 11.

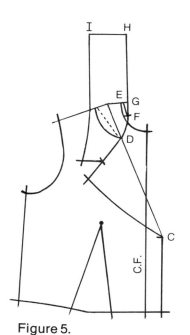

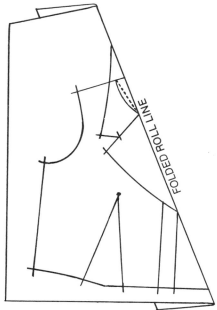

Figure 7.

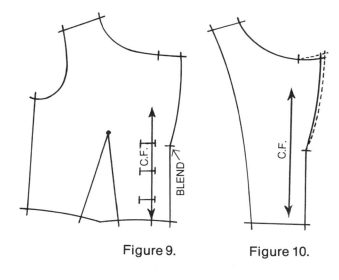

Figure 9.

Figure 10.

Figure 5.

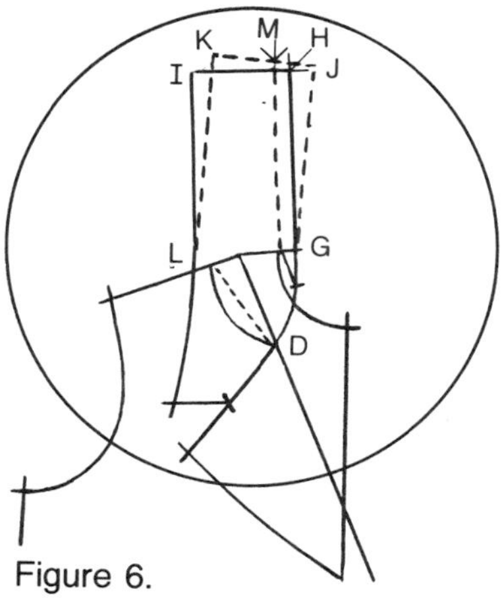

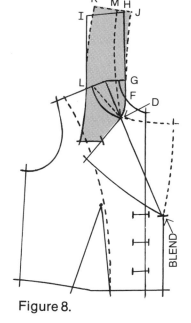

Figure 6.

Figure 8.

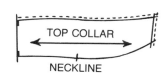

Figure 11.

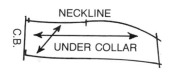

Figure 11A.

DOUBLE-BREASTED NOTCHED COLLAR
sketch 16

Sketch A

Sketch B

Sketch C

Any of the notched collar variations may be applied to a double-breasted notched collar draft. Collar may be developed on any type of waist or torso sloper with or without darts.

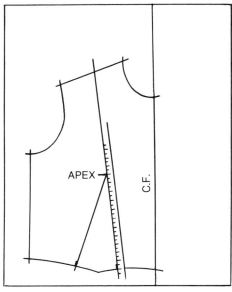

FIGURE 1

A.   Use *one-dart front waist sloper.*

B.   Cut paper approximately 20″ × 30″ (50.8 × 76.2 cm).

C.   Place sloper near left-hand side of paper along bottom edge.

D.   Outline sloper. Dot apex. Crossmark waist dartlines.

E.   Remove sloper. True all lines crossing all intersections.

F.   Place ruler along waist dartline nearest center front touching apex. Draw princess line from waistline to shoulderline.

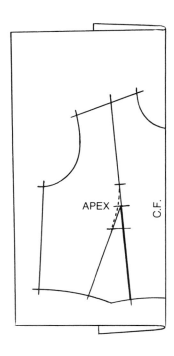

FIGURE 2

A.   Crossmark apex and 2″ (5.1 cm) above and below apex.

B.   Blend at apex (broken line).

C.   Fold paper under on center front line.

D.   Trace princess line from apex to waistline and crossmark on apex to opposite side (darker line).

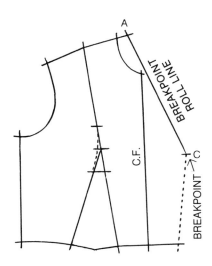

FIGURE 3

A.   Open draft. Pencil in traced lines and apex crossmark

B.   To establish collar stand at neck/shoulderline intersection extend shoulderline 1″ (2.5 cm). Label *A*.

C.   Draw a line from A to C for breakpoint roll line.

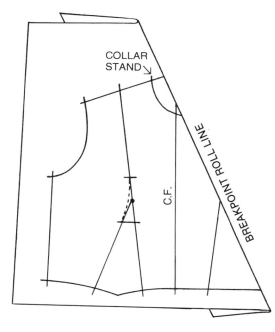

FIGURE 4

A.   Fold paper under on breakpoint roll line.

B.   Trace neckline and collar stand to opposite side.

C.   Open draft. Pencil in traced lines.

To complete collar draft and pattern sections refer to Two-piece Notched Collar, Figures 3 through 11.

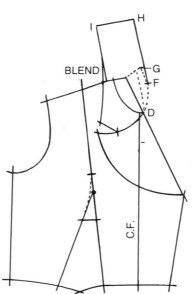

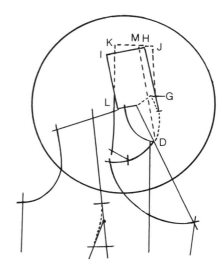

Figure 6A.

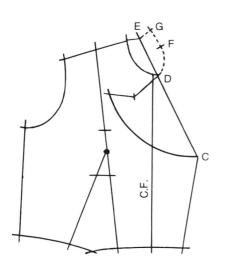

Figure 5.

Figure 6.

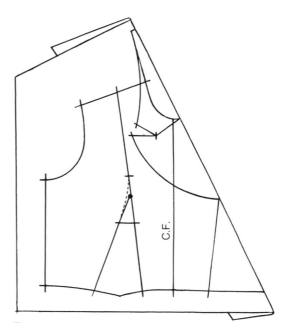

Figure 7.

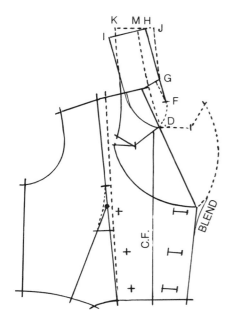

Figure 8.

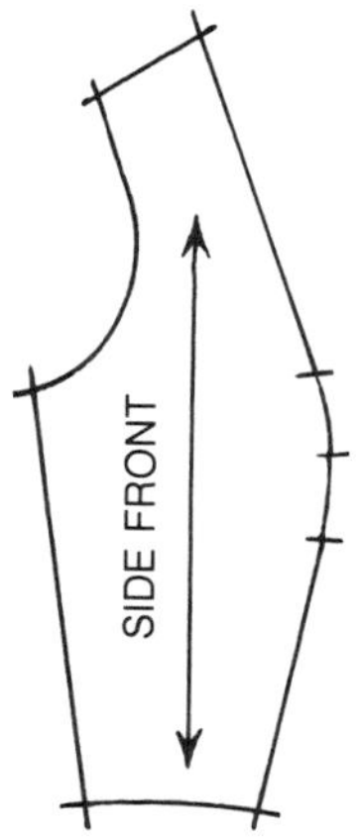

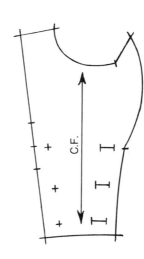

Figure 9.

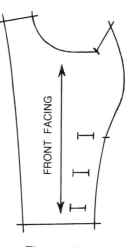

Figure 9A.

Figure 9B.

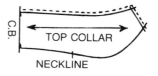

Figure 10.

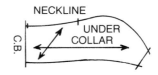

Figure 10A.

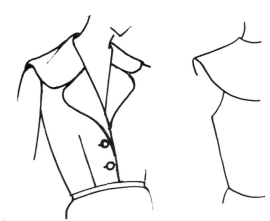

Sketch A Front & Back View

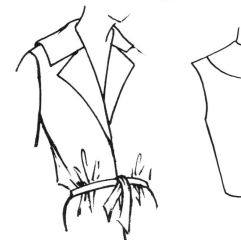

Sketch B Front & Back View

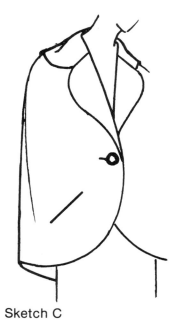

Sketch C

FIGURE 1

A.   Use two-pieced notched collar draft, sketch 13, Figure 1 through Figure 4.

B.   Cut paper approximately 20″ × 30″ (50.8 × 76.2 cm).

C.   Place draft near left-hand side of paper along bottom edge. Outline draft.

D.   Remove draft. True all lines crossing all intersections.

E.   To establish collar roll line on center back line measure in from H 1″ (2.5 cm). Crossmark.

F.   From crossmark square a line down 2″ (5.1 cm). Blend remainder of line (as illustrated).

G.   To establish bias line measure 4″ (10.2 cm) from extension. Draw a broken line parallel to extension. Continue line approximately 7″ (17.8 cm) above height of collar point H. Label J. Square a line from J. Label *K*.

H.   Draw a line through K and label *true bias line* (as illustrated).

I.   Square a line from G to outside edge of collar. Label *L*.

J.   Shaded area is neck section.

K.   Label *neck* and *center back* (as illustrated).

FIGURE 2

A. Copy shaded neck section onto another sheet of paper. Cut away excess paper.

B. Fold neck sections into quarters.

C. Open sections and cut on fold lines towards, but not through, neckline.

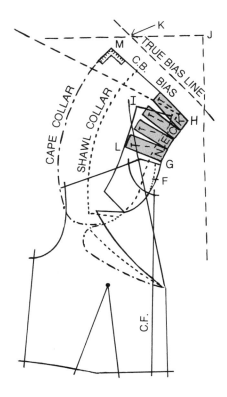

FIGURE 3

A. Place cut neck sections on draft matching L and G.

B. For a *wide flat shawl or cape collar* spread sections until center back of collar is parallel to bias line.

C. For a *wide rolled shawl or cape collar* spread sections until center back of collar is halfway between original position and center back bias line.

D. Draw curved neckline. Square a line from H parallel to bias line the desired length of collar. Illustrated: 7" (17.8 cm). Label *M*.

E. Draw desired notched collar and revere.

F. To complete collar draft and pattern sections refer to Two-piece Notched Collar, Figures 6 through 11.

SLEEVES
introduction

A sleeve is a section of a garment that covers all or part of the arm. There are two major classifications of sleeves:

1.   A mounted sleeve or a sleeve set into an armhole;

2.   A sleeve cut in one with the waist of the garment.

Regardless of the classification sleeves can be short or long, narrow or wide. Some sleeves are designed to add width to the shoulder, others are designed to minimize the shoulder. All sleeves may be fitted or full at the wrist, and may be cut to any desired length. See diagram of *Sleeve Length Variation.* Mounted sleeves may be fitted or full at the armhole. Fitted sleeves may have ease added at the elbow by darts, gathers or soft pleats.

Within the two classifications there are many variations and sub-variations. The following are a few examples:

1.   A mounted sleeve or a sleeve set into an armhole

   A.   Set-in (normal armhole)

      (1)   Puffed
      (2)   Petal
      (3)   Bishop

   B.   Raglan

   C.   Drop shoulder

2.   A sleeve cut in one with the waist of the garment

   A.   Kimono with gusset

      (1)   Shape and size of gusset
      (2)   Style lines introduced within the sleeve

   B.   Bat Wing/Dolman

Within the fitted and full-bottom sleeve classifications are different methods used to finish sleeves.

1.   Fitted sleeves

   A.   Placket opening finished with loops and buttons
   B.   Placket opening finished with buttonholes and buttons
   C.   Placket opening finished with slide fastener
   D.   Placket opening with cuff added

2.   Full-bottom sleeves

   A.   Bottom finished with a self-hem or facing
   B.   Turned back self-cuffs or added cuffs
   C.   Bottom gathered, tucked, or darted into an added cuff

Patterns for the types of sleeves discussed in this Introduction, as well as others, are developed in this section. However, other types of sleeves may be found in our companion book *New Fashion Areas for Designing Apparel through the Flat Pattern.*

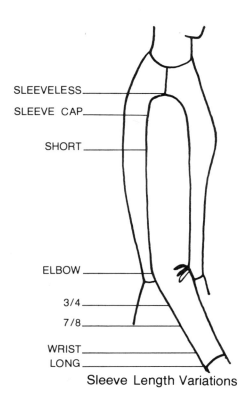

Sleeve Length Variations

The straight sleeve sloper simplifies the development of stylized sleeves such as a bell, shirtwaist, and jack o'lantern sleeve where the elbow dart is not necessary. This sloper cannot be used as a long-fitted sleeve because the elbow ease has been eliminated.

FIGURE 1

A.   Use *fitted sleeve sloper.*

B.   Cut paper approximately 16" × 28" (40.6 × 71.1 cm).

C.   Fold paper in half lengthwise.

D.   Fold sloper in half on grainline.

E.   With fold of paper towards you and back of sloper face up, place fold of sloper to fold of paper.

F.   Outline sleeve cap to underarm seam. Crossmark.

G.   Hold sloper securely in place and lift back of sloper at armhole. Outline front armhole (front armhole is cut deeper) to underarm seam. Crossmark.

H.   Crossmark biceps, elbow and front wristline.

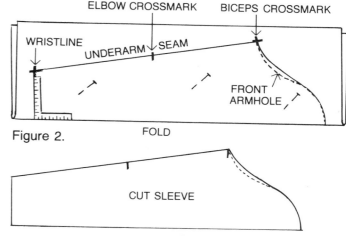

Figure 2.

Figure 2A.

FIGURES 2 & 2A

A.   Remove sloper. Trace elbow and biceps crossmarks and front armhole to opposite side.

B.   On fold at wristline square a line to wristline crossmark.

C.   Draw a straight line from end of wristline to biceps crossmark crossing all intersections. Label *underarm seam.*

D.   Pin sleeve draft and cut on finished lines following *back* armhole line (solid line Figure 2A).

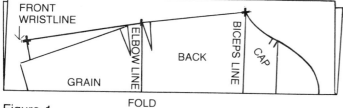

Figure 1.

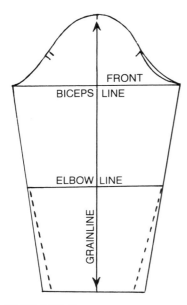

FIGURE 3

A.   Open sleeve draft. Pencil in center line over crease. Label *grainline.*

B.   Extend biceps and elbow lines to traced crossmarks.

C.   Using French curve true front armhole blending line (as illustrated).

D.   Cut away excess paper at front armhole (shaded area).

E.   Place fitted sleeve sloper over straight sleeve draft matching armholes at underarm seams.

F.   Trace front and back armhole crossmarks to draft. *Note:* For a tight-fitting wrist decrease amount desired on either sides of wrist. Crossmark. Draw a line to elbow crossmark (broken line).

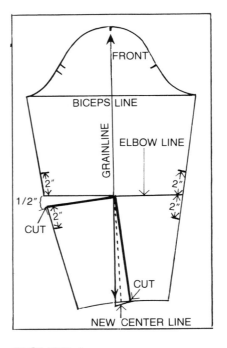

FIGURE 4

A.   If some elbow ease is desired, cut on grainline from wristline to elbow line and on elbow line from back underarm seam to grainline. Overlap draft at wrist and spread elbow ½" (1.3 cm).

B.   Establish crossmarks for control of shirring (as illustrated).

C.   To establish new grainline continue upper sleeve grainline to wrist (broken line).

D.   To establish center line draw a line from center of wrist to elbow line (solid line).

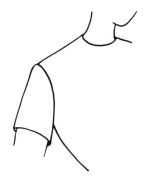

A short sleeve is developed from a basic sleeve sloper.

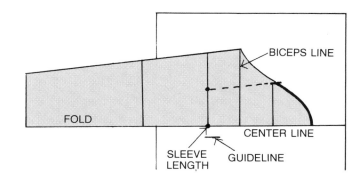

FIGURE 2

A.   Cut paper approximately 15" (38.1 cm) square.

B.   Fold paper in half. Crease.

C.   Open paper. Draw a line over crease. Label *center line*.

D.   With back of sloper face up, place fold of sloper to center line of paper.

E.   Outline sleeve cap to crossmark.

F.   From dot on fold of sloper measure out amount sleeve is to be tightened. Illustrated: 1" (2.5 cm). Draw a short guideline.

FIGURE 1

To prepare sleeve sloper:

A.   Fold sloper in half lengthwise. Work with fold of sloper towards you and back of sloper face up.

B.   Measure desired length of short sleeve and crossmark underarm seam. Illustrated: 3" (7.6 cm). Square a line from fold to crossmark at underarm.

C.   Draw a center line between fold and underarm seam from established sleeve length extending line to cap (broken line).

D.   On this line dot at sleeve length, crossmark at cap and dot on fold (as illustrated).

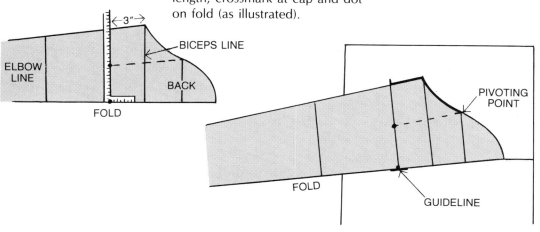

FIGURE 3

A.   Pivoting point is crossmark on sleeve cap.

B.   With pencil hold sleeve at pivoting point and pivot sloper until dot on fold of sleeve touches guideline on paper.

C.   Outline back armhole and underarm seam to crossmark.

D.   Hold sloper securely in place and lift back at armhole. Outline front armhole.

E.   With awl indicate dot on crease line.

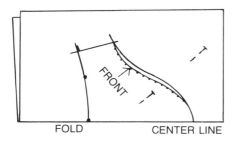

FOLD   CENTER LINE

FIGURE 4

A. Remove sloper. To shape sleeve length line draw a curved line from dot on fold to dot on center line to crossmark on underarm seam.

B. Pin draft. Trace front armhole, underarm seam and sleeve length to opposite side.

C. Open paper. Using French curve true front and back armhole.

D. True all lines crossing all intersections.

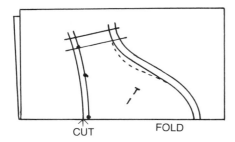

CUT   FOLD

FIGURE 5

Refold paper on center line and pin. Allow seams following back armhole line. Cut and notch seams.

Finished Pattern

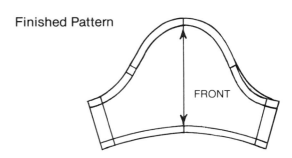

FRONT

FIGURE 6

Open sleeve draft. Adjust front armhole seam allowance and cut away excess paper (shaded area).

ESTABLISHING CROSSMARKS ON SLEEVE

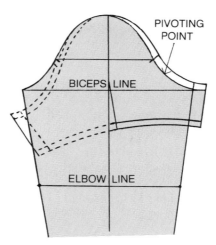

PIVOTING POINT

BICEPS LINE

ELBOW LINE

FIGURE 7

A. Place basic sleeve sloper on draft matching front armhole/underarm intersections. *Note:* Curve of both underarms should be the same— approximately 2″ (5.1 cm) up from underarm intersection.

B. Pivot sloper gradually from this point until front sleeve crossmark touches seamline on draft. Add crossmark to sleeve seam (as illustrated). Remove sloper.
Note: When pivot or cut and spread methods are used to develop sleeve variations, the contour of the original armhole changes. Therefore, crossmarks are established as stated here.

C. Repeat for back.

The tightened sleeve cap is widely used on sleeves in knits and where a narrow-shouldered look is desired. This cap eliminates some of the ease in the armhole seam and achieves a snug-fitting sleeve across the top. Although we have illustrated the tightened sleeve cap on a short sleeve, it may be used on any sleeve length desired.

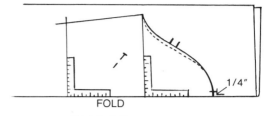

FIGURE 2

A.   Remove sloper. From fold, square a line to biceps intersection. From fold square a line to crossmark for sleeve length.

B.   Using French curve, true front and back armhole.

C.   On sleeve cap from fold measure in ¼″ (0.6 cm). Crossmark. Pin draft. Trace crossmark and front armhole to opposite side.

D.   Cut out sleeve on finished lines following back armhole line.

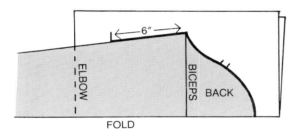

FIGURE 1

A.   Use *basic sleeve sloper.*

B.   Cut paper approximately 15″ (38.1 cm) square.

C.   Fold paper in half.

D.   Fold sloper in half on grainline. Measure desired length of short sleeve. Illustrated: 6″ (15.2 cm).

E.   With fold of paper towards you and back of sloper face up, place fold of sloper to fold of paper.

F.   Outline sleeve cap and underarm seam down to length of sleeve desired. Crossmark.

G.   Indicate back armhole crossmarks.

H.   Hold sloper securely in place and lift back at armhole. Outline front armhole and crossmark.

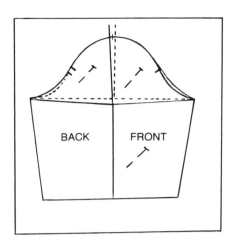

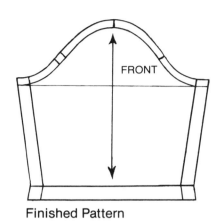

Finished Pattern

FIGURE 3

A. Open draft. Adjust front armhole seam allowance. Cut away excess paper (shaded area). Pencil in crossmark at sleeve cap.

B. Starting at top of sleeve cap, cut through center of sleeve and across biceps line to, but not through, underarm seams.

C. Overlap top of sleeve cap matching crossmarks.

D. Pin draft onto another sheet of paper. Blend top of sleeve cap, if necessary.

E. Outline sleeve draft completely. Remove draft. True all lines crossing all intersections.

F. Establish grainline on center of sleeve.

G. To complete pattern allow seams; cut and notch seams.

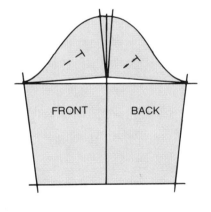

FIGURE 4

The procedure discussed in Figure 3 to tighten the sleeve cap may also be used if a higher or fuller cap is desired. The difference would be to spread the sleeve instead of overlapping.

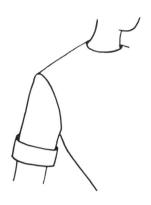

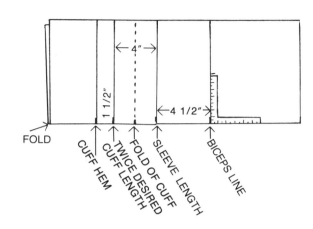

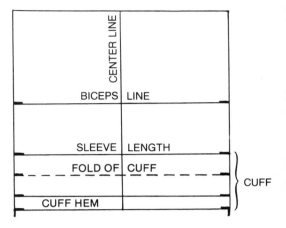

Since a straight hemline is required, a basic sleeve sloper is necessary to develop a sleeve with turned-up self cuff. The short fitted sleeve cannot be used because of the curved hemline. If a cuff is desired on a short fitted sleeve, a separate cuff must be added.

FIGURE 1

A.   Cut paper approximately 20" (50.8 cm) square.

B.   Fold paper in half.

C.   With fold of paper towards you, from right-hand edge measure in 8" (20.3 cm). Crossmark. Square a line from crossmark to edge of paper. Label *biceps line.*

D.   Establish length of sleeve desired from biceps line. Illustrated: 4½" (11.4 cm). Crossmark. Square a line from crossmark to edge of paper.

E.   From length of sleeve measure twice the desired length of cuff. Illustrated: 4" (10.2 cm). Crossmark. Square a line from crossmark to edge of paper.

F.   Establish fold of cuff (center of desired length of cuff) (broken line).

G.   Hem allowance should not exceed length of finished cuff. Illustrated: 1½" (3.8 cm). Crossmark. Square a line from crossmark and cut.

H.   Trace crossmarks to opposite side (darker lines).

FIGURE 2

Open paper. Connect all traced crossmarks. Draw a line over crease for center line on sleeve. Label lines as illustrated.

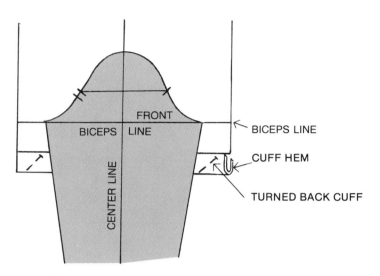

FIGURE 3

A.   Fold up cuff, turn under hem and pin.

B.   Place basic sleeve sloper on draft matching center lines and biceps lines.

C.   Outline sloper. Indicate armhole crossmarks.

D.   Remove sloper. True all lines crossing all intersections.

E.   Trace front and back underarm seam through cuff and hem layers.

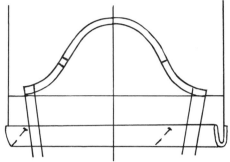

Figure 4.

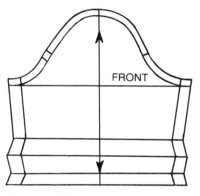

Finished Pattern

FIGURE 4

A.   With draft in pinned position allow seams; cut and notch seams.

B.   Unfold cuff and hem. Pencil in traced cuff lines.

C.   Establish grainline on center fold of sleeve.

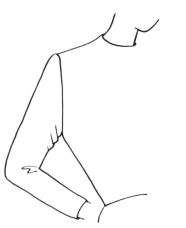

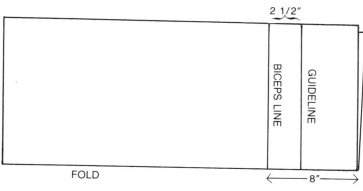

FOLD

2 1/2"

BICEPS LINE

GUIDELINE

8"

FIGURE 2

A. Cut paper approximately 30" (76.2 cm) square.

B. Fold paper in half.

C. With fold of paper towards you, from right-hand edge measure 8" (20.3 cm). Square a line from fold to top edge. Label *biceps line.*

D. Using measurement established between biceps line and guideline on basic sleeve sloper, establish guideline on paper. Crossmark. Square a line from fold to top edge. Label *guideline.*
Note: This measurement varies depending upon size of sleeve. Illustrated: 2½" (6.4 cm).

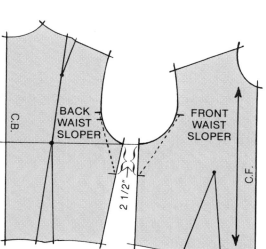

C.B. — BACK WAIST SLOPER — FRONT WAIST SLOPER — C.F. — 2 1/2"

Figure 1.

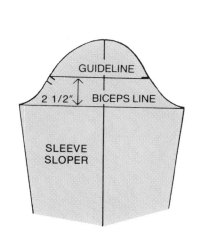

GUIDELINE — 2 1/2" — BICEPS LINE — SLEEVE SLOPER

FIGURE 1

To prepare waist and sleeve slopers:

A. Use *front waist, back waist and basic sleeve slopers.*

B. On *back waist sloper* measure down from armhole/underarm seam intersection 2½" (6.4 cm). Crossmark. Blend a line up to second crossmark on armhole.

C. Repeat on *front waist sloper.*

D. On *basic sleeve sloper,* draw a line parallel to biceps line through crossmarks on sleeve cap. Label *guideline.*

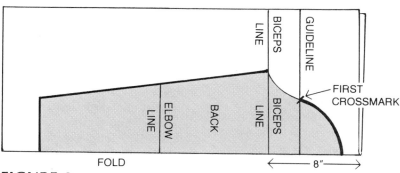

BICEPS LINE — GUIDELINE — ELBOW LINE — BACK — BICEPS LINE — FIRST CROSSMARK — FOLD — 8"

FIGURE 3

A. Fold sleeve sloper in half.

B. With fold of paper towards you and back of sloper face up, place fold of sloper to fold of paper matching biceps lines.

C. Outline sleeve cap to first crossmark. Crossmark paper.

D. Outline underarm seam and wristline (darker line).

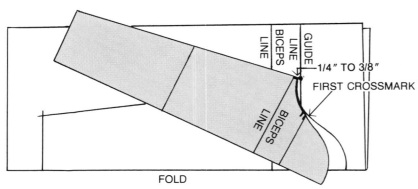

FOLD

FIGURE 4

A.   Use first sleeve cap crossmark as pivoting point.

B.   Hold sloper at pivoting point and pivot sloper until armhole/underarm intersection touches guideline on paper. Dot underarm seam. Outline remainder of armhole (darker line).

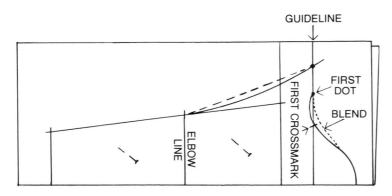

FIGURE 5

A.   Remove sloper.

B.   On guideline measure out from dot at underarm seam 2½" (6.4 cm). Dot. This is equal to the amount on waist slopers that armholes were elongated.

C.   Blend armhole from first dot with a slightly curved line into sleeve cap (broken line).

D.   Draw a straight line from end of new armhole to elbow

(broken line). Blend a slightly curved line (solid line).

E.   Pin draft. Trace all finished lines, crossmark at elbow, adjusted underarm and armhole seamlines and armhole crossmark to opposite side.

F.   Allow seams following back armhole; cut and notch seams. *Note:* Due to the lengthening of the armhole, the sleeve will hang better if the front of the armhole is not shaped.

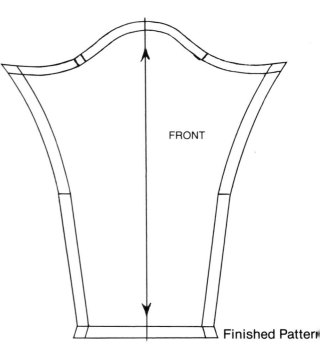

FRONT

Finished Pattern

FIGURE 6

A.   Open paper. Pencil in all traced lines.

B.   Establish grainline on center fold of paper.

C.   Add second crossmark to back armhole ½" (1.3 cm) below first crossmark. Notch.

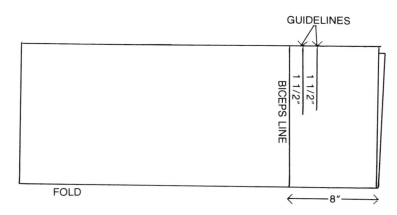

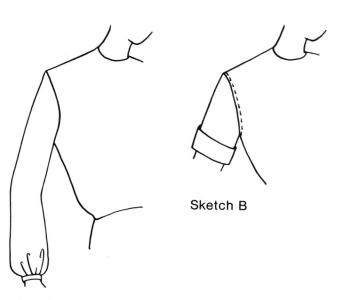

Sketch B

Sketch A

The sleeve with a shortened sleeve cap allows for more freedom of movement and is used in active and casual wear. It usually has a slight pull over the arm due to the shortened cap. The sleeve may be any length desired.

FIGURE 1

A.   Cut paper approximately 20″ × 30″ (50.8 × 76.2 cm).

B.   Fold paper in half lengthwise.

C.   With fold of paper towards you, from right-hand edge measure 8″ (20.3 cm). Square a line from fold to top edge. Label *biceps line.*

D.   Determine the amount the sleeve cap is to be shortened. Illustrated: 3″ (7.6 cm). At the top edge of the paper, draw a short guideline to the right of the biceps line the amount cap is to be shortened. Draw another short guideline halfway between biceps line and first guideline. The space between each line should measure half the width the cap is to be shortened. *Note:* Cap may be shortened a total of 2″ to 3″ (5.1 to 7.6 cm).

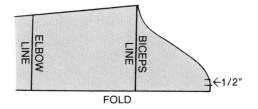

FIGURE 2

To prepare *basic sleeve sloper:*

A.   Fold sloper in half on grainline.

B.   On sleeve cap from fold place two crossmarks ½″ (1.3 cm) apart (as illustrated).

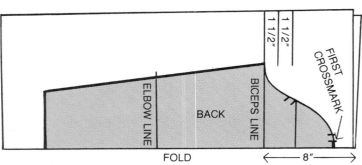

FIGURE 3

A. With fold of paper towards you and back of sleeve face up, place fold of sloper to fold of paper matching biceps lines.

B. Outline underarm seam, wristline and sleeve cap from fold to first crossmark (darker line). Crossmark at elbow line.

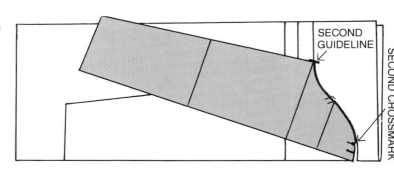

FIGURE 5

A. Second sleeve cap crossmark is pivoting point.

B. Hold sloper at pivoting point and pivot sloper until armhole/underarm seam intersection touches second guideline on paper.

C. Outline remainder of back armhole. Crossmark armhole/underarm seam intersection.

D. Hold sloper securely in place and lift back at armhole. Outline front armhole.

E. Remove sloper. True all lines crossing all intersections.

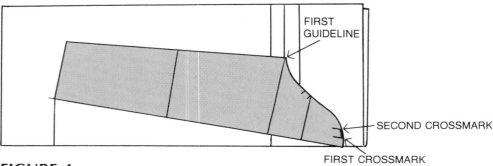

FIGURE 4

A. First sleeve cap crossmark is pivoting point.

B. Hold sloper at pivoting point and pivot sloper until armhole/underarm seam intersection touches first guideline on paper.

C. Outline sleeve cap from first crossmark to second crossmark (darker line).

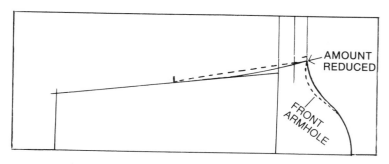

FIGURE 6

Note: The shortened sleeve cap does not require the same amount of armhole ease as the regular sleeve cap. Therefore, the sleeve cap should be reduced with no more than 1" (2.5 cm) armhole ease.

A.   To obtain correct amount of ease, measure front and back waist armholes and add 1" (2.5 cm).

B.   Measure half of this amount on sleeve draft from fold at cap to underarm seam. Crossmark. Label *A*.

C.   Draw a straight line from A to elbow line.

D.   Slightly curve underarm seam (solid line).

E.   Pin draft. Trace front armhole (broken line), underarm seam, wristline, crossmarks at elbow and biceps lines to opposite side.

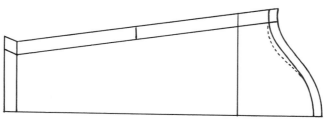

FIGURE 7

To complete pattern allow seams following back armhole; cut and notch seams.

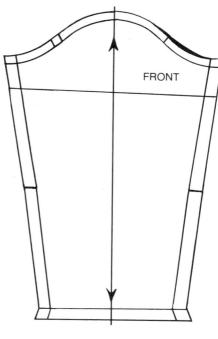

Finished Pattern

FIGURE 8

A.   Open paper. Pencil in all traced lines crossing all intersections.

B.   Establish grainline on center fold of sleeve.

C.   Adjust front armhole seam allowance. Cut away excess paper (shaded area).

D.   To establish armhole crossmarks refer to Short Fitted Sleeve, Figure 7.

CUFFS

A.   To develop shirtwaist sleeve cuff, fitted cuff or French cuff refer to Sleeve Cuffs, sketch 8.

B.   To develop short sleeve with a turned-up self cuff, refer to sketch 4.

SHIRTWAIST SLEEVE
sketch 7

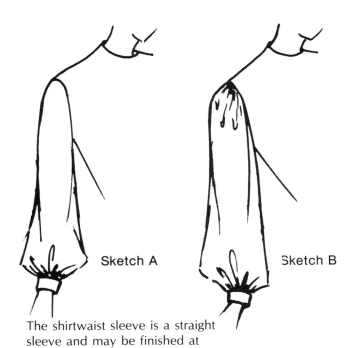

Sketch A   Sketch B

The shirtwaist sleeve is a straight sleeve and may be finished at the wrist with either a fitted or French cuff. The width at the wristline does not exceed the width at the biceps line.

SKETCH A

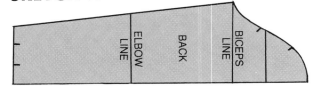

FIGURE 1

To prepare *straight sleeve sloper:*

A. Fold sloper in half on grainline.

B. With back of sloper face up, divide sleeve cap and wrist into three equal parts. Crossmark (as illustrated).

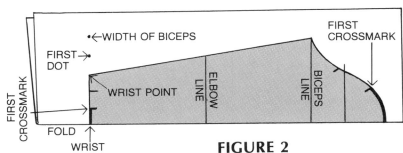

FIGURE 2

A. Cut paper approximately 18″ × 30″ (45.7 × 76.2 cm).

B. Fold paper in half lengthwise.

C. With fold of paper towards you and back of sloper face up, place fold of sloper to fold of paper.

D. Measure width of biceps line. From fold at wristline, measure the width of biceps line. Dot.

E. Divide space between dot and wrist point in half. Dot. Label *first dot.*

F. From fold outline both sleeve cap and wrist to first crossmarks (darker line).

FIGURE 3

A. First crossmark is pivoting point.

B. Hold sloper at pivoting point and pivot bottom of sloper until wrist point touches first dot.

C. Outline both sleeve cap and wrist from first crossmark to second crossmark (darker line).

D. Hold sloper securely in place and lift back at armhole. Outline front armhole.

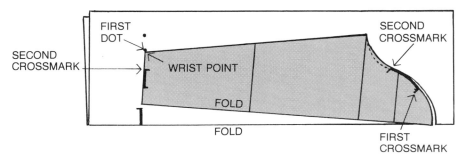

continued

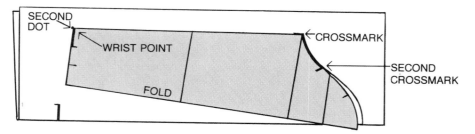

FIGURE 4

A.   Second crossmark is pivoting point.

B.   Hold sloper at pivoting point and pivot bottom of sloper until wrist point touches second dot.

C.   Outline remainder of back armhole and wristline (darker line).

D.   Hold sloper securely in place and lift back at armhole. Outline remainder of front armhole.

E.   Crossmark underarm intersections at armhole and wrist.

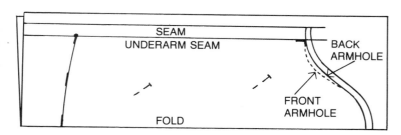

FIGURE 5

A.   Remove sloper.

B.   *Recheck* measurement of width at wrist with width at biceps. If wrist is narrower than biceps, increase to width at biceps and crossmark.

C.   Draw a line between underarm crossmarks extending line at wrist full length of paper.

D.   Using French curve true front and back armholes.

E.   Pin draft. Trace wristline, underarm seam, and front armhole (broken line) to opposite side.

6.   Allow seams on underarm and armhole following back armhole. Cut and notch seams. Leave excess paper at wrist.

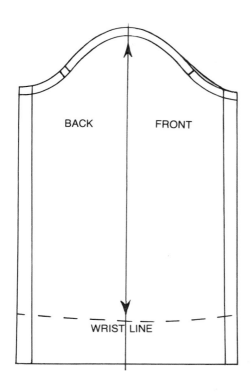

FIGURE 6

A.   Open paper. Pencil in all traced lines.

B.   Adjust front armhole seam allowance. Cut away excess paper (shaded area).

C.   Label *front* and *back* of sleeve.

D.   Establish grainline on center fold of sleeve.

E.   To establish armhole crossmarks refer to Short Fitted Sleeve, Figure 7.

SHIRTWAIST SLEEVE WITH A SHAPED WRISTLINE

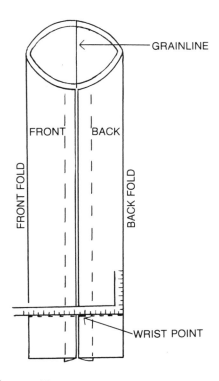

Figure 7

A.   Fold under front and back underarm seams to wrong side of draft and crease.

B.   Match folded seams to established grainline of sleeve with seams touching at armhole intersections. Pin.
Note: 1. When draft is folded in this manner, front of sleeve is now on opposite side. 2. If sleeve is developed accurately, seams will match.

C.   At wristline, square a line from back fold to front fold touching wrist point at underarm seams.

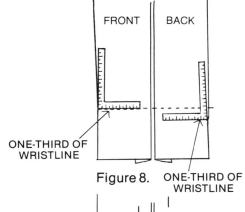

Figure 8.   ONE-THIRD OF WRISTLINE

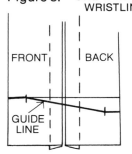

Figure 8A.

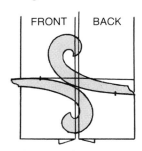

Figure 8B.

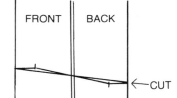

Figure 8C.

FIGURE 8

A.   At wristline on front fold measure one-third of wristline. Crossmark.

B.   At wristline on back fold measure down 1" (2.5 cm) for elbow ease. From this point square a line one-third of wristline. Crossmark.

FIGURE 8A

Draw a straight line between crossmarks. Label *guideline.*

FIGURE 8B

A.   To blend wristline place French curve to back fold touching guideline (as illustrated). Draw back curve to underarm.
Note: To avoid a point at fold end blending of line at right angles to fold approximately $\frac{1}{16}$" (0.2 cm) to scant $\frac{1}{8}$" (0.3 cm) in from fold. See wristline at back fold.

B.   Repeat same for front wrist area using French curve in reverse.

FIGURE 8C

Trace wristline to opposite side.

ADJUSTING SLEEVE LENGTH FOR CUFF

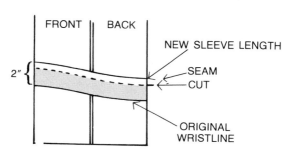

FIGURE 9

Note: Since the shirtwaist sleeve has a cuff, the original length of the sleeve draft must be shortened. The amount the sleeve is shortened is determined by the width of the cuff.

A.   Shorten sleeve ½" (1.3 cm) less than width of the finished cuff. For example for a 2½" (6.4 cm) cuff, shorten sleeve not more than 2" (5.1 cm). Draw new sleeve length line parallel to original wristline.

B.   Allow seam. Cut away excess paper (shaded area).

C.   Open draft. Pencil in traced line.

D.   Adjust front armhole seam allowance. Cut away excess paper (shaded area in Figure 10).

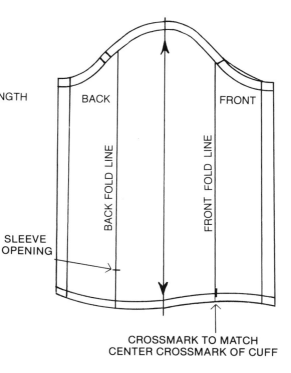

CROSSMARK TO MATCH CENTER CROSSMARK OF CUFF

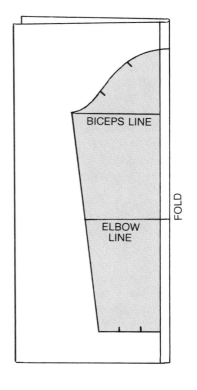

WRIST OPENING

FIGURE 10

Note: The placement of the opening at the wrist of a shirtwaist sleeve is generally on the back fold of the sleeve. The length of the opening depends upon the finish of the slit.

An opening finished with a facing, binding or continuous placket measures 2" to 3" (5.1 to 7.6 cm) in length. An opening finished with a tailored or mannish placket measures 5" to 6" (12.7 to 15.2 cm) long. For this type of placket refer to Tab Openings for Sleeves.

A.   Crossmark length of opening on back fold of sleeve.

B.   Crossmark front fold of sleeve at wristline for matching to center crossmark of cuff.

C.   To establish armhole crossmarks refer to Short Fitted Sleeve, Figure 7.

D.   To develop cuff refer to Sleeve Cuffs, sketch 8.

SKETCH B SHIRTWAIST SLEEVE WITH SLIGHT SHIRRING AT CAP

FIGURE 11

A.   If a slightly fuller cap is desired, draw a vertical line on a sheet of paper. Label *fold.*

B.   From fold measure in ½" (1.3 cm). Draw a line parallel to fold.

C.   Place fold of sloper to line on paper. Pivot. To complete pattern follow the same procedure as for sketch A.

**Sketch A
Fitted or One-Piece Cuff**

Sketch B French Cuff

**Sketch C
Deep Fitted Cuff**

Sketch D Closed Cuff

SKETCH A
FITTED CUFF OR
ONE-PIECE CUFF

The fitted cuff or one-piece cuff is the most popular of the cuffs to be developed in this section. It is part of the shirtwaist sleeve and is generally used on dresses, blouses, jackets, coats and robes.

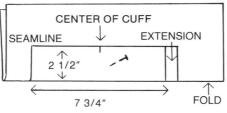

FIGURE 1

A.   Cut paper approximately 12″ (30.5 cm) square.

B.   Fold paper in half.

C.   To determine length of cuff, measure wrist or wristline of fitted sleeve sloper and add ¾″ to 1″ (1.9 to 2.5 cm) for ease. Illustrated: 7¾″ (19.7 cm). *Note:* The fitted cuff is usually made double with a fold on the bottom edge. The lengthwise grain runs around the wrist.

D.   To determine width of cuff, measure up from fold 2½″ (5.1 cm).

E.   Using the planned length and width of cuff, draw a rectangle crossing all intersections.

F.   At seam crossmark center of cuff.

G.   Add 1″ (2.5 cm) extension on right-hand side of draft.

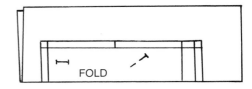

FIGURE 2

Note: To plan buttonholes refer to Buttons & Buttonholes. Pin cuff draft. Allow seams; cut and notch seams.

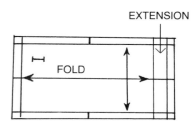

FIGURE 3

Open paper. Establish grainline as desired.

SKETCH B
ONE-PIECE OR
TWO-PIECE
FRENCH CUFF

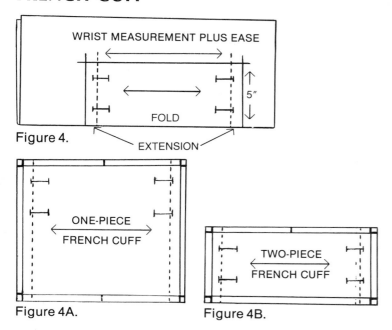

Figure 4.

Figure 4A.

Figure 4B.

FIGURES 4, 4A, 4B

A.   To develop a one-piece French cuff follow the same procedure as for fitted cuff with the following exception:

Width of cuff equals twice the width desired for finished cuff. Illustrated: 5″ (12.7 cm).

B.   To plan buttonholes on cuff as illustrated refer to Buttons & Buttonholes.

C.   To develop a two-piece French cuff follow the same procedure as fitted cuff and one-piece French cuff with the following exception:

Fold should be cut as a seam (Figure 4B).

SKETCH C
DEEP FITTED CUFF

The deep fitted cuff is used on wedding dresses and other types of formal garments.

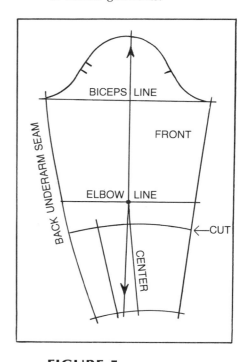

FIGURE 5

A.   Cut paper approximately 16″ (40.6 cm) square.

B.   Use *fitted sleeve sloper*. Place sloper on paper and outline to wristline.

C.   From wrist measure up depth of cuff. Draw a curved line parallel to wristline.

D.   Establish line for opening seam halfway between center line and back underarm seam.

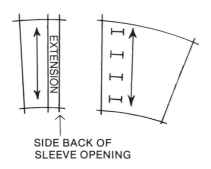

SIDE BACK OF
SLEEVE OPENING

FIGURE 6

A.   Copy cuff in two sections adding extension to left side (as illustrated).

B.   Establish grainline parallel to opening seam.

C.   To plan extension and buttonholes refer to Buttons & Buttonholes.

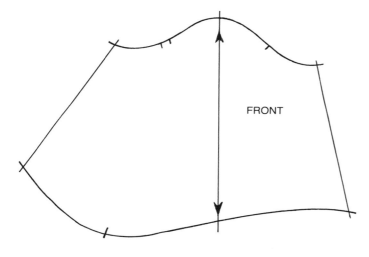

FRONT

FIGURE 6A

To develop full sleeve cut sleeve on cuff line and follow same procedure for Bishop Sleeve with Balanced Fullness.

SKETCH D
CLOSED CUFF

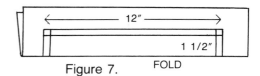

12"

1 1/2"

Figure 7.   FOLD

Figure 7A.

FIGURES 7 & 7A

A.   Cut paper approximately 12" (30.5 cm) square.

B.   Fold paper in half.

C.   To determine length of cuff measure biceps plus at least 1" (2.5 cm) for ease and thickness of fabric. Illustrated: 12" (30.5 cm).

D.   To determine width of cuff measure up from fold desired width. Illustrated: 1½" (3.8 cm).

E.   Using planned length and width, draw a rectangle crossing all intersections.

F.   Crossmark center of cuff seam for matching to center of short sleeve.

G.   Allow seams; cut and notch seams (Figure 7A).

H.   Establish grainline as illustrated in Figure 7A.

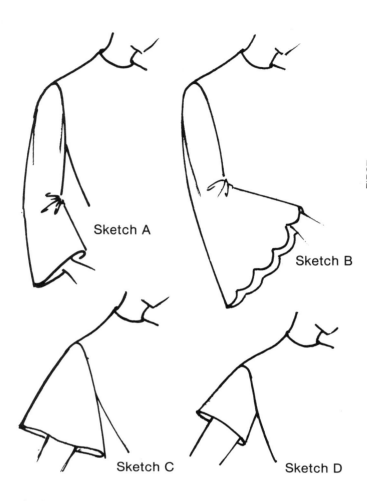

Sketch A

Sketch B

Sketch C

Sketch D

The bell sleeve is an open, free-swinging sleeve and is named for its shape. It measures wider at the wristline than at the biceps line. The width and length may vary as desired. Any sleeve length may have cuffs added, thereby, changing a bell sleeve to a *puffed* sleeve.

SKETCH A

FIGURE 1

To prepare *straight sleeve sloper:*

A.   Fold sloper in half

B.   With back of sloper face up, divide sleeve cap and wrist into three equal parts. Crossmark.

ONE-HALF WIDTH OF BELL SLEEVE

FIRST DOT

FIRST CROSSMARK

FIRST CROSSMARK

WRIST POINT

ELBOW LINE

BICEPS LINE

FOLD

WRIST

FIGURE 2

A.   Cut paper approximately 30″ (76.2 cm) square.

B.   Fold paper in half.

C.   With fold of paper towards you and back of sloper face up, place fold of sloper to fold of paper.

D.   Determine the width desired for bell sleeve. From fold at wrist measure one-half the desired width. Dot.

E.   Divide space between dot and wrist point in half. Dot. Label *first dot.*

F.   From fold outline both sleeve cap and wrist to first crossmarks (darker line).

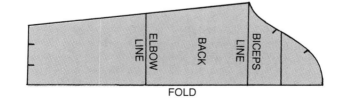

ELBOW LINE

BACK

BICEPS LINE

FOLD

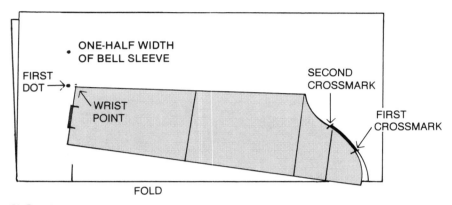

FIGURE 3

A.   First crossmark is pivoting point.

B.   Hold sloper at pivoting point and pivot bottom of sloper until wrist point is in line with first dot.

C.   Outline both sleeve cap and wrist from first crossmark to second crossmark (darker line).

D.   Hold sloper securely in place and lift back at armhole. Outline front armhole.

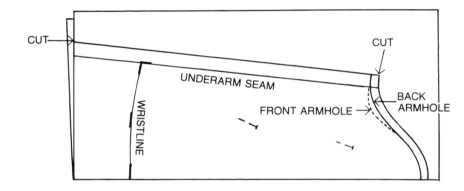

FIGURE 5

A.   Remove sloper.

B.   Draw a line between underarm crossmarks extending line at wrist full length of paper. Label *underarm*.

C.   Using French curve, true front and back armholes.

D.   Pin draft. Trace wristline, underarm seam, and front armhole (broken line) to opposite side.

E.   Allow seam on underarm and armhole following back armhole. Cut and notch seams. Leave excess paper at wrist.

FIGURE 4

A.   Second crossmark is pivoting point.

B.   Hold sloper at pivoting point and pivot bottom of sloper until wrist point is in line with second dot.

C.   Outline remainder of back armhole and wristline.

D.   Hold sloper securely in place and lift back at armhole. Outline remainder of front armhole.

E.   Crossmark underarm intersections at armhole and wrist.

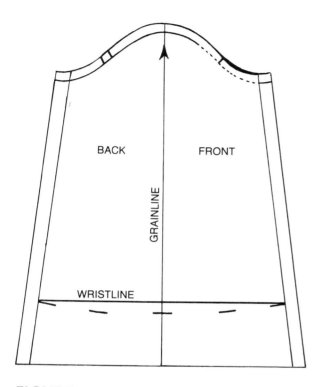

FIGURE 6

A.   Open paper. Pencil in all traced lines.

B.   Adjust front armhole seam allowance. Cut away excess paper (shaded area).

C.   Label *front* and *back* of sleeve.

D.   Draw grainline on center fold of sleeve.

E.   To establish armhole crossmarks refer to Short Fitted Sleeve, Figure 7.

BELL SLEEVE WITH A STRAIGHT WRISTLINE

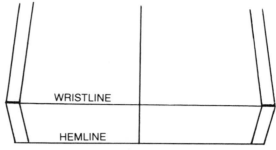

FIGURE 6A

A.   Draw a straight line between wrist crossmarks.

B.   From wristline measure depth of hem desired. Illustrated: 3″ (7.6 cm). Draw a line parallel to wristline.

C.   Cut away excess paper.

D.   To shape hem seam properly, fold paper under on wristline. Trace seamline to hemline.

E.   Open hem. Pencil in all traced lines. Notch seam.

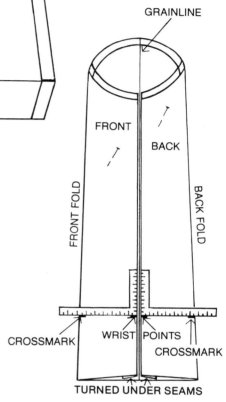

BELL SLEEVE WITH A SHAPED WRISTLINE

FIGURE 7

A.   Fold under front and back underarm seams to wrong side of sleeve draft and crease.

B.   Match folded seams to established grainline of sleeve with seams touching at armhole intersections. Pin.
Note: 1. When draft is folded in this manner, front of sleeve is now on opposite side. 2. If sleeve is developed accurately, seams will match.

C.   At wrist point, square a line from underarm seam to back fold. Crossmark. Repeat for front section.

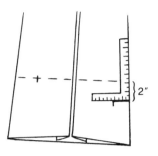

FIGURE 8

A.   On front of sleeve from fold measure one-third of wristline. Crossmark.

B.   At wristline on back fold measure down 2" (5.1 cm) for elbow ease. From this point square a line one-third of wristline. Crossmark.

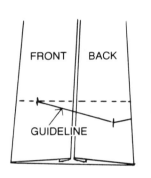

FIGURE 8A

Draw a straight line between crossmarks. Label *guideline.*

FIGURE 8B

A.   To blend wristline place French curve to back fold touching straight guideline. Draw back wrist curve towards underarm seam.
Note: To avoid a point at fold blending of line should end at right angles to fold about a scant ⅛" (0.3 cm) from fold.

B.   Repeat same on front using French curve in reverse.

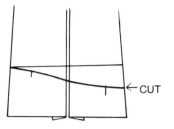

Figure 8C.

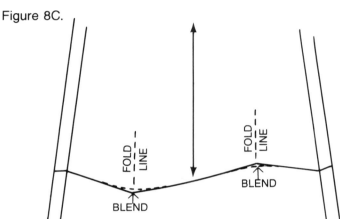

Figure 8D.

FIGURES 8C & 8D

A.   Trace wristline to opposite side.

B.   Open sleeve. Pencil in wristline blending curve, if necessary (Figure 8D).

C.   Allow seams; cut and notch seams.

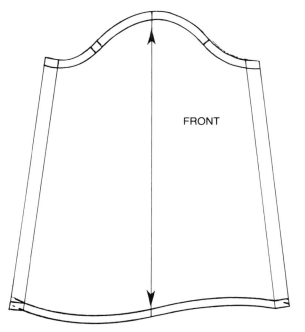

Figure 9. Finished Pattern

FIGURES 9, 9A, 9B, 9C

A. A shaped sleeve requires a shaped facing. From bottom of sleeve measure up desired width of facing (as illustrated in Figure 9A).

B. Copy facing.

Note: For a smoother fit, facing should be made 1/16" to 1/8" (0.2 to 0.3 cm) smaller at underarm seams (broken line in Figure 9B).

C. For finished facing pattern add seam and cut (Figure 9C).

SKETCHES B, C, D

These sketches illustrate bell sleeve variations.

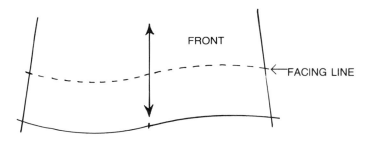

Figure 9A.

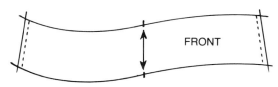

Figure 9B.

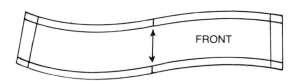

Figure 9C. Finished Pattern

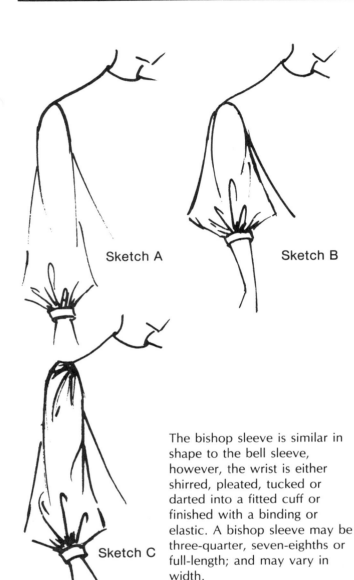

Sketch A

Sketch B

Sketch C

The bishop sleeve is similar in shape to the bell sleeve, however, the wrist is either shirred, pleated, tucked or darted into a fitted cuff or finished with a binding or elastic. A bishop sleeve may be three-quarter, seven-eighths or full-length; and may vary in width.

SKETCH A

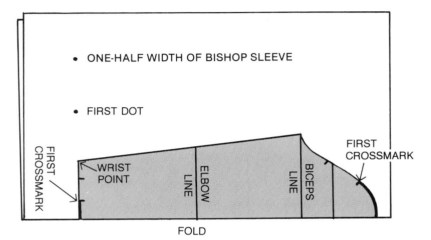

- ONE-HALF WIDTH OF BISHOP SLEEVE
- FIRST DOT

FIRST CROSSMARK

WRIST POINT

ELBOW LINE

BICEPS LINE

FIRST CROSSMARK

FOLD

FIGURE 1

To prepare *straight sleeve sloper:*

A.   Fold sloper in half.

B.   With back of sloper face up, divide cap and wrist into three equal parts. Crossmark.

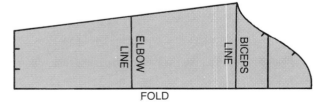

ELBOW LINE

BICEPS LINE

FOLD

FIGURE 2

A.   Cut paper approximately 30″ (76.2 cm) square.

B.   Fold paper in half

C.   With fold of paper towards you and back of sloper face up, place fold of sloper to fold of paper.

D.   Determine the width desired for bishop sleeve. From fold at wrist measure one-half the desired width. Dot.

E.   Divide area between dot and wrist point in half. Dot. Label *first dot.*

F.   From fold outline both sleeve cap and wrist to first crossmarks (darker lines).

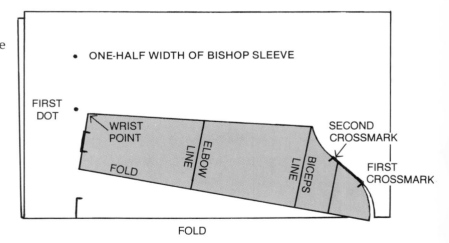

- ONE-HALF WIDTH OF BISHOP SLEEVE

FIRST DOT

WRIST POINT

ELBOW LINE

FOLD

BICEPS LINE

SECOND CROSSMARK

FIRST CROSSMARK

FOLD

FIGURE 3

A.   First crossmark is pivoting point.

B.   Hold sloper at pivoting point and pivot bottom of sloper until wrist point is in line with first dot.

C.   Outline both sleeve cap and wrist from first crossmark to second crossmark (darker line).

D.   Hold sloper securely in place and lift back at armhole. Outline front armhole.

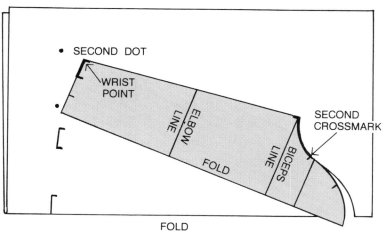

FIGURE 4

A. Second crossmark is pivoting point.

B. Hold sloper at pivoting point and pivot bottom of sloper until wrist point is in line with second dot.

C. Outline remainder of back armhole and wristline.

D. Hold sloper securely in place and lift back at armhole. Outline remainder of front armhole.

E. Crossmark underarm intersections at armhole and wrist.

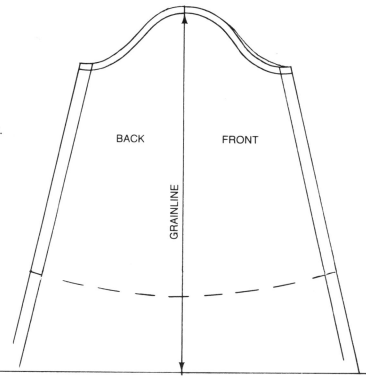

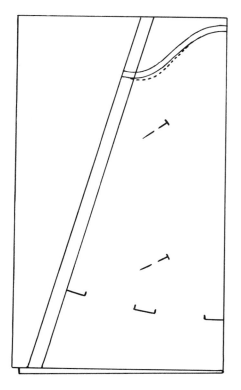

FIGURE 5

A. Remove sloper.

B. Draw a line between underarm crossmarks extending line at wrist full length of paper.

C. Using French curve, true front and back armholes.

D. Pin draft. Trace wristline, underarm seam and front armhole to opposite side.

E. Allow seams on underarm and armhole following back armhole. Cut and notch seams. Leave excess paper at wrist.

FIGURE 6

A. Open paper. Pencil in all traced lines.

B. Adjust front armhole seam allowance. Cut away excess paper (shaded area).

C. Label *front* and *back* of sleeve.

D. Draw grainline on center fold of sleeve and crossmark hemline to match center of cuff.

E. To establish armhole crossmarks refer to Short Fitted Sleeve, Figure 7.

BISHOP SLEEVE WITH A SHAPED WRISTLINE

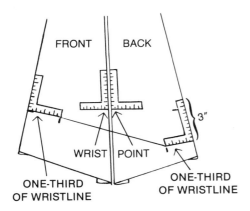

FRONT BACK

WRIST POINT

ONE-THIRD OF WRISTLINE

ONE-THIRD OF WRISTLINE

3"

FIGURE 7

A.   Fold under front and back underarm seams to wrong side of draft and crease.

B.   Match folded seams to established grainline of sleeve with seams touching at armhole intersections. Pin.
Note: 1. When draft is folded in this manner, front of sleeve is now on opposite side. 2. If sleeve is developed accurately, seams will match.

C.   At wristline square a line from underarm seam to back fold. Crossmark. Repeat for front section.

D.   From fold at wristline on front of sleeve square a line one-third of wristline. Crossmark.

E.   At wristline on back fold measure down 3" (7.6 cm) for elbow ease. From this point square a line one-third of wristline. Crossmark.

F.   Draw a straight line between crossmarks.

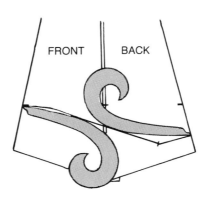

FRONT BACK

FIGURE 7A

Using French curve, blend wristline (as illustrated).

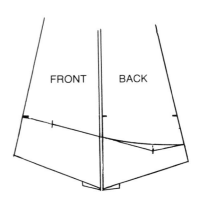

FRONT BACK

FIGURE 7B

Trace wristline to opposite side.

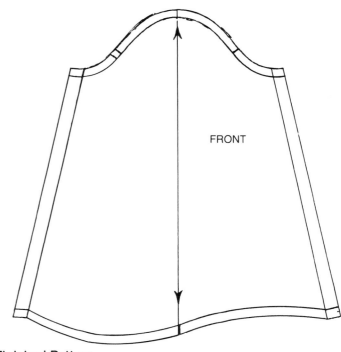

FRONT

Finished Pattern

FIGURE 8

A.   Open sleeve. Pencil in traced line, blending wrist curve if necessary (refer to Bell Sleeve, Figures 8C and 8D).

B.   Allow seams; cut and notch seams.

C.   To develop cuff refer to Sleeve Cuffs, sketch 8.

SKETCH B

To develop this sketch follow the same procedure as for sketch A with the following exception:

Establish three-quarter or length desired on sloper and work from new sleeve length.

SKETCH C
SHIRRED CAP

FIGURE 9

A.   Outline back section of straight sleeve sloper to center line. Indicate biceps and elbow lines. Cut away excess paper.

B.   Fold sleeve at biceps line matching underarm to center line. Crease up to sleeve cap. Crossmark at cap. Label *A*.

C.   Draw a line from A parallel to center line.

D.   Divide area from this line to center into thirds. Draw lines parallel to center line from sleeve cap to wrist.

E.   Number sections (as illustrated). Cut apart sections.

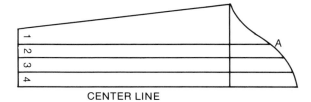

CENTER LINE

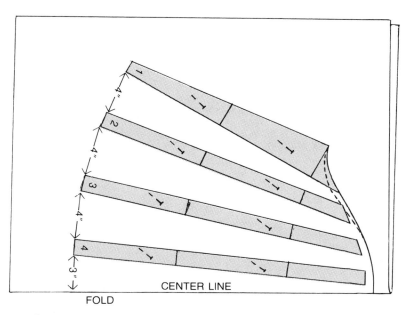

CENTER LINE

FOLD

FIGURE 10

A.   Cut another sheet of paper approximately 30″ (76.2 cm) square.

B.   Fold paper in half. Label center line. Pin section 4 allowing fullness desired at center line. Illustrated: 3″ (7.6 cm) at wrist and ¾″ (1.9 cm) at sleeve cap.

C.   Pin remaining sections spreading amount desired. *Note:* In spreading sections, check that biceps and elbow lines on cut sections form a curved line towards underarm (as illustrated).

D.   Raise cap line for greater puff (as illustrated).

E.   Allow seams on underarm and armhole following back armhole. Cut and notch seams. Leave excess paper at wrist.

F.   To complete shaping of wrist refer to Figures 7, 7A and 7B.

G.   To establish armhole crossmarks refer to Short Fitted Sleeve, Figure 7.

H.   To develop cuff refer to Sleeve Cuffs, sketch 8.

Sketch A

Sketch B

Sketch C

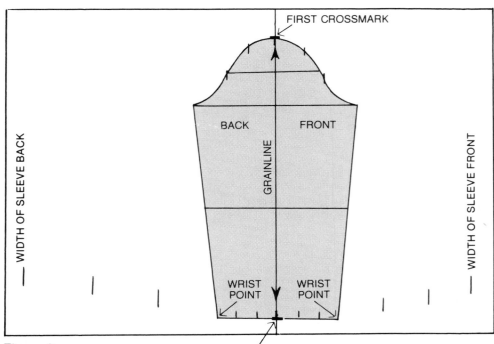

Figure 2.

HORIZONTAL CROSSMARK

FIRST CROSSMARK

BACK FRONT

GRAINLINE

WIDTH OF SLEEVE BACK

WIDTH OF SLEEVE FRONT

WRIST POINT WRIST POINT

When a bishop sleeve is exaggerated in width, it will hang and puff more gracefully if the back is cut wider and longer than the front. A full bishop sleeve may be three-quarter (sketch B), seven-eighths, or full length. All lengths can be push-up sleeves and can be finished with a cuff, binding or elastic.

SKETCH A
FULL LENGTH
BISHOP SLEEVE

FIGURE 1

To prepare *straight sleeve sloper:*

A.   With sloper open divide armhole and wristline into six equal parts (as illustrated). Crossmark.

B.   Crossmark center line at top of cap and wristline.

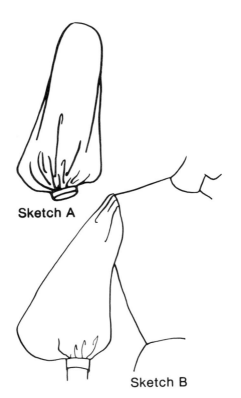

TOP OF CAP

CENTER

BICEPS LINE

BACK FRONT

ELBOW LINE

GRAINLINE

WRISTLINE

FIGURE 2

A.   Cut paper approximately 30" × 45" (76.2 × 114.3 cm).

B.   Draw a vertical line off center leaving more space on left-hand side of paper for developing a fuller sleeve back. Label *grainline.*

C.   With back of sleeve to the left of grainline, place sloper on paper matching grainlines.

D.   With sloper in place, determine width for front and back of bishop sleeve. Crossmark.

E.   Divide space between wrist point on sloper and desired width of bishop sleeve into three equal parts (front and back). Establish crossmarks (as illustrated)

F.   On grainline on paper, place a horizontal crossmark at sleeve cap and at wristline.

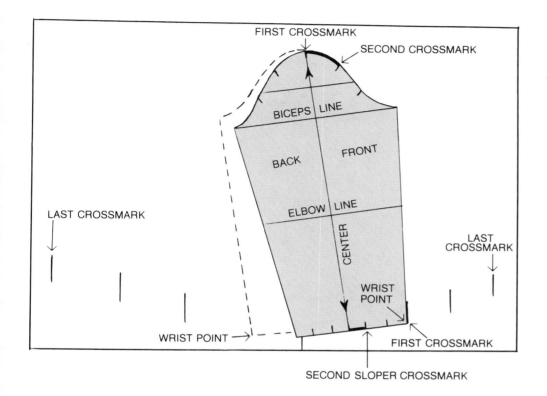

FIGURE 3

Note: The center of the sleeve cap is the first pivoting point. Because of the extreme fullness there will be three pivoting points for each side of the sleeve instead of two as in the bell sleeve. The third pivoting point aids in the equal distribution of the fullness to both cap and wristline of sleeve.

A.   Hold sloper at first crossmark on sleeve cap and pivot bottom of front sleeve until wrist point is in line with first crossmark on paper.

B.   Outline sleeve cap and wristline from first crossmark to second crossmark (darker lines).

C.   Repeat pivoting bottom of sloper and outline armhole and wristline until last crossmark on paper has been reached. Crossmark at biceps line/ underarm intersection and wrist/underarm intersection (Figure 4).

D.   Pivot back of sleeve following the same procedure as for front.

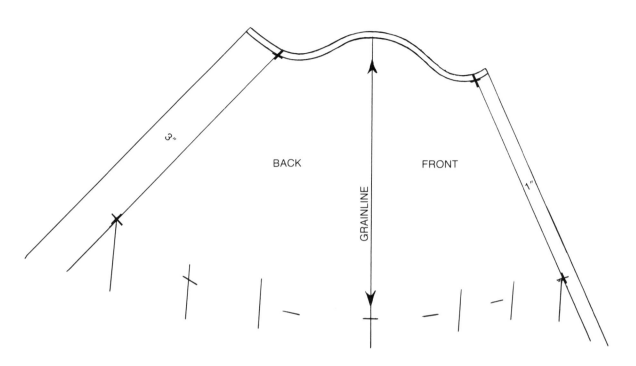

FIGURE 4

A.   Remove sloper. For underarm seam draw a line from crossmarks at biceps line to crossmarks at wristline extending lines at wrist the full length of paper.

B.   Using French curve true armhole. Allow seam and cut.

C.   Allow 1″ (2.5 cm) seam allowance on *front* underarm and 3″ (7.6 cm) on *back* underarm. Cut away excess paper on these two seamlines. *Note:* The additional seam allowance on back of sleeve is needed if an adjustment is to be made, due to the additional fullness added to back of sleeve, crⁱating an unbalanced seam. Since the back seam is more bias than the front seam, it may also need to be shortened. The amount shortened depends upon the stretchability of the fabric used and can only be determined when the pattern is tested in fabric. Refer to Trueing Vertical Seams, Figure 3.

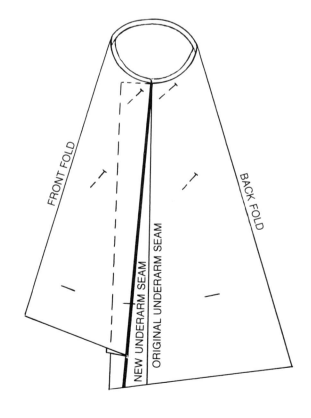

TRUEING UNDERARM SEAMS

FIGURE 5

A.   Fold under front underarm seam to wrong side. Crease.

B.   Match front folded underarm seam to grainline of draft. Crease front sleeve (as illustrated). Pin.

C.   Match back armhole intersection to front armhole intersection. Pin at that point to prevent back underarm from shifting when creasing back sleeve fold.

D.   Unpin front section at armhole and slip 3″ (7.6 cm) seam allowance under front underarm seam. Pin. *Note:* The original back underarm seam will not always match the front underarm seam at the wristline (darker lines). Adjust back seam allowance. Cut away excess paper.

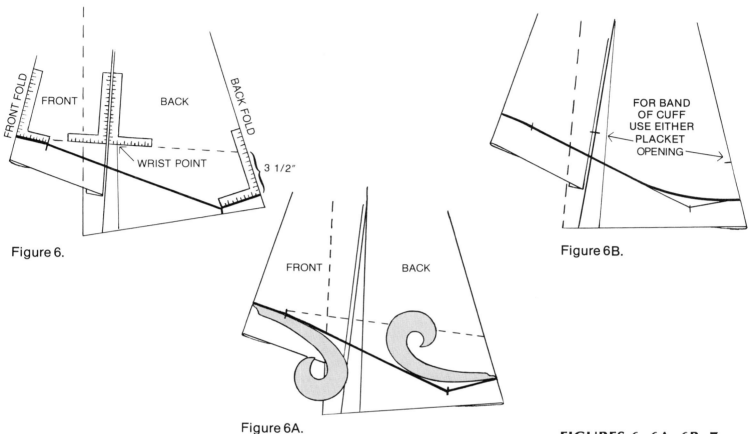

Figure 6.

Figure 6A.

Figure 6B.

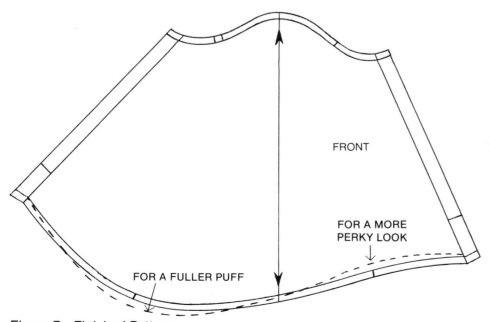

Figure 7. Finished Pattern

FIGURES 6, 6A, 6B, 7

A. To shape wristline for sleeve refer to Bell Sleeve, Figures 7 to 8C with the following exception:

At back fold measure down 3½″ (8.9 cm). Crossmark. The principle is the same regardless of the width of the sleeve.

B. If a cuff is to be added, sleeve may or may not be shortened depending upon amount of puff desired. Refer to Shirtwaist Sleeve, Figure 9.

C. Crossmark center of bottom of sleeve for matching to center of cuff.

D. To develop cuff refer to Sleeve Cuffs, sketch 8.

E. To establish armhole crossmarks refer to Short Fitted Sleeve, Figure 7.

SKETCH B THREE-QUARTER LENGTH BISHOP SLEEVE

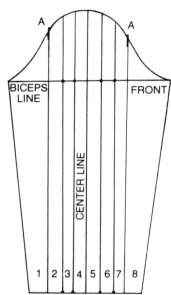

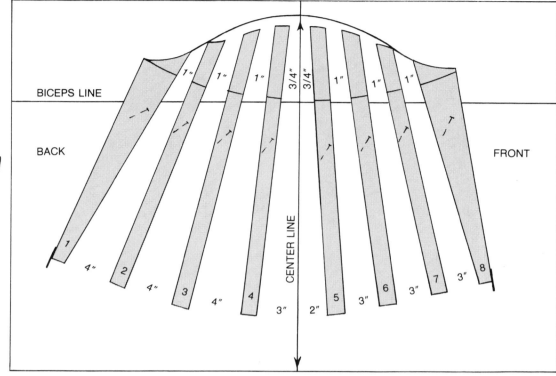

FIGURE 8

To prepare straight sleeve sloper:

A.   Copy and cut sleeve sloper. Indicate biceps line.

B.   Fold front of sleeve at biceps line bringing underarm to center line. Crease only to cap. Crossmark cap. Label *A*. Draw a line parallel to center from A to wrist. Repeat on back of sleeve.

C.   Divide space on front and back of sleeve from this line to center into thirds. Draw lines from armhole to wrist parallel to center.

D.   Number sections. Cut apart sections.

FIGURE 9

A.   Cut paper approximately 32″ × 46″ (81.3 × 116.8 cm).

B.   Draw a vertical line off center leaving more space on left-hand side of paper for developing fuller back sleeve. Label *grainline*.

C.   Square a line on each side of grainline approximately 9″ (22.3 cm) down from top edge of paper. Label *biceps line*.

D.   Pin sections 4 and 5 to paper matching biceps lines allowing fullness desired at center of sleeve. Illustrated: ¾″ (1.9 cm) on each side of center at cap of sleeve.
Note: Since this is an unbalanced sleeve at wristline with more fullness at back, spread front and back as desired (as illustrated).

E.   Pin remaining sections spreading amount desired. *Note:* In spreading sections check that biceps lines on sections form a smooth curve towards underarm.

F.   Raise cap line for greater puff (as illustrated).

G.   To complete sleeve true underarm seam (Figure 5) and shape wrist (Figures 6, 6A, 6B and 7).

SKETCH C EXTREME BALLOON SLEEVE

This sketch illustrates an extreme balloon sleeve. Establish length desired on sloper and follow same procedure as for sketch B adding more width to the sleeve and puff to the back of the sleeve.

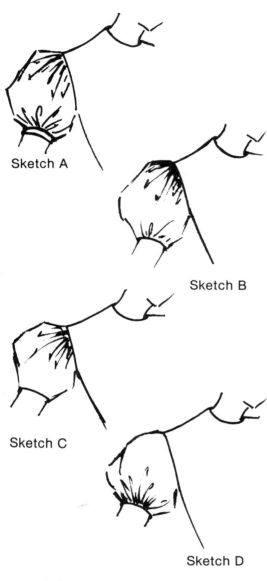

Sketch A

Sketch B

Sketch C

Sketch D

A puff sleeve is a short sleeve gathered either at the armhole or at the cuff or both, producing a rounded shape.

This project will cover:
Sketch A—balanced shirring at armhole (cap) and bottom

Sketch B—shirring at armhole (cap) and slight shirring at bottom

Sketch C—shirring at armhole (cap) and fitted at bottom

Sketch D—fitted cap and shirring at bottom

SKETCH A

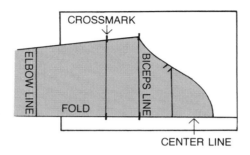

FIGURE 1

A.   To prepare *basic sleeve sloper:*

> 1.   Fold sloper in half. Determine length of sleeve desired. Crossmark. Illustrated: 3″ (7.6 cm).

> 2.   Square a line from fold to crossmark.

B.   Cut paper approximately 10″ × 15″ (25.4 × 38.1 cm).

C.   Draw a horizontal line 1″ (2.5 cm) from bottom edge of paper. Label *center line.*

D.   With back of sloper face up, place fold of sloper to center on paper.

E.   Outline sloper. Crossmark biceps line and length of sleeve at underarm and fold.

F.   Hold sloper securely in place and lift back of sloper at armhole. Outline front armhole (broken line in Figure 2).

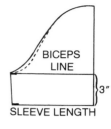

FIGURE 2

A.   Remove sloper. Draw a line connecting crossmarks for biceps and sleeve length.

B.   Cut out sleeve.

FIGURE 3

Fold sleeve draft in half matching underarm seam to center line. Crease.

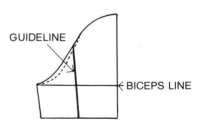

FIGURE 4

Open draft. Draw a line over crease. Label *guideline.*

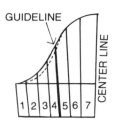

FIGURE 5

A.   Divide sleeve from guideline to center line into *three* equal sections. Divide sleeve from guideline to underarm seam into *four* equal sections.

B.   Number the equal sections *1* to *7* (as illustrated).

FIGURE 6

A.   Cut another sheet of paper 25″ (63.5 cm) square.

B.   Fold paper in half. Crease.

C.   Open paper. Draw a line over crease. Label *center line.*

D.   Square a line 6″ (15.2 cm) from bottom edge of paper and across full width of paper. Label *crosswise grainline.*

E.   On sleeve draft cut sleeve sections numbered 4, 5, 6 and 7. Sections 1, 2 and 3 are not spread in this sleeve.

F.   With paper open, place sleeve sections on paper matching biceps line to crosswise grainline. Spread sections. Pin.
Note: The type of fabric used and the amount of fullness desired determines the amount sections are spread. A spread of ½″ (1.3 cm) produces an average puff; 1″ (2.5 cm) or more produces full puff.

G.   Blend back armhole (solid line) and front armhole (broken line) up towards top of sleeve cap adding ½″ (1.3 cm) or more for a graceful puff line.

H.   Add ½″ (1.3 cm) to bottom of sleeve at center grainline. Draw a slightly curved line from center grainline to underarm seam.

I.   Indicate crossmarks for shirring at bottom of sleeve approximately 2″ (5.1 cm) in from underarm seam.

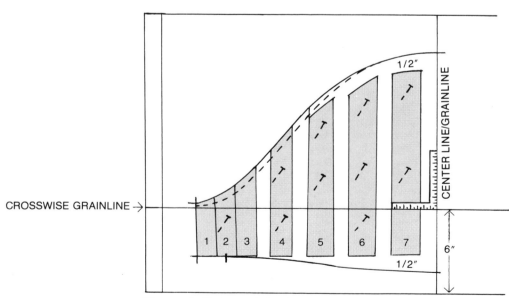

Figure 6. Enlarged Scale

268

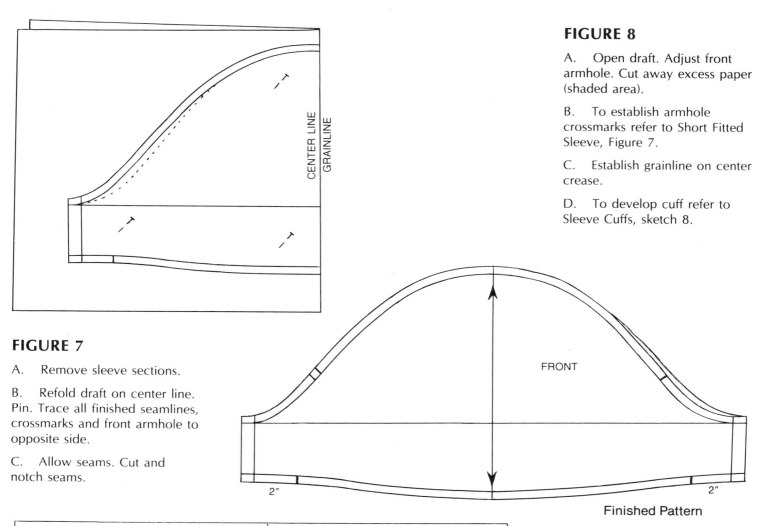

CENTER LINE
GRAINLINE

FIGURE 8

A.　Open draft. Adjust front armhole. Cut away excess paper (shaded area).

B.　To establish armhole crossmarks refer to Short Fitted Sleeve, Figure 7.

C.　Establish grainline on center crease.

D.　To develop cuff refer to Sleeve Cuffs, sketch 8.

FIGURE 7

A.　Remove sleeve sections.

B.　Refold draft on center line. Pin. Trace all finished seamlines, crossmarks and front armhole to opposite side.

C.　Allow seams. Cut and notch seams.

FRONT

2"　　　　　　　　　　　　　　　2"

Finished Pattern

RAISE 1/2"

CENTER LINE / GRAINLINE

FRONT

1　2　3　4　5　6　7

Sketch B

SKETCHES B, C & D

To develop these sketches follow the same procedure as for sketch A with the following exceptions:

Sketch B—Spread armhole more than bottom of sleeve.

Sketch C—Spread only armhole; bottom of sleeve should measure arm circumference plus ½″ (1.3 cm) for ease.

Sketch D—Spread only bottom of sleeve.

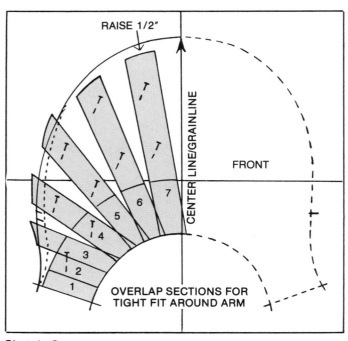

Sketch C

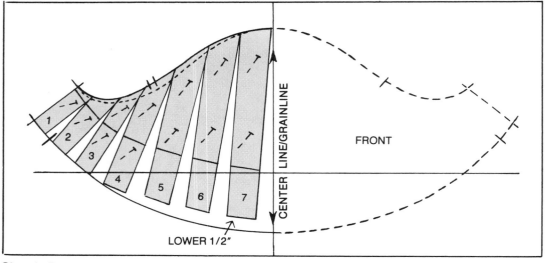

Sketch D

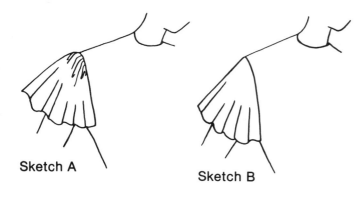

Sketch A   Sketch B

SKETCHES A & B

1.   The type of fabric used and the amount of fullness desired determines the amount sections are spread.

2.   Sleeve may be cut with center on true bias for a softer and more graceful fold.

3.   If a sheer or lightweight fabric is used, sleeve may be cut double with bottom of sleeve on fold of fabric.

4.   To prepare sloper and sleeve draft refer to Puffed Sleeve Variations, Figures 1, 2, 3, 4, 5 and 6, A to D.

5.   On sleeve draft cut sleeve sections and spread sections (as illustrated).

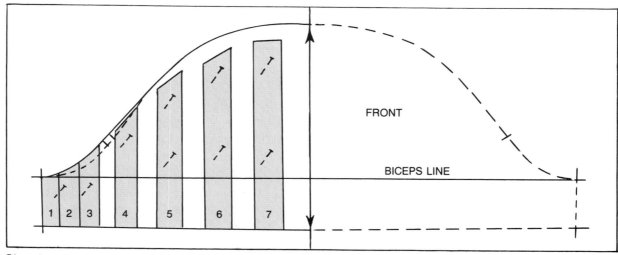

Sketch A

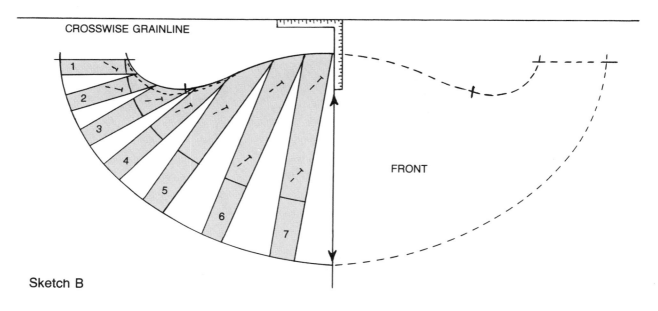

Sketch B

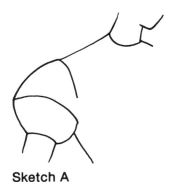

Sketch A

Sketch B

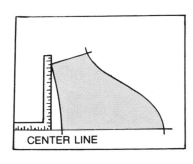

CENTER LINE

A lantern sleeve is a sleeve in two sections—narrow at the shoulder and wrist, wider at mid-arm by a seam forming lantern shape. It may be short, elbow length, three-quarter or full length and may vary in width.

The short lantern sleeve looks smarter if fitted tightly around the arm. To obtain this fit, the sleeve is developed from the Short Fitted Sleeve, sketch 2.

SKETCH A

FIGURE 1

A. Use sleeve developed from Short Fitted Sleeve, sketch 2. Fold sleeve in half.

B. Cut paper approximately 12″ (30.5 cm) square.

C. Draw a horizontal line up from bottom edge and across paper. Label *center line*.

D. With fold of sleeve towards you and back of sleeve face up, place sleeve to center line on paper. Pin. Outline sleeve.

E. Hold sleeve securely in place and lift back of sleeve at armhole. Outline front armhole (broken line in Figure 2).

F. Square a line from center line on paper to bottom of underarm on sleeve.

G. Remove sleeve. True all lines. Cut on all lines.

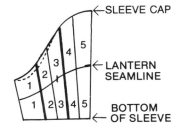

← SLEEVE CAP

← LANTERN SEAMLINE

← BOTTOM OF SLEEVE

FIGURE 2

A. Divide center line between cap and bottom of sleeve in half. Crossmark. Repeat at underarm seam.

B. Draw lantern seamline between crossmarks at center line and underarm seam (follow illustrated line).

C. Divide sleeve into three equal sections (darker lines). Subdivide (as illustrated). Number sections *1* to *5* (as illustrated).

D. To aid in construction, crossmark lantern seamline at center of section three.

E. Cut on lantern seamline.

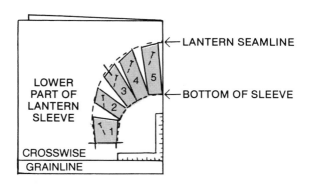

FIGURE 3

A. Use lower part of sleeve. Cut sections from lantern seamline down to, but not through, bottom of sleeve.

B. Cut another sheet of paper 12″ × 25″ (30.5 × 63.5 cm).

C. Fold paper in half. Square a line from fold at bottom edge of paper. Label *crosswise grainline.*

D. Place cut sleeve sections on paper (as illustrated). Spread sections until underarm seam is parallel to crosswise grainline. Pin.
Note: Sections may be spread more or less depending upon shape desired.

E. Outline sections.

F. Trace lantern seamline, crossmark, underarm seam and bottom of sleeve to opposite side.

G. Remove sections. True all lines crossing all intersections. Allow seams; cut and notch seams (Figure 5A).

H. Open paper. Pencil in all traced lines and crossmarks.

I. Establish grainline and crossmarks at center fold.

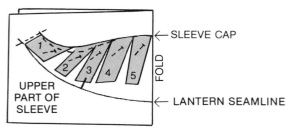

Figure 4.

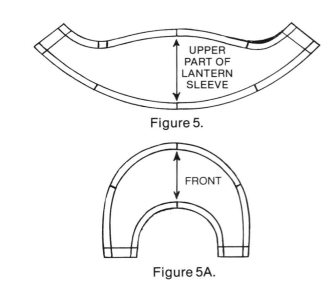

Figure 5.

Figure 5A.

FIGURES 4, 5, 5A

A. Use upper part of sleeve. Repeat instructions from Figure 3. Lantern seamline *must* be spread *the same amount* as in lower part of sleeve so that sections will match when joined.
Note: If developed accurately, crossmarks on upper and lower lantern seamline should match.

B. Adjust front armhole. Cut away excess paper (shaded area in Figure 5).

C. To establish armhole crossmarks refer to Short Fitted Sleeve, Figure 7.

SKETCH B

This sketch illustrates a less extreme short lantern sleeve.

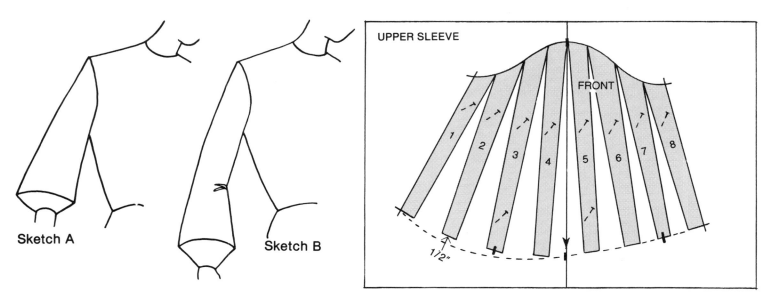

UPPER SLEEVE

FRONT

1 2 3 4 5 6 7 8

1/2"

FIGURE 2

A.   Cut another sheet of paper approximately 24" × 32" (61 × 81.3 cm).

B.   Fold paper in half. Crease.

C.   Open paper. Draw a line over crease. Label *grainline*.

D.   Use upper part of sleeve. Cut sections from lantern seamline up to, but not through, armhole.

E.   Place cut sleeve sections on paper matching center of sleeve to grainline on paper. Spread each section the desired amount. Pin.
Note: For a more graceful puff, the back of the sleeve should be spread more than the front. Also lengthen back sleeve ½" (1.3 cm) beyond lantern seamline (broken line).

F.   Outline sleeve.

G.   Remove sections. True all lines crossing all intersections.

H.   To establish armhole crossmarks refer to Short Fitted Sleeve, Figure 7.

SKETCHES A & B

FIGURE 1

A.   Use *straight sleeve sloper.*

B.   Determine length of sleeve desired.

C.   Cut paper approximately 18" × 26" (45.7 × 66 cm).

D.   Place sloper on paper and outline.

E.   Tighten bottom of sleeve to fit wrist (solid line). Cut out sleeve. Sleeve opening will be at underarm seam.

F.   Determine position of lantern seamline on underarm seams. Draw a straight line between underarm seams. Label *lantern seamline.*

G.   Divide sleeve into eight equal sections. Number the upper and lower sections *1* to *8* (as illustrated).

H.   To aid in construction, crossmark lantern seamline at center of section three and seven.

I.   Cut on lantern seamline.

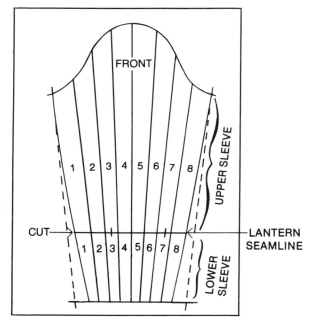

FRONT

1 2 3 4 5 6 7 8

UPPER SLEEVE

CUT

LANTERN SEAMLINE

1 2 3 4 5 6 7 8

LOWER SLEEVE

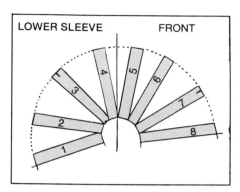

Figure 3.

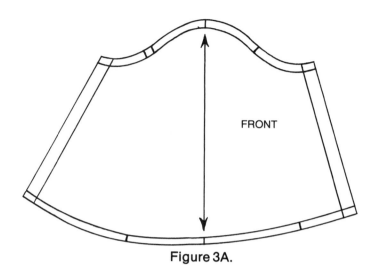

Figure 3A.

FIGURES 3, 3A, 3B

A. Use lower part of sleeve. Repeat instructions from Figure 2, A to G. Lantern seamline *must* be spread the same amount at back and front on lower section as in upper section so that sections will match when joined. Check by measuring seams. Adjust crossmarks, if necessary.

B. To complete patterns of upper and lower sleeve sections allow seams; cut and notch seams.

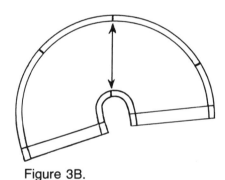

Figure 3B.

The petal sleeve is a short sleeve that crisscrosses over the biceps of the arm. It can be developed with either a fitted or shirred armhole and is used generally on dressy garments.

The petal sleeve is also known as a tulip, crisscross or overlapped sleeve

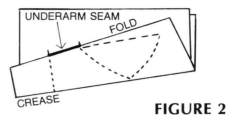

FIGURE 2

Match fold of sleeve to underarm seam. Crease.

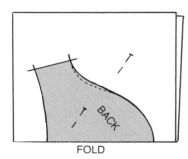

FIGURE 1

A.   Use sleeve developed in Short Fitted Sleeve, sketch 2.

B.   Fold short fitted sleeve in half.

C.   Cut paper 12″ × 25″ (30.5 × 63.5 cm).

D.   Fold paper in half lengthwise.

E.   With fold of paper towards you and back of sleeve face up, place fold of sleeve to fold of paper. Pin.

F.   Outline sleeve.

G.   Hold sleeve securely in place and lift back of sleeve at armhole. Outline front armhole (broken line).

H.   Remove sleeve. True all lines crossing all intersections.

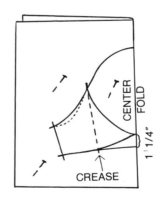

FIGURE 3

A.   Open paper. Draw a broken line over crease. Crossmark armhole.

B.   From crossmark at armhole draw a curved stylized line down to center line fold ending approximately 1¼″ (3.2 cm) up from bottom of sleeve. Label A.

C.   From crease at bottom of sleeve draw a curved line to A.

D.   Trace all lines and crossmark to opposite side.

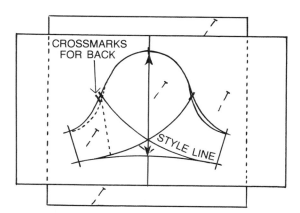

FIGURE 4

A. Open paper. Pencil in all traced lines and crossmark. True front armhole (broken line).

B. Add another crossmark to back armhole ½″ (1.3 cm) below style line crossmark.

C. Establish grainline over center fold line.

D. Cut two sheets of paper approximately 16″ (40.6 cm) square.

E. Pin together. Place sleeve draft on top. Pin.

F. Trace through back sleeve section (shaded area), grainline, back and front armhole (broken line) and all armhole crossmarks.

G. Remove draft. In pinned position true and pencil in all traced lines and crossmarks on both sides.

H. Allow seams following back armhole; cut and notch seams and crossmarks.

PETAL SLEEVE WITH UNDERARM SEAM

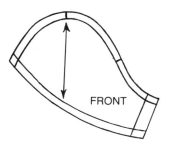 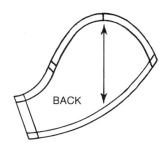

FIGURE 5

A. Separate sections. Place opposite to each other. Label *back* and *front* sleeve sections.

B. Adjust front armhole seam. Cut away excess paper.

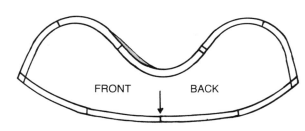

PETAL SLEEVE WITHOUT UNDERARM SEAM

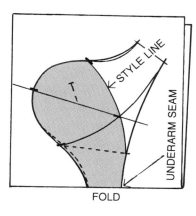

FIGURE 6

A. Cut paper approximately 16″ × 32″ (40.6 × 81.3 cm).

B. Fold paper in half. Place folded underarm seam of sleeve to fold of paper. Pin.

C. Trace through back sleeve section (shaded area), grainline, front and back armhole and armhole crossmarks.

D. Remove draft. In pinned position true and pencil in all traced lines and crossmarks on both sides.

E. Allow seams following back armhole; cut and notch seams.

FIGURE 7

A. Open draft. Draw a line over underarm crease. Label *grainline*.

B. Adjust front armhole seam. Cut away excess paper (shaded area).
Note: Sleeve may be cut double or edge may be finished by facing, rolling, binding or trimming.

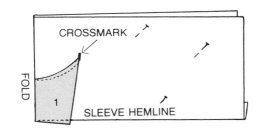

FIGURE 1

A.   Follow procedure for Petal Sleeve, sketch 16, Figures 1 and 2. Since back sleeve is needed, develop draft on single sheet of paper.

B.   Cut away paper at armhole, underarm, center and shaded area.

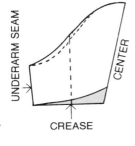

FIGURE 2

A.   Divide sleeve from crease line to center into four equal sections; underarm seam to crease line remains as one section. Number sections 1 to 5 (as illustrated).

B.   Cut on creased line separating section 1 from sections 2 to 5.

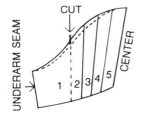

FIGURE 3

A.   Cut paper approximately 12″ × 32″ (30.5 × 81.3 cm).

B.   On length of paper draw a line up from bottom edge of paper allowing 1″ (2.5 cm) for sleeve hem. Cut.

C.   Fold hem under. Pin.

D.   Fold width of paper in half matching folded hem. Pin. Label *fold.*

E.   Match underarm of section 1 to fold and hemline. Pin. *Note:* Section 1 will extend below sleeve hemline.

F.   Measure distance between 2 and 5 (Figure 2).

G.   Measure this amount on draft from hemline of section 1 towards right-hand edge of paper. Crossmark.
Note: If a tighter fit around arm is desired, reduce measurement by ½″ to ¾″ (1.3 to 1.9 cm). Crossmark.

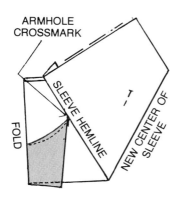

FIGURE 4

A.   At crossmark on sleeve hemline fold paper matching hemline to armhole crossmark.

B.   Crease fold to establish a new center fold of sleeve. Pin.

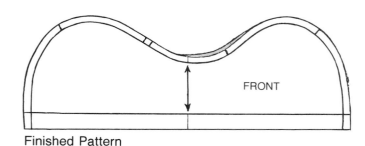

Finished Pattern

FIGURE 6

A.   Open sleeve draft. Establish grainline at underarm and crossmarks at cap on new center sleeve line. Adjust front armhole seam allowance. Cut away excess paper (shaded area).

B.   Add second crossmark at back armhole ½″ (1.3 cm) down from established crossmark. Notch seam.

FIGURE 5

A.   To establish cap of sleeve cut sections 2 to 5 from armhole to, but not through, bottom of sleeve.

B.   Place sections 2 to 5 over folded sleeve. Spread sections to new center fold of sleeve. Pin.

C.   To give a more graceful puff line to sleeve cap, raise capline at center fold at least ½″ (1.3 cm). Blend a new armhole line (broken line).

D.   Trace through front and back armhole. Crossmark. Remove sections 2 through 5.

E.   With draft in pinned position allow seam at armhole. Cut and notch seam.

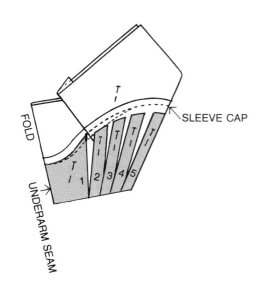

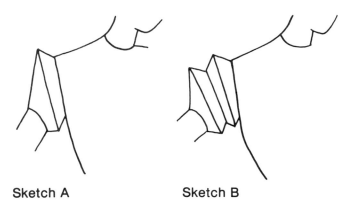

Sketch A   Sketch B

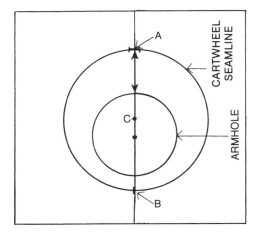

FIGURE 2

A.   Adjust compass point on center dot C and on outer crossmarks A. Draw circle for armhole. Label *cartwheel seamline.*

B.   To aid in joining of cartwheel seams, indicate one crossmark on bottom of circle and two on top of circle.

SKETCH A

FIGURE 1

A.   Cut paper approximately 20" (50.8 cm) square.

B.   Draw a line down center of paper. Label *grainline.*

C.   From top edge of paper on center line measure down approximately 10" (25.4 cm). Dot.

D.   Using a compass, with compass point on dot, draw a circle equal to armhole measurement of waist. *Note:* For circle formula refer to Full Circle Circular Skirt.

E.   From top of circle measure height of sleeve desired. Crossmark. Label *A.*

F.   From bottom of circle measure half the length of underarm seam desired. Crossmark. Label *B.* Illustrated: 1" (2.5 cm).

G.   On grainline crossmark center between A and B. Dot. Label *C.*

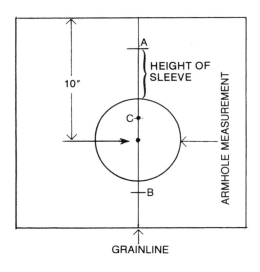

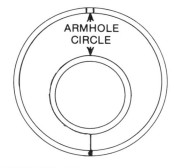

FIGURE 2A

To complete pattern allow seams; cut and notch seams. Label *armhole circle.*

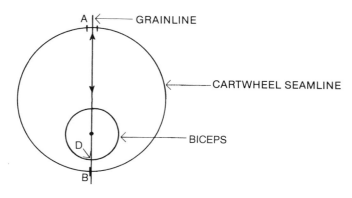

FIGURE 3

A.   Cut another sheet of paper 20″ (50.8 cm) square. Draw a line through center. Label *grainline.*

B.   Draw a second circle identical to cartwheel circle. Label *A* and *B* (as illustrated).

C.   From bottom of circle B measure up half the length of underarm seam desired. Measurement should be the same as on circle in Figure 1. Illustrated: 1″ (2.5 cm). Crossmark. Label *D.*

D.   Adjust compass for circle ending on D. Draw a circle equal to biceps measurement.

E.   To aid in joining cartwheels, indicate one crossmark on bottom of circle and two on top of circle.

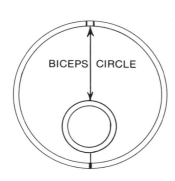

FIGURE 3A

To complete pattern allow seams; cut and notch seams. Label *biceps circle.*

SKETCH B

Copy three armhole circles and one biceps circle.
Note: The principle for cutting multiple cartwheel sleeves is to cut one biceps circle (Figure 3A) and the remaining sleeve sections all armhole circles (Figure 2A).

There are two categories of kimono slopers each with its own characteristics.

1. The slopers retain the original fit, darts and seamlines of the basic waist and sleeve slopers.

2. The slopers are developed for the purpose of matching stripes, plaids and checks on all seamlines.

In the first category, the slopers can be used on all types of fabrics with some limitations in the use of stripes, plaids and checks (see sketch 21). The limitations are due to the unbalanced grain on all seams except for center front and center back.

In the second category, (sketches 30, 31 and 32), the slopers can be used on all types of fabrics. In developing these slopers, there is a small degree of redirecting all seamlines in order to obtain balanced seams for matching. The slopers, however, retain most of the fit of the original basic waist and sleeve slopers.

The three striped kimono slopers, developed for woven striped fabrics, have different common front dart positions, since shifting of darts after slopers are completed will affect matching stripes. It is possible, however, to pivot the shoulder dart of sketch 29 into the neckline or center front without sacrificing matching lines. The dart may also be eliminated by incorporating it into yokelines and other seamlines. The back waist for all three striped kimono slopers is developed with a neck dart.

The slopers developed from the projects on kimono sleeves will be used to show examples of design potential within each sloper as well as how to develop the dolman or batwing sleeve from the basic kimono sloper.

The definition of the kimono sleeve is derived from the historic Chinese garment and is described as a wide straight sleeve set into the garment at right angles or cut in one with the garment. The modified kimono sleeve developed in sketch 19 is cut in one with the waist and is either straight from the biceps to the wrist or fitted to the wrist.

Use the following slopers to develop the one-piece kimono sloper:

1. one-dart front waist sloper

2. back waist sloper with neckline and waistline darts

3. straight sleeve sloper

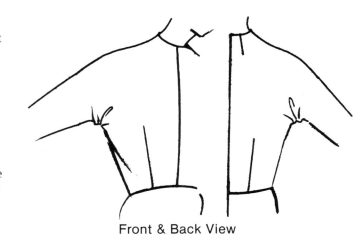

Front & Back View

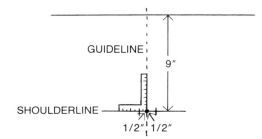

FIGURE 1

A. Cut paper approximately 40" (101.6 cm) square.

B. From the top edge and in the center of the paper, draw a broken vertical line 9" (23 cm) in length. Dot. Label *guideline*.

C. Square a short line on each side of dot. Label *shoulderline*. *Note:* Shoulderline must be a true right angle or it will throw entire pattern off balance as this right angled line is used to balance front and back waists at shoulders.

D. On shoulderline crossmark ½" (1.3 cm) on each side of guideline.

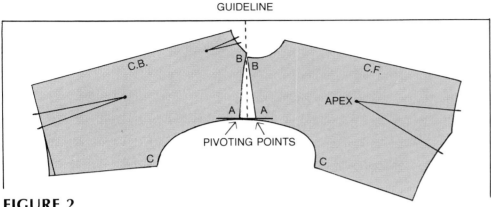

GUIDELINE

PIVOTING POINTS

FIGURE 2

A.   On *front and back waist slopers* label *A, B, C* (as illustrated).

B.   Place sloper on paper matching shoulderlines at A on sloper to crossmarks on paper.

C.   Pivoting point is at A. Hold front sloper at pivoting point and pivot sloper until B touches guideline. Repeat with back. *Note:* Slopers are often planned with ease on back shoulder, therefore, back shoulder will extend slightly.

D.   Outline slopers. Crossmark all darts. With awl indicate end of darts.

FIGURE 3

1.   Remove slopers. True all lines crossing all intersections. Label draft *A, B, C*.

2.   Use *straight sleeve sloper*. Fold sleeve cap under. Place sleeve sloper on paper so that biceps line touches underarm seam at C.

3.   With sleeve sloper properly placed, outline sloper. Crossmark elbow line, center at wristline and center at folded sleeve cap.

4.   Remove sleeve sloper. True all lines crossing all intersections. Draw in biceps line, elbow line and center sleeve line extending center sleeve line to shoulderline (see enlarged area in Figure 3B). *Note:* Center sleeve line, in most cases, may not touch broken guideline.

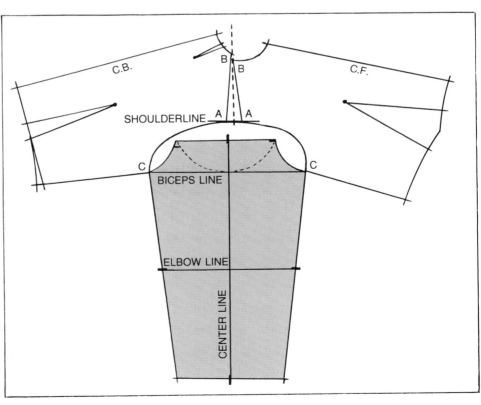

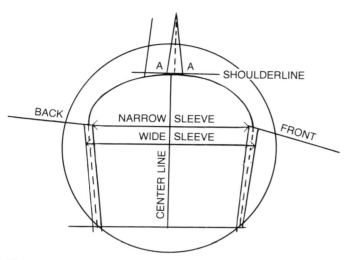

Figure 3A.

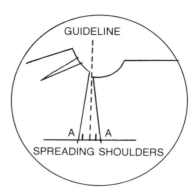

Figure 3B.

FIGURES 3A & 3B

A.   If sleeve is too wide and overlaps underarm seam at biceps line (Figure 3A), spread slopers slightly at shoulder points A (Figure 3B) until biceps line touches underarm seam. (Figure 3B). When spreading shoulder, spread same amount on each side of guideline. Additional spread at shoulder should not exceed ⅛" (0.3 cm) on each side (Figure 3A). If more spread is needed, slopers have not been developed accurately.

B.   If sleeve is too narrow, add to underarm seam on sleeve (as illustrated with broken line Figure 3A). Draw a line from underarm intersection to nothing at wrist.

FIGURE 4

A. To shape shoulder dart extend broken guideline down to 1″ (2.5 cm) above biceps line parallel to center sleeve line. Dot.

B. Draw a *straight* line from front neckline at B to dot. Blend a slightly *curved line* from back shoulder at B to dot.

Note: 1. The position of the shoulder dart depends upon the position of the shoulder on the sloper. The dart may end on the center sleeve line or towards the front (Figure 4) or back of center line. 2. The depth of the dart at center of shoulder should not exceed ¼″ (0.6 cm).

3. Additional alterations for a smooth fitting shoulder may be obtained in a muslin fitting.

D. Blend back neckline to match front neckline at shoulder (broken line).

E. To complete sloper cut away excess paper from draft, *but do not* cut away extended back shoulder as you will need it to develop the two-piece kimono sloper.

Note: To use this sloper as a one-piece kimono pattern, see sketch 20.

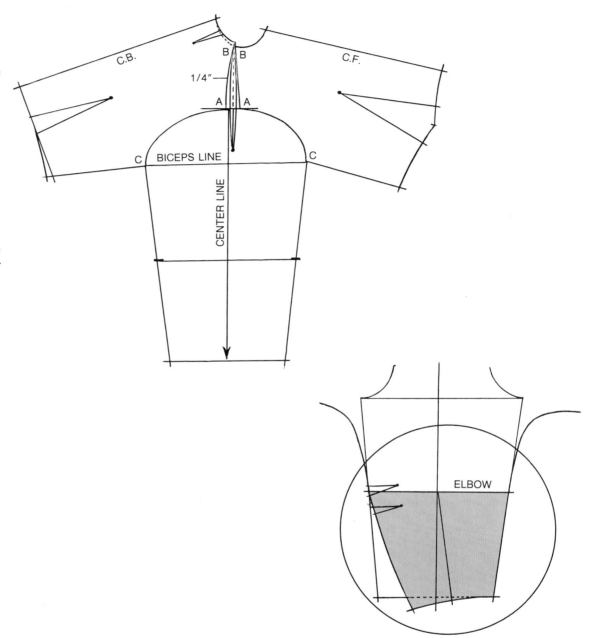

FIGURE 5

If a fitted sleeve is desired, match elbow line on fitted sleeve sloper to elbow line on draft. Outline and indicate darts.

SKETCH A

FIGURE 1

A.   Cut paper approximately 40" (101.6 cm) square.

B.   Copy one-piece kimono sloper developed in sketch 19 with adjusted neckline (broken line).

C.   For shirring, if desired, measure 1½" (3.8 cm) on either side of front and back darts. Crossmark. (sketch B).

D.   True all lines crossing all intersections.

E.   To round underarm, from C measure down 2½" (6.4 cm) on underarm of sleeve and waist. Crossmark.

F.   Draw a line from intersection C 1" (2.5 cm) long. Dot.

G.   Draw a curved underarm line (as illustrated).

H.   Establish grainline desired. Grainline is optional (as illustrated).

Note: 1.   If fabric is wide, center front or center back may be cut on fold thereby eliminating one seam. 2.   If a fitted sleeve is desired, before adding seams to draft match elbow line on fitted sleeve sloper to elbow line on draft. Outline and indicate darts. 3.   Underarm seams of front and back waist are unbalanced, therefore, the overall length of the kimono front underarm seam is shorter than the back. This does not create a problem when using a soft fabric that is susceptible to shrinkage, but seams should be balanced for all other fabrics.

The one-piece kimono sloper developed in sketch 19, Figures 4 or 5, can be used as a pattern with or without balanced seams by making the following adjustments.

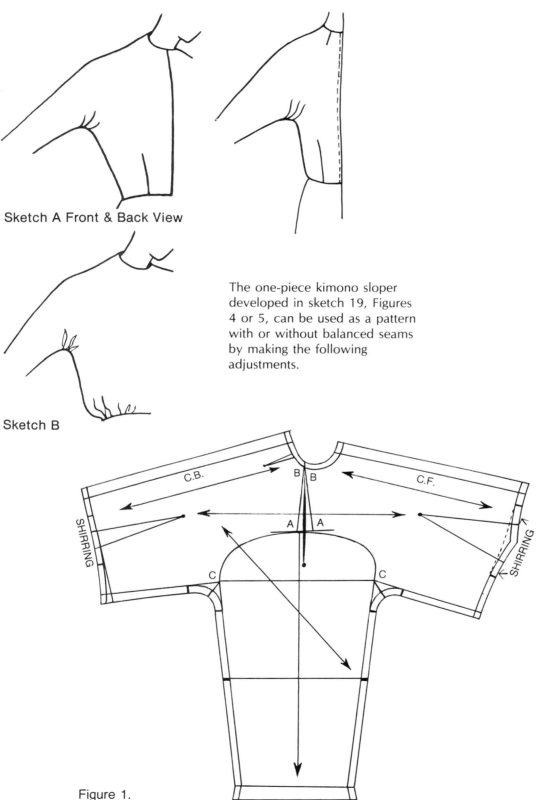

Sketch A Front & Back View

Sketch B

Figure 1.

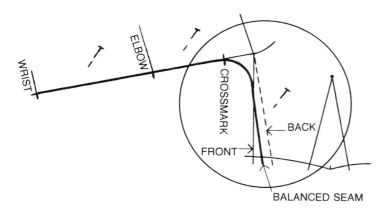

FIGURE 2

A. To balance seams place front (face up) and back underarm seam of kimono sleeve together from wrist to crossmark. Pin.

B. Smooth out waists and pin. Turn draft over and trace back underarm to front of waist.

C. Turn over and draw a line in the center of front and back underarm for new underarm (darker line). Trace adjusted underarm to back waist.

D. To complete pattern allow hem at wrist and seams; cut and notch seams.

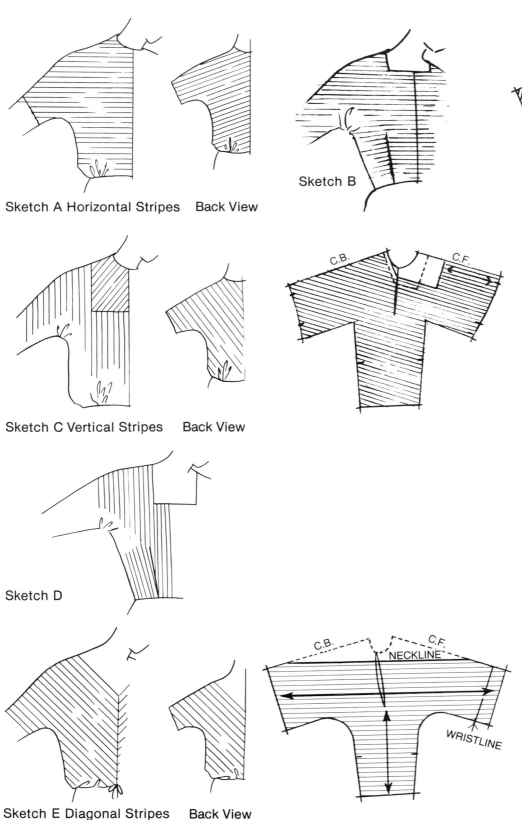

Sketch A Horizontal Stripes   Back View

Sketch B

Sketch C Vertical Stripes   Back View

Sketch D

Sketch E Diagonal Stripes   Back View

1. Many interesting effects may be obtained when using the one-piece kimono sloper by:

   A. re-directing the grainline;

   B. introducing surface details such as yokes;

   C. planning necklines in harmony with the stripes, checks and plaids.

2. Even though the grainline differs at center front and center back, the stripes will match at center seams, but will *not* match at the underarm seam (except in sketch D where grainlines are balanced at front and back underarm seams).

3. Waistline darts in stripes will match only in front when stripes run horizontally or vertically as in sketches B and D, but will not match when stripes are on the diagonal as in sketch E. Plan darts within stripes. For sketch E back and front shirring at waistline is suggested.

4. If a fitted sleeve is desired, match elbow line on fitted sleeve sloper to elbow line on straight sleeve sloper. Outline and indicate darts.

5. For other variations developed from one-piece kimono sloper refer to sketches 22, 23 and 24.

Many designs may be obtained when using the one-piece kimono pattern by introducing style lines.

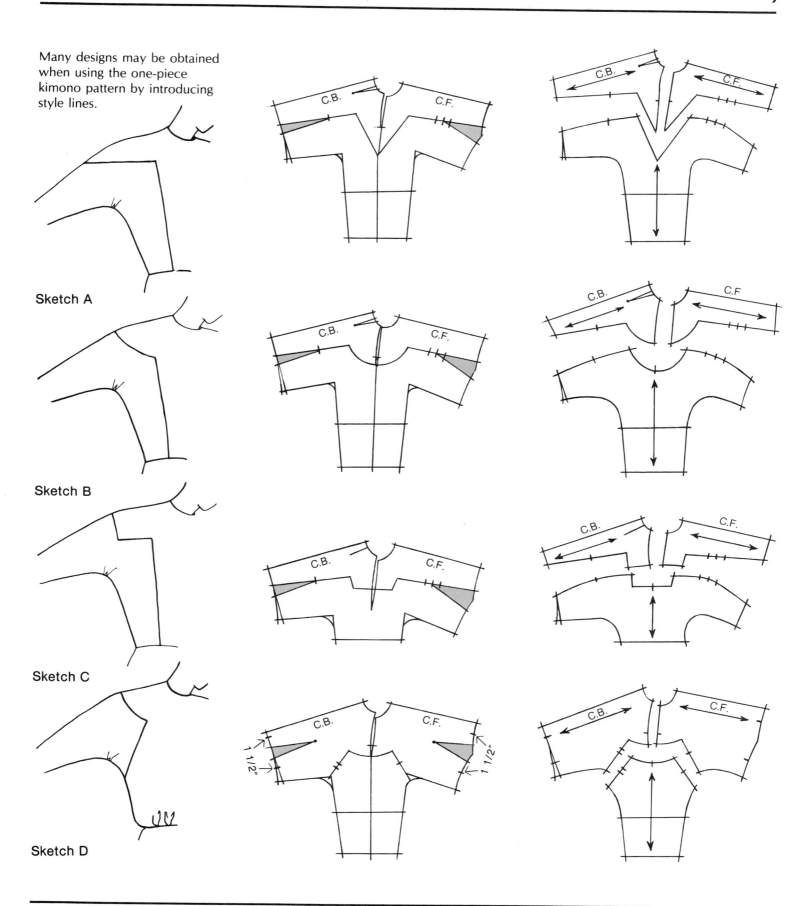

Sketch A

Sketch B

Sketch C

Sketch D

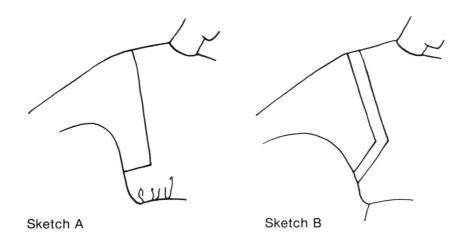

Sketch A   Sketch B

SKETCH A

FIGURE 1

A.   Cut paper approximately 40″ (101.6 cm) square.

B.   Use one-piece kimono sloper, sketch 19. Outline sloper indicate shirring crossmarks 1½″ (3.8 cm) on each side of dart. This squared armhole is more attractive with shirring or soft unpressed pleats at waistline.

C.   To balance underarm seam, if desired, fold draft matching underarm/armhole intersections and wristline. Pin.
Note: If sloper is copied accurately, these points will match and fold will be on center of sleeve.

D.   At waistline crossmark between front and back underarm seam draw a line from crossmark to underarm intersection (darker lines).

E.   From balanced waistline seam crossmark measure up desired height of squared armhole. Label *A*. Illustrated: 3″ (7.6 cm).

F.   Trace balanced underarm seam and crossmarks at A and waistline to opposite side.

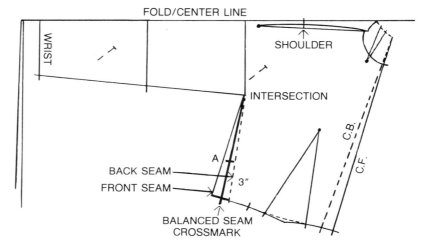

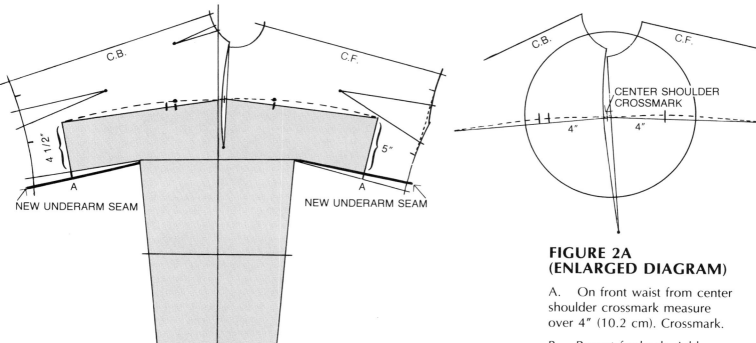

FIGURE 2

A.   Open draft. Pencil in traced back underarm seam and all crossmarks. True all lines crossing all intersections. Label *new underarm seams* for front and back (darker lines).

B.   Crossmark center of shoulder at end of shoulder. See area enlarged in Figure 2A.

C.   For squared armhole:

   1.   On front measure up from A 5″ (12.7 cm). Dot.

   2.   On back measure up from A 4½″ (11.4 cm). Dot.

   3.   On front and back, draw a line parallel to waistline from A to dots and from dots draw a straight line to end of shoulder.

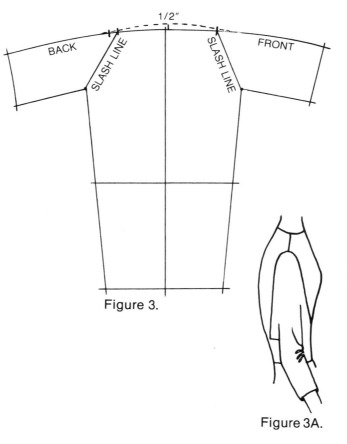

Figure 3.

Figure 3A.

FIGURE 2A
(ENLARGED DIAGRAM)

A.   On front waist from center shoulder crossmark measure over 4″ (10.2 cm). Crossmark.

B.   Repeat for back. Add another crossmark ½″ (1.3 cm) away from first crossmark.

C.   To curve squared armhole line on front and back, measure up ½″ (1.3 cm) from crossmarks. Dot. From dots blend a slightly curved line up to shoulder and down to squared armhole (broken line).
Note: This eliminates a pointed effect on squared armhole line at end of shoulder and achieves the effect of a straight seamline on the body.

FIGURE 3

A.   Copy sleeve following broken line. Do not copy shoulder dart. True all lines crossing all intersections.

B.   This sleeve has the tendency to pull upwards at the overarm. To prevent this upward pull add ½″ (1.3 cm), or more depending upon the stretchability of the fabric used, to top of sleeve. Blend to nothing to crossmarks (broken line).

FIGURE 4

A.   If more freedom of movement is desired at underarm, the underarm seam may be lengthened. To achieve this on front and back sleeve, draw a line from underarm intersections to armhole crossmarks. Label *slash line* and number sections.

B.   Cut out sleeve accurately, cutting each slash line to crossmark.

C.   Cut another sheet of paper approximately 25" (63.5 cm) square. Fold in half. Open and draw a line on crease.

D.   Place sleeve draft onto paper matching center line on sleeve to vertical line on paper.

E.   Spread front and back 1" (2.5 cm), or more depending on fullness desired. Pin. Illustrated: 2" (5.1 cm).
Note: Amount of spread must be the same on front and back.

F.   To check that underarm seams are the same, extend back and front waist and sleeve underarm seams until they intersect.

G.   From intersection measure back and front underarm seam to wrist and from intersection to squared armhole line. If seamline to squared armhole is not the same, increase or decrease spread until lines measure the same from intersections. Pin.

H.   Outline sleeve blending armhole line at crossmarks (broken line). On paper indicate crossmarks at sleeve cap and elbow. Remove draft.

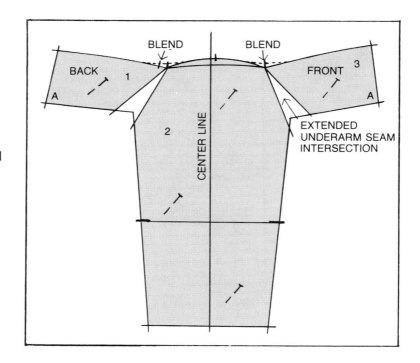

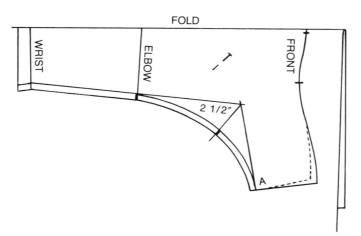

FIGURE 5

A.   To curve and true underarm seam, with front face up fold draft matching underarm of sleeve from wrist to elbow and squared armhole intersections.

B.   Curve underarm as illustrated.

C.   Trace new underarm seam from wrist to waistline, crossmarks at elbow and on underarm curved line to opposite side.

D.   Allow seams at underarm, hem at wrist; cut and notch seams.

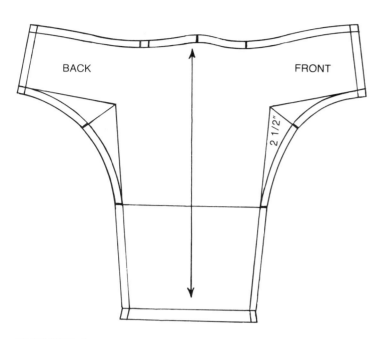

FIGURE 6

A.   Open sleeve draft. Pencil in traced underarm seam.

B.   Establish grainline on center fold of sleeve.

C.   Allow remaining seams; cut and notch seams.
Note: If a fitted sleeve is desired, match elbow line on fitted sleeve sloper to elbow line on draft. Outline and indicate darts.

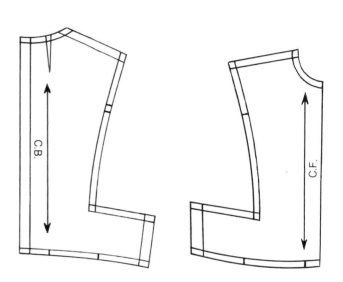

FIGURE 7

A.   Copy front and back waist sections. True all lines crossing all intersections.

B.   Allow seams; cut and notch seams.

C.   Establish grainlines parallel to centers.

SKETCH B

To develop pattern for this sketch, follow procedure discussed for sketch A. Add band line to draft by measuring out desired width from sleeve armhole line.

KIMONO SLEEVE WITH RAGLAN LINE ARMHOLE
sketch 24

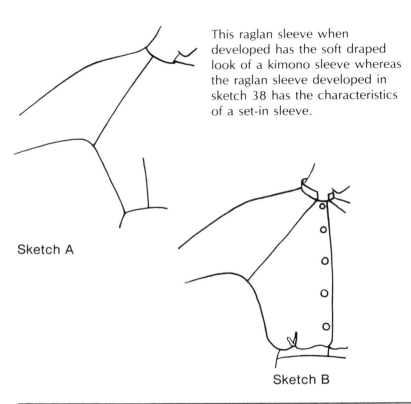

This raglan sleeve when developed has the soft draped look of a kimono sleeve whereas the raglan sleeve developed in sketch 38 has the characteristics of a set-in sleeve.

Sketch A

Sketch B

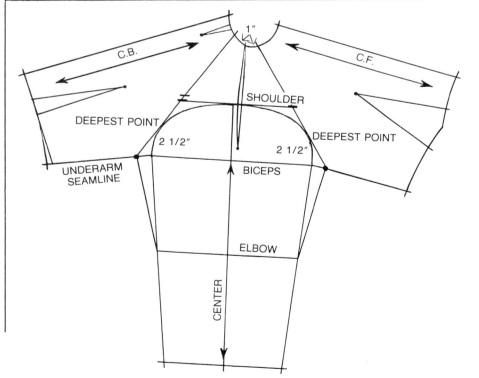

FIGURE 1

A.   Cut paper approximately 40" (101.6 cm) square.

B.   Use one-piece kimono sloper with adjusted neckline, sketch 19, Figure 4.

C.   Outline sloper. Crossmark darts. With awl indicate end of darts. Remove sloper. True all lines crossing all intersections.

D.   Establish grainlines on center front and center back parallel to centers and on center of sleeve.

E.   Measure from front and back neck/shoulder intersections 1" (2.5 cm). Crossmark. This measurement may vary depending upon the raglan style line desired.

F.   To establish raglan line on front, draw a straight line from crossmark at front neckline touching deepest part of armhole to underarm seam. Line may end at any point on underarm seam of waist. Dot.

G.   To establish raglan line on back, measure length of front underarm seam from waistline to dot at end of front raglan line. Measure same length on back and dot.

H.   Draw a line from crossmark at back neckline to underarm dot.

I.   Draw a line parallel to biceps at end of shoulder from front and back raglan lines. Crossmark each end of horizontal line. To indicate back add another crossmark ½" (1.3 cm) above first crossmark.

J.   To complete front and back underarm seams of sleeve, draw a straight line from raglan line dots to elbow.

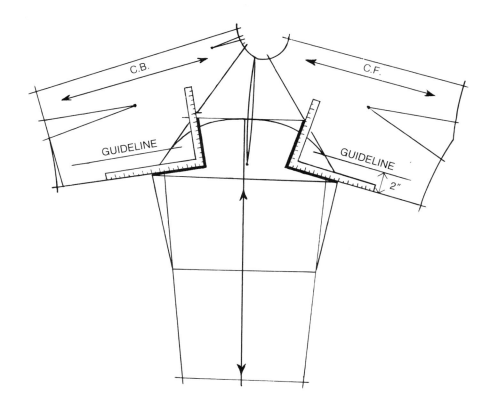

FIGURE 2

A. For a better hang and fit of sleeve, lengthen underarm seam of sleeve. To lengthen underarm seam, place an L-square in line with back underarm and move L-square until it touches crossmark on raglan armhole line. Draw in a right angle (darker lines).

B. Repeat on front.

C. From underarm seam on front measure up 1″ to 2″ (2.5 to 5.1 cm). Draw a line parallel to underarm seam extending line through raglan line. Label *guideline*.

D. Repeat on back.

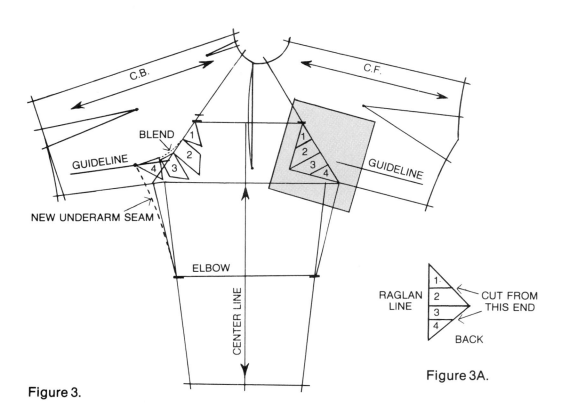

Figure 3.

Figure 3A.

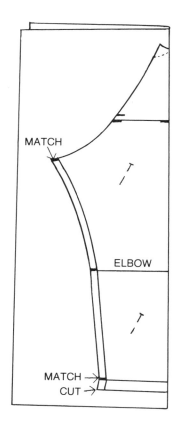

FIGURES 3 & 3A

Note: The sections to be copied are not true triangles. Therefore, it is important *to follow instructions carefully* to obtain accurate results.

A.   Place a piece of paper over each triangle on draft (see front). Copy, true lines and label *front:* Repeat for back. Cut away excess paper.

B.   Fold back triangle into quarters. Open and number sections *1, 2, 3, 4* and label *raglan line* (Figure 3A).

C.   Cut up to but not through raglan line (Figure 3A).

D.   Place raglan line of back triangle to back raglan line of sleeve with section 1 touching crossmark (as illustrated).

E.   Spread remaining sections until section 4 touches guideline. Pin and blend armhole (broken line).

F.   For new underarm seam draw a slightly curved line to elbow line (broken line).

G.   Repeat for front.

H.   Copy sleeve, center line, armhole crossmarks, shaped shoulder dart. Crossmark elbow. With awl indicate end of shoulder dart.

FIGURE 4

A.   To true and balance underarm seam, fold sleeve matching underarm/armhole intersections and wristline. Pin. *Note:* If sloper is developed accurately, fold will be on center line of sleeve.

B.   True underarm. Trace underarm seam and crossmarks at armhole, elbow and wrist to opposite side.

C.   Allow seams at underarm and hem at wrist; cut and notch seams.

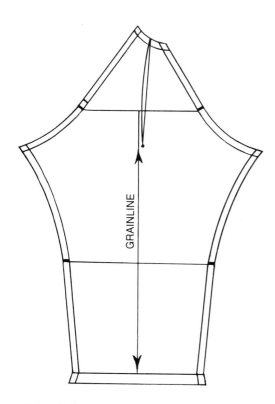

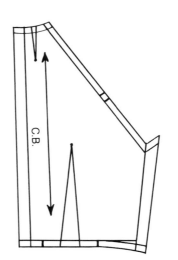

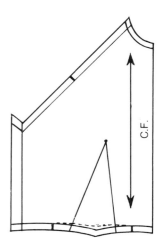

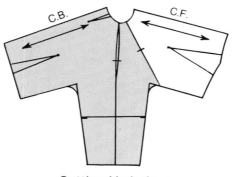

Cutting Variations

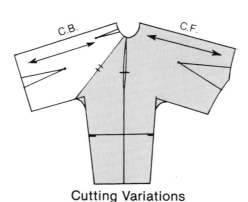

Cutting Variations

FIGURE 5

A.   Open sleeve draft. Pencil in traced underarm seam. Draw a line between elbow crossmarks. Redirect armhole crossmarks at right angles to seams.

B.   Establish grainline on center fold of sleeve.

C.   Allow remaining seams; cut and notch seams.
Note: If a fitted sleeve is desired, match elbow line on fitted sleeve sloper to elbow line on draft. Outline and indicate darts.

FIGURE 6

A.   Copy front and back waist sections. True all lines crossing all intersections.

B.   Allow seams; cut and notch seams.

C.   Establish grainlines parallel to centers.

SKETCH B

A.   At waistline measure 1½" (3.8 cm) on either side of front and back darts for shirring. Crossmark.

B.   To develop collar refer to Mandarin Collar.

CUTTING VARIATIONS

Illustrated are some cutting variations for raglan style lines. However, the underarm seams of sleeves on these variations cannot be lengthened. Therefore, pattern pieces must be copied from draft as in Figure 1. Underarm may be rounded as desired.

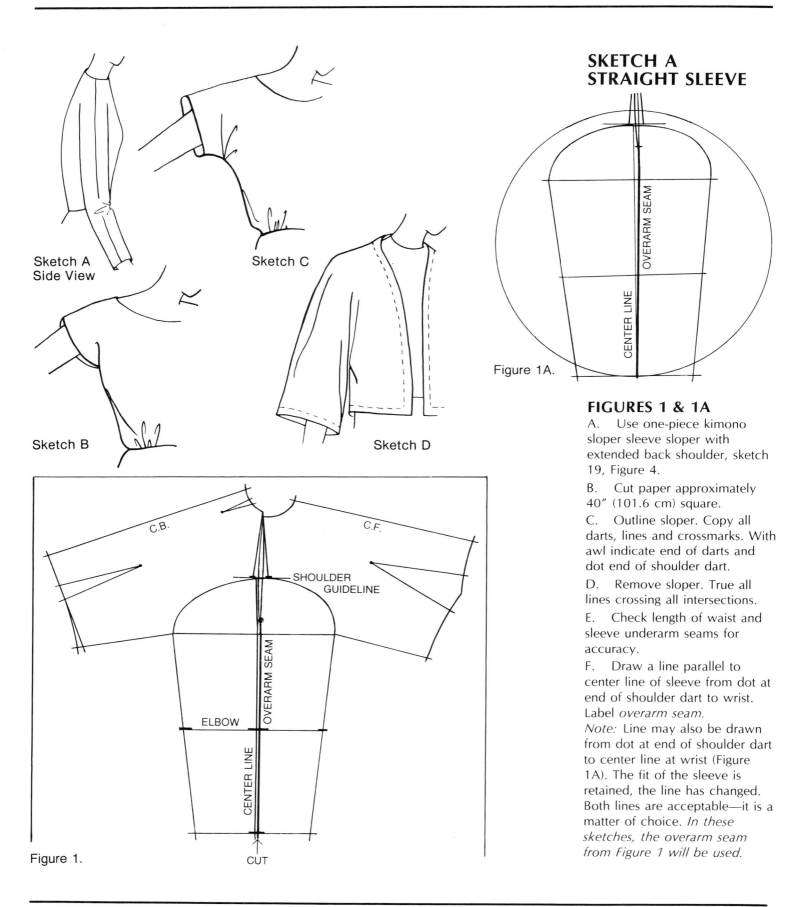

**SKETCH A
STRAIGHT SLEEVE**

Sketch A
Side View

Sketch C

Sketch B

Sketch D

OVERARM SEAM

CENTER LINE

Figure 1A.

C.B.

C.F.

SHOULDER GUIDELINE

OVERARM SEAM

ELBOW

CENTER LINE

Figure 1.

CUT

FIGURES 1 & 1A

A.   Use one-piece kimono sloper sleeve sloper with extended back shoulder, sketch 19, Figure 4.

B.   Cut paper approximately 40" (101.6 cm) square.

C.   Outline sloper. Copy all darts, lines and crossmarks. With awl indicate end of darts and dot end of shoulder dart.

D.   Remove sloper. True all lines crossing all intersections.

E.   Check length of waist and sleeve underarm seams for accuracy.

F.   Draw a line parallel to center line of sleeve from dot at end of shoulder dart to wrist. Label *overarm seam.*

Note: Line may also be drawn from dot at end of shoulder dart to center line at wrist (Figure 1A). The fit of the sleeve is retained, the line has changed. Both lines are acceptable—it is a matter of choice. *In these sketches, the overarm seam from Figure 1 will be used.*

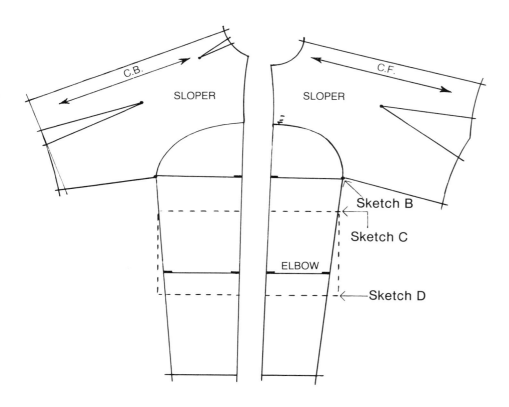

FIGURE 2

A.   Cut away paper from draft. Cut draft apart through overarm seam following front and back shaped shoulder dartlines.

B.   Establish grainlines parallel to centers.

C.   Since this is a sloper, underarm intersection should be at an angle. Patterns are curved at underarm seams.

SKETCHES B, C, D

The sleeve lengths for these sketches are illustrated by broken lines in Figure 2.

Sketch A Side View

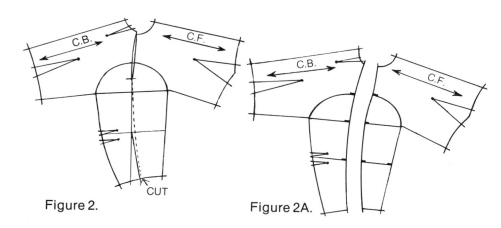

Figure 2.

Figure 2A.

FIGURES 2 & 2A

For a curved overarm seam, blend center line of sleeve at elbow area (broken line). See Figure 2A for finished sloper.

TWO-PIECE FITTED KIMONO SLEEVE SLOPER

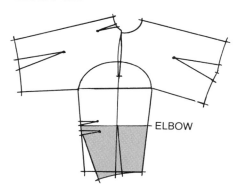

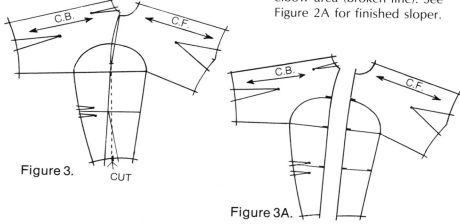

Figure 3.

Figure 3A.

FIGURES 3 & 3A

For a straight overarm seam, crossmark on wristline between grainline and center line of sleeve. Draw a straight line from crossmark to end of shoulder dart (broken line). See Figure 3A for finished sloper.

FIGURE 1

A.   Cut paper approximately 40" (101.6 cm) square.

B.   Outline one-piece kimono sleeve sloper with extended back shoulder, sketch 27, Figures 1 and 2 (as illustrated).

C.   To convert straight sleeve into a fitted sleeve place fitted sleeve sloper to draft matching elbow lines. Outline and indicate darts.

Two-Dart Front Waist Kimono

FIGURE 4

Both Figures 2 and 3 may be converted into a two-dart front waist kimono with fitted sleeve by following instructions given for two-piece kimono sleeve sloper, sketch 27, Figures 1 and 2.

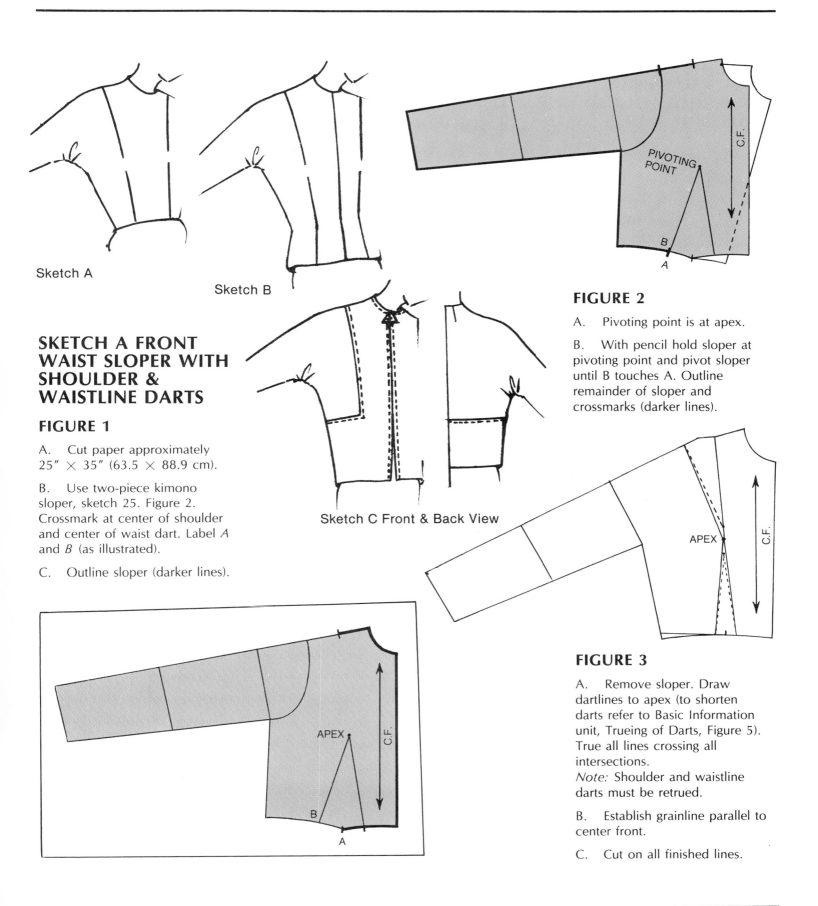

Sketch A

Sketch B

Sketch C Front & Back View

SKETCH A FRONT WAIST SLOPER WITH SHOULDER & WAISTLINE DARTS

FIGURE 1

A.   Cut paper approximately 25" × 35" (63.5 × 88.9 cm).

B.   Use two-piece kimono sloper, sketch 25. Figure 2. Crossmark at center of shoulder and center of waist dart. Label *A* and *B* (as illustrated).

C.   Outline sloper (darker lines).

FIGURE 2

A.   Pivoting point is at apex.

B.   With pencil hold sloper at pivoting point and pivot sloper until B touches A. Outline remainder of sloper and crossmarks (darker lines).

FIGURE 3

A.   Remove sloper. Draw dartlines to apex (to shorten darts refer to Basic Information unit, Trueing of Darts, Figure 5). True all lines crossing all intersections.
Note: Shoulder and waistline darts must be retrued.

B.   Establish grainline parallel to center front.

C.   Cut on all finished lines.

SKETCH B FRONT TORSO SLOPER WITH SHOULDER & WAISTLINE DARTS

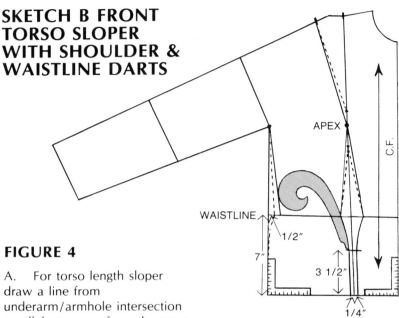

FIGURE 4

A. For torso length sloper draw a line from underarm/armhole intersection parallel to center front the torso length desired. Illustrated: 7″ (17.8 cm) down from waistline grainline at side seam.

B. Square a line across bottom and up center front to waistline.

C. Continue center line of dart to hipline. On center line from hipline measure up 3½″ (8.9 cm). Crossmark. From crossmark draw parallel lines ¼″ (0.6 cm) on each side of center line down to hipline.

D. Curve darts with French curve (as illustrated). Repeat on opposite side.
Note: End of bustline dart will vary depending upon size of bust. Adjustments should be made when testing sloper in muslin. The larger the bust the greater the bust dart underlay at waistline and space at hipline.

E. For shaped side seam, measure in at waistline/underarm intersection ½″ (1.3 cm). Dot. Draw in new lines (broken lines).
Note: Line from waist to hipline is curved.

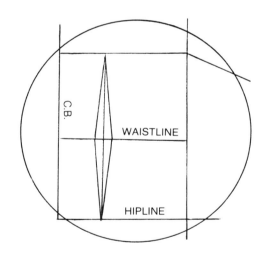

FIGURE 5

A. For back repeat as for front Figure 4, A and B.

B. Continue center line of dart to hipline. Draw in lower section of dart (as illustrated).

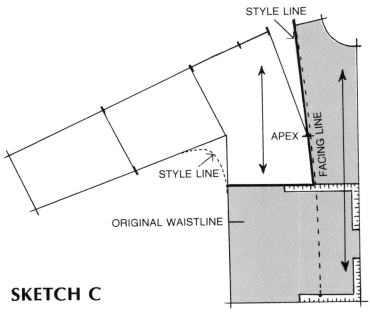

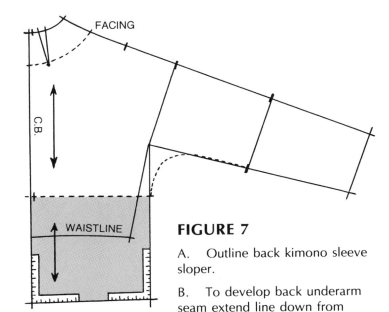

SKETCH C

FIGURE 6

A. Outline torso length sloper, Figure 4, indicating only shoulder dart crossmarks and apex.

B. Establish horizontal style line desired below apex by squaring a line from center front to underarm seam (darker lines).

C. Place ruler on dartline crossmark nearest neckline and draw line to style line (darker line).
Note: Line may not touch apex.

D. Draw dartline nearest armhole to new dartline in line with apex.

E. Establish length and underarm curve desired (broken line).

FIGURE 7

A. Outline back kimono sleeve sloper.

B. To develop back underarm seam extend line down from underarm intersection parallel to center back same length as front underarm seam. Crossmark.

C. Square a line to center back and up center back.

D. Establish horizontal style line and underarm curve to match front (broken line).

E. To complete pattern indicate facing lines on back and front (as illustrated). Copy sections; allow hem at bottom of sleeve and waist. Allow seams; cut and notch seams.

Sketch A
Underarm View

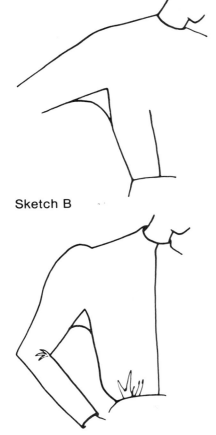

Sketch B

Sketch C

The procedure for developing the kimono sleeve sloper with gusset is the same regardless of the angle to which the sleeve is pivoted downward. However, the more the sleeve is pivoted downward the shorter the underarm seam becomes. The shorter the underarm seam the longer the gusset and the gusset slash lines.

Use two-piece kimono sleeve sloper developed in sketch 25, Figure 2.

FIGURE 1

Diagram illustrates pivoted positions for sleeve:

Position 1—original kimono sloper (shaded area).

Position 2—a lowered position. Other variations may be achieved by pivoting to any point between 1 and 2.

Position 3—sleeve is pivoted to 45° angle, the maximum position for this sleeve. It has the characteristics of a set-in sleeve and requires the longest gusset.

Depending upon the sloper used, the sleeve, when pivoted to the 45° angle, may end too close to the waistline at the underarm seam. In this case it is advisable to style the gusset as shown in sketch 29, Figure 1.

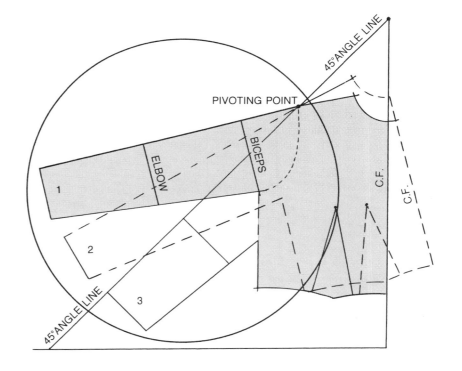

FIGURE 2

A.   Cut paper approximately 36" (91.4 cm) square.

B.   Draw a right angle 28" (71.1 cm) long across the bottom and along the right-hand edge of the paper. Dot each end. Draw a diagonal line between the dots. Label diagonal line *45° angle* and vertical line, *center front.*
Note: Right angle and diagonal line must be drawn accurately or problems will arise when developing draft.

C.   Place sloper on paper matching center front of sloper to center front on paper and shoulder crossmark to 45° angle line.

D.   Dot underarm/armhole intersection. Outline underarm, waistline, neckline and shoulder. Crossmark end of shoulder. Label *A.*

E.   With awl indicate apex. Crossmark waistline dart and trace armhole.

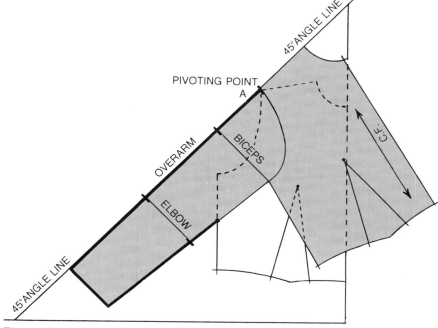

Figure 3.

FIGURE 3

A.   Pivoting point is A.

B.   Pivot sleeve from A downwards until overarm touches 45° line. Outline sleeve (as illustrated). Crossmark elbow and biceps lines.

C.   With awl indicate end of darts. Remove sloper. True all lines crossing all intersections. Pencil in traced armhole.

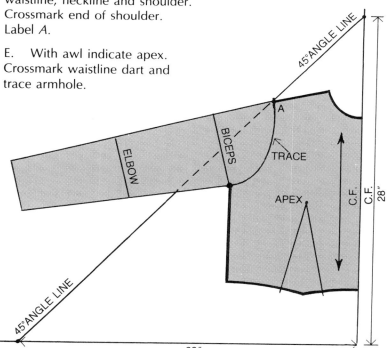

Figure 2.

FIGURE 4

A.   Allow 1" (2.5 cm) seam for trueing at waistline, wristline, overarm and shoulder; cut.

B.   Cut on neck, center front and underarm seamlines.

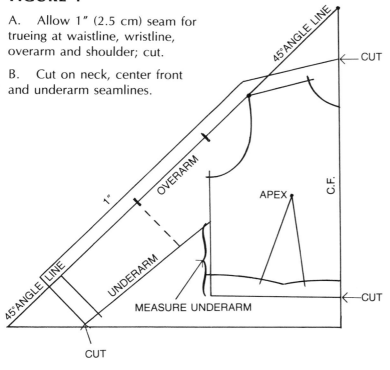

BACK KIMONO SLEEVE WITH GUSSET

FIGURES 5 & 5A

A.   Cut paper approximately 36" (91.4 cm) square.

B.   Place center back of kimono sleeve sloper on left-hand side of paper near top edge.

C.   Outline waist section of sloper. Crossmark waist and neckline darts and trace armhole. With awl indicate end of darts.

D.   Label end of shoulder A.

E.   Measure underarm seam of front from waistline to new underarm/armhole intersection (Figure 4). Measure this amount on back from waistline on underarm (Figure 5A). Dot. *Note:* 1.   Back sleeve cannot be pivoted to a 45° angle since underarm seams would *not* be the same length. 2.   Overarm seam of front and back will not balance on grainline as this kimono sleeve sloper retains the original fit and seamlines of the basic front and back sloper.

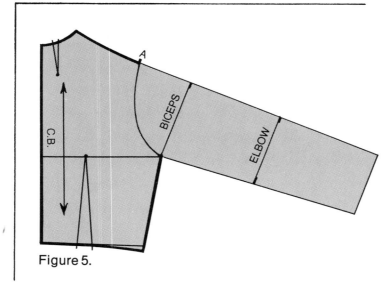

Figure 5.

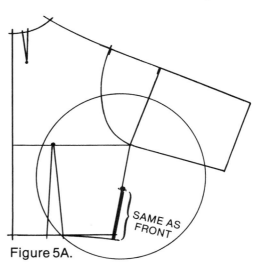

Figure 5A.

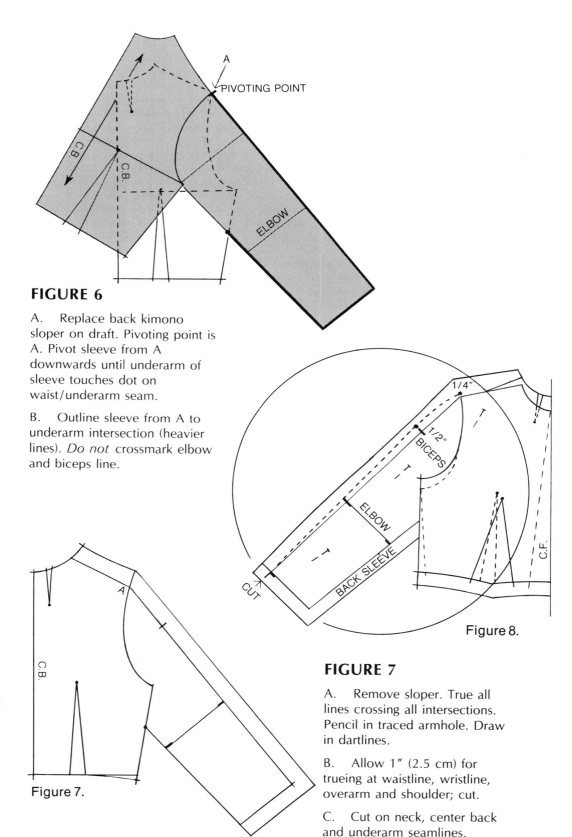

Figure 7.

Figure 8.

FIGURE 6

A.   Replace back kimono sloper on draft. Pivoting point is A. Pivot sleeve from A downwards until underarm of sleeve touches dot on waist/underarm seam.

B.   Outline sleeve from A to underarm intersection (heavier lines). *Do not* crossmark elbow and biceps line.

FIGURE 7

A.   Remove sloper. True all lines crossing all intersections. Pencil in traced armhole. Draw in dartlines.

B.   Allow 1" (2.5 cm) for trueing at waistline, wristline, overarm and shoulder; cut.

C.   Cut on neck, center back and underarm seamlines.

FIGURE 8

A.   To true overarm seam, with front draft face up match front to back at shoulder crossmark and wrist. Pin.
Note: 1.   Back sleeve will extend at underarm as it is wider than front sleeve. 2.   If pattern is developed accurately, shoulder and wrist will match. 3. Back shoulder should be ¼" (0.6 cm) longer than front shoulder.

B.   To true seam measure up from shoulder crossmark ¼" (0.6 cm) and ½" (1.3 cm) from biceps line and dot. Blend a slightly curved line from shoulder dot down through dots to nothing at wrist (broken line).

C.   Trace new overarm seam, crossmarks at biceps, elbow and wrist to opposite side.

D.   With draft in pinned position, cut excess paper away on new overarm seam up to dot on shoulder.

E.   Notch elbow, biceps and shoulder.

F.   Separate drafts. Blend a slightly curved line in front and back from shoulder dot to about 1" (2.5 cm) away from neckline.

G.   Check for accuracy of sleeve and waist underarm seams from underarm intersections. Adjust, if necessary, at wristline and waistline and cut away excess paper from front and back waistlines and wristlines.

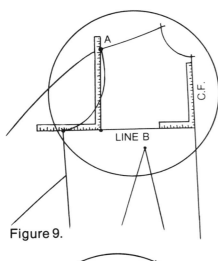

Figure 9.

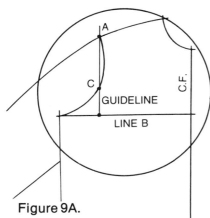

Figure 9A.

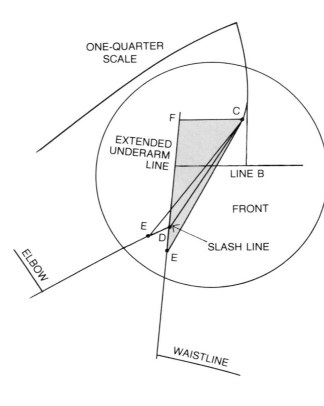

ONE-QUARTER SCALE

FIGURE 10 (ENLARGED DIAGRAM)

A.   To establish front gusset slash line, draw a line from C to underarm/armhole intersection. Dot. Label *D*.
Note: The front gusset slash line may be extended slightly higher or lower depending upon the fit desired. The higher the front gusset slash line, the closer the fit. Adjustment for fit and effect desired should be made when testing sloper in fabric.

B.   To establish front gusset seamline, measure down from D on waist and sleeve underarm seams 1" (2.5 cm) and dot. Label *E*.

C.   Draw lines from E to C.

D.   To develop front gusset section, extend underarm seam up above line B. Draw a line parallel to line B from C to extended underarm line. Label *F*. *Note:* Shaded area is the gusset section.

PLANNING FRONT GUSSET SLASH LINE FOR BALANCED GUSSET

FIGURES 9 & 9A

A.   Place an L-square on center front and square a line from center front to underarm. Label *line B*.

B.   Place L-square on line B touching A (as illustrated). Draw a line, very lightly, to line B and dot. Label *guideline* (Figure 9A).

C.   Measure line between dot and A. Place a dot on armhole one-third of measurement minus ¼" (0.6 cm). Label *C* (close up in Figure 9A).

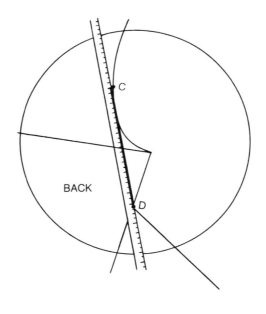

PLANNING BACK GUSSET SLASH LINE

FIGURE 11

Place ruler at underarm intersection touching a point on armhole equal to the length of front slash line. Label *C*. Draw line (darker line).

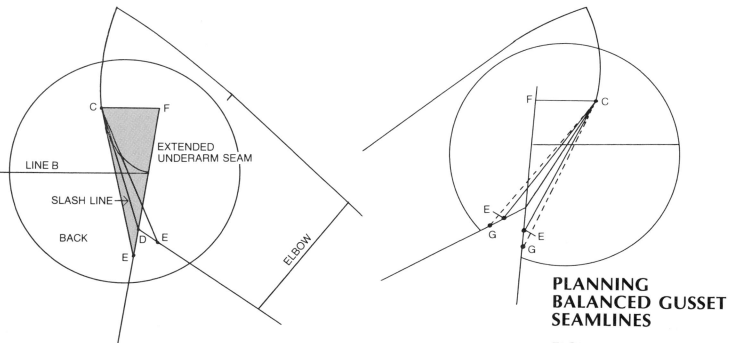

FIGURE 12

A.   To establish back gusset seamlines on waist and sleeve underarm seams measure down from D 1" (2.5 cm). Dot. Label each side *E.*

B.   Draw lines from E to C.

C.   To develop back gusset section extend underarm seam up above line B. Draw a line parallel to line B from C to extended underarm line. Label *F.* Note: Shaded area is the gusset section.

PLANNING BALANCED GUSSET SEAMLINES

FIGURE 13

Note: For a balanced gusset the four gusset seamlines must be the same length. It does not matter that the area between the seamlines varies. *However,* if the seam allowance is not sufficient on any one line, the crossmark at E must be lowered to obtain a ½" (1.3 cm) seam allowance. This adjustment must be made on all *four* seamlines in order to maintain the same length on front and back underarms.

If necessary, lower all lines at E ½" (1.3 cm). Dot. Label *G.* Draw lines from G to C (broken lines).

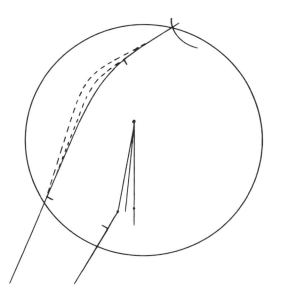

FIGURE 14

To achieve the look of a leg-o-mutton sleeve, as in sketch C, curve overarm seam (as illustrated).

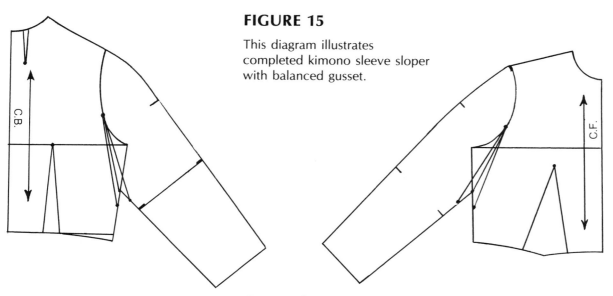

FIGURE 15

This diagram illustrates completed kimono sleeve sloper with balanced gusset.

Finished Sloper

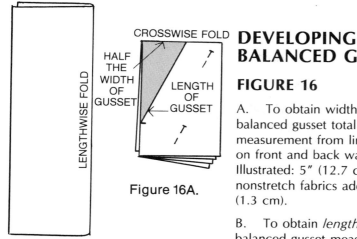

Figure 16A.

Figure 16.

DEVELOPING BALANCED GUSSET

FIGURE 16

A. To obtain width of balanced gusset total measurement from line F to C on front and back waists. Illustrated: 5″ (12.7 cm). For nonstretch fabrics add ½″ (1.3 cm).

B. To obtain *length* of balanced gusset measure line C to E. Illustrated: 6¼″ (15.9 cm).

C. Cut paper approximately 18″ (45.7 cm) square.

D. Accurately fold paper in half lengthwise and then in half crosswise. Pin.

E. On crosswise fold measure one half the total gusset width. Crossmark.

F. From crossmark draw a line down to lengthwise fold to equal length of gusset.

G. With gusset draft in pinned position cut.

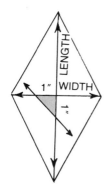

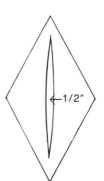

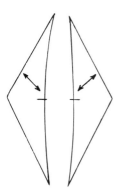

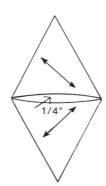

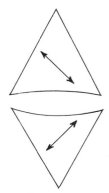

Figure 17.
One-Piece
Gusset

Figure 17A.
Gusset with
Vertical Dart

Figure 17B.
Two-Piece
Gusset

Figure 17C.
Gusset with
Horizontal Dart

Figure 17D.
Two-Piece
Gusset

FIGURES 17, 17A, 17B, 17C, 17D

Open gusset. Establish lengthwise and crosswise grainlines on creased lines and establish bias grainlines (as illustrated).

Note: For gusset to fit the contour of the underarm a ½" (1.3 cm) vertical dart may be picked up at the center of gusset or a ¼" (0.6 cm) horizontal dart. Gussets may also be cut in two pieces (Figures 17A, B, C D).

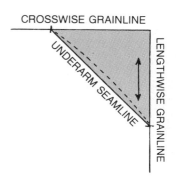

FIGURE 18

Note: The development of the gussets described in Figures 16 and 17 gives maximum arm movement whereby the arm can be raised directly above the head (as illustrated). However, if a shorter gusset is preferred, develop as follows:

A.   On single sheet of paper draw a right angle. Label corner *A*.

B.   From A measure on lengthwise and crosswise grain, the length of gusset required. Crossmark each end.

C.   Draw a line between crossmark and A. Curve seam if desired.

Note: 1.   With this method the seamlines joined to the garment are on the straight grain and act as a stay, therefore, preventing the gusset slash line from stretching. 2.   This sloper may be used as a pattern. Allow seams on kimono sleeve waist and gusset developed.

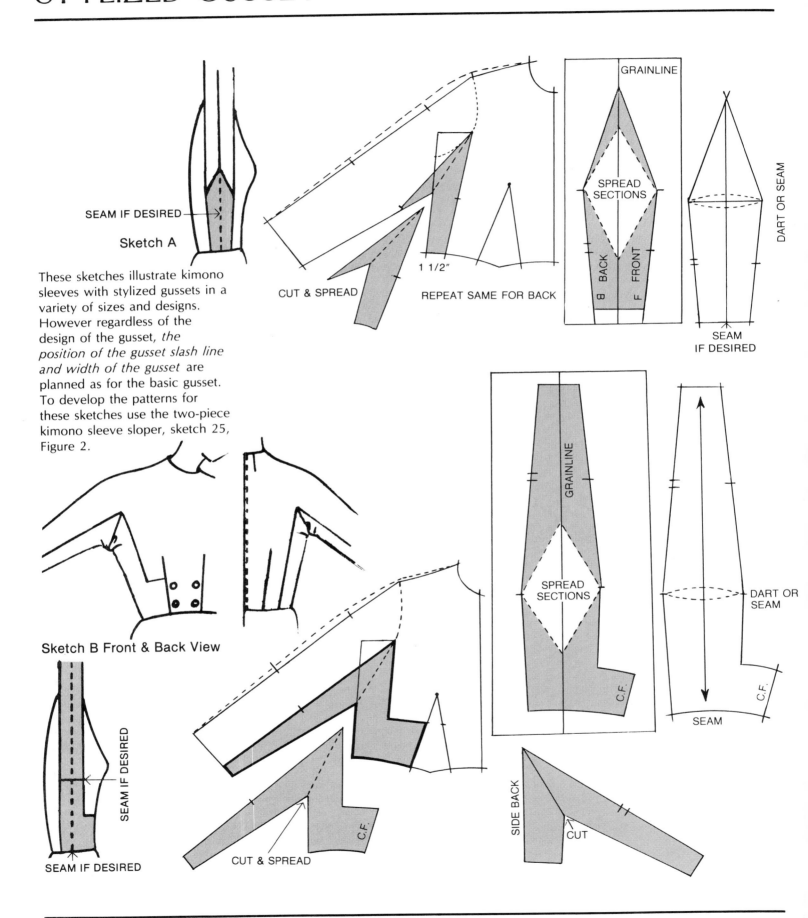

SEAM IF DESIRED

Sketch A

These sketches illustrate kimono sleeves with stylized gussets in a variety of sizes and designs. However regardless of the design of the gusset, *the position of the gusset slash line and width of the gusset* are planned as for the basic gusset. To develop the patterns for these sketches use the two-piece kimono sleeve sloper, sketch 25, Figure 2.

CUT & SPREAD

1 1/2"

REPEAT SAME FOR BACK

GRAINLINE

SPREAD SECTIONS

BACK

FRONT

B

F

DART OR SEAM

SEAM IF DESIRED

Sketch B Front & Back View

SEAM IF DESIRED

SEAM IF DESIRED

CUT & SPREAD

C.F.

GRAINLINE

SPREAD SECTIONS

C.F.

DART OR SEAM

SEAM

C.F.

SIDE BACK

CUT

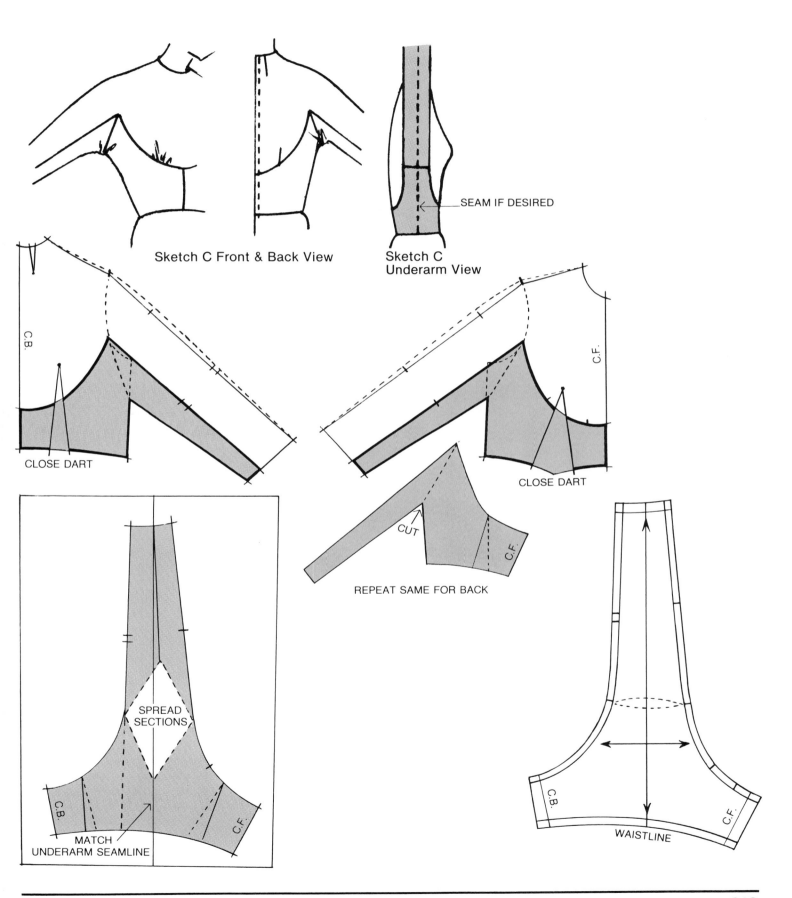

Sketch C Front & Back View

SEAM IF DESIRED

Sketch C
Underarm View

C.B.

CLOSE DART

C.F.

CLOSE DART

CUT

C.F.

REPEAT SAME FOR BACK

SPREAD
SECTIONS

C.B.

C.F.

MATCH
UNDERARM SEAMLINE

C.B.

C.F.

WAISTLINE

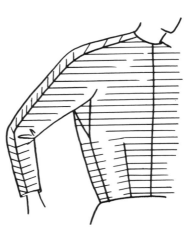

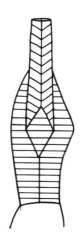

Sketch A Front & Underarm View

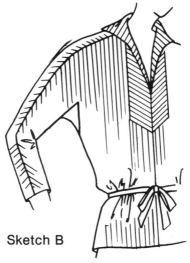

Sketch B

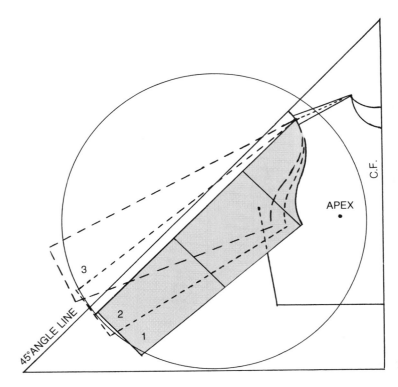

FIGURE 1

Diagram illustrates pivoted positions for sleeve:

Position 1—Sleeve is pivoted to 45° angle, the maximum position for this sleeve. It has the characteristics of a set-in sleeve and requires the longest gusset. Depending upon the sloper used, the sleeve, when pivoted to the 45° angle may end too close to the waistline at the underarm seam. In this case it is advisable to style the gusset as shown in sketch 29, Figure 1.

Positions 2 and 3—These sleeves will not hang like set-in sleeves and require smaller gussets. Sleeve may also be pivoted up to point where wrist end of underarm of sleeve is in line with waistline, the highest position for this kimono which still requires a gusset.

Matching stripes, plaids and checks can only be achieved when working with designs which have been woven into the fabric. Printed designs are often printed off grain, therefore, making it difficult to match the pattern and keep the garment cut on the proper grain.

Use the following basic slopers

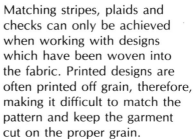

　　1.　two-dart front waist sloper

　　2.　back waist sloper with shoulder and waistline darts

　　3.　straight sleeve sloper

FIGURE 2

A.   Cut paper approximately 36″ (91.4 cm) square.

B.   Draw a right angle 31″ (78.7 cm) long across the bottom and up the right-hand edge of the paper. Dot each end. Draw a diagonal line between dots. Label diagonal line, *45° angle* (true bias) and vertical line, *center front*.
Note: Right angle and diagonal line must be accurate or problems will arise when developing draft and matching pattern on fabric.

C.   Place front waist sloper on paper matching center front on sloper to center front on paper with shoulder/armhole intersection ½″ (1.3 cm) away from 45° angle line.

D.   Crossmark shoulder dartline nearest center front and dot neck/shoulderline intersection. Outline neckline, center front, underarm seam to armhole and dot. Crossmark waistline/center front intersection. Indicate apex with awl.
Note: It is not necessary to indicate waistline dart. If dart or darts are desired, they should be planned within the pattern of the fabric used.

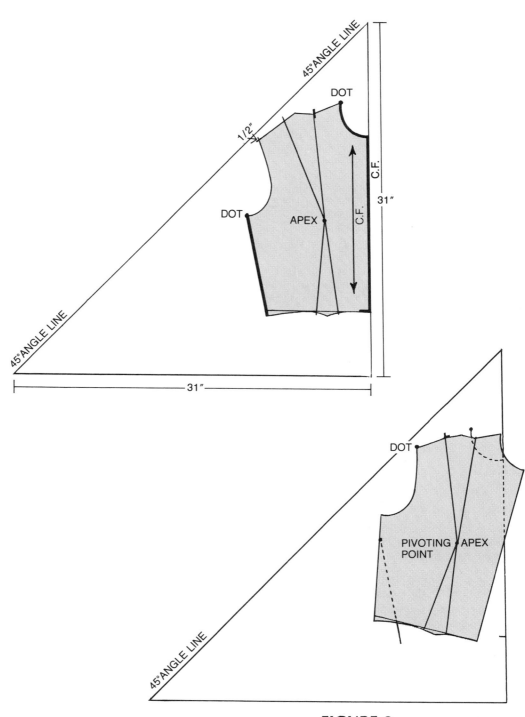

FIGURE 3

A.   Pivoting point is apex.

B.   Pivot sloper from apex and close shoulder dart. Dot end of shoulderline.

FIGURE 4

A. Remove sloper. Draw a straight line between shoulder dots.

B. Square a line from center front to dot at underarm. Draw a short line from dot for guideline (darker line).

C. Square a line from waistline to underarm. Label *new waistline.*

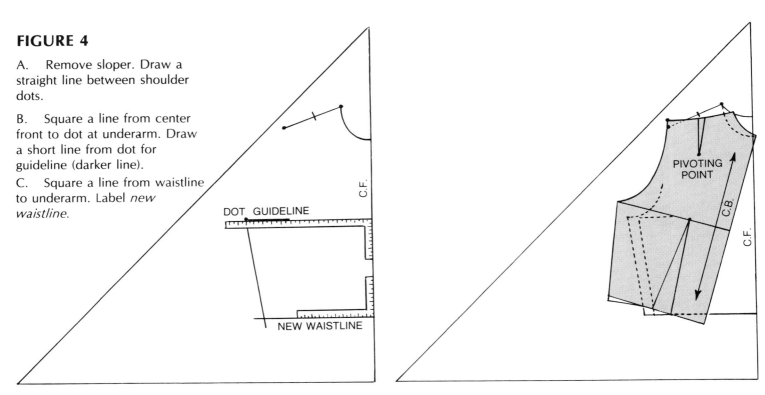

FIGURE 5

A. Match underarm of back waist sloper to dot on front underarm. Move sloper on guideline until center back touches center front.

B. Dot neck/shoulderline intersection. Outline neck, underarm and lower half of armhole (darker lines).
Note: Position of front and back neck/shoulderline intersections may differ than illustrated in Figure 5. The difference depends upon the position of the shoulderlines on the sloper. Regardless of the shoulder position, adjustment will be shown in Figure 7 to balance shoulder for matching stripes, plaids and checks.

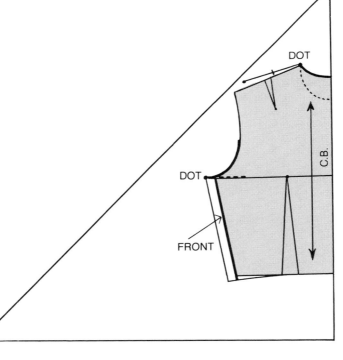

FIGURE 6

To eliminate back shoulder dart pivot sloper from end of shoulder dart until end of back shoulder is in line with front shoulder dot. Back shoulder may fall above, below or on front shoulder. Dot end of back shoulder. Remove sloper. Draw a line from shoulder dot to back neckline dot.

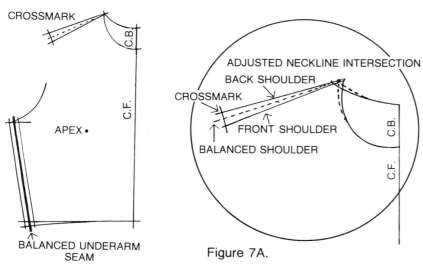

Figure 7

Figure 7A.

FIGURES 7, 7A, 7B, 7C

A.   To balance shoulderline draw a line between back and front shoulderlines to neckline intersection (broken line). Crossmark end of shoulder.

B.   The following are examples of balancing shoulder and neckline variations (enlarged diagrams):

> 1.   *Figure 7A*—adjusting neckline, if necessary, (broken lines of neck and shoulder).
>
> 2.   *Figure 7B*—end of front and back shoulders touching.
>
> 3.   *Figure 7C*—overlapping shoulder at neckline (broken line of neck and shoulder).

C.   To balance underarm seam draw a line between original front and back seams (as illustrated).

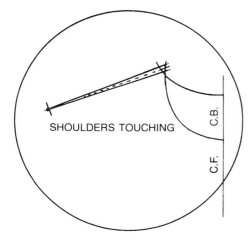

Figure 7B.

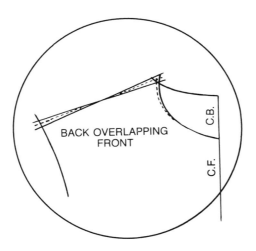

Figure 7C.

FIGURE 8

A.   With sleeve sloper folded, match top of sleeve cap to crossmark of adjusted shoulderline on draft.

B.   Pivot sloper from this point downwards until fold of sleeve is parallel to 45° angle line.

C.   Outline sleeve ending at adjusted underarm seam (heavier lines). Crossmark elbow and biceps lines. Remove sloper. True all lines crossing all intersections.

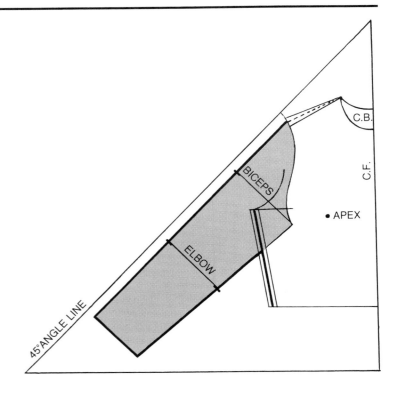

FIGURE 9

A.   To true overarm seam measure up ¼" (0.6 cm) from shoulder crossmark and ½" (1.3 cm) from biceps line and dot. Blend a slightly curved line from center of back shoulder through dots and down to nothing at wrist.

B.   Establish stripe guideline by squaring a line through apex.

C.   Drop waistline at underarm ¼" (0.6 cm). Blend a slightly curved line into waistline.

D.   To develop gusset slash and seamlines refer to sketch 28, Figures 9, 9A and 10.
Note: To regain some of the width lost across bust, due to balancing seams, back armhole will be used for planning gusset.

E.   To develop *gusset* refer to sketch 28, Figures 9 through 18 with the following exception:

Do not allow ½" (1.3 cm) for ease on gusset as stripe on fabric will not match.

F.   By balancing all seams for matching stripes on fabric, front and back slopers must be the same with the exception of the front and back necklines. To develop back sloper, place front draft onto another sheet of paper. Pin securely to prevent shifting when cutting and tracing.

G.   Cut accurately on all finished lines following back neckline. Lift front neck section and cut on front neckline.

H.   Notch crossmarks at shoulder, stripe guideline, biceps and elbow on underarm seam.

I.   Trace both gusset lines to opposite side. With awl indicate top of gusset lines.

J.   Turn draft to opposite side and draw a line between crossmarks. Label *stripe line.* Pencil in gusset lines and dot. Label *center back.*

K.   Separate slopers.

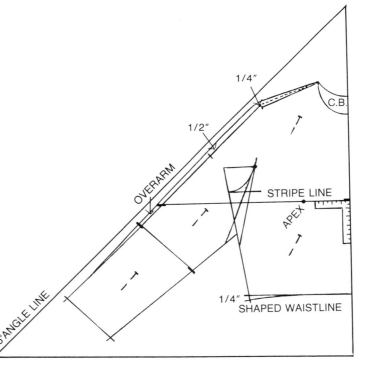

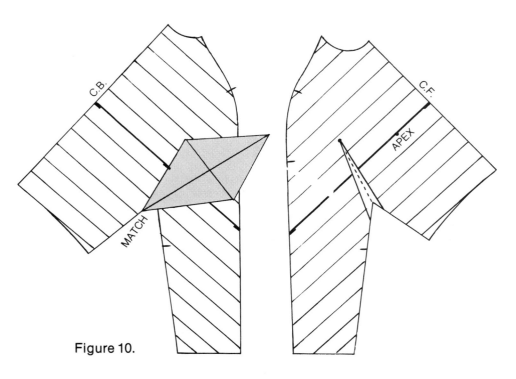

Figure 10.

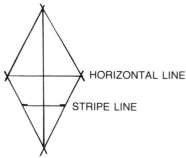

HORIZONTAL LINE

STRIPE LINE

FIGURE 10

A.   To establish stripe line on gusset match one side of gusset to gusset seamline on waist. Dot stripe line on gusset (as illustrated).

B.   Remove gusset. Draw a line from dot parallel to horizontal crease line. Label *stripe line*.
Note: 1.   Stripes on gusset will match *only* at waist/underarm seam not at sleeve underarm. .
2.   Diagram has been drawn to illustrate how stripes will match on garment and gusset.

SKETCH B
TORSO WAIST

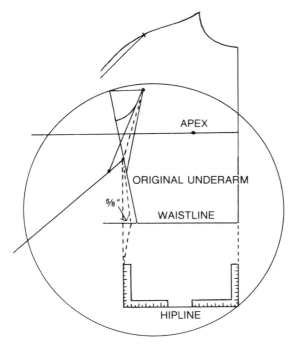

FIGURE 11

A.   Establish torso lines by squaring lines (as illustrated).

B.   If desired, shape waistline ⅝" (1.6 cm).

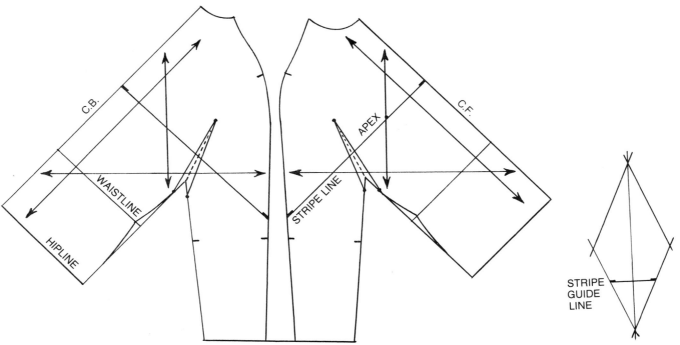

Figure 12. Finished Long Torso Sloper

FIGURE 12

A.   This diagram illustrates a Finished Torso Length Sloper showing stripe line variations which may also be applied to a waist length sloper.

B.   Gusset stripe line must be adjusted to match torso stripe line selected.

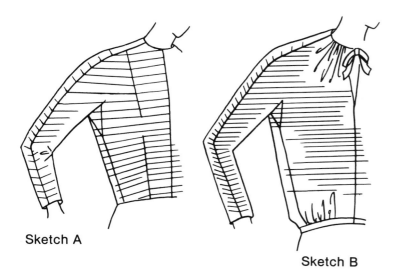

Sketch A

Sketch B

SKETCH A

This kimono sloper with shoulder and waistline darts retains:

A.   The original fit across the bustline as that of the basic two-dart front waist sloper, however, the shoulder dart underlay will not be as deep as the shoulder dart on the basic front waist sloper since seams must balance so that stripes, plaids and checks will match.

B.   The matching of stripes on all major seams.

C.   The hang of the set-in sleeve.

Use the following basic slopers:

   1.   two-dart front waist sloper

   2.   back waist sloper with neckline dart

   3.   straight sleeve sloper

FIGURE 1

A.   Cut paper approximately 36″ (91.4 cm) square.

B.   Draw a vertical line the full length of the paper near right-hand edge. Label *guideline*.

C.   From guideline measure in 2″ (5.1 cm). Label *center back*. Draw a right angle 31″ (78.7 cm) long across the bottom and up center back. Dot each end. Draw a diagonal line between dots. Label diagonal line *45° angle line* (true bias).

D.   Place back waist sloper on paper matching center back on sloper to center back on paper with end of shoulder ½″ (1.3 cm) away from 45° angle line.

E.   Dot both ends of shoulder. Outline neckline, neckline dart, armhole, underarm seam. Crossmark waistline at center back intersection. With awl indicate bottom of neck dart.

F.   Remove sloper. Draw a straight line between shoulder dots.

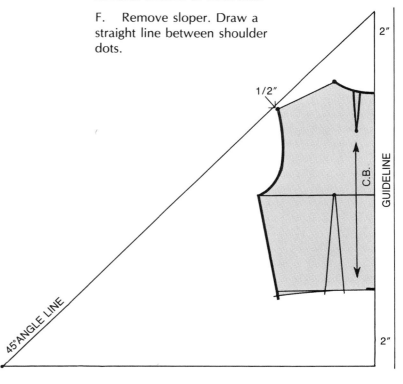

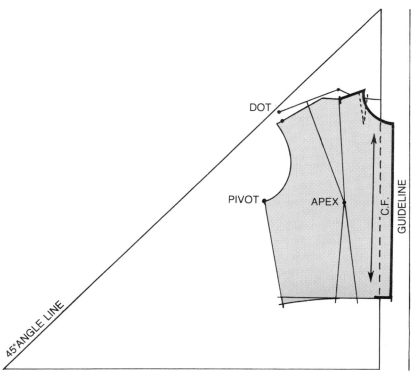

Figure 2.

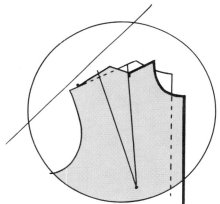

Figure 2A.

FIGURES 2 & 2A

A.   Match underarm of front waist sloper to back underarm/armhole intersection. Pivot sloper from this point until center front is parallel to guideline on paper.
Note: Center front will extend beyond center back from ½" to 2" (1.3 to 5.1 cm) depending upon the size of the bust.

B.   Front shoulder may end below back shoulder (Figure 2) touch back shoulder (Figure 2A) or end above back shoulder (not illustrated). Front shoulder will extend beyond back shoulder regardless of position. Dot end of front shoulder in line with back shoulder dot.

C.   Crossmark dartline nearest neckline. From crossmark outline shoulder, neckline, center front. Crossmark waistline at center front intersection.

D.   Indicate apex with awl.

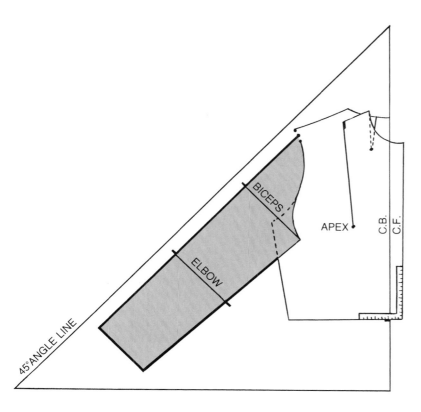

FIGURE 4

A.   Remove sloper. Square a line from center front through apex across paper. Label *stripe line.*

B.   To true overarm seam measure up ¼" (0.6 cm) from shoulder dot and ½" (1.3 cm) from biceps line and dot. Blend a slightly curved line from center of back shoulder through dots and down to nothing at wrist.

C.   To develop *gusset slash* and *seamlines* refer to sketch 28, Figures 9 through 18.

D.   To develop *gusset* refer to sketch 28, Figure 16 with the following exception:

Do not allow ½" (1.3 cm) for ease on gusset as stripes on fabric will not match.

E.   Drop waistline at underarm ¼" (0.6 cm). Blend a slightly curved line into waistline.

FIGURE 3

A.   Remove sloper. Square a line from crossmarks at waistline/center front to back underarm seam.

B.   Draw a line from shoulder crossmark to apex.

C.   To balance shoulder, dot between back and front shoulders at armhole.
Note: If shoulders touch as in Figures 2A, use original dot.

D.   With sleeve sloper folded match sleeve to center shoulder dot on draft. Pivot sloper from this point downwards until fold of sleeve is parallel to 45° angle line.

E.   Outline sleeve (darker lines). Crossmarks biceps and elbow lines.

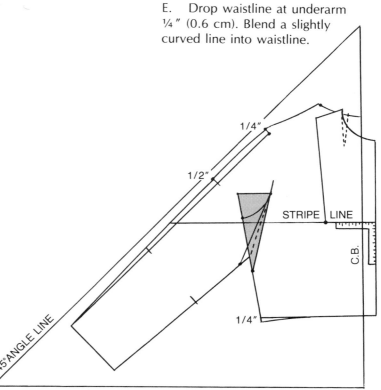

FIGURE 5

A.   By balancing all seams for matching stripes, front and back slopers are the same with the exception of the front and back shoulderlines. To develop back sloper, place front draft onto another sheet of paper. Pin securely to prevent shifting when cutting and tracing.

B.   Cut accurately starting with *center front,* waistline, underarm at waist and sleeve, wrist and overarm to shoulder dot. At dot cut above shoulder, allowing paper to true neck and front shoulderlines.

C.   Trace back shoulder, neckline, neckline dart, center back, gusset seamlines and a shoulder crossmark through shoulder dots to opposite side. With awl indicate top of gusset lines.

D.   Notch crossmarks at stripe guide line, shoulder biceps and elbow on over- and underarm seams.

E.   Turn draft to opposite side and draw a line between stripe crossmarks. Label *stripe line.* Pencil in all traced lines.

F.   Separate sections. Cut excess paper from back shoulder, neckline and center back. Label *center back.*

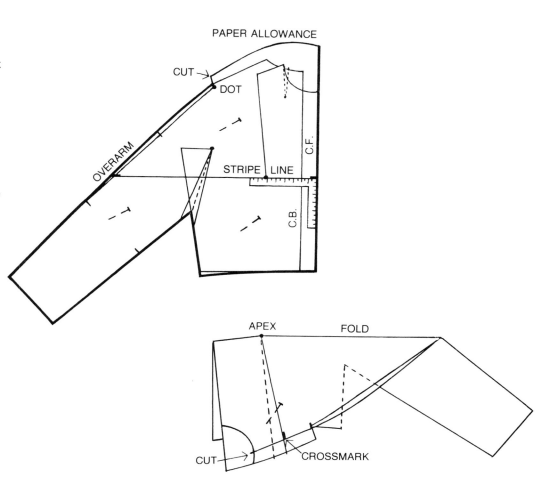

FIGURE 6

A.   To true front shoulder dart:

1.   Measure length of back shoulder.

2.   Crease front dartline. Cup at apex and move fold of dart towards armhole until front shoulder measures the same as back shoulder. Crease and pin.

B.   Draw a straight line from neckline to shoulder crossmark. Blend line into overarm.

C.   Crossmark against fold of dartline.

D.   With dart in pinned position, cut excess paper from front shoulder and neckline.

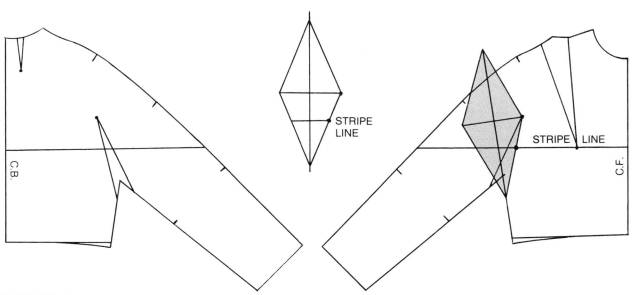

FIGURE 7

A.   Open draft. Draw a straight line from crossmark at shoulder dart to apex.

B.   To establish stripe line in gusset match side of gusset to gusset seamline on waist. Dot stripe line on gusset.

C.   Remove gusset. From dot draw a stripe line parallel to horizontal line. Label *stripe line*. Note: 1.   Stripes on gusset will match only at waist/underarm seam not at sleeve underarm.
2.   If fitted waistline is desired, plan darts within the stripes.

SKETCH B
TORSO WAIST

A.   To develop torso length sloper follow instructions given for sketch 30, Figure 11.

B.   To develop pattern for this sketch pivot shoulder dart into neckline for shirring.

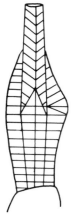

**Sketch A
Underarm View**

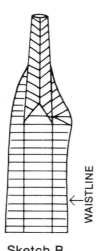

**Sketch B
Underarm View**

WAISTLINE

Sketch C

With the introduction of an underarm dart on a 45° angle kimono sleeve, the space between gusset seamlines is often lost since seamline may extend to or beyond waistline. Therefore, it is advisable to develop a stylized gusset. The seamlines will not be obvious as they will be absorbed when matching the stripes.

Use the kimono sloper with gusset developed in sketch 30, Figure 10.

SKETCH A

FIGURE 1

A.   Cut paper approximately 30″ (76.2 cm) square.

B.   Draw a vertical line the full length and near right-hand edge of paper. Label *center front.*

C.   Place center front of kimono sloper to center front of paper. Outline sloper.

D.   Indicate all crossmarks, dots at end of gusset lines and underarm intersection. With awl indicate top of gusset line and apex.

E.   Remove sloper. True all lines crossing all intersections and extend waistline at underarm seam (as illustrated).

F.   Pencil in stripe and gusset lines. Dot underarm intersection and apex. Dot top of gusset line and label *A.*

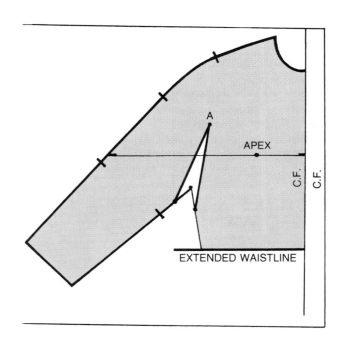

FIGURE 2

A.   Square a line up from extended waistline to underarm dot.

B.   Place back waist sloper over draft matching centers and shoulders. Outline back neckline. Remove sloper.

C.   To establish stylized gusset line, draw a line parallel to center front from A extending line below waistline.

D.   Place draft onto another sheet of paper. Pin securely to prevent shifting when cutting and tracing.

E.   Cut out draft following heavier lines (as illustrated). Lift front neck section and cut on front neckline.

F.   Trace all gusset lines and waistline to opposite side.

G.   Notch shoulder, stripe, biceps and elbow lines.

H.   Turn draft to opposite side. Pencil in traced gusset lines and connect stripe line notches. Label *center back.*

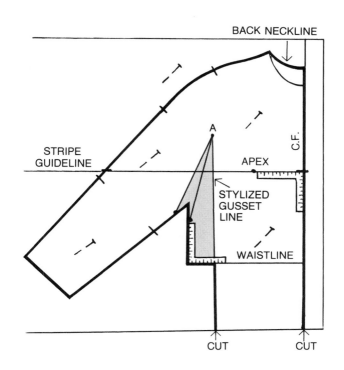

FIGURE 3

Separate sections and cut away excess paper from *back stylized gusset lines* and *waistline.* Note: Diagram and following diagrams have been drawn to illustrate how stripes will match on garments and gussets.

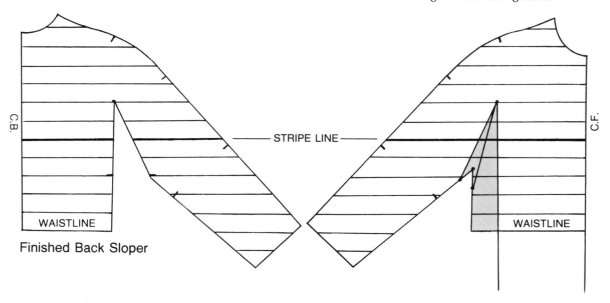

Finished Back Sloper

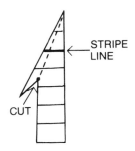

FIGURE 4

A.   Copy front stylized gusset section (shaded area in Figure 3). Indicate stripe line.

B.   Cut on all finished lines. Draw a broken line from intersection to A.

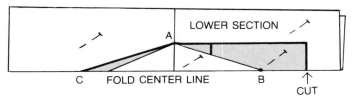

FIGURE 5

Since front and back stylized gusset lines are the same, the gusset may be developed on the fold.

A.   Cut paper approximately 10″ × 27″ (25.4 × 68.6 cm).

B.   Fold paper in half lengthwise. Approximately at center of paper square a line from fold to edge.

C.   Cut gusset section from intersection up to A (see Figure 4).

D.   Pin lower section to fold with A at center line of paper. Pin and label *B* (as illustrated).

E.   If sleeve section of gusset is too narrow to handle, measure from B to center line on fold and repeat this measurement to the left of center line. Dot and label *C*. Draw a line between A and C (darker line).

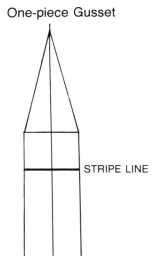

One-piece Gusset

FIGURE 6

A.   Cut on all finished lines. Trace stripe line to opposite side. Open paper and continue stripe line across paper.

B.   This one-piece gusset when set into the garment results in a boxy look (sketch B). If a semi- or fitted garment is desired as in sketch A, refer to Figure 6A.

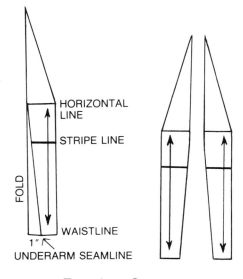

Two-piece Gusset

FIGURE 6A

A.   Refold gusset. From fold at waistline measure in 1″ (2.5 cm). Draw a line to fold at horizontal line. Cut on new line. Open paper and cut on fold line making a two-piece gusset.

B.   For a fitted waist, plan a dart at waistline of front and back waists.

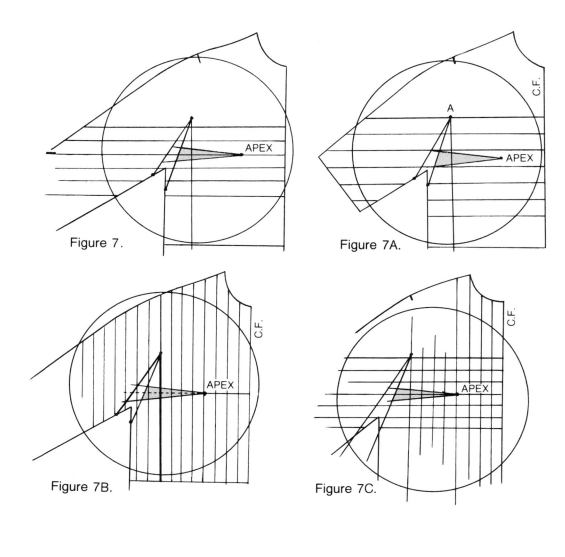

Figure 7.

Figure 7A.

Figure 7B.

Figure 7C.

DEVELOPING UNDERARM DART

FIGURES 7, 7A, 7B, 7C

The stripes on the fabric must be analyzed as to how the dart will fit into a "repeat."

Figure 7—the dart, starting at the apex, may be in line with the stripe.

Figure 7A—the dart may start at the center of a repeat.

Figure 7B—the center of the dart must be on grain when working with vertical stripes.

Figure 7C—the center of the dart must be on grain when working with checks and plaids.

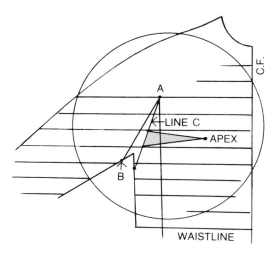

WAISTLINE

FIGURE 8

A.   Label gusset lines *B* and *C* (as illustrated).

B.   Establish two dartlines from apex to line C for dart underlay. *Note:* To match stripes from dart to hemline follow these rules: 1.   Illustrated: 1½" (3.8 cm) repeat. Center of repeat was planned to be in line with apex. 2.   For smaller repeats such as ¼", ½" or ¾" (0.6, 1.3, 1.9 cm), two or more repeats may be used for underlay. Underlay should not exceed 1½" (3.8 cm). 3.   When working on large figure types, dart underlay may need to be deeper than 1½" (3.8 cm). Regardless of size of garment, the darts must be planned within the repeat.

FIGURE 9

A.   Cut sleeve gusset line from B to A.

B.   Square a line from center front to apex and cut (broken line).

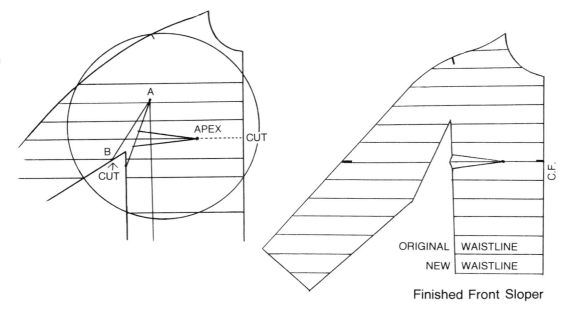

Finished Front Sloper

FIGURE 10

A.   Close dart by creasing lower dartline and pin onto upper dartline.

B.   To obtain a smooth working area, lift sleeve section over extended end of pinned dart.

C.   With dart in pinned position, blend line at dart (as illustrated). Cut excess paper from gusset line starting at C and up to A.

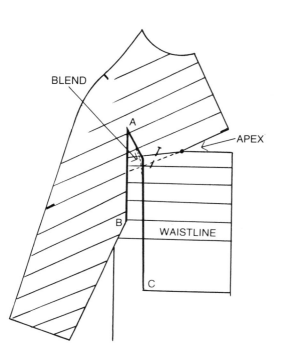

FIGURE 11

A.   With the introduction of the underarm dart, the front waistline and underarm seam is shortened the depth of the dart underlay or repeat. In this project the repeat was 1½" (3.8 cm). To restore the original length to the front, add amount at waistline to equal the depth of the dart underlay (as illustrated).

B.   Cut away excess paper from new waistline.

SKETCH C

A.   To develop this sketch lengthen sloper from new waistline length desired.

B.   Use straight gusset as in Figure 6 and lengthen gusset same amount as in waist.

C.   Add a stitched band to front of garment and at bottom of sleeve.

D.   To plan buttonholes refer to Buttons & Buttonholes.

E.   To develop collar refer to Mandarin Collar.

The procedure for developing the dolman/batwing sleeve is to use the kimono sloper and pivot the sleeve section upwards. The higher the sleeve is pivoted, the longer the underarm seam resulting in a draped look.

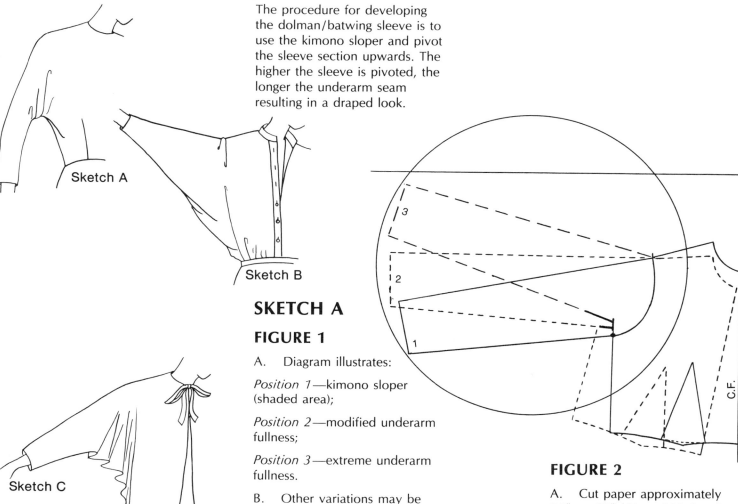

Sketch A

Sketch B

Sketch C

SKETCH A

FIGURE 1

A.   Diagram illustrates:

Position 1—kimono sloper (shaded area);

Position 2—modified underarm fullness;

Position 3—extreme underarm fullness.

B.   Other variations may be achieved by pivoting to any point between positions 1 and 3 (as illustrated).

FIGURE 2

A.   Cut paper approximately 24″ × 40″ (61 × 101.6 cm).

B.   Use two-piece kimono sloper, sketch 25.

C.   Place center front of sloper towards right-hand side and near bottom edge of paper.

D.   Dot shoulder and label *A*. Outline sloper from A to underarm intersection (heavier lines). Label overarm/wrist intersection *B*.

E.   With sloper in this position, place a ruler in line with wrist. Measure up from B height of dolman sleeve desired. Illustrated: 4″ (10.2 cm). Place a crossmark parallel to B on overarm seam. Label *C*.

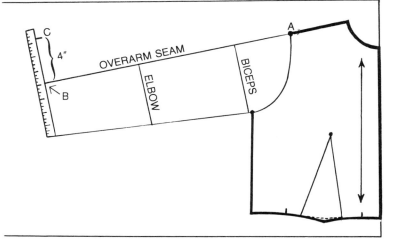

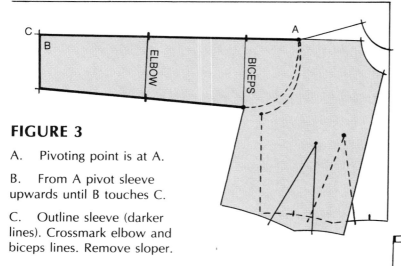

FIGURE 3

A.   Pivoting point is at A.

B.   From A pivot sleeve upwards until B touches C.

C.   Outline sleeve (darker lines). Crossmark elbow and biceps lines. Remove sloper.

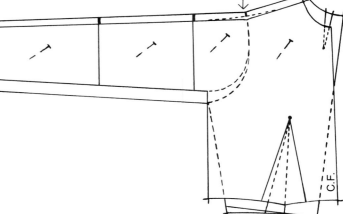

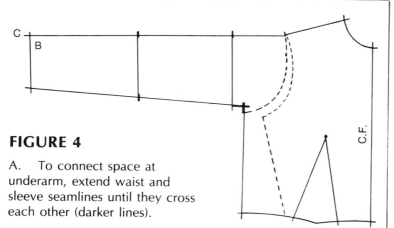

FIGURE 4

A.   To connect space at underarm, extend waist and sleeve seamlines until they cross each other (darker lines).

B.   True all lines crossing all intersections.

C.   To develop pattern for back, follow same procedure as for front with the following exception:

Do not crossmark at elbow and biceps lines.

FIGURE 5

A.   To true front and back overarm seam, with front face up match overarm from shoulder crossmarks to wrist. Pin patterns.
Note: If patterns are developed accurately, these points should match and the back shoulder should extend ¼" (0.6 cm) at neckline for the back shoulder ease.

B.   Blend at shoulder (broken line). Trace shoulder, biceps, elbow and wrist crossmarks on overarm seam to opposite side (heavier lines).

C.   With drafts in pinned position, allow seam and cut overarm seam to neckline. Notch crossmarks. Separate drafts.

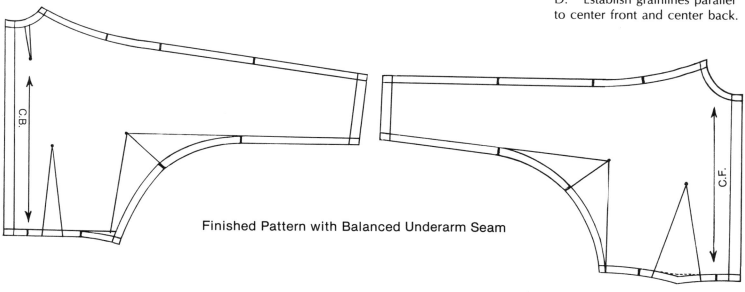

FIGURE 6

A. To true front and back underarm seam, with front face up match underarm from armhole intersection to wrist. Pin patterns.

B. Draw a diagonal line from intersection through the approximate center between elbow and waistline.

C. Draw desired underarm curve from wrist or elbow to depth desired to diagonal line. Heavier and broken lines indicate variations.

Note: Depth of underarm curve depends upon height to which sleeve is pivoted. The higher the sleeve is pivoted, the lower the curve may be planned as the length of the underarm lost in lowering the curve has been made up by the lengthening of the seam when the sleeve is pivoted upwards.

D. To complete pattern with *unbalanced underarm seams* place a crossmark at elbow and diagonal line. From wrist trace crossmarks and underarm curve to diagonal line to opposite side.

FIGURE 7

A. Separate drafts. Place opposite to each other. Pencil in traced lines and crossmarks.

B. Continue underarm curve from diagonal line down to waistline on both front and back waist.

C. Allow seams on remainder of pattern; cut and notch seams.

D. Establish grainlines parallel to center front and center back.

Finished Pattern with Balanced Underarm Seam

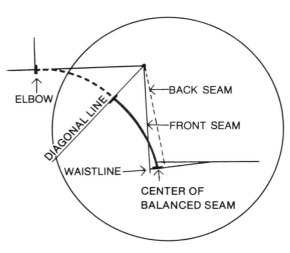

FIGURE 7A

To complete pattern with *balanced underarm seams:*

A.   With drafts in pinned position, continue underarm curve from diagonal line to *center* between front and back underarm seam at waistline. Trace to opposite side (darker line).

B.   Place a crossmark at waistline/underarm intersection. Trace to opposite side.

C.   Allow seam on underarm; cut and notch seam.

D.   Separate drafts. Pencil in traced lines and crossmarks. Blend front and back waistline to crossmark at underarm intersection.

E.   Allow seams on remainder of pattern; cut and notch seams.

F.   Establish grainline parallel to center front and center back.

SKETCH B

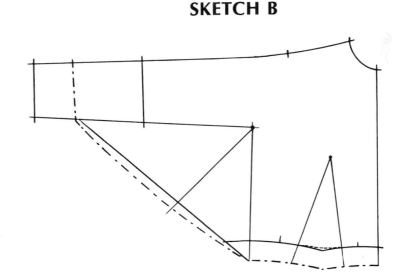

FIGURE 8

A.   To develop pattern for this sketch, follow same procedure as for sketch A.

B.   See illustration for shaping of dolman sleeve line.

C.   For a more blouson effect, lower waistline at center front desired amount. Draw a new waistline from center front to underarm seam before planning the curved underarm seam.

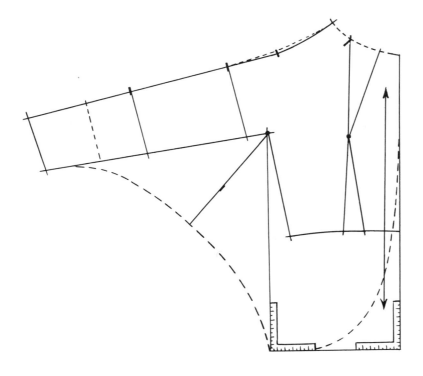

SKETCH C

FIGURE 9

A.   To develop this pattern use two-dart kimono sloper and follow same procedure as for sketch A.

B.   Pivot shoulder dart into neckline for neckline shirring.

C.   Draw a line parallel to center front from underarm intersection to desired length of tunic.

D.   Square a line from underarm towards and up at center front.

E.   Establish desired sleeve length and underarm curve. Blend underarm to bottom of tunic (broken line).

F.   Establish desired center front curved line to underarm seam (broken line).

G.   To develop pattern for back extend underarm seam same amount as front.

H.   To true and complete overarm and underarm seams follow instructions given for sketch A, Figure 5 (overarm seam) and Figure 6 (underarm seam).

I.   Establish grainline parallel to center front and center back.

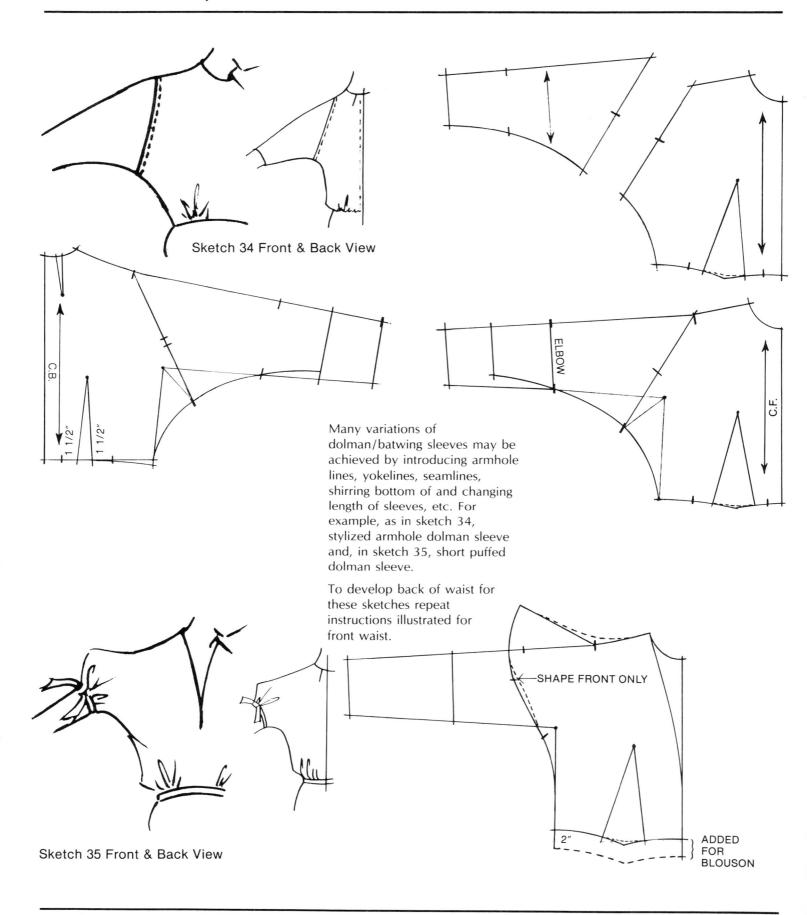

Sketch 34 Front & Back View

C.B.

1 1/2" 1 1/2"

ELBOW

C.F.

Many variations of dolman/batwing sleeves may be achieved by introducing armhole lines, yokelines, seamlines, shirring bottom of and changing length of sleeves, etc. For example, as in sketch 34, stylized armhole dolman sleeve and, in sketch 35, short puffed dolman sleeve.

To develop back of waist for these sketches repeat instructions illustrated for front waist.

SHAPE FRONT ONLY

2"

ADDED FOR BLOUSON

Sketch 35 Front & Back View

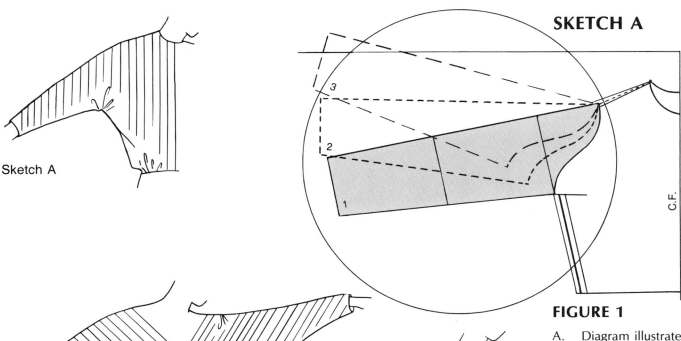

Sketch A

SKETCH A

Sketch B

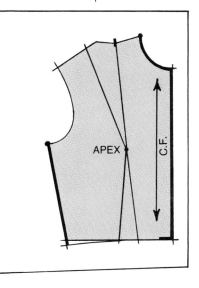

Sketch C

The procedure for pivoting the sleeve when developing the dolman/batwing sloper for stripes, plaids and checks is the same as for the basic dolman. However, the preparation of the front and back waist differs in that all seams must be balanced for matching before sleeve sloper can be applied for pivoting and establishing sleeve position.

Use the following basic slopers to develop this sloper:

1. two-dart front waist sloper

2. back waist sloper with shoulder and waistline darts

3. straight sleeve sloper

APEX C.F.

FIGURE 1

A.   Diagram illustrates:

Position 1—minimum underarm fullness. Sleeve armhole/underarm intersection touches waist underarm line;

Position 2—modified underarm fullness;

Position 3—extreme underarm fullness.

B.   Other variations may be achieved by pivoting sleeve to any point between positions 1 and 3.

FIGURE 2

A.   Cut paper approximately 36″ (91.4 cm) square.

B.   Place center front of sloper towards right-hand side and near bottom edge of paper.

C.   Crossmark shoulder dartline nearest neckline. Dot neck/shoulder and armhole/underarm intersections. Outline sloper (darker lines).

D.   Crossmark waistline/center front intersection (darker lines). With awl indicate apex.

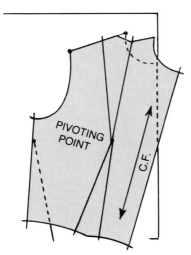

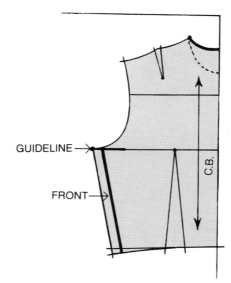

FIGURE 5

A. Match back waist underarm to front underarm dot. Move sloper on guideline until center back touches center front. *Note:* Back and front neck/shoulder intersections may differ than illustrated here. The difference depends upon the position of back and front shoulderlines on a sloper. Regardless of their position, adjustment will be made to balance neck/shoulder intersections for matching.

B. Dot back neck/shoulder intersection. Outline neck and underarm (darker line).

FIGURE 3

Pivot sloper from apex closing shoulder dart. Dot end of shoulder.

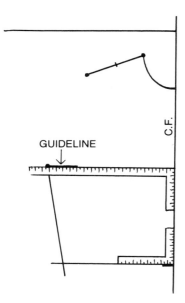

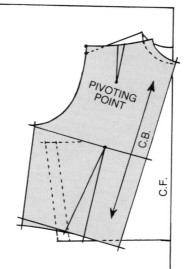

FIGURE 6

A. To eliminate back shoulder dart pivot sloper from bottom of shoulder dart until end of shoulder is directly above, below or touching end of front shoulder. Dot end of back shoulder.

B. Remove sloper.

FIGURE 4

A. Remove sloper. Draw a line between dots at shoulder.

B. Place L-square from center front to underarm dot (as illustrated). Draw a short guideline from dot (darker line).

C. Square a line from crossmark at center front to underarm seam (as illustrated).

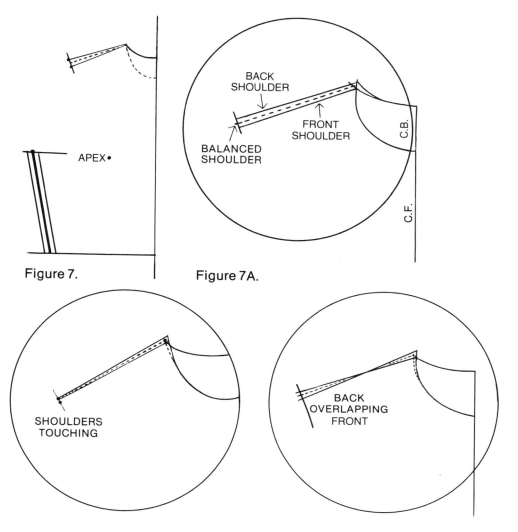

Figure 7.   Figure 7A.

Figure 7B.   Figure 7C.

FIGURE 8

A.   Place cap of folded sleeve sloper to adjusted shoulder. Pivot sleeve from this point upwards to height desired. Illustrated: Position 1—minimum underarm fullness.

B.   Outline sleeve and crossmark elbow and biceps.

C.   Remove sloper. True all lines crossing all intersections.

FIGURES 7, 7A, 7B, 7C

A.   To balance shoulderline draw a broken line between back and front shoulders to neckline intersection. Adjust neckline if necessary (Figures 7A, 7B, 7C).

B.   Crossmark shoulder (as illustrated).

C.   To balance underarm seam draw a line between original front and back seams (darker line).

Figure 8.

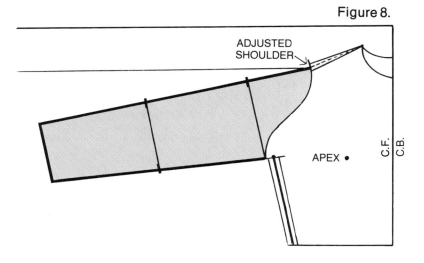

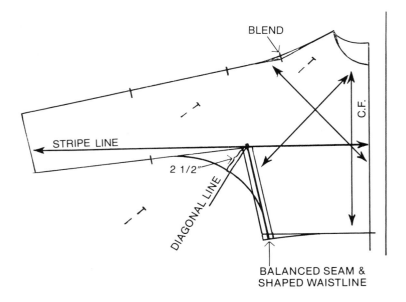

BLEND

STRIPE LINE

2 1/2"

DIAGONAL LINE

C.F.

BALANCED SEAM & SHAPED WAISTLINE

FIGURE 9

Note: Depth of underarm curve depends upon height to which sleeve is pivoted. Refer to Basic Dolman/Batwing Sleeve, Figure 6, C and Note.

A.   Draw a diagonal line from dot at underarm intersection through approximate center between elbow and waistline. Illustrated: 2½" (6.4 cm).

B.   Draw a curved line from elbow through diagonal line down to the balanced underarm seam at waistline.

C.   Establish stripe guideline by squaring a line from center front across draft crossing through dot. See illustration for other stripe line variations.

D.   Blend line at shoulder crossmark.

E.   Add ¼" (0.6 cm) to waistline at underarm. Blend into waistline with a curved line (as illustrated).

F.   Due to balancing all seams for matching stripes, front and back are the same with the exception of the necklines. To develop back sloper place front draft onto another sheet of paper. Pin securely to prevent shifting when cutting and tracing.

G.   Cut accurately on all finished lines following back neckline. Lift front neck section and cut on front neckline.

H.   Notch crossmarks at shoulder, biceps, elbow line, diagonal line on underarm and stripe line. With awl indicate dot at underarm intersection.

I.   Turn draft to opposite side. Draw a line between stripe line crossmarks. Pencil in dot. Label *center back.* Separate drafts.

SKETCH B

To develop pattern follow same procedure as for sketch A with this exception:

Pivot sleeve as high as desired for batwing. Plan neckline.

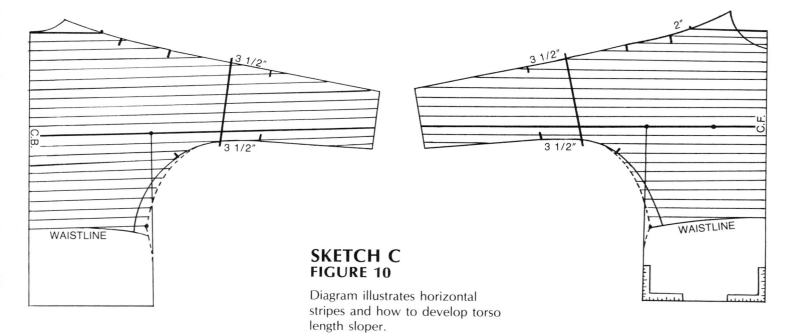

SKETCH C
FIGURE 10

Diagram illustrates horizontal stripes and how to develop torso length sloper.

A.   Copy waistline length sloper.

B.   Draw a new underarm seam parallel to center front from dot to desired torso length. Square a line across to and up center front.

C.   At waistline measure in ⅝" (1.6 cm) if desired and dot.

D.   Draw a new underarm line, slightly curved, from crossmark to waistline dot and down to hipline (broken line).

Plan neckline and sleeve length 3½" (8.9 cm) up from elbow (darker lines on Finished Sloper).

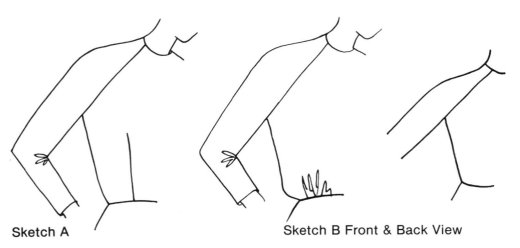

Sketch A

Sketch B Front & Back View

This raglan sleeve sloper when developed has the characteristics of a set-in sleeve.

Use the following basic slopers to develop this sloper:

1. one-dart front waist sloper

2. back waist sloper with neckline and waistline darts

3. straight sleeve sloper

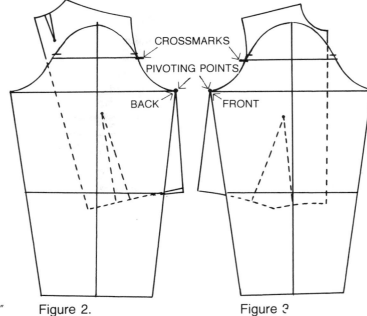

Figure 2.

Figure 3

FIGURE 1

To prepare straight sleeve sloper:

A. On front and back sleeve from biceps line measure up 2¾" (7 cm). Draw a line across sleeve cap.
Note: This line may correspond with the original armhole crossmarks.

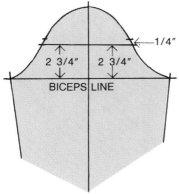

B. On front and back sleeve from this line measure up ¼" (0.6 cm). Crossmark.
Note: This additional ¼" (0.6 cm) on sleeve cap allows for area lost when curving and blending angles on raglan style line.

FIGURES 2 & 3

To prepare front and back armholes:

A. Match front of sleeve to front waist sloper at underarm intersection (see arrow). Pivot sleeve following contour of waist armhole up to line crossmark on sleeve cap. Crossmark front waist armhole.

B. Repeat on back waist.

PREPARATION OF RAGLAN SLEEVE SLOPER

FIGURE 4

A.   Cut paper approximately 40" (101.6 cm) square.

B.   Fold paper in half. Open paper and draw a vertical line on crease.

C.   From top edge of paper on vertical line measure down 10" (25.4 cm). Label A. Square a short line on each side of A. Label *guideline*.
Note: This guideline is for balancing front and back waist shoulders at sleeve cap. Line *must* be a true right angle or it will throw entire pattern off balance.

D.   Place grainline of sleeve sloper to vertical line on paper with sleeve cap touching guideline at A.

E.   Outline sleeve. Crossmark elbow and biceps lines and at crossmarks on both sides of sleeve cap.

F.   Remove sloper. True all lines crossing all intersections. Draw elbow and biceps lines.

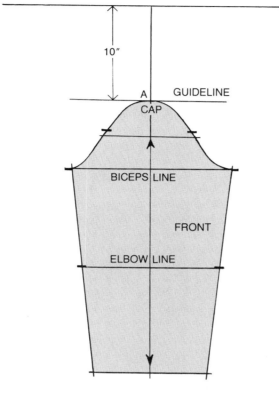

FIGURES 5 & 5A

A.   Place front waist sloper to sleeve draft matching armhole crossmarks. Hold in place with a push pin at crossmarks.

B.   Repeat for back.

C.   Using crossmarks as pivoting points, pivot back and front slopers until waist and sleeve armholes touch *(but do not overlap)* approximately 2" (5.1 cm) above pivoting points. *Note:* Front and back shoulder intersections may touch above or below guideline (Figures 5 and 5A). Adjustment and blending of shoulder will be explained later.

D.   When positioned accurately, outline back and front slopers.

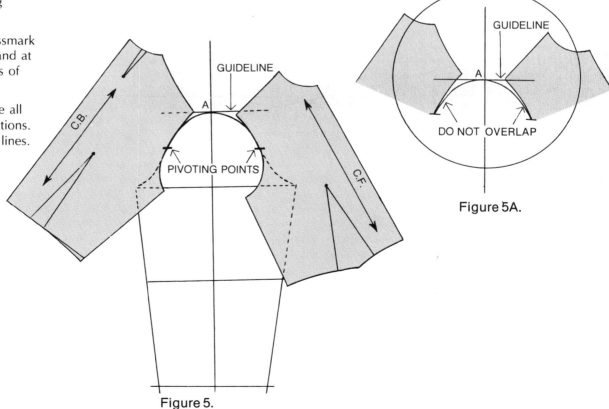

Figure 5.

Figure 5A.

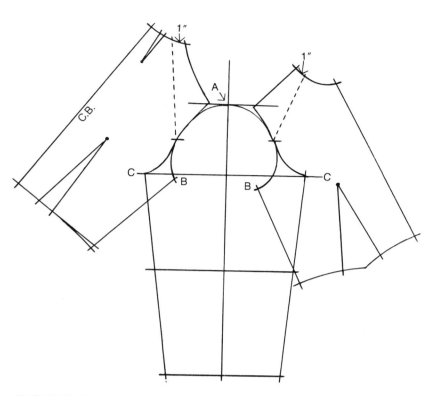

FIGURE 7

A.   Draw front waist armhole starting at B up to ½" (1.3 cm) away from broken line at crossmark and up to neckline (heavier line).

B.   Repeat on back.

C.   Blend armhole of front sleeve starting at C up to crossmark (broken line).

D.   Repeat on back.

Note: In this diagram the distance from line A to shoulder point of back is shorter than the distance from A to shoulder point of front (see dots). However, this will vary depending upon the position of shoulder seams of basic sloper. Figures 8A, 8B and 8C illustrate a few variations.

FIGURE 6

A.   Remove slopers. True all lines crossing all intersections.

B.   From front neck/shoulder intersection measure over 1" (2.5 cm). Crossmark. This measurement may vary depending upon effect desired.

C.   Draw a light broken line from crossmark to armhole.

D.   Repeat on back.

E.   On front and back waist at underarm/armhole intersection and sleeve, label *B* and *C* (as illustrated).

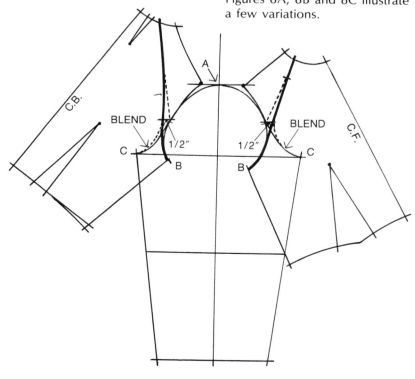

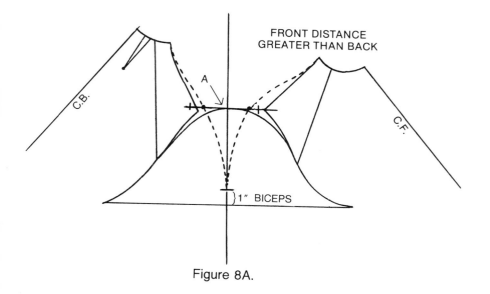

Figure 8A.

FIGURES 8A, 8B, 8C, 8D

When the distance between A and the two shoulders is not equal, shoulder seam must be balanced. To do this, measure the distance between the end of the shoulders. Divide measurement in half and measure equally on each side of line A on guideline and crossmark.

A. For ease over shoulder point, from crossmarks on guideline measure ½" (1.3 cm) towards line A and dot (Figure 8A).

B. To complete shoulder seam blend a curved line from shoulder/neckline intersection to ½" (1.3 cm) dots and down center of sleeve to 1" (2.5 cm) above biceps line and crossmark (broken line in Figure 8A).
Note: If shoulder pads are used in the garment or if more ease is desired for broader shoulders, dart may be shortened (Figure 8D) when testing pattern in fabric.

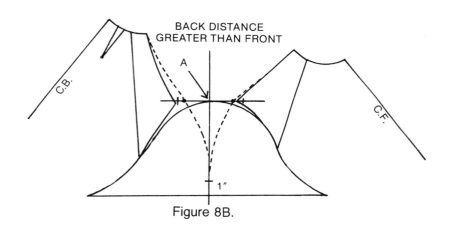

Figure 8B.

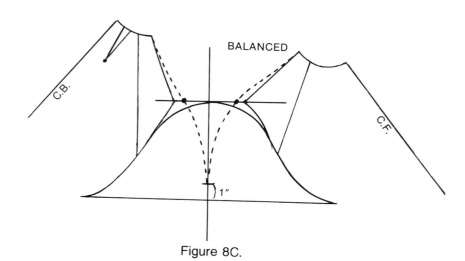

Figure 8C.

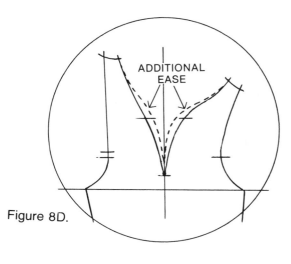

Figure 8D.

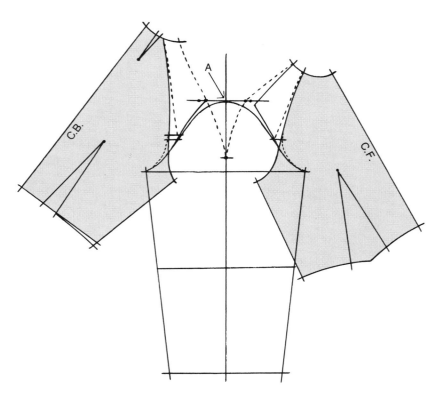

FIGURE 9

A.   Extend front and back armhole crossmarks to new raglan line.

B.   On back add a second crossmark ½″ (1.3 cm) above first.

C.   Copy front and back waists (shaded area). True all lines crossing all intersections.

FIGURE 10

A.   Establish grainlines parallel to centers.

B.   Cut away excess paper and adjust armhole crossmarks to right angles to seams (as illustrated).
Note: Sleeve will be completed later.

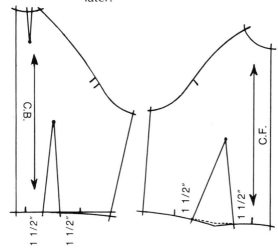

FIGURE 11

Note: To eliminate a slight break at front raglan armhole and for better fit over bustline, it is advisable to pivot a portion of the waistline dart to raglan line between neck intersection and armhole crossmark. This additional fullness will be eased into the raglan line of sleeve between crossmarks.

A.   Cut paper approximately 15″ × 25″ (38.1 × 63.5 cm).

B.   Outline front raglan waist sloper starting at dartline A to center front, up center front, neckline and 1″ (2.5 cm) of raglan line. Crossmark and label *B*. With awl indicate apex.

C.   From A on waistline measure towards center ¼″ to ½″ (0.6 to 1.3 cm). Crossmark and label *C*.

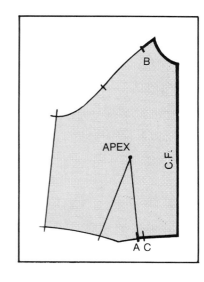

FIGURE 12

A.   Pivot sloper at apex until A touches C.

B.   Outline remainder of sloper starting at armhole crossmark down and around to dartline. Crossmark and label *D*.

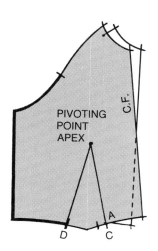

FIGURE 13

A.   Remove sloper. Blend armhole line between crossmarks (broken line).

B.   Establish grainline in center of new dart. Dot at apex.

C.   Draw decreased dart and true (broken line).

D.   To develop shirred waistline crossmark 1½" (3.8 cm) on either side of dartlines. Blend dart area (broken line).

E.   Establish grainline parallel to center. Cut on finished lines.

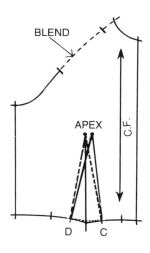

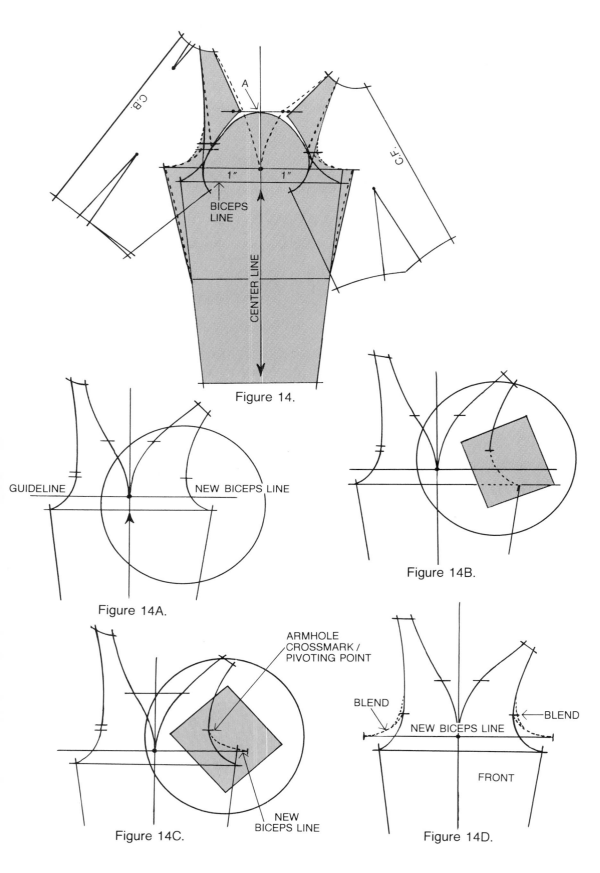

Figure 14.

Figure 14A.

Figure 14B.

Figure 14C.

Figure 14D.

ONE-PIECE RAGLAN SLEEVE

FIGURES 14, 14A, 14B, 14C, 14D

A.   For freedom of movement, from biceps line at back and front of sleeve measure up 1" (2.5 cm). Draw a line parallel to biceps line extending line beyond sleeve. Label *new biceps line* (Figure 14A).

B.   Copy front armhole line from crossmark to underarm intersection. Crossmark underarm intersection (broken line in Figure 14B).

C.   Hold paper securely in place at armhole crossmark and pivot paper upwards until underarm crossmark touches new biceps line. Pin. (Figure 14C).

D.   Trace new armhole and underarm crossmark on new biceps line to opposite side (broken line).

E.   Remove paper. Pencil in traced line and crossmark.

F.   Repeat on back.

G.   Blend sharp corners on back and front armholes at crossmark (Figure 14D).

H.   To complete underarm on front of sleeve draw a new underarm to elbow line using a straight or curved line (broken and solid lines in Figure 14).

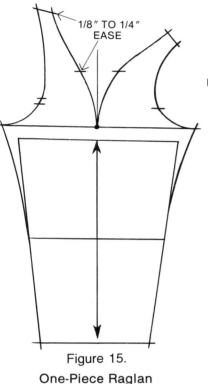

Figure 15.

One-Piece Raglan Sleeve Sloper

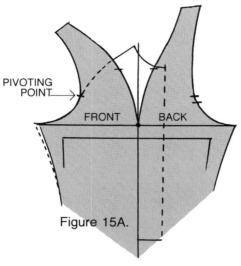

Figure 15A.

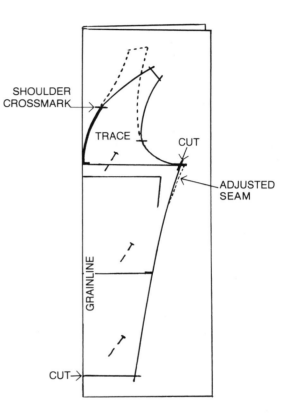

FIGURES 15 & 15A

A.   Copy sleeve (shaded area in Figure 14).

B.   To true sleeve armholes match front crossmark of sleeve to crossmark on front waist draft. Pivot sleeve from crossmark down to armhole/underarm seam intersection. If sleeve is too small, add to sleeve seam measurement matching underarm seam of waist. Blend into seam (broken line in Figure 15A).

C.   To true raglan line of waist and sleeve up to neckline, rematch sleeve crossmark to front waist crossmark. Pivot sleeve from crossmark up to neckline. If one line is longer than the other, adjust by compromising the difference at the neckline.

E.   To true shoulder dart measure from dart crossmarks to neckline.
Note: Back shoulder should have ⅛″ to ¼″ (0.3 to 0.6 cm) ease. If difference is more, adjust by compromising.

FIGURE 16

A.   With front face up, fold sleeve in half on grainline matching original armhole and wrist intersections. Pin. If developed accurately, these points will match.

B.   Trace adjusted armhole/underarm seam intersection, elbow and shoulder crossmarks and curved line from shoulder crossmark down to crossmark on fold to opposite side (darker lines).

C.   Cut excess paper from underarm seam and wristline.

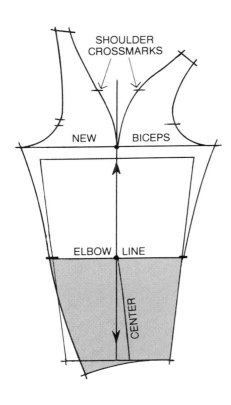

FIGURE 17

A.   Open draft. Pencil in traced crossmarks and curve from shoulder crossmark down to dot on new biceps line.

B.   Draw new elbow and biceps lines if necessary.

C.   Cut excess paper from rest of draft and adjust crossmarks to right angle to seams. Label *one-piece raglan sleeve sloper*.

D.   To develop fitted sleeve place fitted sleeve sloper over raglan sleeve matching elbow lines. Outline bottom of sleeve sloper (shaded area).

TWO-PIECE RAGLAN SLEEVE

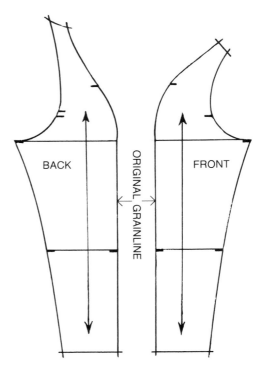

FIGURE 18

A.   Copy front section of sleeve to grainline. Draw new grainline parallel to original grainline.

B.   Establish crossmark at elbow on center of sleeve.

C.   Repeat for back.

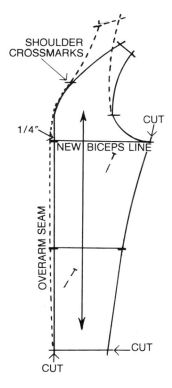

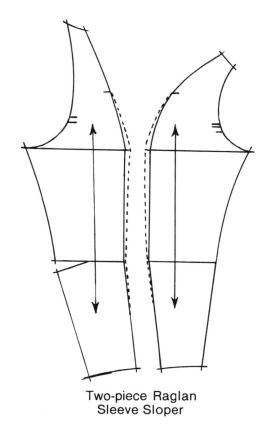

Two-piece Raglan Sleeve Sloper

FIGURE 20

For a two-piece fitted raglan sleeve, copy adjusted sleeve (Figure 17) and adjust overarm seam (broken line).

Note: 1. If either of these raglan sleeve slopers are to be used as patterns, copy sections. True all lines crossing all intersections. Allow seams and hem at wrist; cut and notch seams. 2. The original drafts, as well as the finished sloper, should be retained as they can be used to develop many variations of raglan sleeve patterns (see sketches 39, 40 and 41).

FIGURE 19

Note: With a two-piece raglan sleeve, it is possible to allow additional ease over biceps if needed or desired.

A. To shape overarm seam accurately, pin overarm seams together from shoulder crossmark to wrist. Smooth and pin.

Note: Check elbow crossmarks for accuracy. Trace front crossmark to back if necessary.

B. Add ¼ " (0.6 cm) at biceps line. Blend to nothing up to shoulder crossmark and down to wrist (broken line).

C. Cut paper away from sleeve starting at shoulder crossmark down around wrist and up underarm seam.

D. Separate sleeve. Cut away excess paper from remainder of sleeve.

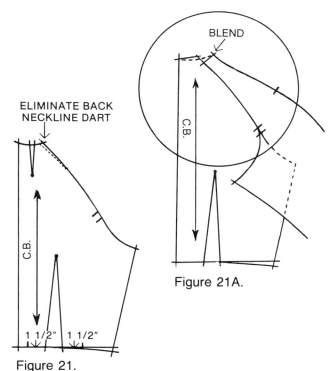

Figure 21.

Figure 21A.

FIGURES 21 & 21A

A. If back neckline dart is not desired, it can be eliminated. From raglan line measure in depth of dart. Blend to nothing (broken line).

B. With this change, a slight adjustment must be made at neckline of waist and sleeve. To adjust match back sleeve and waist armholes from crossmarks to neckline. Blend neckline (Figure 21A).

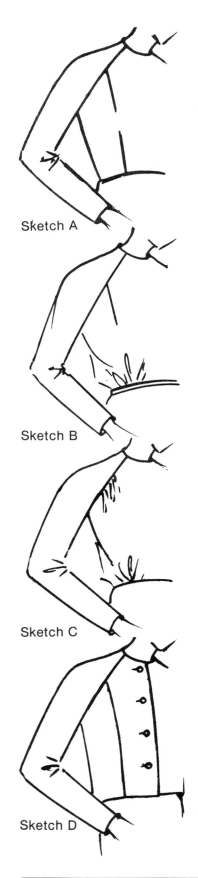

Sketch A

Sketch B

Sketch C

Sketch D

SKETCHES A, B, C

FIGURES 1 & 2

A. To develop patterns for these sketches copy front waist from raglan sleeve sloper, sketch 37.

B. To introduce a shoulder dart or shirring to front waist follow same procedures as in sketch 37, Figures 11 and 12, with the following exceptions:

　　1. Pivot *half* of waistline dart.

　　2. Outline 2" *(5.1 cm)* of raglan line and crossmark.

FIGURE 3

Draw new shoulder dart to apex.

FIGURE 4

Crease, cup and close dart. Pin. True raglan line. Trace dart underlay to opposite side.

FIGURE 5

A. Open draft. Pencil in traced lines. True all lines crossing all intersections. Shorten darts (broken lines for sketch A).

B. To develop shirring at shoulder and/or waistline establish crossmarks (as illustrated). Blend shoulderline (broken line for sketch C and waistline for sketches B and C).

C. To complete pattern copy remaining sections from draft, allow hem at wrist and seams on all sections; cut and notch seams.

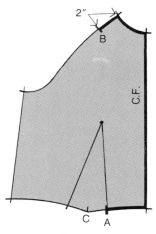

Figure 1.

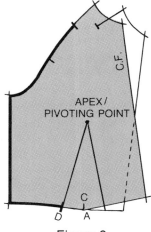

Figure 2.

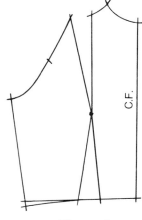

Figure 3.

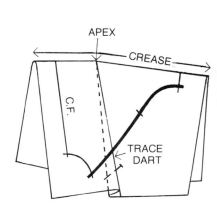

Figure 4.

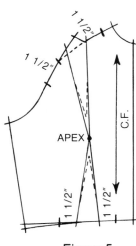

Figure 5.

SKETCH D

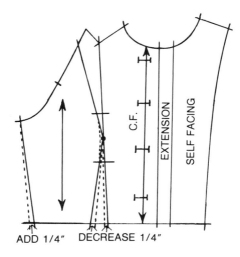

FIGURE 6

A. To develop pattern for this sketch follow same procedures as in sketches A, B and C eliminating crossmarks for shirring.

B. On side section of front waist establish grainline parallel to center front.

C. Plan extension, buttonholes and facing desired.

D. Crossmark and blend princess line (as illustrated).

E. For width at waistline decrease dart ¼" (0.6 cm) on each side of dartlines and add ¼" (0.6 cm) at underarm.

F. Copy sections. True all lines crossing all intersections.

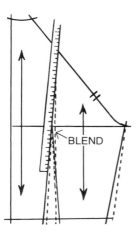

FIGURE 7

A. Copy back waist eliminating neckline dart on raglan line (sketch 37, Figure 21 and 21A). Allow ease as on front waist.

B. For princess line balance ruler on dartline from waistline up through top of dart to raglan line.

C. Blend princess line (as illustrated).

D. On side section establish grainline parallel to center back.

E. To complete pattern copy back section and raglan sleeve. Allow hem on bottom of sleeve and bolero. Allow seams; cut and notch seams.

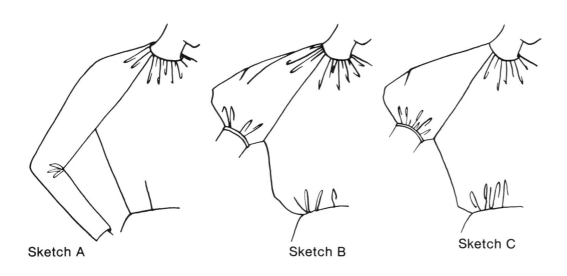

Sketch A   Sketch B   Sketch C

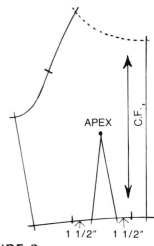

FIGURE 3

A. Blend neckline (broken line).

B. Indicate shirring crossmarks at waistline (as illustrated).

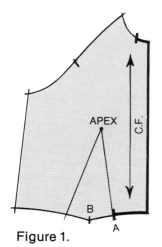

Figure 1.

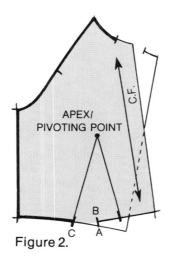

Figure 2.

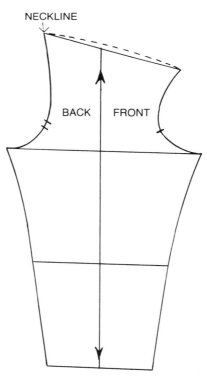

WAISTS

FIGURES 1 & 2

A. To develop waist patterns for these sketches copy front and back waist from sketch 37, Figure 14.

B. To develop neckline shirring pivot half of waistline dart to neckline.

SKETCH A FULL LENGTH SLEEVE WITH SHIRRING AT NECKLINE

FIGURE 4

A. To develop long sleeve with shirring at neckline of sleeve copy raglan sleeve, sketch 37, Figure 14, eliminating shoulder dart.

B. Draw a straight line between back and front armhole/neckline intersections.

C. From center of neckline measure up ½″ (1.3 cm). Draw a new neckline (broken line).

SKETCH B
PUFF SLEEVE WITH SHIRRING AT NECKLINE & BICEPS

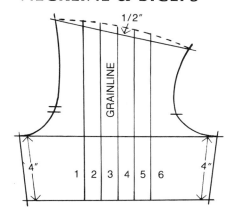

FIGURE 5

A.   Copy raglan sleeve eliminating shoulder dart length desired. Illustrated: 4″ (10.2 cm). Cut excess paper from all seamlines.

B.   Draw a straight line between back and front armhole/neckline intersections.

C.   From center of neckline measure up ½″ (1.3 cm). Draw a new neckline (broken line).

D.   Establish slash lines 1½″ (3.8 cm) apart on either side of grainline and number (as illustrated).

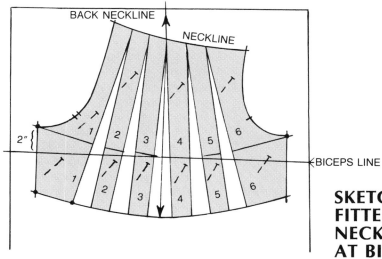

FIGURE 6

Note: Since front and back of sleeve are different shapes, sleeve must be developed as illustrated.

A.   Fold another sheet of paper in half. Open and draw a line over crease. Label *grainline.*

B.   From neckline of back of sleeve measure down to biceps line plus 2″ (5.1 cm). Square a line across paper from each side of grainline. Label *biceps line.*

C.   Cut sleeve sections up to top of sleeve; spread both sides of sleeve equal amount from grainline. Pin.

D.   Outline sleeve. Remove sections. True all lines crossing all intersections.

E.   Fold on grainline matching seams. Retrue underarm seam if necessary.

SKETCH C
FITTED AT NECKLINE, SHIRRED AT BICEPS

FIGURE 7

A.   Copy raglan sleeve sketch 37, Figure 14, *with* shoulder dart in length desired. Illustrated: 3″ (7.6 cm). Cut excess paper from seams.

B.   Slash on center of sleeve. Close dart at neckline.

C.   Pin sections to another sheet of paper. Copy blending neckline and hemline (as illustrated).

D.   Remove sections. True all lines crossing all intersections.

E.   Fold sleeve in half matching underarm seams. Crease. Open and draw a line over crease. Label *grainline.*
Note: To complete pattern sections add seams and hem at wrist; cut and notch seams.

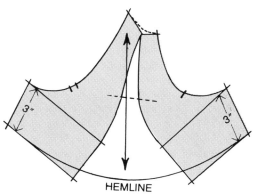

RAGLAN SLEEVE WITH STYLIZED ARMHOLES
sketch 40

A. To develop patterns for these sketches copy raglan draft, sketch 37, Figure 14.

B. Plan style lines (as illustrated). The principles are the same, the designs vary.

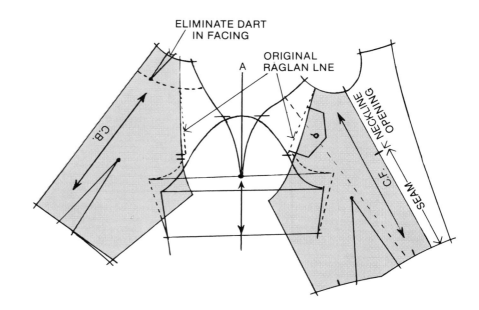

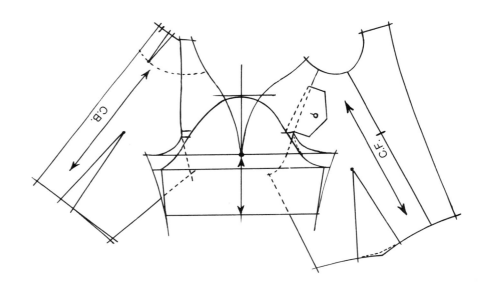

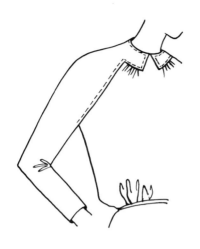

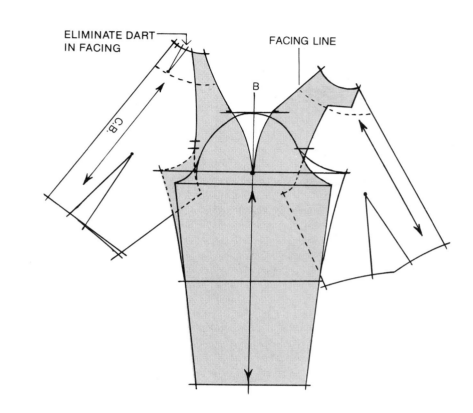

ELIMINATE DART IN FACING

FACING LINE

C.B.

B

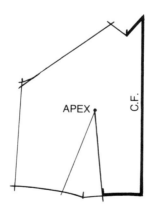

APEX

C.F.

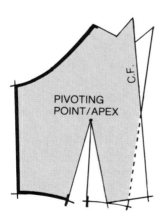

PIVOTING POINT/APEX

C.F.

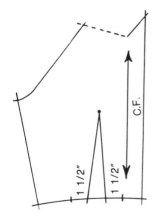

C.F.

1 1/2" 1 1/2"

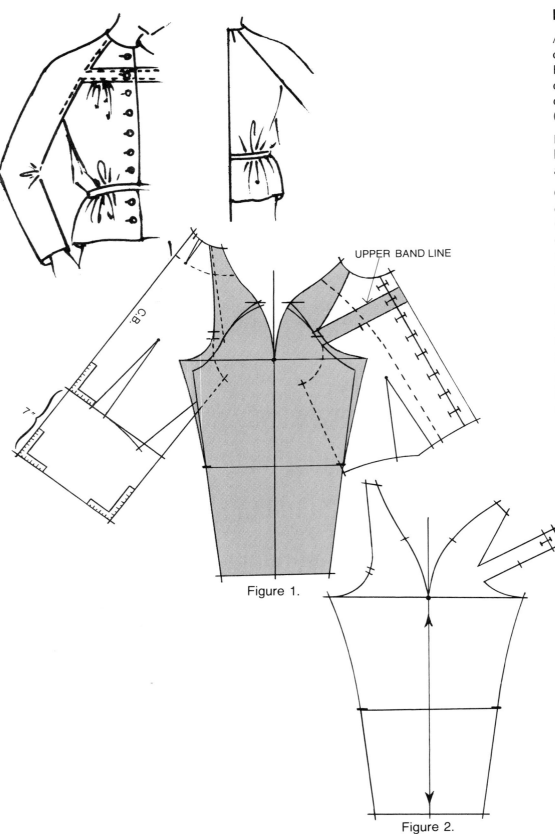

UPPER BAND LINE

C.B.

7"

Figure 1.

Figure 2.

FIGURE 1

A.   To develop this pattern copy raglan draft, sketch 37, Figure 14, extending center back down from waistline the length desired. Illustrated: 7" (17.8 cm) (hipline).

B.   Square a line across at hipline and up underarm to armhole intersection.

C.   On front waist plan width of band desired. Illustrated: 1½" (3.8 cm). From neckline at center front measure down width of band plus ¼" (0.6 cm). Dot. Square a line across to armhole. Label *upper band line.*

D.   From this line measure down established width of band minus ¼" (0.6 cm). Draw a line parallel to upper band line.

E.   Crossmark on lower band line halfway between center front and armhole.

F.   Plan extension line. Illustrated: ¾" (1.9 cm) and facing.

G.   Mark buttonholes:

   1.   Plan first buttonhole in center of band;

   2.   Plan second buttonhole towards neckline same distrance from upper band line as first buttonhole on band.

   3.   Plan remaining buttonholes equal distance apart as the first and second buttonholes down to waistline.

FIGURE 2

For a one-piece sleeve copy sleeve and band section (shaded area) in Figure 1 and redirect crossmarks to right angles of seams.

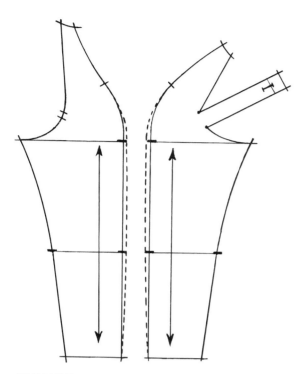

FIGURE 3

For a two-piece sleeve refer to sketch 37, Figures 18, 19 and 20.

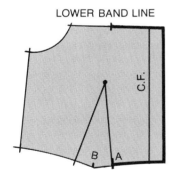

FIGURE 4

A.   Copy front waist section up to lower band line. Copy crossmark. Cut away paper on seamlines and use as sloper. Label dartline nearest center front *A* and crossmark center of dart *B*.

B.   On another sheet of paper outline waist (darker lines) and crossmark B on paper.

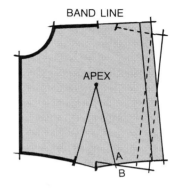

FIGURE 5

Pivot dart from apex until crossmark B touches A. Outline remainder of waist (darker lines). Add crossmark on paper at band line.

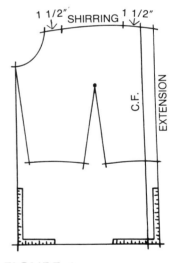

FIGURE 6

A.   Blend shirring line. Establish position for shirring by measuring in from center front and armhole 1½″ (3.8 cm). Crossmark.

B.   Extend side seam from underarm/armhole intersection parallel to center front same length as back underarm seam.

C.   Square a line across paper.

D.   Continue center front and extension lines down to hipline. Recheck that all lines are parallel to each other.

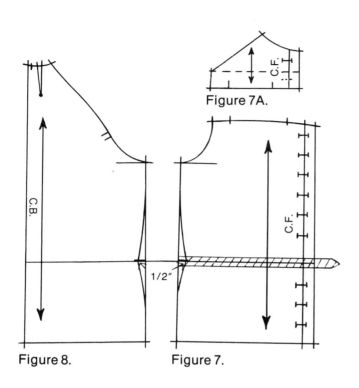

Figure 7A.

Figure 8.

Figure 7.

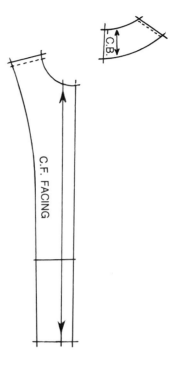

FIGURES 7 & 7A

A.   Finish marking buttonholes allowing space for belt (as illustrated).

B.   Copy front neck section up to upper band line (Figure 7A).

FIGURE 8

Copy back section.
Note: Front and back underarm seams at waistline may be slightly shaped if desired.

FIGURE 9

A.   Plan and copy front and back neck facing (broken line in Figure 1). Lengthen front facing to hipline.
Note: Front facing is in one piece and joined to extension line.

B.   Establish grainline on all sections parallel to centers.

C.   True all lines crossing all intersections.

D.   To complete pattern sections allow seams, hem at wrist and bottom of overblouse; cut and notch seams.

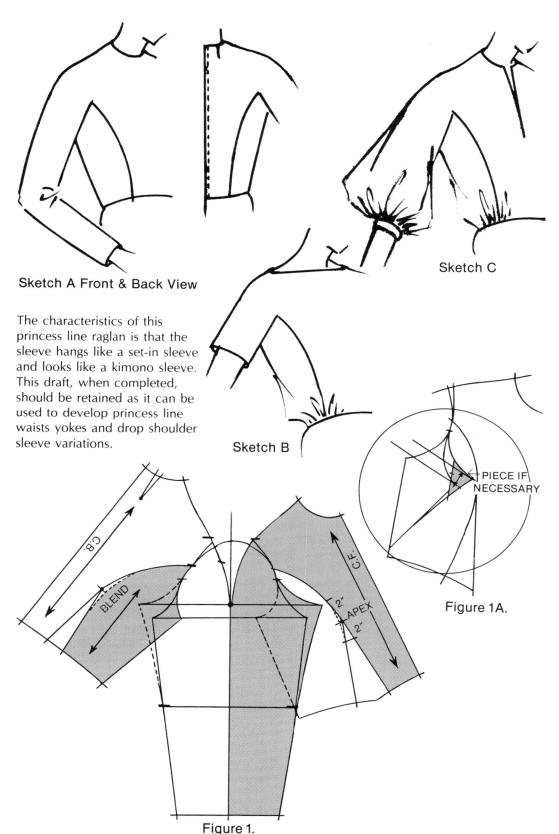

Sketch A Front & Back View

The characteristics of this princess line raglan is that the sleeve hangs like a set-in sleeve and looks like a kimono sleeve. This draft, when completed, should be retained as it can be used to develop princess line waists yokes and drop shoulder sleeve variations.

Sketch B

Sketch C

Figure 1A.

Figure 1.

SKETCH A

FIGURES 1, 1A, 1B

A.   To develop pattern follow same procedure as for sketch 37, Figures 1 through 5 with the following exception: Eliminate the ¼″ (0.6 cm) ease allowed on sleeve cap.

B.   To shape shoulder refer to sketch 37, Figures 8A through 8D.

C.   Indicate princess style line on front and back waists (as illustrated). For graceful lines start princess line approximately 1″ (2.5 cm) above armhole crossmarks and blend into dartlines nearest centers.

D.   On front waist establish three crossmarks. One at apex and one above and below 2″ (5.1 cm) apart.

E.   On back waist add one crossmark at top of dart. Blend (broken line).

F.   On side back section establish grainline parallel to center back.

G.   On center front and back waist establish grainlines parallel to centers.

H.   To allow for freedom of underarm movement refer to sketch 37, Figure 14A to 14D. Draw a new back underarm to elbow as on front of sleeve.

I.   Copy center front and sleeve (shaded area) and crossmarks at shoulder, biceps, elbow and bustline.

K.   If area between style line and new underarm does not allow for sufficient seam allowance, sleeve must be pieced (Figure 1A, front).

361

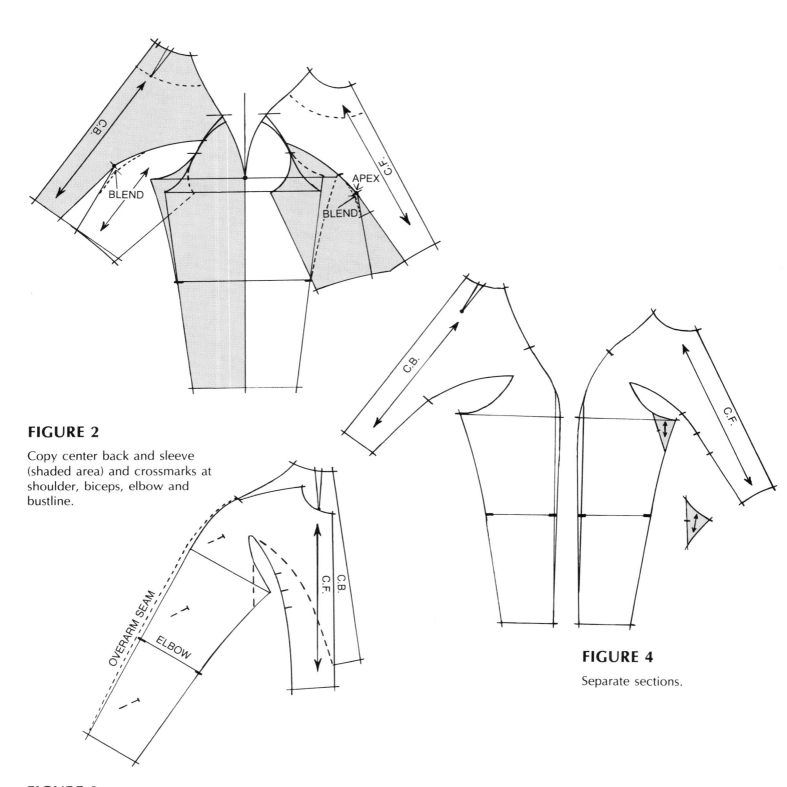

FIGURE 2

Copy center back and sleeve (shaded area) and crossmarks at shoulder, biceps, elbow and bustline.

FIGURE 4

Separate sections.

FIGURE 3

To true overarm seam refer to sketch 37, Figure 19.

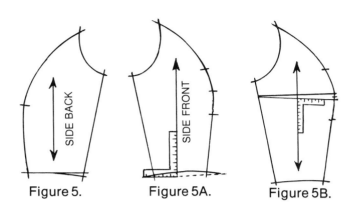

Figure 5.   Figure 5A.   Figure 5B.

FIGURES 5, 5A, 5B

A.   Copy front and back waist side sections, crossmark and back grainline (shaded areas in Figures 1 and 2).

B.   On side front waist establish grainline by squaring a line up from waistline (Figure 5A).

Note: Additional ease may be added across bustline if necessary (Figure 5B):

1.   Square a line across bustline to center crossmark. 2.   Slash side front bustline to underarm seam and spread ⅛″ to ¼″ (0.3 to 0.6 cm) depending upon the fabric's properties of shrinkage.

3.   Recopy waist. Establish new crossmark in center of spread.

FIGURE 6

A.   Plan neckline facing on draft Figure 2 and copy.

B.   To eliminate back neckline dart in facing close dart when copying facing.

C.   To complete pattern sections allow hem at wrist and seams; cut and notch seams.

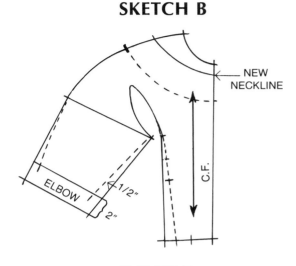

NEW NECKLINE

ELBOW   1/2″   2″

C.F.

FIGURE 7

A.   For shirred waistline establish princess lines through center of darts.

B.   Copy sleeve to length desired.

C.   To tighten bottom of sleeve, if desired, see illustration.

D.   Establish new neckline and facing (as illustrated).

SKETCH C

FIGURE 8

A.   Establish princess lines through center of darts.

B.   Copy sleeve to elbow line.

C.   See diagram for:

1.   introducing fullness to width of sleeve;

2.   lengthening center of sleeve for a deeper puff;

3.   establishing crossmarks for end of slit opening and facing (as illustrated).

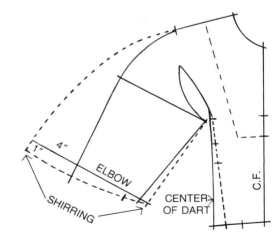

1″   4″   ELBOW   C.F.   SHIRRING   CENTER OF DART

KIMONO–TYPE RAGLAN SLEEVE WITH PRINCESS LINE & BUSTLINE DART

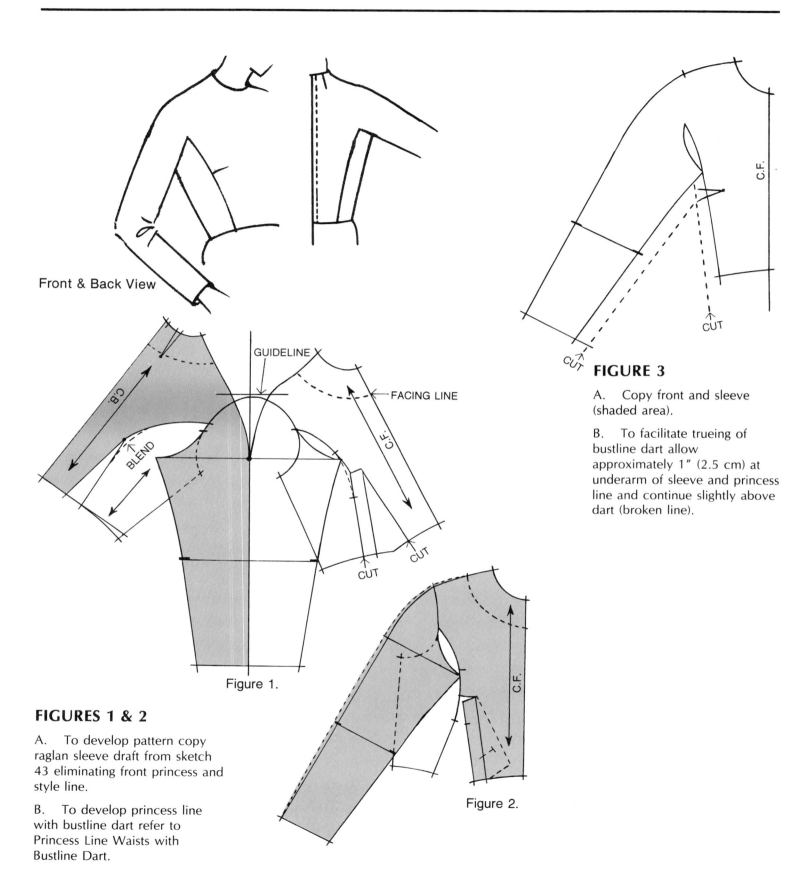

Front & Back View

GUIDELINE

FACING LINE

C.B.

BLEND

C.F.

CUT

CUT

Figure 1.

Figure 2.

C.F.

C.F.

CUT

CUT

FIGURE 3

A.   Copy front and sleeve (shaded area).

B.   To facilitate trueing of bustline dart allow approximately 1″ (2.5 cm) at underarm of sleeve and princess line and continue slightly above dart (broken line).

FIGURES 1 & 2

A.   To develop pattern copy raglan sleeve draft from sketch 43 eliminating front princess and style line.

B.   To develop princess line with bustline dart refer to Princess Line Waists with Bustline Dart.

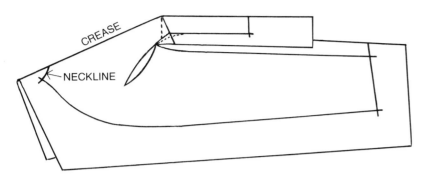

FIGURE 4

A.   Crease upper dartline to apex. Fold, cup and close dart creasing draft above and below from apex.

B.   Lift front section over sleeve. Blend dartline at apex (broken line). Trace on adjusted line.

C.   Open draft. Cut away excess paper on all lines (Figure 5).

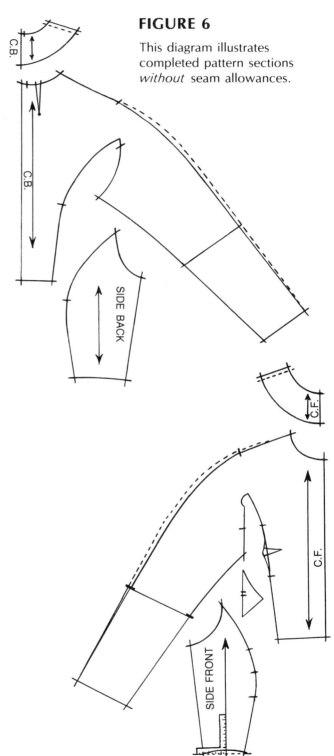

FIGURE 6

This diagram illustrates completed pattern sections *without* seam allowances.

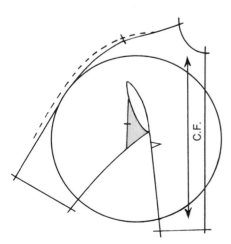

FIGURE 5

This diagram illustrates piecing on underarm of sleeve if necessary.

FIGURES 1 & 2

A. To develop pattern copy raglan sleeve draft, sketch 43.

B. Plan yokeline as desired.

C. Plan facing (as illustrated). Front yoke can also be fully faced.

D. Plan buttonholes as desired.

E. Copy sections. True all lines crossing all intersections.

F. To complete pattern allow hem and seams; cut and notch seams.

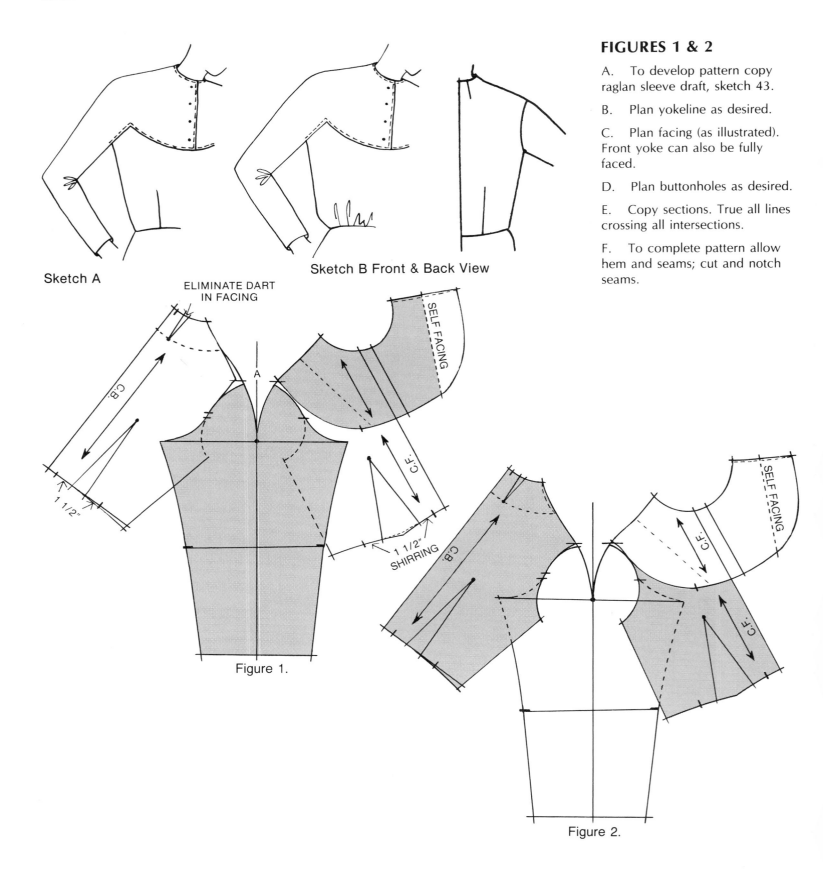

Sketch A

Sketch B Front & Back View

Figure 1.

Figure 2.

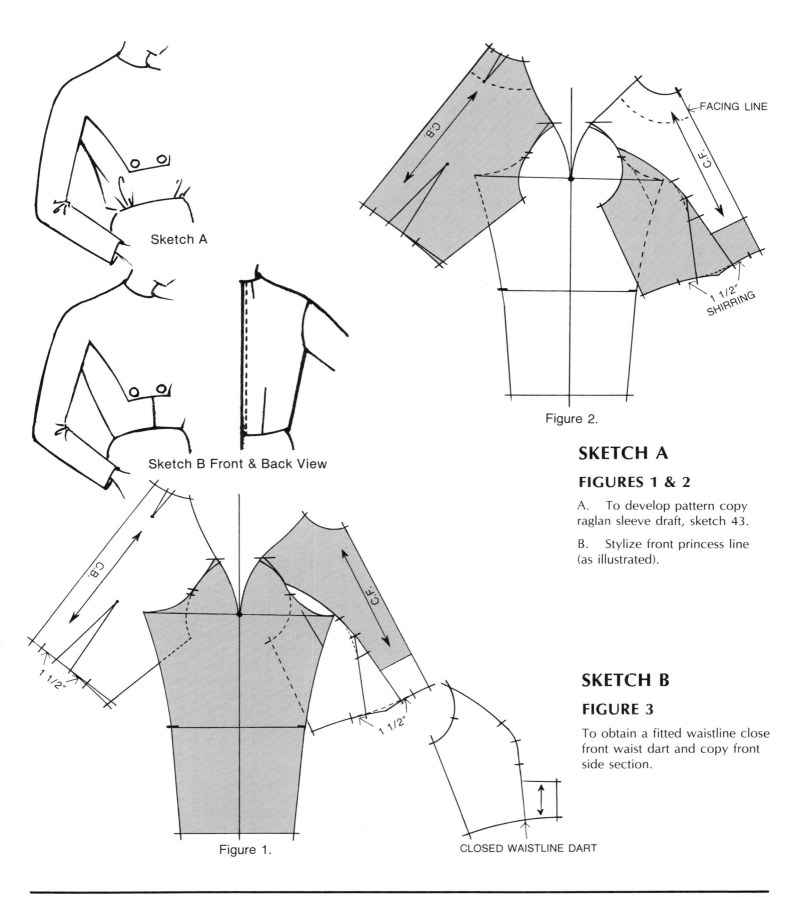

Sketch A

Sketch B Front & Back View

Figure 2.

Figure 1.

FACING LINE

C.F.

1 1/2"
SHIRRING

C.B.

1 1/2"

C.F.

1 1/2"

CLOSED WAISTLINE DART

SKETCH A

FIGURES 1 & 2

A.   To develop pattern copy raglan sleeve draft, sketch 43.

B.   Stylize front princess line (as illustrated).

SKETCH B

FIGURE 3

To obtain a fitted waistline close front waist dart and copy front side section.

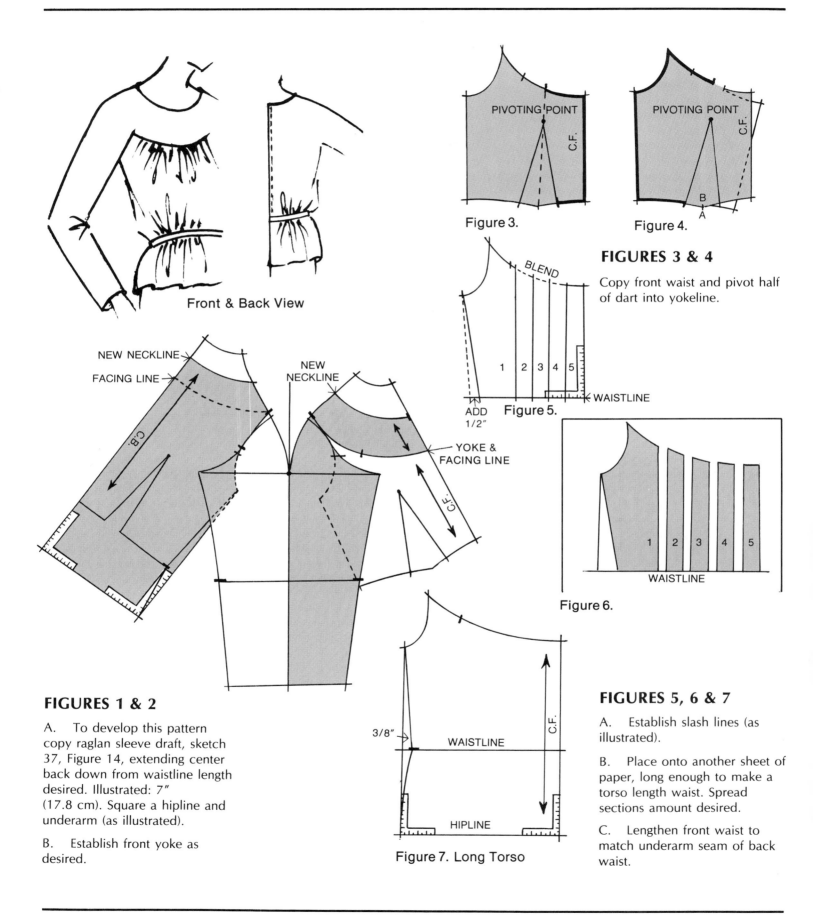

Front & Back View

NEW NECKLINE

FACING LINE

C.B.

NEW NECKLINE

YOKE & FACING LINE

C.F.

Figure 3.

Figure 4.

PIVOTING POINT

C.F.

PIVOTING POINT

B
A

C.F.

FIGURES 3 & 4

Copy front waist and pivot half of dart into yokeline.

BLEND

1 2 3 4 5

WAISTLINE

ADD 1/2" Figure 5.

1 2 3 4 5

WAISTLINE

Figure 6.

3/8"

WAISTLINE

C.F.

HIPLINE

Figure 7. Long Torso

FIGURES 1 & 2

A.   To develop this pattern copy raglan sleeve draft, sketch 37, Figure 14, extending center back down from waistline length desired. Illustrated: 7" (17.8 cm). Square a hipline and underarm (as illustrated).

B.   Establish front yoke as desired.

FIGURES 5, 6 & 7

A.   Establish slash lines (as illustrated).

B.   Place onto another sheet of paper, long enough to make a torso length waist. Spread sections amount desired.

C.   Lengthen front waist to match underarm seam of back waist.

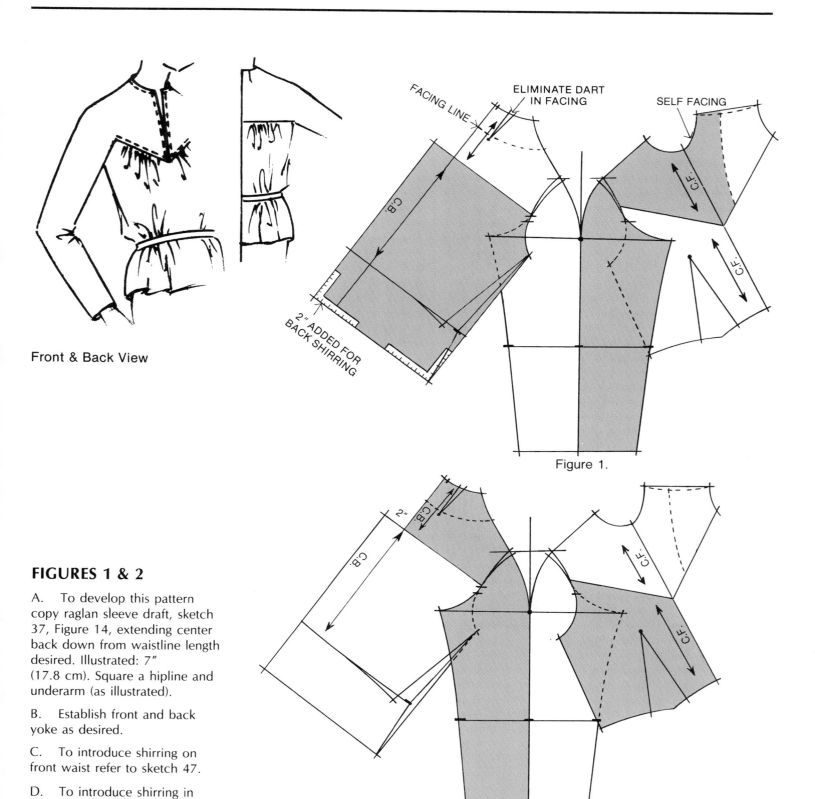

Front & Back View

Figure 1.

Figure 2.

FIGURES 1 & 2

A.   To develop this pattern copy raglan sleeve draft, sketch 37, Figure 14, extending center back down from waistline length desired. Illustrated: 7" (17.8 cm). Square a hipline and underarm (as illustrated).

B.   Establish front and back yoke as desired.

C.   To introduce shirring on front waist refer to sketch 47.

D.   To introduce shirring in back waist add amount desired at center back. Illustrated: 2" (5.1 cm). Draw a new center back line.

DROP SHOULDER
sketch 49

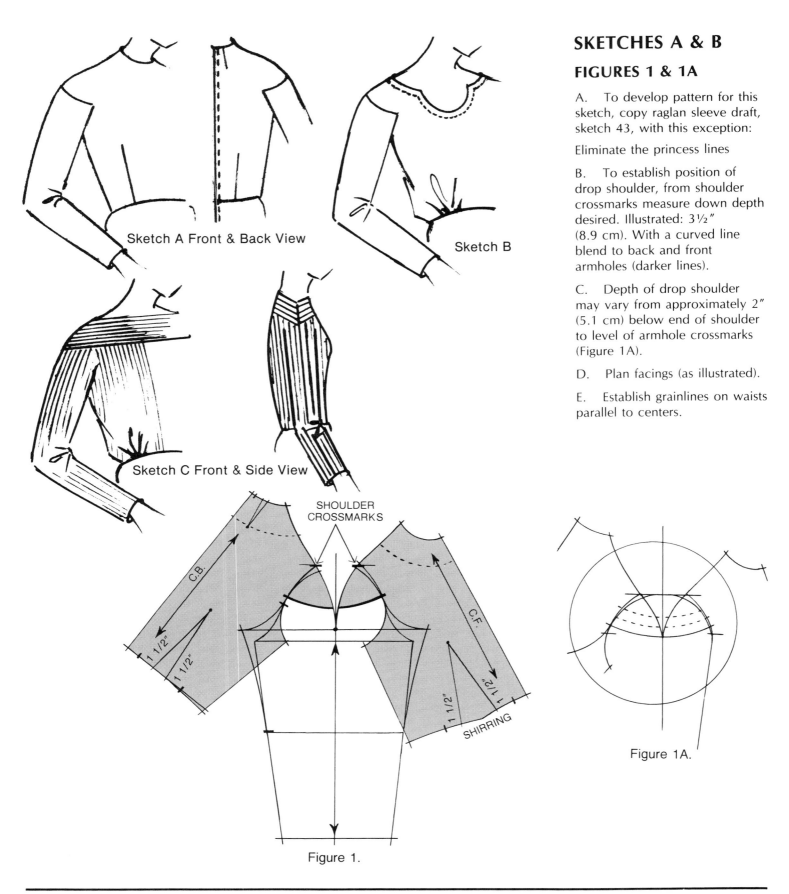

Sketch A Front & Back View

Sketch B

Sketch C Front & Side View

SKETCHES A & B
FIGURES 1 & 1A

A. To develop pattern for this sketch, copy raglan sleeve draft, sketch 43, with this exception:

Eliminate the princess lines

B. To establish position of drop shoulder, from shoulder crossmarks measure down depth desired. Illustrated: 3½" (8.9 cm). With a curved line blend to back and front armholes (darker lines).

C. Depth of drop shoulder may vary from approximately 2" (5.1 cm) below end of shoulder to level of armhole crossmarks (Figure 1A).

D. Plan facings (as illustrated).

E. Establish grainlines on waists parallel to centers.

SHOULDER CROSSMARKS

C.B.

1 1/2"

1 1/2"

C.F.

1 1/2"

1 1/2"

SHIRRING

Figure 1.

Figure 1A.

continued

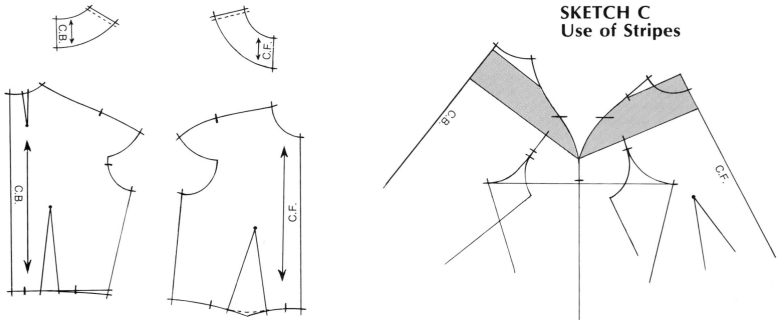

**SKETCH C
Use of Stripes**

FIGURE 2

A.   Copy waists with crossmarks and grainlines (shaded area in Figure 1)
Note: It is advisable to true shoulderline to capline for shape and length since one shoulderline may be longer than the other. To correct patterns, place front over back matching shoulder crossmarks to bottom of capline. Blend a new overarm line to capline.

B.   Copy facings. To eliminate back neckline dart fold, cup and close dart on draft. Pin.

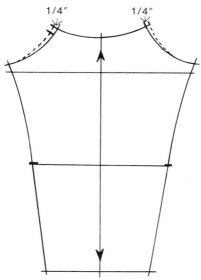

FIGURE 3

A.   Copy sleeve with grainline.

B.   For a better hang of sleeve, add ¼" (0.6 cm) at sides of capline (as illustrated).

C.   To complete pattern section allow hem at wrist and seams on all sections; cut and notch seams.

FIGURE 4

To develop the pattern for this sketch, follow same procedure as for sketches A and B establishing yokeline (as illustrated). Depth of yokeline is limited to the depth of the normal drop shoulder.

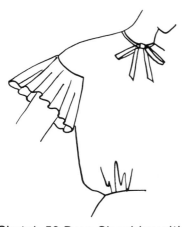

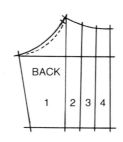

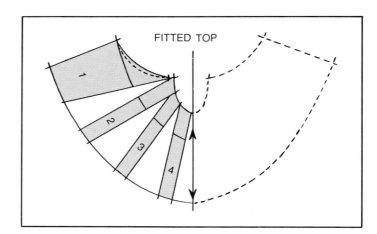

FITTED TOP

BACK

1 | 2 | 3 | 4

Sketch 50 Drop Shoulder with Fitted Cap & Flared Sleeve

1. Sleeves with drop shoulders may be left loose at biceps or wristline.

2. To develop short flared and puffed sleeves refer to Flared Sleeve Variations and Puffed Sleeve Variations.

3. To develop shape at wristline for sketch 52 refer to Bishop Sleeve with Balanced Fullness.

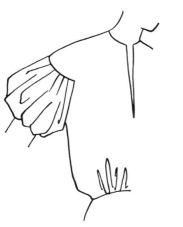

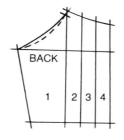

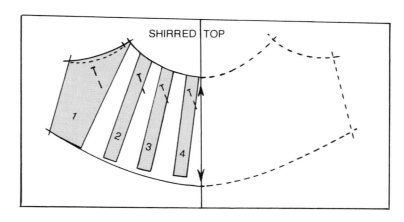

SHIRRED TOP

BACK

1 | 2 | 3 | 4

Sketch 51 Drop Shoulder with Shirred Cap & Puffed Sleeve

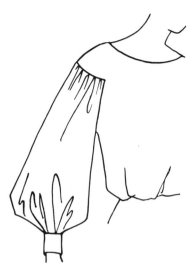

Sketch 52 Drop Shoulder with Bishop Sleeve

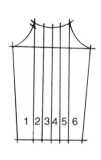

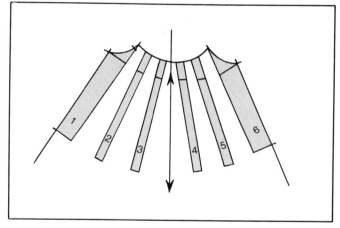

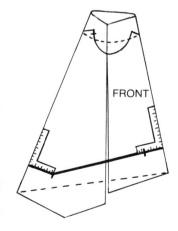

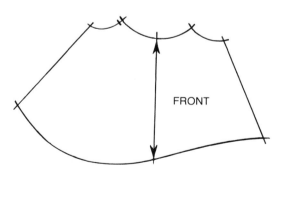

SKIRTS
introduction

A skirt is defined as (1) the lower part of a dress from the waist to the hem and (2) a separate garment starting at the waist and ending in any length desired.

Skirts play a major role in the classification of a silhouette. If a slim skirt is attached to a bodice, the silhouette achieved is the *sheath.* If the skirt is extended above the waistline and stops below the bustline, it becomes the *empire.* Regardless of the silhouette, skirts are classified as slim, full or shaped. Within these skirt classifications, the degree of width at the hemline and/or waistline varies.

The slim skirt is not necessarily devoid of all fullness. It may have some soft fullness introduced at the waistline and not at the hemline; it may be developed with one or several flat pressed pleats or straight gores. In either case, the skirt retains a slim look.

The full and shaped skirts achieve their width at the waistline or yokeline and/or hemline through the use of gores, pressed or unpressed pleats, gathers, tiers and circles.

Skirt lengths play an important role in the fashion picture. All the lengths illustrated in Skirt Length Variations have been in vogue at one time or another. Most of the skirts in this text have been developed as a mid-calf length, but all the skirts can be interpreted in any length desired.

This text attempts to cover the more popular skirts within the three skirt classifications. The companion book, *New Fashion Areas for Designing Apparel through the Flat Pattern,* covers a complete series on pleated skirts.

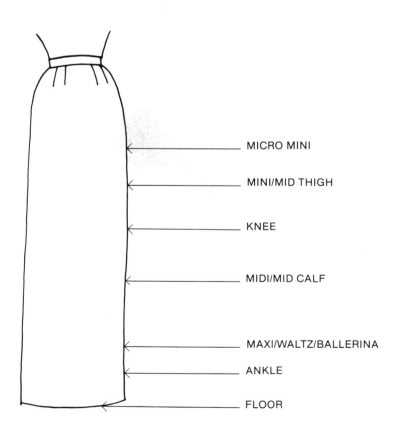

MICRO MINI

MINI/MID THIGH

KNEE

MIDI/MID CALF

MAXI/WALTZ/BALLERINA

ANKLE

FLOOR

Skirt Length Variations

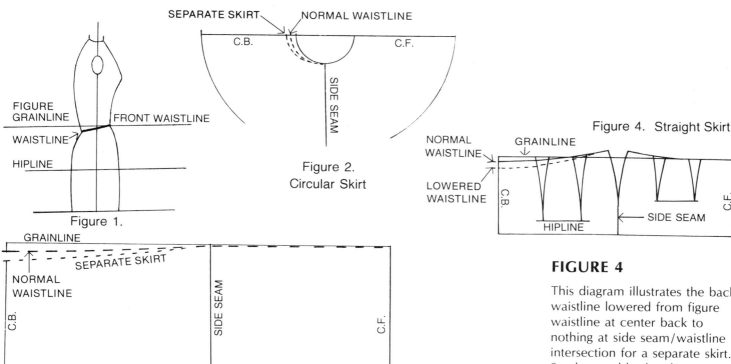

Figure 1.

Figure 2.
Circular Skirt

Figure 3.   Dirndl Skirt

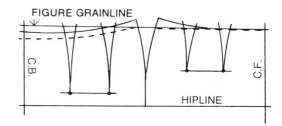

Figure 4. Straight Skirt

FIGURE 4

This diagram illustrates the back waistline lowered from figure waistline at center back to nothing at side seam/waistline intersection for a separate skirt. See lowered broken line.

FIGURE 5

This diagram illustrates back waistline lowered from figure waistline at center back to nothing at figure *grainline* at side seam on sloper for a separate skirt. When the shaping ends on the figure grainline, the skirt hikes up at side seams giving skirt a slight A-line silhouette. See broken line.

Note: Fitted Waistlines. If a waistline increases in measurement when lowered, the extra ease may be eliminated on: 1. circular-skirts—at center back seam; 2. gored skirts—on gore seams; 3. basic skirts—make darts deeper.

FIGURES 1, 2, 3

A.   Figure 1 illustrates the grainline in relation to the waistline on the model form. The front waistline starts on the figure grainline and the back waistline normally drops ¼" to ½" (0.6 to 1.2 cm) below the grainline. Therefore, when developing a skirt without a sloper, such as circular and dirndl skirts (Figures 2 and 3). It is important to lower back waistline before completing skirts. If waistline is not lowered, the skirt will not hang properly. The hemline will be longer in the back than in the front and the side seam will swing towards the front.

B.   When a skirt is made as a separate garment, the waistline must be lowered another ½" to 1½" (1.3 to 3.8 cm) as the skirt has a tendency to drop even lower or buckle at the center back waistline. See lowered broken lines in Figures 2 and 3.

SKIRT WAISTBANDS
sketch 2

The waistline of a skirt may be finished in one of the following methods:

1. with a waistband;

2. turned back with belting;

3. with a hem and a drawstring or elastic inserted and pulled through.

The finish selected depends upon the effect desired.

The waistbands developed in this section may be applied to any type of skirt—full or slim, long or short—and to all types of pants, shorts and culottes. The waistbands developed are for skirts with left-hand side or center back openings and for wraparound skirts. If tie ends are desired, as often used in wraparound skirts, all one has to do is add the needed length at each end of the waistband. The length at each end will vary depending upon where and how the skirt is to be tied.

Since all the skirts covered in this unit fall into one of the above categories, we have omitted repeating the instructions for waistbands in the development of the skirt patterns.

WAISTBAND FOR LEFT SIDE OPENINGS

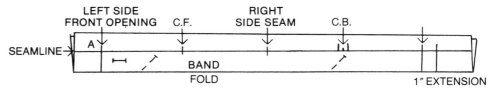

FIGURE 1

A. Cut paper approximately 6" × 36" (15.2 × 91.4 cm).

B. Fold paper in half lengthwise. Pin.

C. With fold towards you, measure up from fold the desired width of belt. Illustrated: 1½" (3.8 cm). Draw a line parallel to fold. Label *seamline*.

D. Square a line up from fold at left end of waistband. Label *left side front opening*.

E. Plan length of waistband. Measure from left side opening amount determined and square a line up from fold. Label *left side back opening*.
Note: Additional length should be added to waistline measurement before marking pattern to allow for thickness of seams, darts and shirring. The amount needed may range from ½" to 1½" (1.3 to 3.8 cm). If this additional ease is not added, waistband will be too tight.

F. From left side opening measure amount of front waistline measurement plus half of the ease allowed. Crossmark. Label *right side seam*.

G. Crossmark center between left side opening and side seam. Label *center front*.

H. Crossmark center between side seam and left side back opening. Label *center back*.

I. Crossmark ¼" (0.6 cm) on either side of center back to facilitate identification of back.

J. From left side back opening measure out 1" (2.5 cm) for extension. Square a line up from fold.

K. Trace all lines and crossmarks to opposite side.

L. Allow seams; cut and notch seams.

M. To plan buttonholes refer to Buttons & Buttonholes.

Finished Waistband Pattern

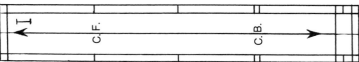

FIGURE 2

1.   Open paper. Pencil in all traced lines and crossmarks.

2.   Establish grainline on fold.

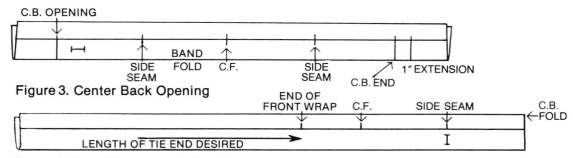

Figure 3. Center Back Opening

Figure 4. Front Wraparound Opening

WAISTBAND FOR CENTER BACK OPENINGS OR WRAPAROUND SKIRTS

FIGURES 3 & 4

To develop waistbands for center back openings or wraparound skirts follow the same procedure discussed for left side openings with the following exception:

Begin marking and measuring from center back or wraparound end instead of left side seam.

FOUR-GORED FLARED SKIRT
sketch 3

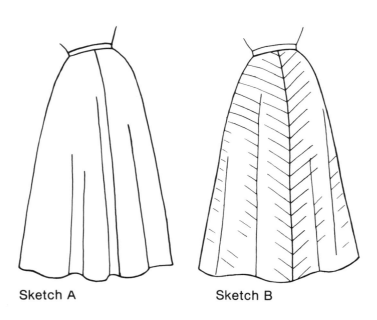

Sketch A   Sketch B

A gored skirt is made in panels which are triangular shaped, narrow at the waistline and wider at the hemline. The skirt usually hugs the hips.

Two methods will be illustrated to develop a four-gored flare skirt:

    1.   the Pivoting Method;

    2.   the Cut/Slash and Spread Method.

The *Pivoting Method* is the shifting of a sloper on pattern paper from a marked position towards a designated point. The *Cut/Slash and Spread Method* is the cutting of a copied sloper along predetermined guide lines and spreading apart the pieces towards a designated measurement.

THE PIVOTING METHOD

FIGURE 1

A.   Cut paper approximately 25″ × 35″ (63.5 × 88.9 cm) for a 28″ (71.1 cm) skirt length.

B.   Use *two-dart front skirt sloper.*

C.   To prepare sloper, draw a line parallel to center front from the bottom of each dart to hemline. Label dartlines *A, B, C, D.*

D.   Place sloper on paper with center front near bottom right-hand edge of paper.

E.   Outline sloper (darker line). Crossmark on paper dartline A and hemline.

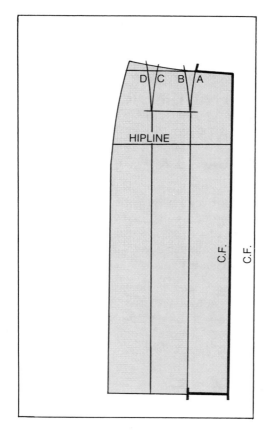

FIGURE 2

A.   First pivoting point is bottom of dart closest to center front. Hold sloper at first pivoting point and pivot sloper away from center front until B touches crossmark.

B.   Crossmark on paper dartline
C. Crossmark at hemline and draw line (as illustrated heavier line).

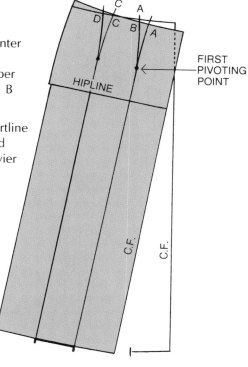

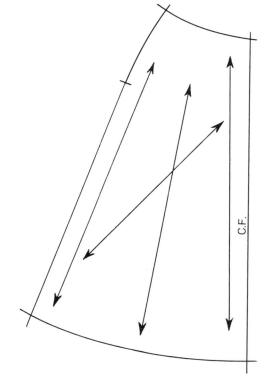

FIGURE 4

A.   Remove sloper. Establish grainline as follows:

> 1.   Parallel to side seam (sketch A).

> 2.   At a 45° angle from center front (sketch B).

> 3.   Parallel to center front or through center of gore.

Note: Skirts will hang or drape differently depending upon the position of the grainline.

B.   To develop the back skirt repeat the same procedure as for front skirt.

C.   To balance side seams refer to Trueing Vertical Seams.

D.   To complete pattern allow hem and seams; cut and notch seams.

To develop waistband, if needed, refer to Skirt Waistbands.

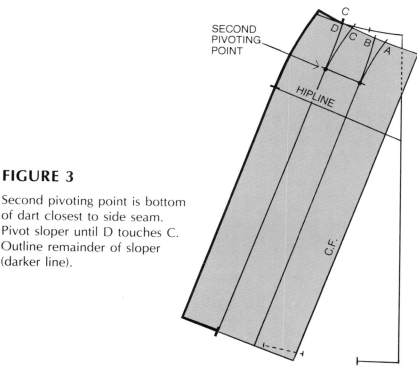

FIGURE 3

Second pivoting point is bottom of dart closest to side seam. Pivot sloper until D touches C. Outline remainder of sloper (darker line).

THE CUT/ SLASH & SPREAD METHOD
FIGURE 5

A.   Cut paper approximately 25" × 30" (63.5 × 76.1 cm) for a 28" (71.1 cm) skirt length.

B.   Use *two-dart front skirt sloper.*

C.   Place sloper on paper. Outline sloper and indicate darts and hipline.

D.   Remove sloper. True all lines crossing all intersections.

E.   Draw two lines parallel to center front from bottom of each dart to hemline. Number sections *1, 2, 3.*

F.   Cut draft on all finished lines and cut sections apart.

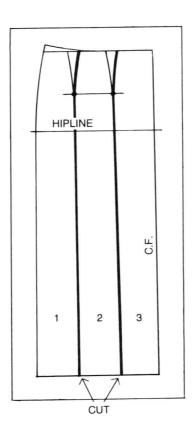

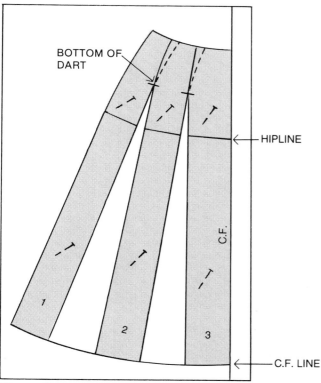

Figure 6.

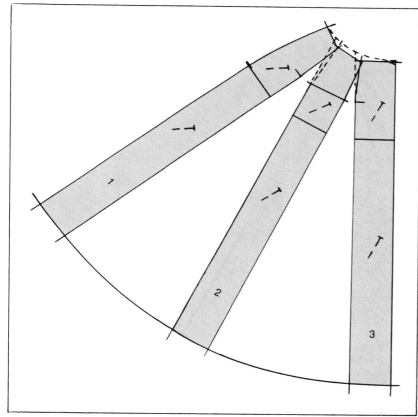

Figure 7.

FIGURES 6 & 7

A.   Cut another sheet of paper 25″ × 35″ (63.5 × 88.9 cm) for a 28″ (71.1 cm) skirt length. Draw a vertical line 1″ (2.5 cm) in from right-hand edge of paper. Label *center front line.*

B.   Pin center front of skirt section to center front line on paper towards bottom edge of paper.

C.   Place sections 2 and 1 matching bottom of darts and closing top of darts, thereby spreading skirt sections at hemline and retaining fit at hip area.
Note: For a fuller flared skirt, the spread at the hemline can be increased by spreading darts up to waistline (Figure 7).

D.   Outline skirt. Crossmark hipline at side seam.

E.   Remove sections. True all lines crossing all intersections.

F.   Establish grainline as follows:

>   1.   Parallel to side seam.

>   2.   At a 45° angle from center front.

>   3.   Parallel to center front or through center of gore.

Note: Skirts will hang or drape differently depending upon the grainline used.

G.   To develop the back skirt repeat the same procedure as for front.

H.   To balance side seams refer to Trueing Vertical Seams.

I.   To complete pattern allow hem and seams; cut and notch seams.

To develop waistband, if needed, refer to Skirt Waistbands.

SIX-GORED FLARED SKIRT
sketch 4

Front & Back View

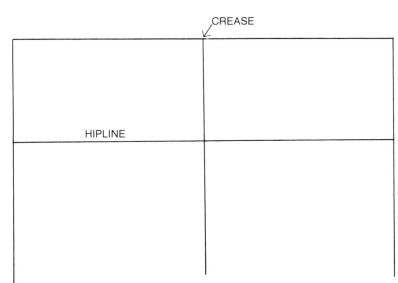

FIGURE 2

A.　Open paper. Draw a line between crossmarks. Label *hipline.*

B.　Draw a line over crease the full length of paper.

Many silhouettes may be obtained by using the gored skirt as a pattern. This is achieved simply by changing the:

    1.　position of the flare points;

    2.　number of seams used;

    3.　degree of flare added to each seam;

    4.　addition of shirring and/or pleating.

FIGURE 1

Preparation of the paper insures the accurate development of the front and back skirt.

A.　Cut paper approximately 35″ (88.9 cm) square for a 28″ (71.1 cm) skirt length.

B.　Fold paper in half. With fold of paper on right-hand side, from top at left-hand side measure down 9″ (22.9 cm). Crossmark. Trace crossmark to opposite side.

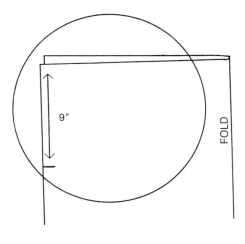

FIGURE 3

A.   Use *two-dart front skirt sloper.*

B.   Place sloper on paper approximately 1" (2.5 cm) in from right-hand edge matching hiplines.

C.   Outline sloper. Indicate waistline dartlines.

D.   Remove sloper. True all lines crossing all intersections.

E.   Draw a grainline parallel to center front from the bottom of the dart closest to center front to hemline. Label *gore line.*

F.   Establish flare points as desired.
Note: On a gored skirt with a fitted hipline, flare points start at the hipline (as illustrated). On a loose-fitting gore skirt, flare points may be placed anywhere between the hipline and waistline.

G.   On each side of gore line, establish width of flare at hemline. Illustrated: 1½" (3.8 cm). Dot. Draw a broken line from dots to flare point.
Note: Width of flare may be ½" (1.3 cm) or more as desired. However, the width of the flare must be the same on each side of the gore line for a balanced flare. Refer to Trueing Vertical Seams.

H.   To establish flare at side seams, on hemline measure out 2" (5.1 cm). Dot. Draw a line from dot to flare point.

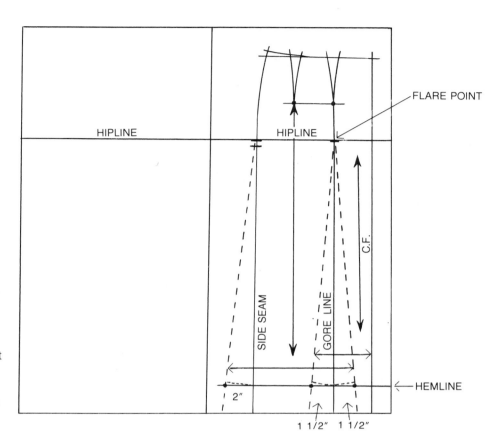

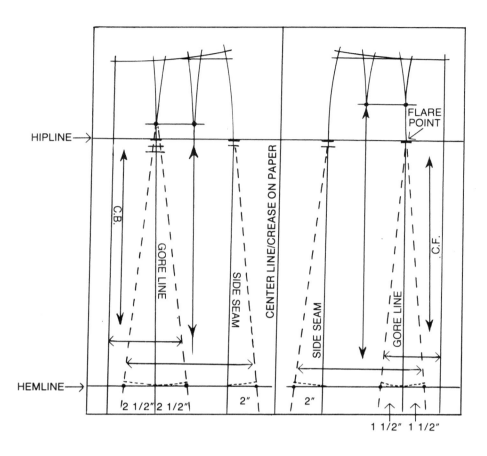

FIGURE 4

A.   To develop back skirt repeat the same procedure as for front.

Note: Increasing the flares towards the back of the skirt creates a more graceful look to the figure. The amount added must be in proportion to the flare added to the front of the skirt. For example in the skirt developed in this sketch:

front flare—1½" (3.8 cm)

side seam flare—2" (5.1 cm)

back flare—2½" (6.4 cm)

B.   Establish crossmarks at flare points. One crossmark for front gore joining; two crossmarks for side seams; three crossmarks for back gore. Crossmarks should be ½" (1.3 cm) apart.

C.   Establish grainline parallel to centers.

D.   On side gores, establish grainline parallel to centers from the bottom of the darts.

E.   Shape hemline at flare lines. Length must measure the same as at grainline from hipline to hemline (slightly curved broken lines).

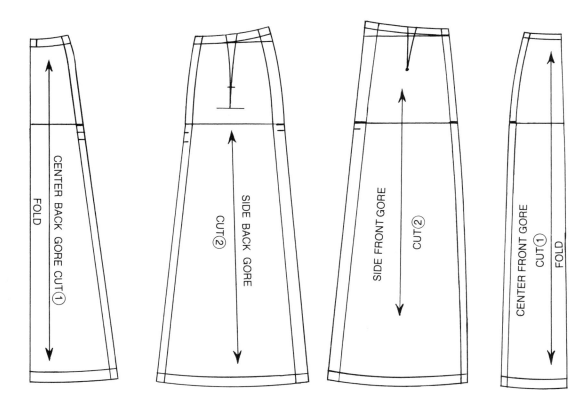

FIGURE 5

A. Copy center front gore as indicated by arrow at hemline in Figure 4.

B. Copy crossmarks and grainline.

C. To develop each gore repeat the procedure.

D. Allow hem on each gore. Illustrated: 1" (2.5 cm).

E. To complete pattern true seamlines. Refer to Trueing Vertical Seams.

To develop waistband, if needed, refer to Skirt Waistbands.

Front & Back View

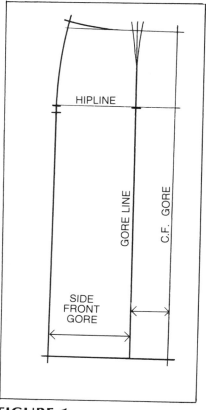

FIGURE 1

A.   Cut paper approximately 20″ × 35″ (50.8 × 88.9 cm) for a 28″ (71.1 cm) skirt length.

B.   Use *two-dart front skirt sloper.*

C.   Place sloper on paper and outline. Indicate dart nearest center front and hipline. (Side dart will be absorbed in shirring.)

D.   Remove sloper. True all lines crossing all intersections. Establish crossmarks on hipline: one below dart nearest center front; two at side seam ½″ (1.3 cm) apart (as illustrated).

E.   Draw a grainline parallel to center front from bottom of dart closest to center front to hemline and through dart up to waistline. Label *gore line.*

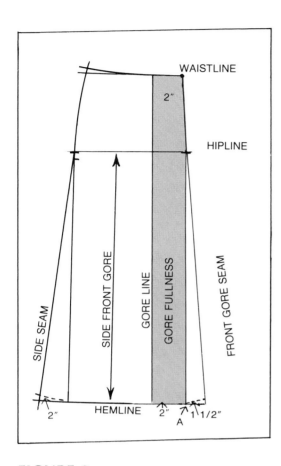

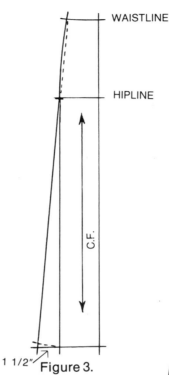

1 1/2" Figure 3.

FIGURE 3

A.   Copy center front gore, hipline and crossmark. Label *center front*.

B.   At hemline for flare measure out 1½" (3.8 cm). Dot. Draw a line from dot to waistline.

C.   To develop center back and side back gores repeat same procedure.
Note: Allow the same amount of flare at side seam. Add three crossmarks ½" (1.3 cm) apart on back gore for joining.

FIGURE 2

A.   On another sheet of paper, allowing more paper on right-hand side, copy side front gore and hipline crossmarks. Extend waistline, hipline and hemline to right-hand edge of paper.
Note: Do not copy waistline darts as they will be absorbed into shirring.

B.   Establish grainline by squaring a line from hipline through center of gore.

C.   At waistline and hemline from gore line measure out amount desired for shirring. Illustrated: 2" (5.1 cm). Dot. Draw a line between dots. Label *A* at hemline.

Note: Amount of fullness added for shirring depends upon the fabric used and the effect desired:

D.   At hemline from A measure out 1½" (3.8 cm) for flare. Dot. Draw a line from dot to waistline. Label *front gore seam.*

E.   At hemline from side seam measure out 2" (5.1 cm) for flare. Dot. Draw a line from dot to widest part of hipline.

F.   Shape hemline at flare lines. Length must measure the same as at grainline from hipline to hemline (slightly curved broken lines).

FIGURE 4

A.   Allow hem on each gore. Illustrated: 1" (2.5 cm).

B.   To complete pattern true seamlines. Refer to Trueing Vertical Seams.

To develop waistband, if needed, refer to Skirt Waistbands.

SIX-GORED FLARED SKIRT WITH SHIRRED FRONT GORE

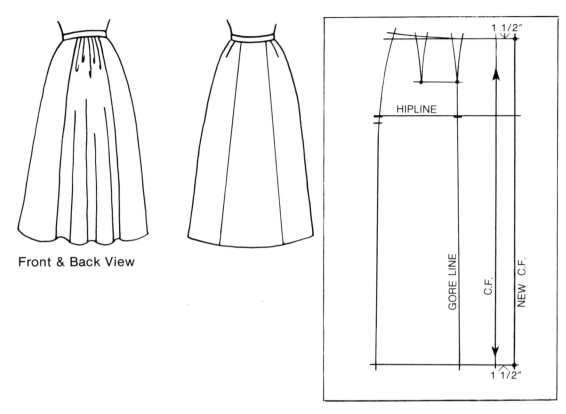

Front & Back View

FIGURE 1

A.   Cut paper approximately 20" × 35" (50.8 × 88.9 cm) for a 28" (71.1 cm) skirt length.

B.   Use *two-dart front skirt sloper.*

C.   Center sloper on paper and outline. Indicate darts and hipline.

D.   Remove sloper. True all lines crossing all intersections. Establish crossmarks on hipline: one below dart closest to center front; two at side seam ½" 1.3 cm) apart (as illustrated).

E.   Draw a grainline parallel to center front from bottom of dart closest to center front to hemline. Label *gore line.*

F.   At waistline and hemline from center front, measure out desired amount for front gore fullness. Illustrated: 1½" (3.8 cm). Dot.
Note: Amount of fullness added for shirring depends upon the fabric used and the effect desired.

G.   Draw a line between dots. Label *new center front.*

H.   Establish grainline parallel to center front.

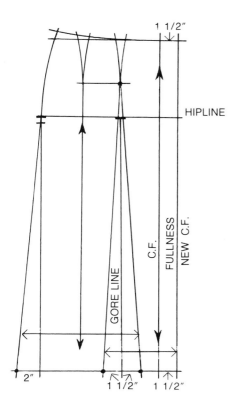

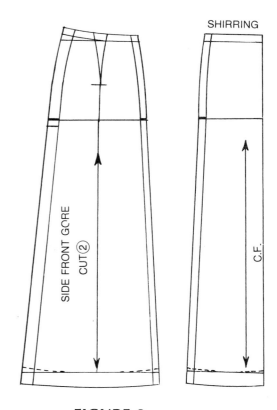

FIGURE 2

A.   On both sides of gore line at hemline measure out 1½" (3.8 cm) for flare. Dot. Draw flare lines from dots to bottom of dart.

B.   At hemline from side seam measure out 2" (5.1 cm) for flare. Dot. Draw a line from dot to widest part of hipline.

C.   Establish grainline parallel to center front by dropping line from bottom of dart.

D.   Shape hemline at flare lines. Length must be the same as at grainline from hipline to hemline. See curved broken lines in Figure 3.

FIGURE 3

A.   Copy center front gore, side front gore, hipline, crossmarks. grainlines and dart (as illustrated).

B.   Allow hem on each gore. Illustrated: 1" (2.5 cm).

C.   To develop center back skirt refer to Six-Gored Flared Skirt.

D.   To complete pattern true seamlines. Refer to Trueing Vertical Seams.

To develop waistband, if needed, refer to Skirt Waistbands.

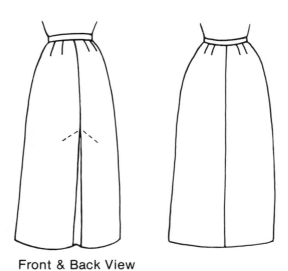

Front & Back View

FIGURE 1

A.   Cut paper approximately 20″ × 35″ (50.8 × 88.9 cm) for a 28″ (71.1 cm) skirt length.

B.   Use *two-dart front skirt sloper*.

C.   Place sloper 5″ (12.7 cm) from right-hand edge of paper and outline. Indicate darts and hipline.

D.   Remove sloper. True all lines crossing all intersections. Establish two crossmarks on side seam at hipline ½″ (1.3 cm) apart (as illustrated).

E.   At hemline from center front measure out ½″ (1.3 cm). Dot. Draw a line from dot to waistline. Label *new center front*.
Note: 1. The ½″ (1.3 cm) flare prevents the inverted pleat from spreading when not in motion.
2. The ½″ (1.3 cm) flare is for a 28″ (71.1 cm) skirt length. For a longer skirt extend the line. The flare will widen automatically as the skirt is lengthened and will become narrower as the skirt is shortened.

F.   At hemline from side seam measure out 1½″ (3.8 cm) for flare. Dot. Draw a line from dot to widest part of hipline.

G.   Shape hemline at flare lines. Length must be the same as at grainline from hipline to hemline (slightly curved broken lines).

H.   Plan and draw stitching line for kick pleat. Illustrated: height, 13″ (33 cm); depth from center front, 3″ (7.6 cm) at hemline, 2″ (5.1 cm) at end of pleat. Crossmark stitching line (as illustrated).
Note: Kick pleat may be higher on skirt depending upon the effect desired.

I.   Fold paper under on new center front.

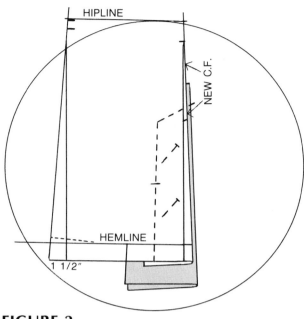

FIGURE 2

To prepare paper for kick pleat backing:

A.   Cut paper approximately 18″ (45.7 cm) square. Fold paper in half.

B.   Place fold of skirt draft to fold of paper (shaded area). Pin.

C.   Trace planned kick pleat line (broken line), crossmark and hemline to paper.

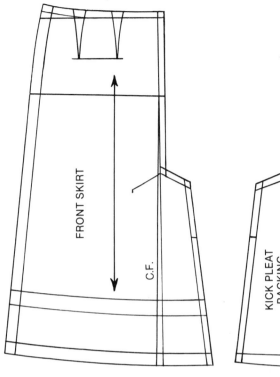

Figure 3.   Figure 3A.

FIGURE 3

A.   Remove skirt draft.

B.   Open paper of skirt draft. Pencil in traced lines and crossmark.

C.   Establish grainline parallel to original center front.

D.   To complete pattern allow hem and seams; cut and notch seams.

FIGURE 3A

A.   Pin kick pleat backing in folded position. True traced lines crossing intersections.

B.   Allow hem and seams; cut and notch seams.

C.   Open pleat. Pencil in remainder of traced lines. Establish grainline on fold.

FOUR-GORED FLARED SKIRT WITH CENTER FRONT INVERTED KICK PLEAT   sketch 7 continued

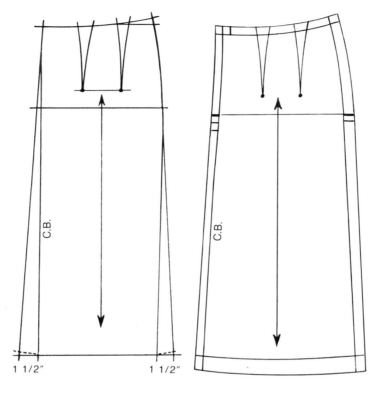

Figure 4.   Figure 4A.

FIGURE 4

A.   Copy *two-dart back skirt sloper.*

B.   True all lines crossing all intersections.

C.   At hemline from side seam measure out the same amount for flare as on front skirt. Illustrated: 1½" (3.8 cm). Dot. Draw a line from dot to hipline.

D.   At hemline from center back measure out 1½" (3.8 cm) for flare. Dot. Draw a line from dot to waistline.

E.   Establish grainline parallel to original center back.

FIGURE 4A

To complete pattern allow hem and seams; cut and notch seams.
Note: To true and balance back side seam with front side seam refer to Trueing Vertical Seams.

To develop waistband, if needed, refer to Skirt Waistbands.

Front & Back View

FIGURE 1

A.   Cut paper approximately 20″ × 35″ (50.8 × 88.9 cm) for a 28″ (71.1 cm) skirt length.

B.   Use *two-dart front skirt sloper.*

C.   Center sloper on paper and outline. Indicate darts and hipline.

D.   Remove sloper. True all lines crossing all intersections. Establish crossmarks on hipline: one below dart closest center front; two at side seam ½″ (1.3 cm) apart (as illustrated).

E.   Draw a grainline parallel to center front from bottom of dart closest to center front to hemline. Label *gore line.*

F.   On both sides of gore line at hemline measure out ½″ (1.3 cm) for slight flare. Dot. Draw flare lines from dots at hemline to bottom of dart. Label each line *flare line.* (see Note in sketch 7, Figure 1).

G.   On side gore establish grainline parallel to center front by dropping a line from end of dart.

H.   On center gore establish grainline parallel to center front.

I.   From side seam at hemline measure out 1½″ (3.8 cm) for flare. Dot. Draw a line from dot to widest point of hipline.

J.   Shape hemline at flare lines. Length must be the same as at grainline from hipline to hemline (slightly curved broken lines).

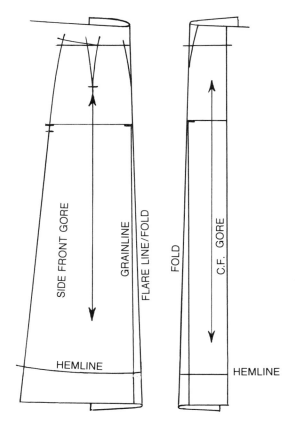

FIGURE 2

A.   On another sheet of paper, allow 5″ (12.7 cm) at right-hand side of paper, copy side front gore (follow arrow near hemline).

B.   On another sheet of paper, allow 5″ (12.7 cm) at left-hand side of paper, copy center front gore (follow arrow near hemline).

C.   True all lines crossing all intersections.

D.   Fold paper under on flare line of each gore.

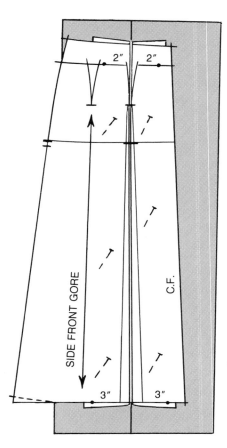

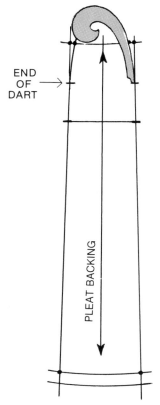

FIGURE 3

FIGURE 4

FIGURE 3

A.   To develop separate pleat backing, cut paper 10″ × 35″ (25.4 × 88.9 cm).

B.   Fold paper in half. Crease. Open paper and draw a line over crease. Label *grainline*.

C.   Pin skirt gores to paper matching hipline crossmarks and folded edges of skirt gores to grainline of paper.

D.   On both sides of waist dartlines at fold measure in 2″ (5.1 cm). Dot.

E.   On both sides of hemline at fold measure in 3″ (7.6 cm). Dot.

F.   Trace waistline and hemline from dot to dot across hipline to center front and end of dart. Indicate all dots with awl.

G.   Remove skirt sections.

FIGURE 4

A.   On pleat backing draw a line from dots at hemline through dots at waistline. Pencil in traced lines across waistline, hipline and hemline.

B.   Measure up from hipline distance to end of dart. Crossmark. Repeat on opposite side (as illustrated).

C.   Pleat backing must measure the same as the pleat underlay at waistline. To make this adjustment on pleat backing, from grainline at waistline measure out 2″ (5.1 cm). With French curve, draw a line to end of dart crossmark (as illustrated). Repeat on opposite side.

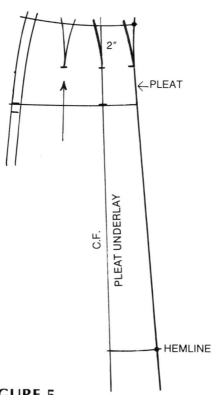

FIGURE 5

A.   On center front skirt gore open pleat. Draw a line from dot at waistline to dot at hemline.

B.   Shape pleat seam from end of dart up to waistline. Underlay at waistline should also measure 2″ (5.1 cm).

C.   Pencil in traced hipline on pleat underlay.

D.   Repeat on front side gore. *Note:* Back skirt may be a duplicate of the front skirt or may be a basic back or two-gore back as in sketch 7.

E.   Allow hemline on all gores.

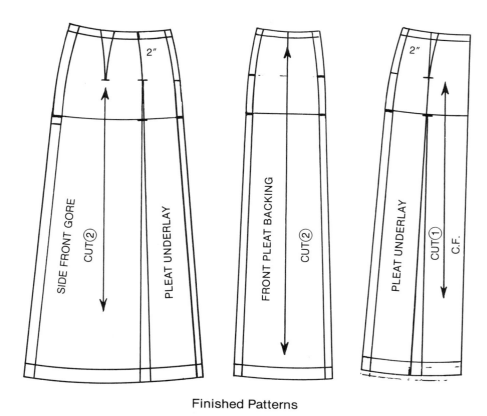

Finished Patterns

FIGURE 6

To complete pattern true seamlines, allow seams and hem; cut and notch seams.

To develop waistband, if needed, refer to Skirt Waistbands.

EIGHT-GORED FLARED SKIRT
sketch 9

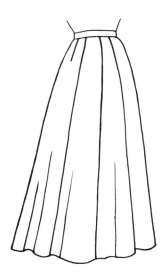

To develop the pattern for this sketch refer to Six-Gored Flared Skirt. To develop pattern for a ten-gored flared skirt, add additional flare line at bottom of second dart.

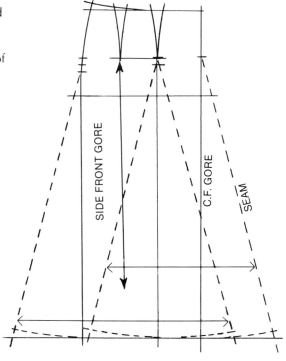

SIDE FRONT GORE

C.F. GORE

SEAM

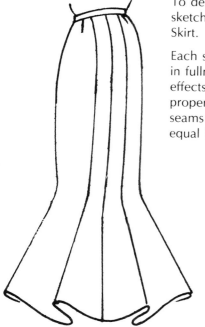

To develop the pattern for this sketch refer to Six-Gored Flared Skirt.

Each seam in this skirt may vary in fullness to achieve different effects. However, to obtain a properly balanced flare, the two seams that are joined must be equal in fullness.

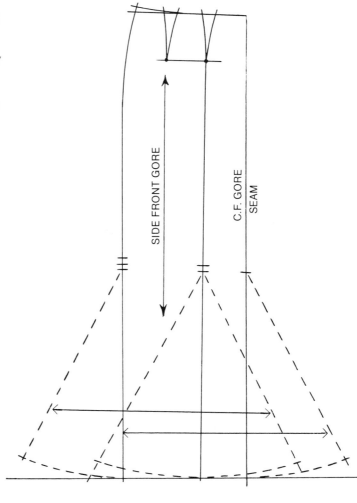

SIDE FRONT GORE

C.F. GORE

SEAM

GORED SKIRT WITH BACK FULLNESS
sketch 11

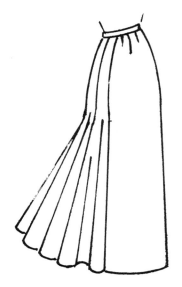

To develop the pattern for this sketch refer to Six-Gored Flared Skirt.

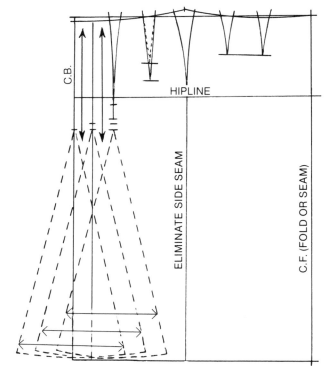

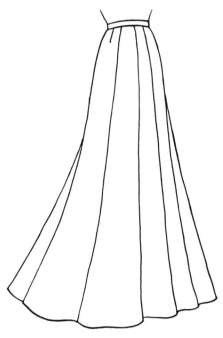

To develop the pattern for this sketch refer to Six-Gored Flared Skirt.

Each seam in this skirt may vary in fullness to achieve different effects. However, to obtain a properly balanced flare, the two seams that are joined must be equal in fullness.

To develop pattern for a ten-gored flared skirt add additional flare line at bottom of second dart.

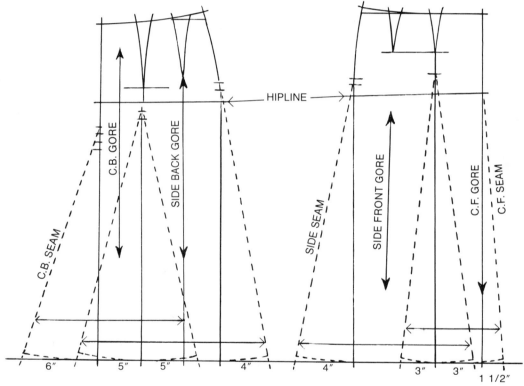

MULTIPLE GORED/UMBRELLA SKIRT
sketch 13

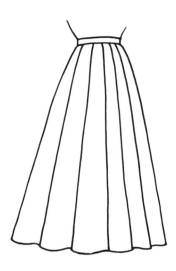

When a skirt is designed with twelve or more gores, it is not necessary to develop the pattern from the basic skirt sloper. All the gores in the skirt could be cut the same. However, a final adjustment must be made at the waistline from the center back to the side seam for the skirt to fit and hang properly (refer to Skirt Waistline Adjustments).

TWELVE-GORED SKIRT

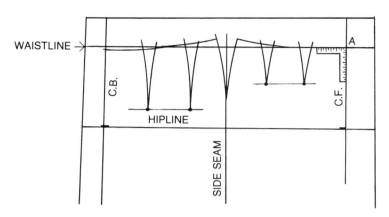

WAISTLINE & FLARE POINT MEASUREMENTS

FIGURE 1

A.   Cut paper approximately 15″ × 25″ (38.1 × 63.5 cm).

B.   Fold paper in half. Crease. Open paper and draw a line over crease. Label *side seam.*

C.   Use *two-dart front and back skirt slopers.* Place slopers on paper matching side seams at hipline and side seam on paper. Outline upper sections. Crossmark hipline and darts. Indicate bottom of darts with awl.

D.   Remove slopers. Draw a line between hipline crossmarks. Label center front waistline *A* (as illustrated).

E.   From A square a line across and through a center back. Label *waistline.*

FIGURE 2

A.   From A measure down desired flare point. Illustrated: 4″ (10.2 cm). Square a line across through center back. Label *flare point line.*

B.   Draw a line halfway between waistline and flare point line. Label *center line.*

C.   To obtain size of gore measure waistline (*do not* include dart underlay, center line and flare point line).

D.   Divide each line into six equal parts. This represents half of the twelve-gored skirt. *Note:* 1. When dividing each area use the larger fraction as this ease will be absorbed by the thickness of the seam allowance. 2. The one gore will be developed on the fold (Figure 3) so the measurement of the gore must again be divided in half. The following illustrates how to obtain final measurements.

Measurement of *half* of twelve-gored skirt

14″ (30.6 cm) waistline

17″ (43.2 cm) center line

19″ (48.3 cm) flare point line

Six gores (half of skirt) ⅙ of measurements

⅙ of 14″ = 2⅜″ (6 cm)

⅙ of 17″ = 3″ (7.6 cm)

⅙ of 19″ = 3¼″ (8.3 cm)

Half of gore to be used for developing gore

½ of 2⅜″ = 1¼″ (3.8 cm)

½ of 3″ = 1½″ (3.8 cm)

½ of 3¼″ = 1⅝″ (4.1 cm)

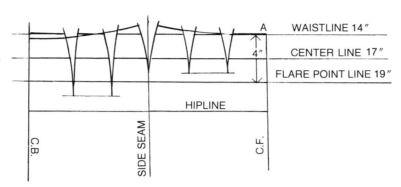

DEVELOPING GORE
FIGURE 3

A.   Cut paper approximately 16″ × 34″ (40.6 × 86.4 cm) for a 28″ (71.1 cm) skirt length.

B.   Fold paper in half lengthwise and pin.

C.   From fold measure down approximately 2″ (5.1 cm) from top edge of paper. Square a line across paper. Label *waistline.* From waistline measure down desired flare point. Illustrated: 4″ (10.2 cm). Square a line across paper. Label *flare point line.* Draw a line halfway between waistline and flare point line. Label *center line.*

D.   From fold on waistline measure in 1¼″ (3.2 cm). Dot. From fold on center line measure in 1½″ (3.8 cm). Dot. From fold on flare point line measure in 1⅝″ (4.1 cm). Dot.

E.   From waistline on fold measure down desired length of skirt. Illustrated: 28″ (71.1 cm). Square a line across paper. Label *hemline.*

F.   Square a line from dot at flare point line to hemline. Line *must* be parallel to fold. Label *gore line.*

G.   From gore line at hemline measure out desired amount for flare. Dot. Illustrated: 2½″ (6.4 cm). Draw a line from dot to flare point line.

H.   Draw a line from flare point dot to waistline. Line may be slightly curved depending upon shape of figure.

I.   Length at side seam must be the same as length at gore line from flare point line to gore line to hemline. Shape hemline to gore line (slightly curved broken line).

J.   On side seam crossmark halfway between hemline and flare point line and at flare point.

K.   Trace waistline, flare point line, gore seamline, hemline and all crossmarks to opposite side.

L.   With gore folded allow hem and seam *except* at waistline. Cut.

M.   Allow 1¼″ (3.2 cm) seam at waistline for further adjustment. Cut.

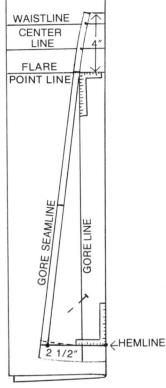

Figure 3.

FIGURE 4

A.   Open gore. Pencil in traced lines and crossmarks. Establish grainline on crease.

B.   Label pattern piece *front skirt gore.* Indicate *cut* ⑥.

Note: Additional gore patterns are necessary to shape back waistline (see finished patterns). If the following steps are followed carefully, the results will be more accurate than if gores are copied and cut individually.

C.   To prevent shifting while tracing and cutting, pin complete front gore securely onto three sheets of paper.

D.   Carefully trace waistline, gore line, flare point line, hemline, grainline and all crossmarks.

E.   Cut away paper along seam allowance. To prevent gores from shifting while cutting pin securely.

F.   Separate gores. Pencil in all traced lines and crossmarks.

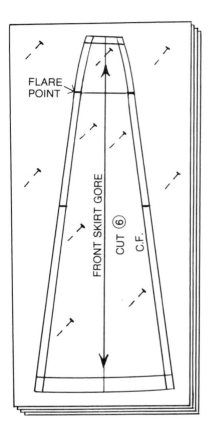

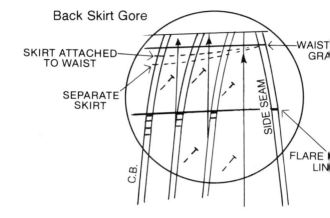

FIGURE 5

A.   To shape back waistline match and pin the finished seamlines at the waistline overlapping seam allowance. *Note:* When pinned the waistlines and flare point lines must be straight and parallel to each other (darker lines).

B.   Label *center back* and *side seam.*

C.   If skirt is to be *attached to garment,* lower center back waistline ¼" to ½" (0.6 to 1.3 cm). If skirt is a *separate garment,* lower center back waistline 1" to 1½" (2.5 to 3.8 cm). Blend a curved line to side seam or waistline grainline (broken line). Refer to Skirt Waistline Adjustments.

D.   To aid in joining gores correctly establish additional crossmarks ½" (1.3 cm) apart (as illustrated).

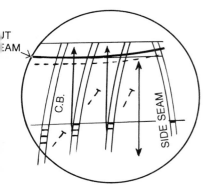

FIGURE 6

A.   In pinned position allow ½″ (1.3 cm) seam at new waistline. Cut away excess paper.

B.   Separate gores. Match each gore at seamline from waistline to flare point line. Trace additional crossmarks to opposite seamlines. Pencil in crossmarks.

**FIGURE 7
FINISHED PATTERN**

The finished pattern shows shaping of back waistline in relation to front waistline and grainline and shows correct placement for crossmarks. *Note:* Since front waistline from center front to side seam is a straight grain, only one pattern is necessary. See front gore, cut⑥.

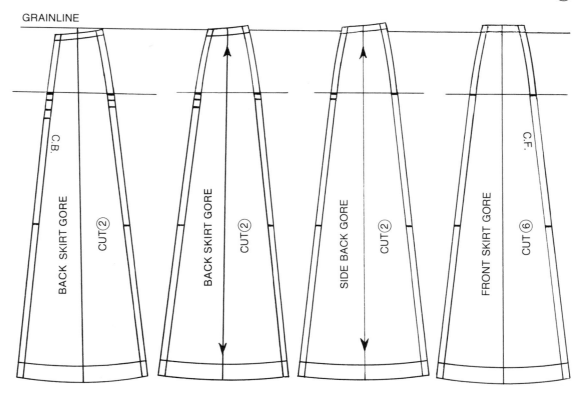

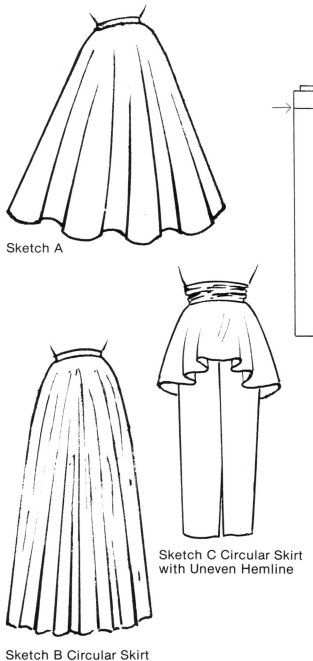

Sketch A

Sketch C Circular Skirt with Uneven Hemline

Sketch B Circular Skirt in Soft Fabric

CIRCULAR SKIRT WITH CENTER FRONT & CENTER BACK SEAMS

FIGURE 1

A. To determine radius of full-circle circular skirt measure waistline. Subtract 1″ (2.5 cm). Multiple this result by $\frac{1}{6}$. For example: 25″ (63.5 cm) waistline minus 1″ (2.5 cm) = 24″ (61 cm) × $\frac{1}{6}$ = 4″ (10.2 cm) radius.

B. Cut paper 25″ × 70″ (63.5 × 177.8 cm) for a 28″ (71.1 cm) skirt length.

C. Fold paper in half and pin. On fold from top edge of paper measure down 1″ (2.5 cm). Label *A*. From A square a line across paper.

D. From A measure in on line the determined radius—4″ (10.2 cm). Label *B*.

E. Use a compass and with pointed end on A and pencil on B, draw waistline.
Note: If compass is not available, from A to B measure down the determined radius and continue measurements over to fold.

F. From B on line measure desired length of skirt. Label *C*.

G. To indicate hemline measure down the desired length from various points on waistline. Draw hemline.

H. Trace waistline to opposite side. *Cut hemline only.*

A circular skirt is made by using a full, three-quarter, one-half or one-quarter circle. The formulas discussed in the following sketches to obtain the various circular skirts are quick and easy to develop. The results are approximate measurements and are adequate for workroom purposes.

The lengths of all the circular skirts have not been developed to scale since the pattern diagrams would be too large for the size of the page. All circular skirts are developed without seams to facilitate showing styling and cutting variations.

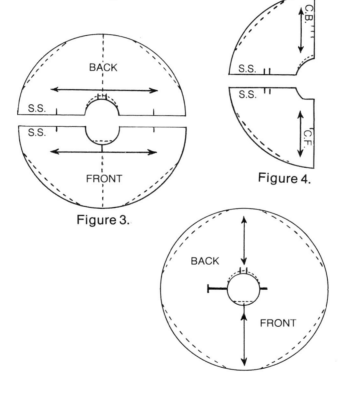

Figure 2.

Figure 3.

Figure 4.

FIGURE 2

A. Open draft. Pencil in traced waistline. Draw a line over crease. Label *side seam*.

B. Label *center front* and *center back*. Establish grainline parallel to centers. Crossmark center front and center back seams (as illustrated).

C. Lower center back waistline ¼" (0.6 cm) and draw a new waistline to side seam line (broken line). Refer to Skirt Waistline Adjustments.

D. For a flattened appearance and more graceful look at center front, the flare of the skirt can be moved slightly away from the center. On center front measure in 1½" (3.8 cm). Crossmark. Square a line back to center front.

E. Cut on adjusted front and back waistline (broken line).

F. Cut circular skirt in fabric and pin to model form to allow bias area to stretch before finishing hemline.

G. With skirt on form measure up from floor new hemline. Transfer adjusted hemline to pattern (dotted lines).
Note: Amount of adjustment depends upon stretchability of fabric. For example crepe has more stretch than cotton.

To develop waistband, if needed, refer to Skirt Waistbands.

CIRCULAR SKIRT WITH SIDE SEAMS

FIGURE 3

The draft in Figure 2 equals one-half of a skirt and has a center front and center back seam. If side seams are preferred, cut two half circles, label pattern and shape waistline (as illustrated).

CIRCULAR SKIRT WITH CENTER FRONT, CENTER BACK & SIDE SEAMS

FIGURE 4

If four seams are desired, cut apart on side seam line. Crossmark seams (as illustrated).

CIRCULAR SKIRT WITHOUT SEAMS

FIGURE 5

If no seams are desired, such as in a very short skirt, cut pattern with center front and center back on fold. Plan placket opening by slashing through waistline on grainline at center back or on left-hand side of skirt. Establish crossmarks on waistline (as illustrated).

SKETCH C CIRCULAR SKIRT WITH UNEVEN HEMLINE

FIGURE 6

If an uneven hemline is desired, shape hemline (as illustrated). Skirt may be developed without any seams, with two seams or with four seams.

CIRCULAR SKIRT WITH CENTER BACK SEAM

FIGURE 1

A. To determine radius of a three-quarter circle circular skirt measure waistline. Subtract 1″ (2.5 cm). Multiply this result by $\frac{1}{5}$. For example: 25″ (63.5 cm) waistline minus 1″ (2.5 cm) = 24″ (61 cm) × $\frac{1}{5}$ = 4 $\frac{4}{5}$″ (10.7 cm).

B. Cut paper 70″ (177.8 cm) square for a 28″ (71.1 cm) skirt length.

C. Fold paper in quarters and pin. Label A (as illustrated).

D. From A measure in the determined radius—4 $\frac{4}{5}$″ (10.7 cm). Crossmark. Label B.

E. Use a compass and with pointed end on A and pencil on B, draw waistline.

F. From B on line measure desired length of skirt. Label C.

G. To indicate hemline measure down the desired length from various points on waistline. Draw hemline.

H. Trace waistline to opposite side. Cut hemline.

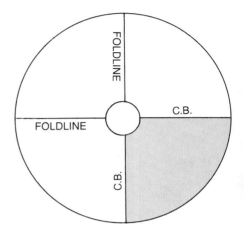

FIGURE 2

A. Open draft. Pencil in traced waistline. Draw very light lines over creases.

B. Cut away one-quarter section of draft (shaded area). Label *center back* (as illustrated).

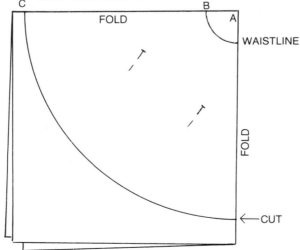

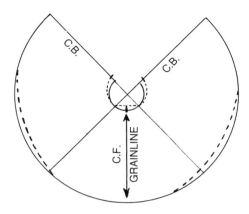

FIGURE 3

A.   To establish center front match the two cut edges. Crease. Open and draw a line over new crease. Label *center front* and *grainline*.

B.   On each side of center back lower center back waistline ¼" (0.6 cm) and flatten center front. Refer to Full Circle Circular Skirt, Figure 2.

C.   Cut on adjusted waistline (broken line).

D.   As in full circle circular skirt, cut skirt in fabric and adjust hemline. Transfer new hemline to pattern. Cut away paper on new hemline.

CIRCULAR SKIRT WITH SIDE SEAMS

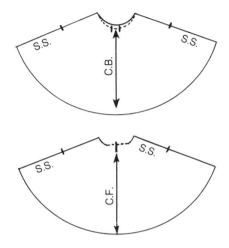

FIGURE 4

A.   To develop three-quarter circle circular skirt with side seams, copy skirt pattern, retain original waistline and hemline. Cut on center front line. Refold each section in half for new centers. Open and draw line on each crease. Label *center front, center back, side seam* and *grainline*.

B.   Lower center back waistline ¼" (0.6 cm).
Note: Adjust center front waistline and hemline after testing pattern in fabric. Amount of adjustment may differ as bias is now on side seam instead of center back.

C.   Transfer adjustments to pattern.

D.   Cut away paper on adjusted waistline and hemline.

E.   Add all crossmarks (as illustrated).

To develop waistband, if needed, refer to Skirt Waistbands.

ONE-HALF CIRCLE CIRCULAR SKIRT
sketch 16

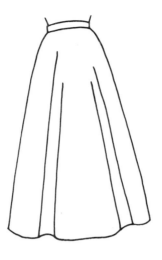

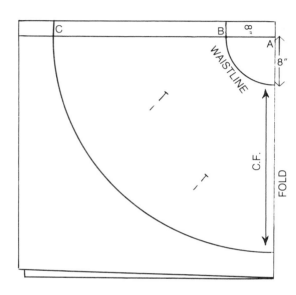

CIRCULAR SKIRT WITH CENTER BACK SEAM

FIGURE 1

A. To determine radius of one-half circle circular skirt measure waistline. Subtract 1" (2.5 cm). Multiply this result by $\frac{1}{3}$. For example: 25" (63.5 cm) waistline minus 1" (2.5 cm) = 24" (61 cm) $\times$ $\frac{1}{3}$ = 8" (20.3 cm) radius.

B. Cut paper 25" $\times$ 75" (63.5 $\times$ 190.5 cm) for a 28" (71.1 cm) skirt length.

C. Fold paper in half and pin. On fold from top edge of paper measure down 1" (2.5 cm). Label A. From A square a line across paper.

D. From A on line measure in the determined radius—8" (20.3 cm). Label B.

E. Use a compass and with pointed end on A and pencil on B, draw waistline.

F. From B on line measure desired length of skirt. Label C.

G. To indicate hemline measure down the desired length from various points on waistline. Draw hemline.

H. Trace waistline to opposite side. Cut on seamline and hemline.

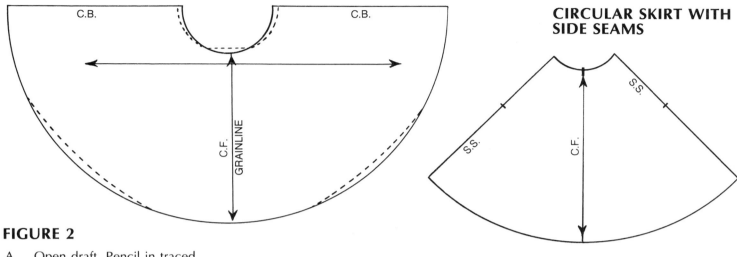

FIGURE 2

A.   Open draft. Pencil in traced waistline. Draw a line over crease. Label *center front* and *grainline.*

B.   Label seam *center back.*

C.   Lower center back waistline ¼″ (0.6 cm).
Note: Adjust center front waistline and hemline after testing pattern in fabric. Amount of adjustment may differ from full-circle circular skirt as there is less fullness and bias is now on side seam.

D.   Transfer adjustments to pattern.

E.   Cut away paper on adjusted waistline and hemline.

F.   Add crossmarks (as illustrated).

CIRCULAR SKIRT WITH SIDE SEAMS

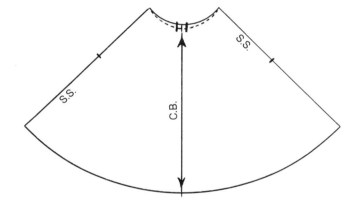

FIGURE 3

To develop one-half circle circular skirt with side seams refer to Three-quarter Circle Circular Skirt, Figure 4, A through E.

To develop waistband, if needed, refer to Skirt Waistbands.

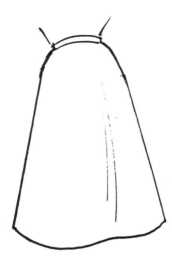

The one-quarter circle gives the skirt an A-line look.

CIRCULAR SKIRT WITH CENTER BACK SEAM

FIGURE 1

Note: To determine the radius of a one-quarter circle circular skirt, 1" (2.5 cm) is not subtracted from the waistline measurement. The one-quarter circle circular skirt is a hip-fitting skirt and the inch is needed for ease over the hips. The extra fullness at the waistline can be eased into the waistband or may be darted at the side seam. If skirt is cut into two sections, shape as illustrated in Figure 4.

A.   Measure waistline and multiply by $\frac{2}{3}$. For example: 25" (63.5 cm) waistline $\times \frac{2}{3} =$ 16 $\frac{2}{3}$" (42.3 cm) radius.

B.   Cut paper approximately 50" (127 cm) square.

C.   Draw two lines at right angles to each other (as illustrated). Label *A*.

D.   From A measure down the determined radius—16 $\frac{2}{3}$" (42.3 cm). Label *B*.

E.   Use a compass and with pointed end on A and pencil on B, draw waistline.

F.   From B on line measure desired length of skirt. Label *C*.

G.   To indicate hemline measure down the desired length from various points on waistline. Draw hemline.

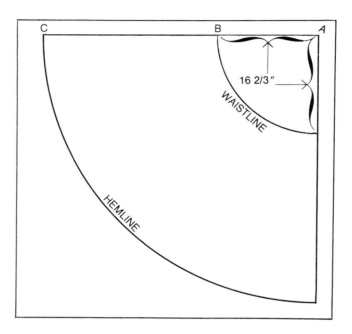

FIGURE 2

A.   To establish center front fold draft in half matching seams. Crease. Pin.

B.   Add $\frac{1}{2}$" (1.3 cm) for ease at seam (broken line). Label *new center back seam*.

C.   With draft pinned cut on all seamlines.

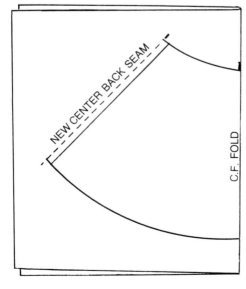

One-Piece Skirt

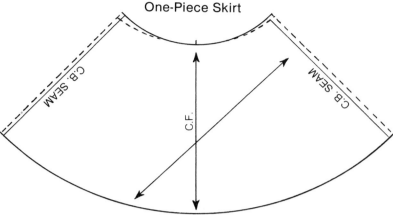

FIGURE 3

A.   Open draft. Draw a line over crease. Label *center front* and *grainline.* On waistline crossmark center front. *Note:* For bias center front redirect grainline (as illustrated).

B.   On each side of center back lower waistline ¼" (0.6 cm) (broken lines). *Note:* Center front of this skirt needs no adjustment.

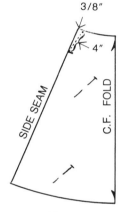

Figure 4.

CIRCULAR SKIRT WITH SIDE SEAMS

FIGURES 4 & 4A

A.   To develop one-quarter circle circular skirt with center front and center back seams retain original back waistline and hemline. Cut apart draft at center front.

B.   Refold sections in half. Pin. Label side seam and center front (Figure 4).

C.   To eliminate ease on waistline, with pattern folded, measure in at waistline/side seam intersection ⅜" to ½" (0.9 to 1.3 cm). Dot. From waistline measure down 4" (10.2 cm). Crossmark.

D.   Draw a curved line from dot to crossmark. Trace line and crossmark to opposite side.

E.   Repeat same procedure on back section.

F.   Cut on all finished lines.

G.   Open sections. Draw a line over crease. Label *center front, center back* and *grainline.* Pencil in crossmarks.

H.   Add crossmarks to waistline (as illustrated).

I.   Adjust back waistline (as illustrated).

To develop waistband, if needed, refer to Skirt Waistbands.

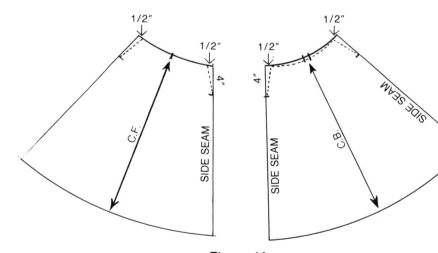

Figure 4A:

Sketch A

To determine the radius for this circular skirt and develop the pattern, refer to Full Circle Circular Skirt. To mark the hemline:

A.   Measure from waistline on two right angles length desired. Crossmark.

B.   Square a line from crossmark to complete hemline.

C.   Shorten points at hemline to length desired (broken line).

D.   Shirr waistline as in sketch B. Refer to Circular Skirt with Shirred Waistline.

Sketch B

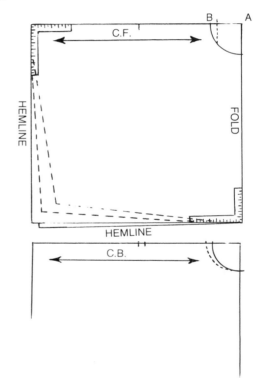

Sketch A

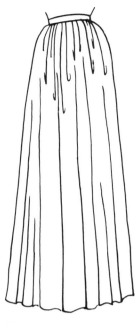

Sketch B Dirndl Skirt
in Soft Fabric

SKETCH A

To develop pattern for a shirred
waistline with average fullness,
double the waistline
measurement and multiply by $\frac{1}{6}$.
To complete pattern for sketch
A refer to Full Circle Circular
Skirt.

SKETCH B

When more shirring at waistline
is desired, such as when using
sheer soft fabrics, more than one
circle is used to achieve the
effect desired.
Notes: Shirring may be added to
any of the circular skirts
discussed following this
principle.

CIRCULAR SKIRT WITH SHIRRED WAISTLINE & PEPLUM

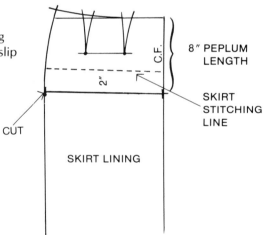

FIGURE 1

Skirt lining may be cut as long as the skirt to serve as a self slip or may be cut away at the peplum line.

8" PEPLUM LENGTH

C.F.

2"

SKIRT STITCHING LINE

CUT

SKIRT LINING

FIGURE 2

To develop pattern for this sketch refer to Full Circle Circular Skirt, increasing the radius to obtain desired shirred fullness at waistline of peplum and hipline of skirt.

FIGURE 1

A. To determine radius for this skirt refer to Full Circle Circular Skirt.

B. Cut paper same width as for full circle and add to length the amount needed for number and depth of tucks planned.

C. Fold paper and draw waistline.

D. Plan and draw number and depth of tucks desired (as illustrated).

1. By varying the depth, number and placement of tucks, many design features may be obtained.

2. If fabric is not wide enough to develop the circular skirt with tucks, piece fabric under one of the tucks.

3. If tucks are planned in a small space or in groups, fabric is sent to a professional to be tucked and pressed before cutting skirt.

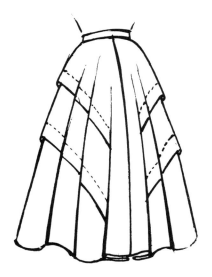

E. Trace tuck lines and waistline to opposite side. Open paper. Pencil in traced tuck lines and waistline.

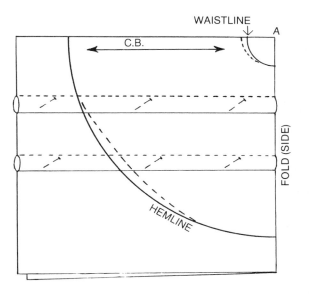

FIGURE 2

Recheck tuck lines for accuracy.

A. Fold and pin tucks.

B. Refold draft and pin.

C. To complete pattern refer to Full Circle Circular Skirt, Figure 1, F and G and Figure 2, A through G and *Notes.*

D. Adjust back waistline (as illustrated broken lines).

E. To adjust front waistline, refer to Full Circular Skirt, Figure D.

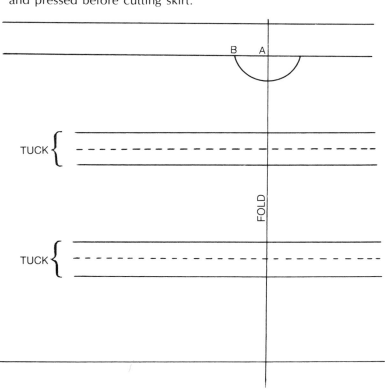

EIGHT-GORED CIRCULAR SKIRT
sketch 22

1.   The principle of dividing the circular skirt into gores may be applied to the three-quarter, one-half and one-quarter circle circular skirts.

2.   All the circle patterns may be folded into thirds, quarters, etc. until the number of gores desired have been obtained.

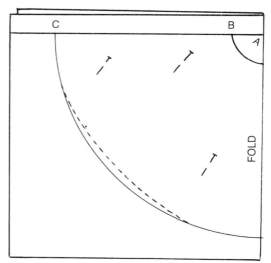

Figure 1.

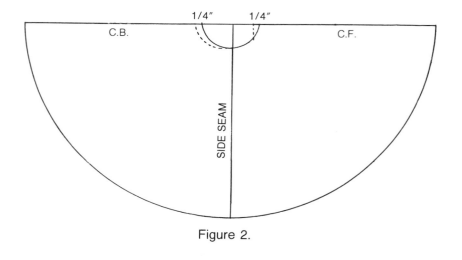

Figure 2.

FIGURES 1 & 2

To determine the radius for this skirt and develop the pattern refer to Full Circle Circular Skirt.

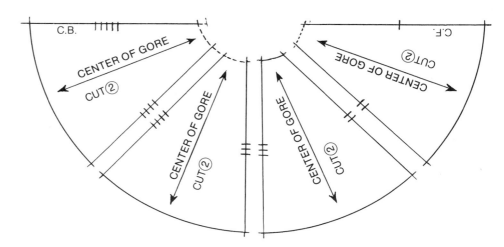

FIGURE 4

A. Cut apart on seamlines. Copy sections. True all lines crossing all intersections.

B. Establish grainline in center of each gore. Fold gores in half for accurate placement of grainlines.

FIGURE 3

A. To develop pattern for an eight-gored circular skirt refold draft in half and then in half again. Crease.

B. Open draft. Draw a line over each crease.

C. Indicate crossmarks for joining gores starting with one crossmark at center front, two at gore line, three on side seam, four at gore line and five at center back (as illustrated). Crossmarks should be ½" (1.3 cm) apart.

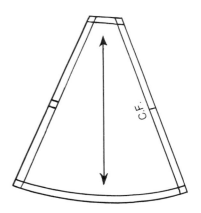

Finished Front Gore Pattern

FIGURE 4A

This diagram illustrates completed center front gore.

To develop waistband, if needed, refer to Skirt Waistbands.

CIRCULAR SKIRT WITH PLEATED WAISTLINE
sketch 23

The principle of adding pleats to the circular skirt may be applied to the three-quarter, one-half and one-quarter circle skirts.

FIGURES 1 & 2

A. Plan the number of pleats desired.

B. Plan the depth of each pleat and then double the depth for pleat underlay.

C. Multiply number of pleats by the size of each pleat. For example: 4" (10.2 cm) total size of pleat; 2" (5.1 cm) for pleat and 2" (5.1 cm) for pleat underlay. Eight side pleats or four inverted pleats multiplied by 4" (10.2 cm) = 32" (81.3 cm) total allowance for pleats.

D. Add this total to waistline measurement and multiply by 1/6.

E. Cut paper 25" × 70" (63.5 × 177.8 cm) for a 28" (71.1 cm) skirt length.

F. To develop pattern for this sketch refer to Full Circle Circular Skirt, Figures 1 and 2.

G. With crossmarks indicate placement of pleats as desired. Illustrated: center of quarter circle.

FIGURE 3

This diagram illustrates pleats in fabric.

To develop waistband, if needed, refer to Skirt Waistbands.

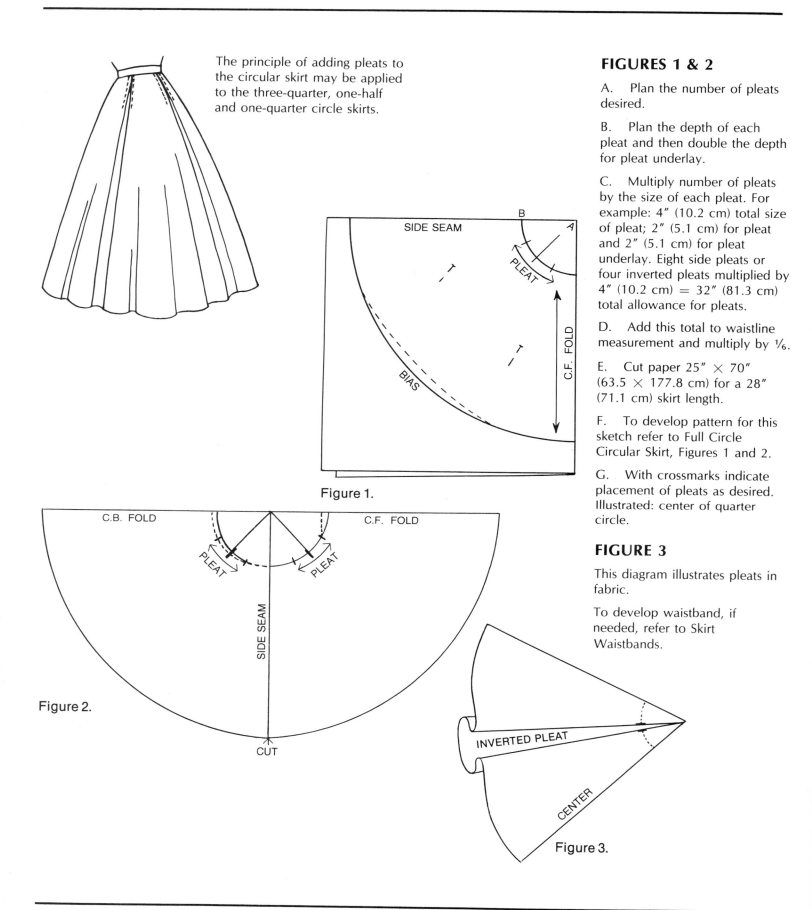

Figure 1.

Figure 2.

Figure 3.

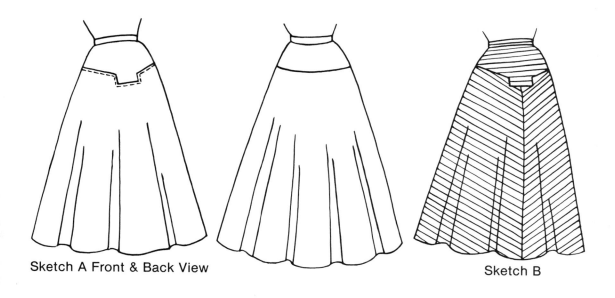

Sketch A Front & Back View

Sketch B

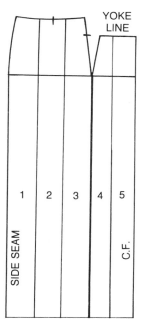

YOKE LINE

1 2 3 4 5

SIDE SEAM

C.F.

HIP YOKE SECTION

FIGURE 1

A.   Cut paper approximately 12″ × 30″ (30.5 × 76.2 cm) for a 28″ (71.1 cm) skirt length.

B.   Use *one-dart front skirt sloper*. Place sloper on paper and outline. Indicate dart and hipline. Remove sloper. True all lines crossing all intersections. Cut on all seamlines.
Note: If stylized hip yoke is planned below the hipline, use the *two-dart front skirt sloper*. The dart nearest the center front will be eliminated when developing the skirt yoke, but the side dart should be retained for better fit.

C.   Cup and close skirt dart. Pin. Draw stylized hip yoke desired. Establish crossmark on yokeline for joining to skirt.

D.   With dart closed, cut on yokeline.

E.   Pin yoke onto another sheet of paper and trace. Remove yoke draft. True all lines crossing all intersections.

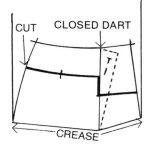

CUT   CLOSED DART

CREASE

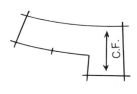

C.F.

FIGURE 2

A.   Label *center front*.

B.   Establish grainline parallel to center front.

SKIRT SECTION

FIGURE 3

A.   Open dart on skirt draft. Draw a line parallel to center front from bottom of dart to hemline (darker line).

B.   Divide front skirt section in half and side skirt section in thirds. Draw lines parallel to center front from hemline to yokeline. Number each section (as illustrated).

C.   Cut away excess paper from skirt draft.

D.   Cut slash lines from hemline up to but not through yokeline except at dartline nearest center front.

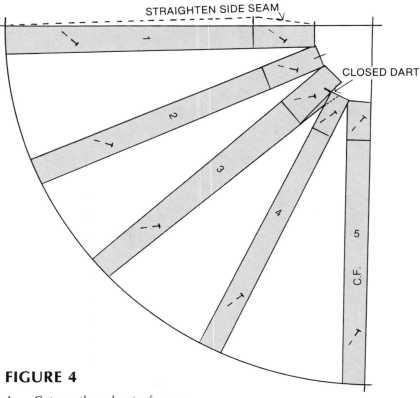

STRAIGHTEN SIDE SEAM

CLOSED DART

FIGURE 4

A.   Cut another sheet of paper approximately 45" (114.3 cm) square.

B.   Draw two lines at right angles to each other.

C.   Place cut skirt sections on paper matching center front, #5, and side seam, #1, to right angle lines of paper.

D.   Close dart matching crossmark at yoke intersection. Spread sections evenly to form circular skirt.

E.   Blend skirt yokeline. Straighten side seam. Draw hemline and yokeline crossmark.

F.   Remove skirt draft. True all lines crossing all intersections. Establish grainline parallel to center front.

G.   As in Full Circle Circular Skirt, cut skirt in fabric adjust hemline, transfer new hemline to pattern and cut away paper on new hemline.

HIP YOKE & SKIRT SECTIONS

FIGURES 5 & 5A

A.   To complete pattern allow hem and seams; cut and notch seams.

B.   To develop back follow same procedure as for front.

To develop waistband, if needed, refer to Skirt Waistbands.

Finished Patterns

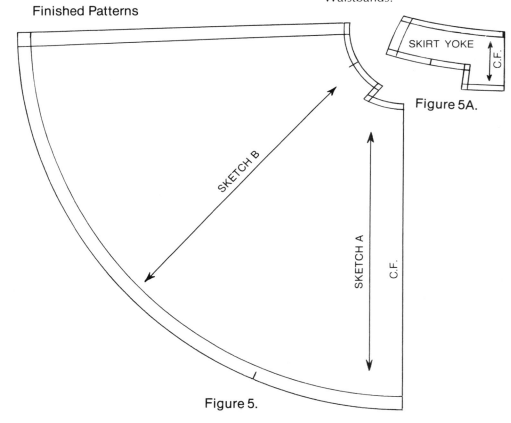

Figure 5A.

Figure 5.

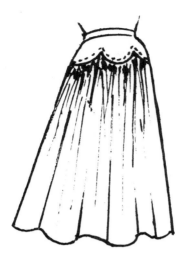

Sketch A Front & Back View

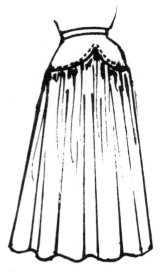

Sketch B

A dirndl skirt is a full skirt gathered into waistband or bodice or as illustrated in these sketches into a hip yoke.

HIP YOKE SECTION

FIGURE 1

A.   Cut paper approximately 12″ × 30″ (30.5 × 76.2 cm) for a 28″ (71.1 cm) skirt length.

B.   Use *one-dart front skirt sloper.* Place sloper on paper and outline. Indicate dart and hipline.

C.   Cup and close skirt dart. Pin. Draw stylized hip yoke desired. Establish crossmark on yokeline for joining to skirt.

D.   With dart closed, cut on yokeline.

E.   Pin yoke onto another sheet of paper and trace. Remove yoke draft. True all lines crossing all intersections.

FIGURE 2

A.   Label *center front.*

B.   Establish grainline parallel to center front.

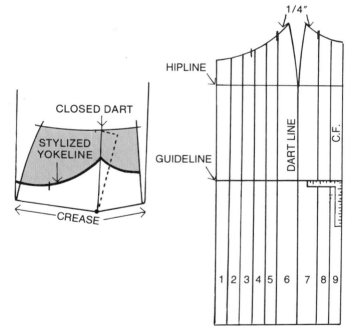

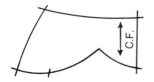

SKIRT SECTION

FIGURE 3

A.   Open dart on skirt draft. Draw a line parallel to center front from bottom of dart to hemline. Label *dartline.*

B.   On yokeline measure 1¼″ (3.2 cm) on either side of dartline. Draw lines parallel to dartline from yokeline to hemline.

C.   Divide remainder of yokeline into sections approximately 1″ (2.5 cm) apart. Draw lines parallel to dartline from yokeline to hemline.

D.   Number sections (as illustrated). From center front square a line halfway between hemline and yokeline. Label *guideline.*

E.   Cut away excess paper from skirt draft.

F.   Cut apart skirt sections. Close dart and pin.
Note: This is only necessary when yoke style line has a point at the dart.

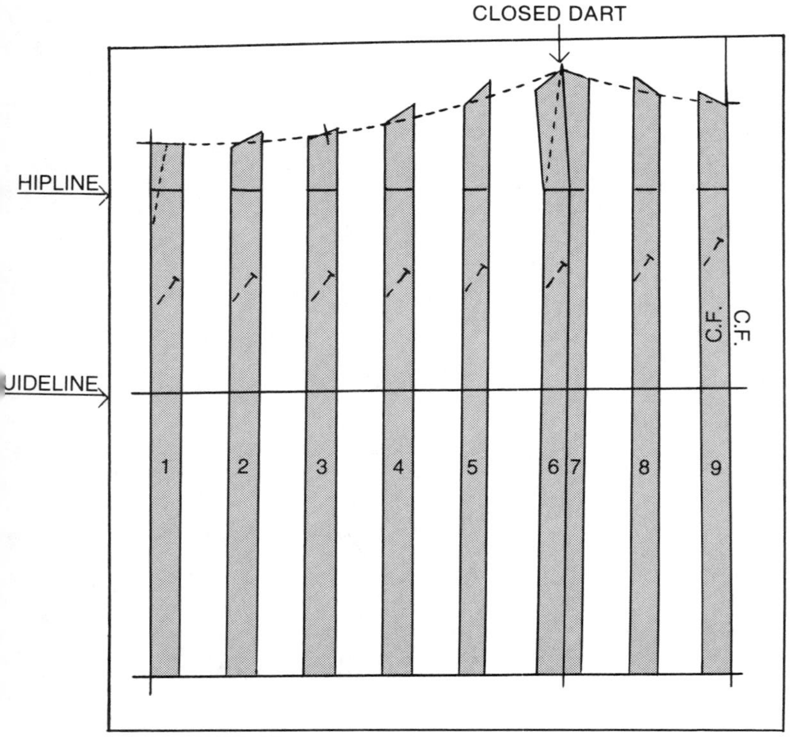

CLOSED DART

HIPLINE

GUIDELINE

1 2 3 4 5 6 7 8 9

C.F.

FIGURE 4

A.   Cut another sheet of paper approximately 35″ (88.9 cm) square.

B.   Fold paper in half and crease. Open paper. Draw a line over crease. Label *guideline*. Square a line at right angles to guideline length of paper. Label *center front*.

C.   Place cut skirt sections to paper matching guidelines and center front. Spread each section desired amount. Illustrated: 2″ (5.1 cm).

D.   Blend skirt yokeline. Indicate crossmark. Square a line at hemline from center front.

E.   Remove skirt draft. True all lines crossing all intersections. Establish grainline parallel to center front.

FIGURE 5

A.   To complete pattern allow hem and seams; cut and notch seams.

B.   To develop back follow same procedure as for front.

To develop waistband, if needed, refer to Skirt Waistbands.

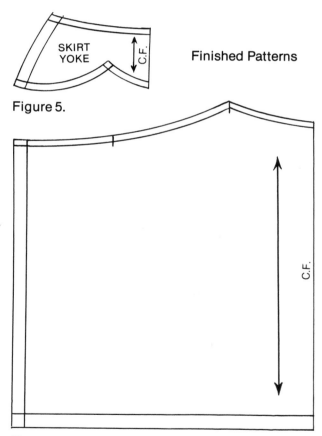

SKIRT YOKE

C.F.

Finished Patterns

Figure 5.

C.F.

Figure 5A.

Front View   **Two-Gored Back Skirt**

A peg-top skirt has fullness introduced at the waistline and no fullness at the hemline. The principle for establishing slash lines for this skirt is to place lines on sloper in the direction in which the desired fullness is to drape. The fullness may be in the form of shirring or unpressed pleats (sketch 27).

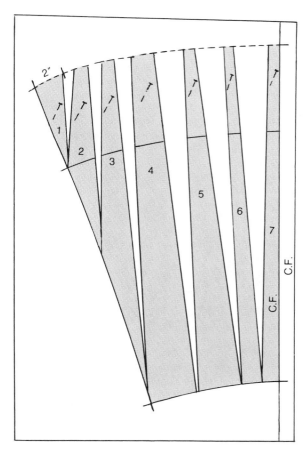

FIGURE 2

A.   Cut another sheet of paper approximately 25″ × 35″ (63.5 × 88.9 cm).

B.   Draw a vertical line near right-hand edge of paper. Label *center front.*

C.   Place cut skirt draft to paper matching center fronts. Spread remaining sections desired amount and pin. *Note:* The fullness allowed between sections may be equal or may vary depending upon the effect desired. For example, if more fullness is desired at center front, spread front sections more than others.

D.   Outline waistline, side seam and hemline and indicate hipline crossmark.

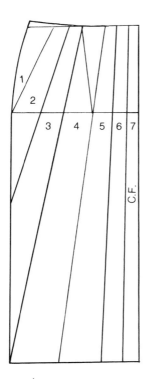

FIGURE 1

A.   Cut paper approximately 12″ × 30″ (30.5 × 76.2 cm) for a 28″ (71.1 cm) skirt length.

B.   Use *either one- or two-dart front skirt sloper.* Place sloper on paper and outline. Indicate hipline.

C.   At waistline establish slash lines approximately 1″ (2.5 cm) apart. Direct lines to side seam and hemline (as illustrated).

D.   Number sections. Cut slash lines starting at waistline to side seam and hemline, but not through side seam and hemline.

E.   Cut away excess paper from skirt draft.

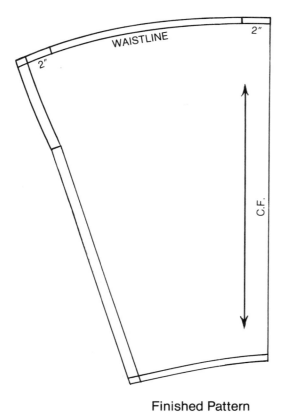

Finished Pattern

FIGURE 3

A. Remove skirt sections. True all lines crossing all intersections.

B. Establish grainline parallel to center front. Indicate waistline crossmarks (as illustrated).

C. Back skirt section may be a basic skirt, two-gored skirt without side seam flare or pegged skirt.

D. The peg-top skirt hemline is slightly concave and, therefore, needs to be finished with a facing. Refer to Facings.

E. To complete pattern allow hem and seams; cut and notch seams.

To develop waistband, if needed, refer to Skirt Waistbands.

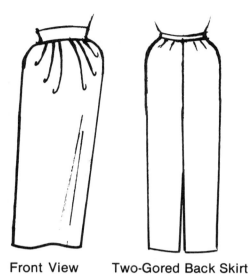

Front View   Two-Gored Back Skirt

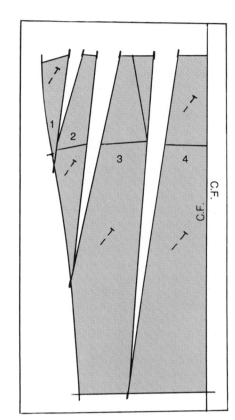

FIGURE 2

A.   Cut another sheet of paper approximately 25″ × 35″ (63.5 × 88.9 cm).

B.   Draw a vertical line near right-hand edge of paper. Label *center front.*

C.   Place cut skirt sections on paper matching center fronts. Spread remaining sections desired amount and pin. *Note:* The fullness allowed for each pleat may be equal or may vary depending upon the effect desired. For example if a deeper pleat is desired at center front, spread front sections more than others.

D.   Indicate direction of pleats at waistline with a crossmark on each side of slash.

E.   Outline waistline, side seam, hemline and indicate hipline crossmark and crossmarks at end of slash lines at side seam and hemline.

F.   Remove sections.

G.   Draw a light line from waistline crossmarks to crossmarks at side seam and hem (guidelines for trueing waistline pleats).

FIGURE 1

A.   Cut paper approximately 12″ × 30″ (30.5 × 76.2 cm) for a 28″ (71.1 cm) skirt length.

B.   Use *one-dart front skirt sloper.* Place sloper on paper and outline. Indicate hipline and dart.

C.   To establish position of pleats at waistline, measure 1″ (2.5 cm) from dartline nearest side seam and another 1″ (2.5 cm). Crossmark (as illustrated).

D.   From these crossmarks draw straight lines to side seam (as illustrated).

E.   Extend dartline nearest center front to hemline. *Note:* If more pleats are desired, add an additional slash line for each additional pleat.

F.   Number sections. Cut away excess paper from skirt draft.

G.   Cut slash lines from waistline down to but not through side seam and hemline.

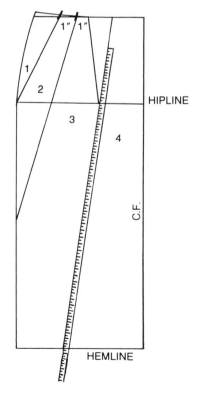

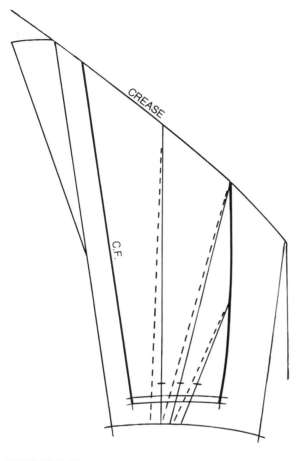

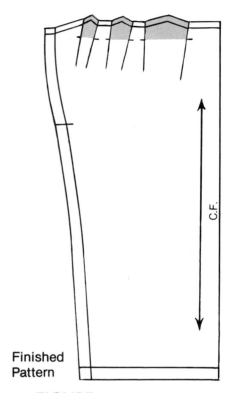

**Finished
Pattern**

FIGURE 3

A.   Crease lines nearest center front. Cup and close pleats following direction of pleat lines. Pin.

B.   True waistline through pleat underlay. From waistline measure down length desired for stitching pleats. Illustrated: 1″ (2.5 cm). Crossmark.

C.   Trace waistline and pleat crossmarks.

D.   With pleats pinned, allow seam at waistline only. Cut away excess paper.

E.   Open draft. Pencil in all traced lines.

FIGURE 4

A.   True side seam and hemline. Establish grainline parallel to center front.

B.   Back skirt section may be a basic skirt, two-gored flared skirt without side seam flare or pegged skirt.

C.   The peg-top skirt hemline is slightly concave and, therefore, needs to be finished with a facing. Refer to Facings.

D.   To complete pattern allow seams; cut and notch seams. To develop waistband,, if needed, refer to Skirt Waistbands.

Front & Back View

A wraparound skirt has two free edges, one of which is folded and wrapped over the other.

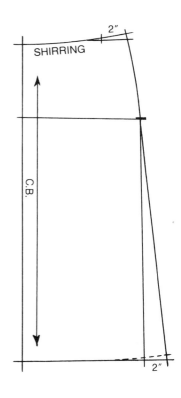

FIGURE 2

A.   Develop back skirt section (as illustrated).

B.   Match side seams of front and back skirt for accuracy. Pin. Allow seams; cut sections together and notch.

C.   On back section establish grainline parallel to center back.

D.   To complete pattern allow seams and hem to remainder of pattern; cut and notch seams.

To develop waistband, if needed, refer to Skirt Waistbands.

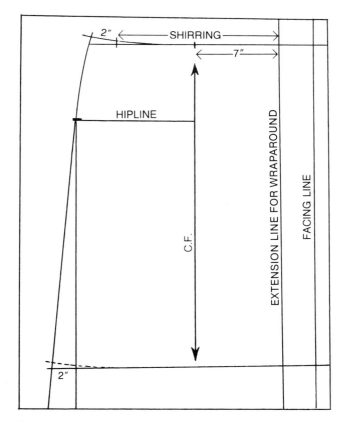

FIGURE 1

A.   Cut paper approximately 25″ × 35″ (63.5 × 88.9 cm) for a 28″ (71.1 cm) skirt length.

B.   Use *one-dart front skirt sloper*. Place sloper near left-hand edge of paper, allowing a margin for side seam and flare.

C.   Outline sloper. Indicate hipline. If shirring is desired, *do not* indicate dart.

D.   Remove sloper. True all lines crossing all intersections. Extend waistline at center front across paper.

E.   To establish crossmarks for waistline shirring, from side seam measure in 2″ (5.1 cm). Crossmark.

F.   To establish wraparound extension, from center front

measure out a total of 7″ (17.8 cm): 5″ (12.7 cm) for wraparound and 2″ (5.1 cm) for shirring. Draw a line parallel to center front. Label *extension line*.

G.   For a slight A-line look, at side seam/hemline intersection measure out 2″ (5.1 cm). Draw a line up to widest part of hipline.

H.   Shape hemline at new side seam. Length must be the same as at original side seam from hipline down (broken line).

I.   Add self facing to extension line the desired width. Illustrated: 3″ (7.6 cm).

J.   Establish grainline on center front line of skirt.

Front & Back View

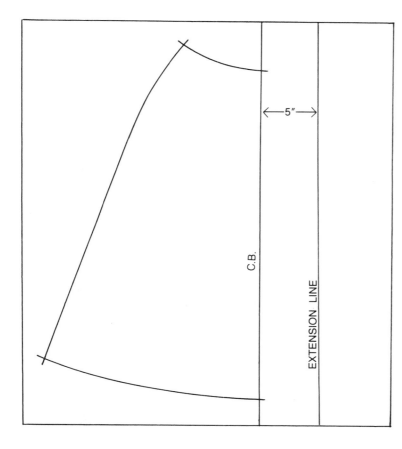

FIGURE 1

A.   Cut paper approximately 25″ × 35″ (63.5 × 88.9 cm) for a 28″ (71.1 cm) skirt length.

B.   To develop patterns for front and back sections of wraparound flared skirt refer to Four-Gored Flared Skirt.

C.   To establish wraparound extension from center back measure out 5″ (12.7 cm). Draw a line parallel to center back. Label *extension line.*

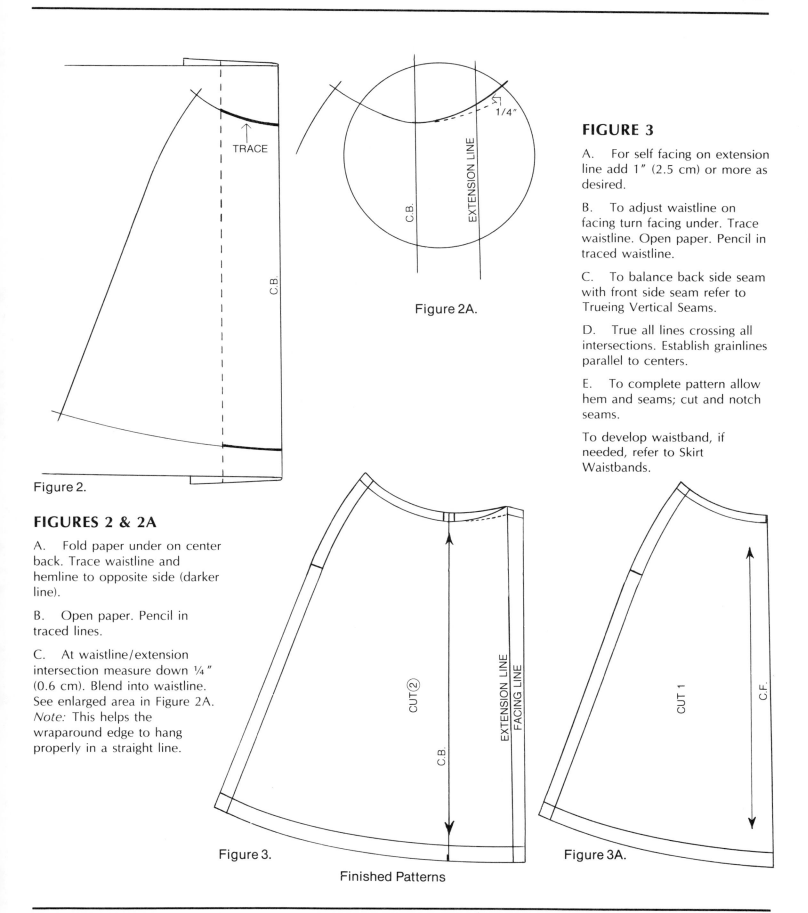

Figure 2.

Figure 2A.

FIGURES 2 & 2A

A. Fold paper under on center back. Trace waistline and hemline to opposite side (darker line).

B. Open paper. Pencil in traced lines.

C. At waistline/extension intersection measure down ¼″ (0.6 cm). Blend into waistline. See enlarged area in Figure 2A. *Note:* This helps the wraparound edge to hang properly in a straight line.

FIGURE 3

A. For self facing on extension line add 1″ (2.5 cm) or more as desired.

B. To adjust waistline on facing turn facing under. Trace waistline. Open paper. Pencil in traced waistline.

C. To balance back side seam with front side seam refer to Trueing Vertical Seams.

D. True all lines crossing all intersections. Establish grainlines parallel to centers.

E. To complete pattern allow hem and seams; cut and notch seams.

To develop waistband, if needed, refer to Skirt Waistbands.

Figure 3.
Finished Patterns

Figure 3A.

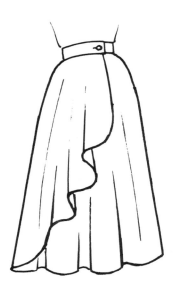

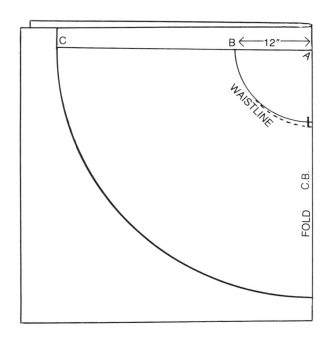

FIGURE 1

A. To determine radius of circular skirt measure waistline. Add a total of 10" (25.4 cm): 5" (12.7 cm) for skirt overlap and 5" (12.7 cm) for skirt underlap. Multiply by 1/6.

B. Cut paper 25" × 75" (63.5 × 190.5 cm) for a 28" (71.1 cm) skirt length.

C. To develop pattern for this sketch refer to Full Circle Circular Skirt, Figure 1, C to G.

D. Lower center back ¼" (0.6 cm). Blend back waistline (broken line). Refer to Full Circle Circular Skirt, Figure 2, C.

E. Add waistline crossmark ¼" (0.6 cm) from fold.

F. Trace crossmark to opposite side. Cut on seamline, hemline and adjusted waistline.

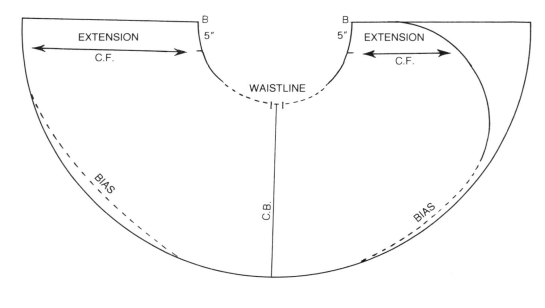

FIGURE 2

A. Open draft. Pencil in waistline crossmarks. Draw a line over crease. Label *center back* (as illustrated).

B. From B at both sides of waistline measure in 5" (12.7 cm). Crossmark. Label *extension* and *center front* (as illustrated).

C. Curve front skirt from B at right-hand side of draft to hemline as desired.

D. As in full circle circular skirt, cut skirt in fabric, adjust hemline, transfer new hemline to pattern and cut away paper on new hemline.

To develop waistband, if needed, refer to Skirt Waistbands.

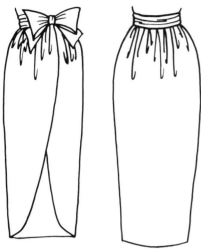

Sketch A Front & Back View

Sketch B

SKETCH A

FIGURE 1

A. Cut paper approximately 40″ (101.6 cm) square.

B. Draw a vertical line full length of paper 5″ (12.7 cm) in from left-hand edge. Label *center back.*

C. Square a line across paper from center back 9″ (22.9 cm) below top edge of paper. Label *hipline.*

D. Use *back skirt sloper.* Place sloper on paper matching center backs and hiplines.

Crossmark waistline and bottom of skirt sloper. Label *A* and *B* (as illustrated).

E. Outline side seamline extending line full length of paper.

F. Remove sloper. Square line from A and B across paper. Label *new waistline* and *bottom of sloper* (as illustrated).

G. Measure width of front sloper at hipline. Draw a line parallel to side seamline. Label *center front, C* and *D* (as illustrated).

			NEW WAISTLINE	
A				
9″				
		HIPLINE	C	
C.B.	C.B.	SIDE SEAMLINE	C.F.	
	B	BOTTOM OF SLOPER	D	

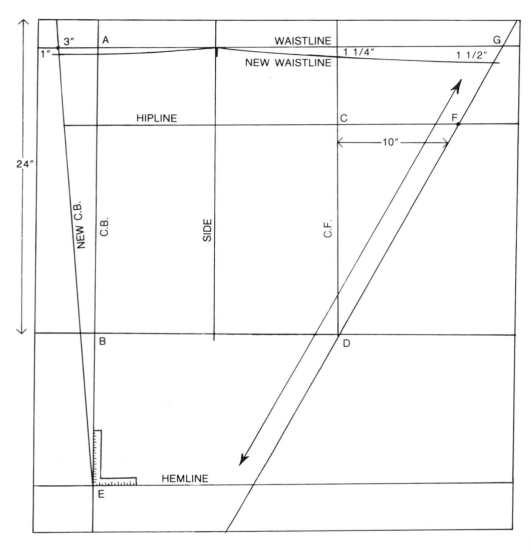

FIGURE 2

A. To develop front skirt wraparound extension, from C measure out 10" (25.4 cm). Dot. Label *F*.

B. Draw a line from F to D extending line full length of paper. Label *G* at waistline.

C. For length of skirt from center back measure down length desired. Illustrated: 38" (96.5 cm). Crossmark. Label *E*.

D. Square a line from E. Label *hemline*.

E. For back waistline fullness from A measure out 3" (7.6 cm). Dot. Draw a line from dot to E. Label *new center back*.
Note: This added amount of fullness is in harmony with the fullness at the front waistline.

F. To adjust waistline measure down:

    1. from G 1½" (3.8 cm);

    2. at center front 1¼" (3.2 cm);

    3. at center back 1" (2.5 cm).

Blend new waistline (as illustrated).
Note: Final adjustment of waistline can only be made when testing skirt in fabric.

G. Establish grainline parallel to wraparound extension. Crossmark at waistline/side seam intersection.

H. To complete pattern allow hem and seams; cut and notch seams.

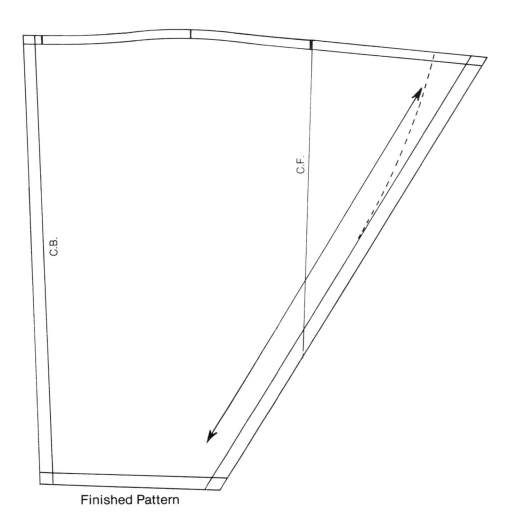

C.B.

C.F.

Finished Pattern

FIGURE 3

If less fullness is desired at waistline, the wraparound extension may be shaped (broken line).

SASH ON SKIRT

Cut a bias strip length and width desired. Sash may be cut on single or double piece of fabric depending upon fabric used.

SKETCH B

To develop pattern follow same procedure as for sketch A adding the amount desired for ruffle above the waistline.

To develop waistband, if needed, refer to Skirt Waistbands.

SHIRRED TIERED/BROOMSTICK SKIRT
sketch 32

Sketch A

Sketch B

Sketch C

SKETCH A

FIGURE 1

A.   Cut paper approximately 12″ × 45″ (30.5 × 114.3 cm).

B.   Use *one-dart front skirt sloper.* Place sloper on paper and outline. *Do not* copy darts as they will be absorbed in the shirring. Remove sloper.

C.   Establish length of skirt desired. Illustrated: 40″ (101.6 cm).

Note: For mass production, the last tier is usually longer so that if shortened for a specific individual, the proportion in relation to the other tiers will not be lost.

Tiered skirts may be made in any length and may be divided in any number of tiers desired. The tiers may be all the same length or graduated. They may be pleated, shirred or flared. The hemline of each tier may be trimmed by adding fringe, colored binding, ribbon, etc.

These diagrams are worked out on a 1/16″ (0.2 cm) scale.

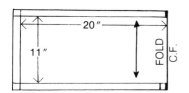

FIGURE 2

First Tier—Double width of basic skirt.

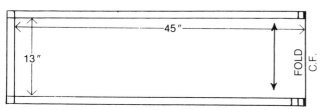

FIGURE 3

Second Tier—Double width of the first tier and add 5″ (12.7 cm).

FIGURE 4

Third Tier—Double width of the second tier and add 10″ (25.4 cm).
Note: Fullness given is suitable for sheer fabrics. Increase or decrease fullness as desired depending upon the type of fabric used.

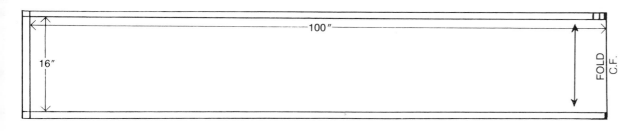

FOR ALL TIERS

A. Establish grainline parallel to center front.

B. Crossmark each tier (as illustrated).

C. To complete pattern allow hems and seams; cut and notch seams.
Note: 1. Depth of hem depends upon the finish planned.
2. Placement of seams on each tier depends upon the width of the fabric used.

To develop waistband, if needed, refer to Skirt Waistbands.

SKETCH B

To develop pattern for this sketch follow same procedure as for sketch A with the following exceptions:

A. For ruffle add to length of each tier amount desired above stitching line.

B. Increase fullness for each additional tier.

SKETCH C

A. *First Tier*—Copy from a *two-dart front skirt sloper.*

B. *Second Tier*—Double width of bottom of first tier.

C. *Third Tier*—Double width of the second tier and add 5″ (12.7 cm).

FLARED TIERED SKIRT
sketch 33

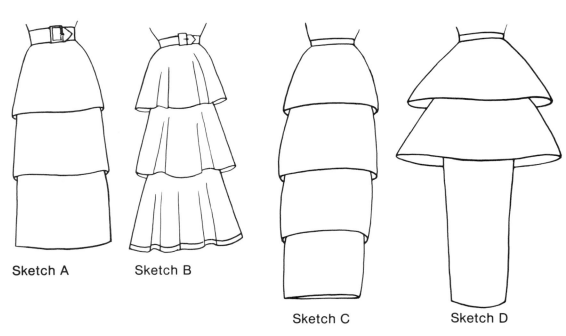

Sketch A   Sketch B

Sketch C   Sketch D

FIGURE 1

A.   Cut paper approximately 15" × 30" (38.1 × 76.2 cm) for a 28" (71.1 cm) skirt length.

B.   Use *two-dart front skirt sloper.* Place sloper on paper and outline. Indicate darts. Remove sloper.

C.   Draw slash lines parallel to center front from end of darts to hemline.

D.   Divide skirt into number of tiers desired in the lengths desired. If belted, consider width of belt when proportioning tiers.

E.   Label: *bottom of first tier, bottom of second tier, bottom of third tier* (as illustrated).

F.   Establish sewing lines 2" (5.1 cm) above tier lines (broken lines).

G.   Indicate one crossmark on sewing line at waistline, two crossmarks on sewing line at bottom of first tier and three crossmarks on sewing line at bottom of second tier.

H.   Copy each tier separately from sewing line to bottom of tier line. Indicate crossmarks on each tier and cutting lines. Cut away excess paper.

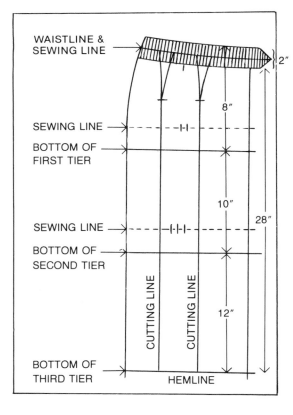

FIGURE 2

A. Number sections *1* to *9* (as illustrated).

B. Cut on lines up to but not through sewing lines.

C. Cut another sheet of paper 25" × 50" (63.5 × 127 cm).

D. Draw a line 1" (2.5 cm) from right-hand edge of paper. Label *grainline*.

E. Place center front of first tier to grainline of paper. Spread sections determined amount by closing darts and pin. Illustrated: 13½" (34.3 cm).

F. Place center front of second tier to grainline of paper. To determine amount of spread for second tier, measure bottom of first tier and add 1" (2.5 cm). Illustrated: 14½" (36.8 cm). Spread second tier and pin.

G. Place center front of third tier to grainline of paper. To determine amount of spread for third tier, measure bottom of second tier and add 1" (2.5 cm). Illustrated: 15½" (39.4 cm). Spread third tier and pin.

H. Outline each tier. Indicate sewing line crossmarks (as illustrated).

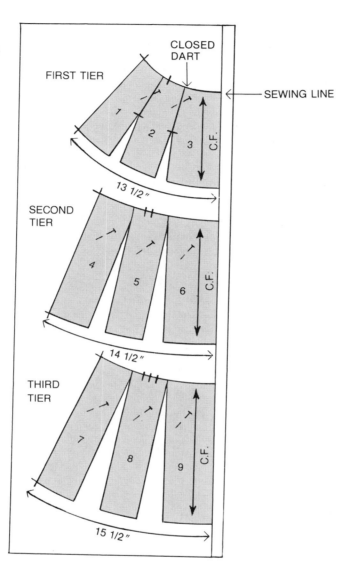

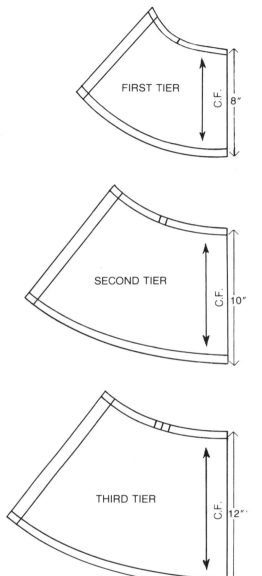

FIGURE 3

A.   Remove tier sections. True all lines crossing all intersections.

B.   Establish grainlines parallel to center front.

C.   To develop back skirt, follow the same procedure as for front.

D.   To complete pattern allow hems and seams; cut and notch seams.

Note: 1.   Before allowing side seams on each tier, the front and back side seams for each tier should be checked for grain balance. 2.   Hem allowance on tiers depends upon the finish planned:

    A.   machine-stitched edge;

    B.   shaped facing;

    C.   binding or other trim;

    D.   narrow hem.

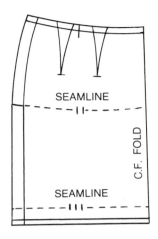

FIGURE 4

Copy underskirt for attaching tiers from draft and complete as illustrated.
Note: The underskirt may be extended the full length of the skirt to act as a slip or allow just a few inches below last seamline.

To develop waistband, if needed, refer to Skirt Waistbands.

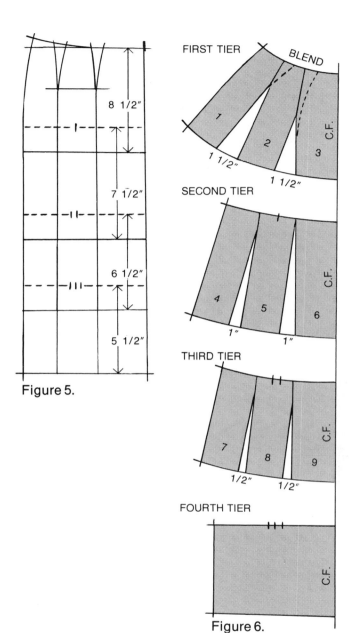

Figure 5.

FIRST TIER BLEND

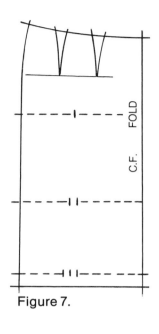

8 1/2"

7 1/2"

6 1/2"

5 1/2"

1 1/2"   1 1/2"

SECOND TIER

1"   1"

THIRD TIER

1/2"   1/2"

FOURTH TIER

Figure 6.

Figure 7.

SKETCHES B, C, D

To develop patterns for sketches B, C and D, follow instructions as for sketch A with the following exceptions:

Sketch B—First tier may be spread the desired fullness with second and third tiers increased the same amount as discussed in sketch A.

Sketch C—The desired fullness is worked in reverse as illustrated in Figures 5, 6, 7

Sketch D—Plan length of skirt and tiers as desired and work the desired fullness as in sketch A spreading *only* the two top tiers to width desired.

PANTS
introduction

Pants are garments that enclose the hips and legs between the waist and ankle. They may be fitted, loose, contoured, straight, bell- or peg-shaped. Pants lengths and names vary from season to season as illustrated in *Pants Length Variations*. Pants are an integral part of a woman's wardrobe and are styled and worn for all occasions—streetwear, sportswear, loungewear, evening wear.

Within the pants silhouette, attractive styling can be achieved by introducing such design features as pleats, flounces, godets, flares and yokes. Surface details such as pockets, beading, embroidery and appliqué also add to the design of pants. Fabrics also play an important part in the design of pants. Fabrics may range from sheer to heavyweight in all types of fibers, weaves and knits.

The many fashion variations discussed in this unit will be developed from the basic pants sloper. To develop the one- or two-dart pants sloper, refer to the companion text *How to Draft Basic Patterns*.

The diagrams have not been developed to scale as they would be too large for this page size.

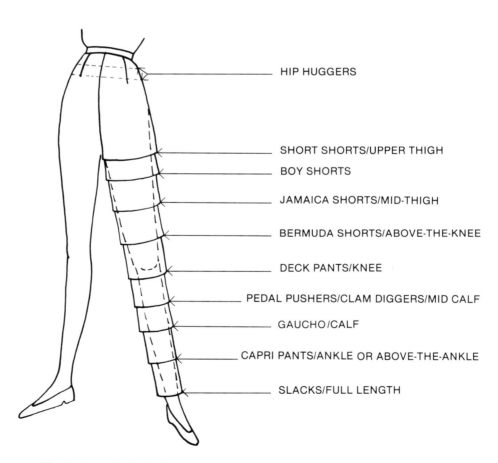

- HIP HUGGERS
- SHORT SHORTS/UPPER THIGH
- BOY SHORTS
- JAMAICA SHORTS/MID-THIGH
- BERMUDA SHORTS/ABOVE-THE-KNEE
- DECK PANTS/KNEE
- PEDAL PUSHERS/CLAM DIGGERS/MID CALF
- GAUCHO/CALF
- CAPRI PANTS/ANKLE OR ABOVE-THE-ANKLE
- SLACKS/FULL LENGTH

Pants Length Variations

Pants waistlines may be treated in a variety of ways depending upon the effect desired. The most popular waistline is the fitted look achieved by darts. Throughout this chapter the *two-dart pants sloper* is used more often than the *one-dart pants sloper*. However, these darts may easily be converted into one or two short front pleats, groups of shirring or total waistline shirring as illustrated in this sketch. Other waistline variations such as stylized seamlines and yokes will be developed in this unit.

To develop the one- or two-dart pants sloper refer to *How to Draft Basic Patterns*.

CONVERTING TWO FRONT DARTS INTO TWO FRONT PLEATS

FIGURE 1

These diagrams illustrate converting front darts into two pleats (broken line). Depth: 1″ (2.5 cm).

CONVERTING TWO FRONT DARTS INTO ONE FRONT DART

FIGURE 2

A.   Measure depth of dart underlays on sloper.

B.   For one dart crossmark on draft dartline nearest center front.

C.   From crossmark measure total depth of dart underlays. Crossmark. Indicate center between crossmarks. Dot. Square a line from hipline up to dot on waistline. Label *grainline*.

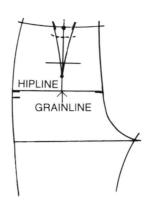

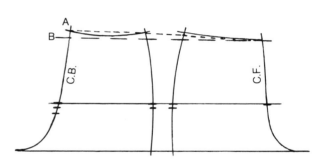

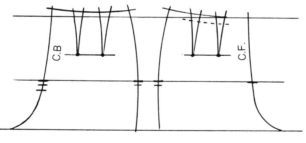

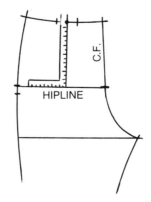

FIGURE 2A

A.   For dart from hip on grainline measure up 1″ (2.5 cm). Draw in curved dart.

B.   For pleat from waistline measure down 1″ (2.5 cm). Draw line through dartlines parallel to waistline (broken line).

SHIRRED WAISTLINE

FIGURE 3

A.   Broken line A retains the ease allowed at center back from crotch to waistline. Draw a straight line from A ending 1″ (2.5 cm) from center front.

B.   Broken line B, although it shortens the center back seam, retains the straight grainline from center back to center front for stripe, plaid or checked fabrics.

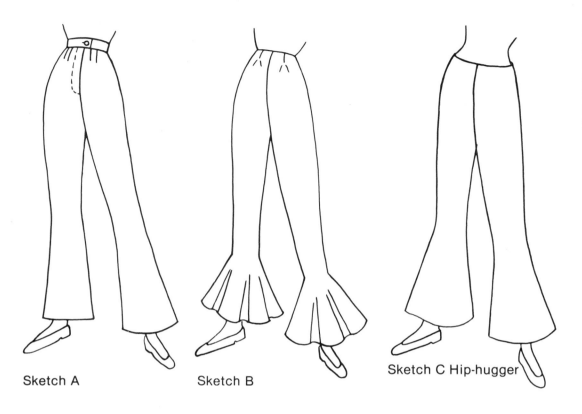

Sketch A   Sketch B   Sketch C Hip-hugger

Bell bottom pants are flared from the knee down to give a bell shape at the hemline. The principles for developing the flare at the bottom of the pants are the same for developing the flare on gored skirts.

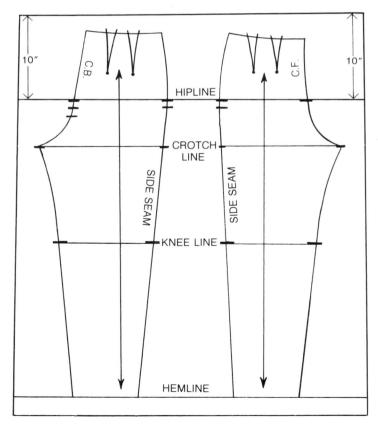

SKETCHES A & B

FIGURE 1

A.   Cut paper approximately 30" × 45" (76.2 × 114.3 cm) for a 41" (104.1 cm) pants length.

B.   From top edge of paper measure down 10" (25.4 cm). Draw a horizontal line across paper. Label *hipline*.

C.   Use *two-dart front and back pants slopers.* Place slopers on paper matching hiplines. Allow space between side seams for width of flares desired.

D.   Outline slopers. Crossmark darts at waistline. With awl indicate bottom of darts. Indicate grainlines, hiplines, crotch lines and knee lines.

FIGURE 2

A. Remove slopers. True all lines crossing all intersections. *Note:* If shirred waistline is desired, do not indicate darts.

B. Draw a line between crossmarks on crotch line, knee line and hemline. All lines must be parallel to hipline. Recheck lines and grainlines for accuracy.

C. For an average bell bottom flare, at each seam measure out 2″ (5.1 cm). Draw a line from each flare point to knee line. *Note:* The depth of the flare and the flare point at the side seam and inner leg seam may vary to achieve different design effects (see Figure 3). However, to obtain a properly balanced garment the *two seams that are joined* must be equal in length and width.

D. For a shaped hemline on the back pants section, measure down ½″ (1.3 cm) from hemline at center of leg. Dot. Draw a curved line to seams (as illustrated).

E. For a shaped hemline on the front pants section, measure up ½″ (1.3 cm) from hemline to center of leg. Dot. Draw a curved line to seams (as illustrated).

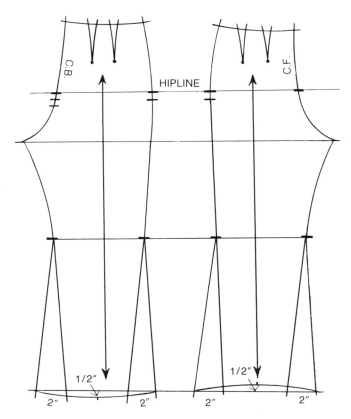

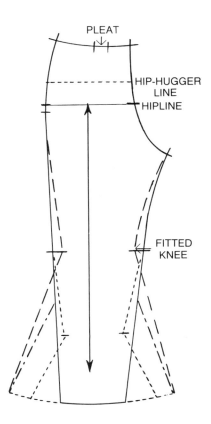

FIGURE 3

A. If a fitted knee is desired see shaping in illustration.

B. If a hip-hugger line is desired, as in sketch C, draw a straight line at desired depth (broken line).

C. Pants may also be more form fitting above any of the flare points. Refer to Contoured/Body Fitting Pants.

D. If front pleats are desired refer to Pants Waistline Dart Variations.

FIGURE 4

A.   For a fly-front placket add 1½″ (3.8 cm) extension to center front of right-hand side of pants draft. Draw a line 6″ (15.2 cm) long parallel to center front.

B.   Fold extension under on center front. Trace waistline to opposite side. Open paper. Pencil in traced line.
Note: Dotted line illustrates stitching line of fly-front placket.

FIGURE 4A

On left-hand side of pants for underside of placket add ⅜″ (1 cm) for extension. Draw a line 6″ (15.2 cm) long parallel to center front. Crossmark (as illustrated).

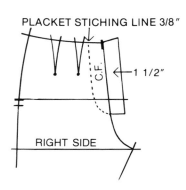

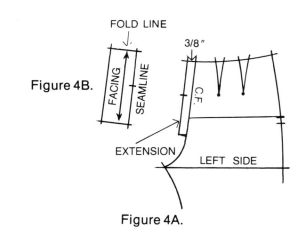

Figure 4B.

Figure 4A.

FIGURE 4B

A.   For left-hand side placket facing cut another sheet of paper. Draw a line 6″ (15.2 cm) long. Crossmark. Label *seamline.*

B.   Square a line at top and bottom of crossmarks of seamline towards left-hand side of paper.

C.   From seamline measure out ⅜″ (1 cm). Draw line parallel to seamline. Label *fold line.*

D.   From fold line measure out 1″ (2.5 cm). Draw a line parallel to foldline.

E.   Establish grainline on fold line.

F.   Crossmark on seamline to match crossmark on pants placket extension line.

G.   To complete pants pattern allow hem and seams; cut and notch seams.

To develop waistband refer to Skirt Waistbands.

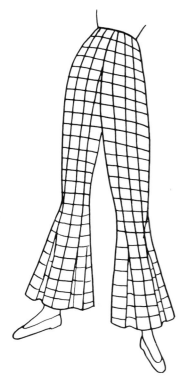

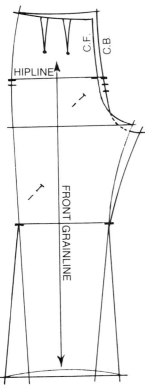

To match stripes, plaids or checks in bell bottom, tapered, peg-top, etc. pants, the lengthwise pants grainline on the back pants pattern must be redirected.

The following instructions are given for pants with side seams.

FIGURES 1 & 1A

A.   With front pants pattern face up, place front pants to back pants matching hipline crossmarks, hemline and side seam. Pin.

B.   Trace front grainline to back. Separate sections. Draw new grainline on back traced line. Label *grainline for stripes.*

Figure 1.

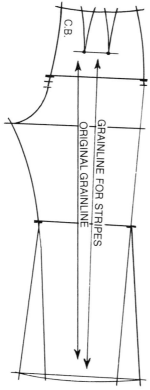

Figure 1A.

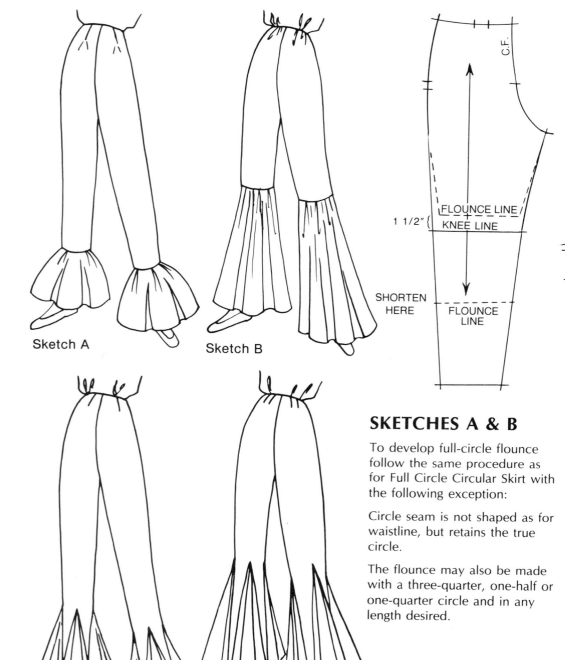

Sketch A

Sketch B

Sketch C

Sketch D

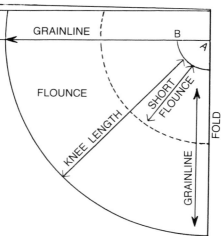

FIGURE 1

Plan flounce line (broken line).

SKETCHES A & B

To develop full-circle flounce follow the same procedure as for Full Circle Circular Skirt with the following exception:

Circle seam is not shaped as for waistline, but retains the true circle.

The flounce may also be made with a three-quarter, one-half or one-quarter circle and in any length desired.

FIGURE 2

Diagram illustrates developed short and knee-length flounce.

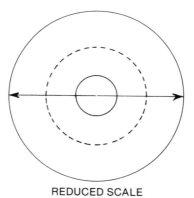

REDUCED SCALE

FIGURE 3

Diagram illustrates reduced scale of full circle flounce.

SKETCHES C & D

A godet is a triangular piece, in some cases round at top flaring at the bottom and varies in fullness. A godet is either set into a seam or a slash line on skirts, sleeves, pants, etc. to give added fullness and style details.

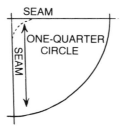

FIGURE 5

A.   Cut paper for size of godet planned plus 4″ (10.2 cm).

B.   Draw a right angle. Label top of angle *A*. From A measure on straight lines length desired. Draw curved hemline.

C.   True lines. Allow seams; cut and establish grainline.

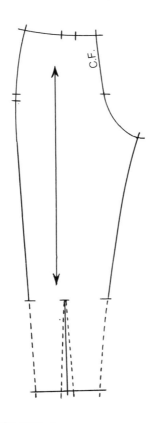

FIGURE 4

Plan slash lines for godet inserts. Follow illustration (broken lines).

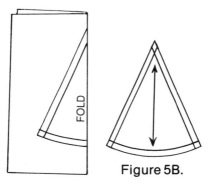

Figure 5A.

Figure 5B.

FIGURES 5A & 5B

A.   For godet with less fullness, fold paper in half. Draw a line from fold to width and length desired. Draw hemline.

B.   Trace lines to opposite side. Allow seams; cut and notch seams.

C.   Open paper. Pencil in traced lines. Draw grainline on crease (Figure 5B).

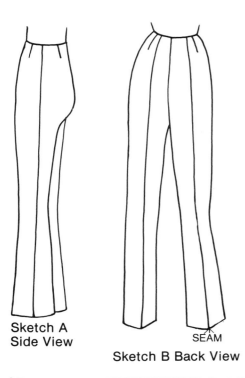

**Sketch A
Side View**

Sketch B Back View

SEAM

**Sketch C
Side View**

Contoured, tapered or body fitting pants are well fitted by shaping seams to conform to the lines of the body. To achieve this body fit, final adjustments must be made after testing pants in fabric. With new fabrics constantly being introduced, retesting patterns is a must.

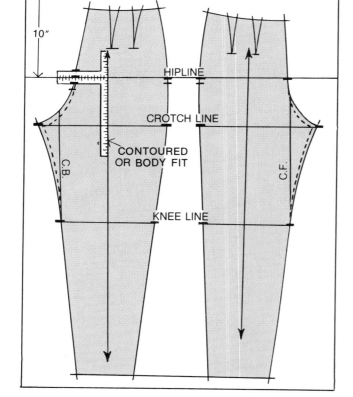

10"

HIPLINE

CROTCH LINE

CONTOURED
OR BODY FIT

C.B.

C.F.

KNEE LINE

SKETCHES A, B, C
FIGURE 1

A. Cut paper approximately 30" × 45" (76.2 × 114.3 cm) for a 41" (104.1 cm) pants length.

B. From top edge of paper measure down 10" (25.4 cm). Draw a horizontal line across paper. Label *hipline*.

C. Use *two-dart front and back pants slopers*. Place slopers on paper matching hiplines. Allow space between side seams for flare of bell bottoms, if desired, and seam allowance.

D. Outline slopers. Crossmark waistline darts, hipline, crotch line, knee line and hemline. With awl indicate bottom of darts. Indicate grainline.

E. Remove slopers. True all lines crossing all intersections.

F. Draw a line between crossmarks on crotch line, knee line and hemline. *All* lines must be parallel to hipline.

G. For a tighter fitting crotch reduce original crotch line:

    1. From center front on crotch line measure out one-fifth of front hipline. Blend a new crotch line up to hipline and curve slightly down to knee line (broken line).

    2. From center back of crotch line measure out two-fifths of back hipline. Blend a new crotch line up to hipline and curve slightly down to knee line (broken line).

Note: To obtain a contoured or body fit at pants back you may introduce a shaped dart or seamline from crotch line up to hipline and down to knee line.

H. Square a line from hipline up to dart nearest center back. Extend line down full length of pants.

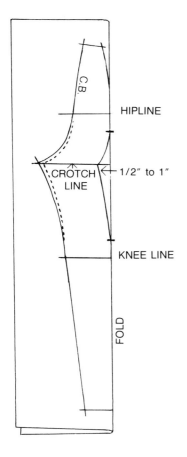

FIGURE 2

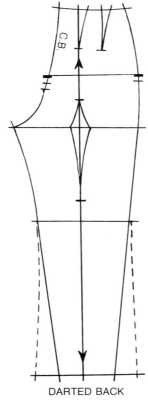

DARTED BACK

FIGURE 3

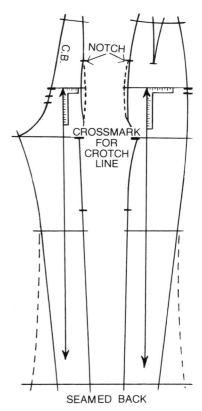

SEAMED BACK

FIGURE 2

A.   With center back face up fold draft on line.

B.   On crotch line from fold measure in ½″ to 1″ (1.3 to 2.5 cm) depending upon fit desired. Dot.

C.   Draw a short curved line from dot up to hipline and a slightly curved line down towards knee line (as illustrated).

D.   Place a crossmark at end of dart.

E.   To complete dart trace to opposite side.

FIGURE 3

A.   Open draft. Pencil in traced dart.

B.   For tapered pants retain original pants line at hemline.

C.   For bell bottom pants add desired flare (as illustrated).

D.   For yokeline as in sketch C refer to Peg-Top Pants with Hip Yoke & Unpressed Pleats. Follow procedure for back yoke making yoke desired depth. *Note:* Darts may be eliminated by shaping of yoke.

E.   To complete pattern allow hem and seams; cut and notch seams.

FIGURE 4

If pants are designed to be cut apart as in sketches B and C the seam at hipline should be blended slightly (broken line).

A.   Establish crossmarks at crotch line and above hipline (as illustrated).

B.   Establish grainline on each section by squaring a line from hipline.

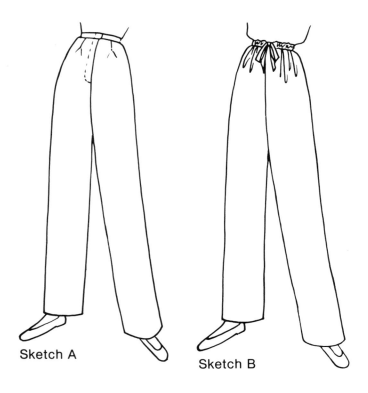

Sketch A

Sketch B

Straight leg or stovepipe pants are tight-fitting pants with narrow legs. The width at the crotch is the same at the hemline.

1.   This straight leg style may be cut with or without side seams.

2.   Side seam dart *must* be retained for less bulk at the waistline particularly when using heavyweight fabrics.

3.   Side seam dart can be used for side placket opening.

4.   If pants are to be cut in a striped, plaid or checked fabric, match grainline to stripe on fabric.

SKETCH A STRAIGHT LEG PANTS WITH SIDE SEAMS

FIGURE 1

A.   Cut paper approximately 30″ × 45″ (76.2 × 114.3 cm) for a 41″ (104.1 cm) pants length.

B.   From top edge of paper measure down 10″ (25.4 cm). Draw a horizontal line across paper. Label *hipline.*

C.   Use *two-dart front and back pants slopers.* Place slopers on paper matching hiplines. Allow space between side seams for seam allowance.

D.   Outline slopers to crotch line. Dot (as illustrated). Crossmark waistline dart and all crossmarks at hipline. With awl indicate bottom of darts. *Note:* If shirred waistline is desired, do not indicate darts.

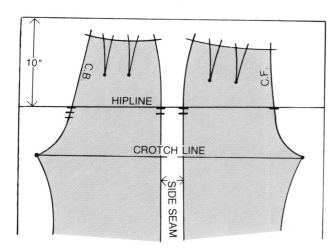

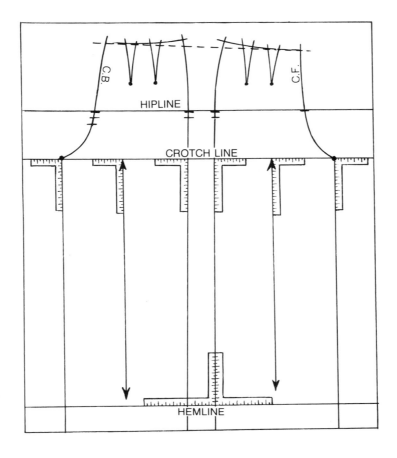

FIGURE 2

A.   Remove slopers. True all lines crossing all intersections.

B.   Draw a line between dots for crotch line.

C.   Square lines from crotch line to bottom of paper for inner leg seams and side seams.

D.   From waistline at side seam measure down length of pants desired. Square a line across paper. Label *hemline.*

E.   Square a grainline from crotch line down center of pants.

Note:

1.   If *shirred waistline with a separate waistband* is desired, retain original shaped waistline.

2.   If *shirred waistline with self facing* for an elasticized waistline is desired, draw a straight line from center front to center back (broken line). From straight line measure up twice the width of elastic plus ¼" (0.6 cm).

3.   If *front waistline pleat* is desired, refer to Pants Waistline Dart Variations.

4.   For waistband refer to Skirt Waistbands.

STRAIGHT LEG PANTS WITHOUT SIDE SEAMS

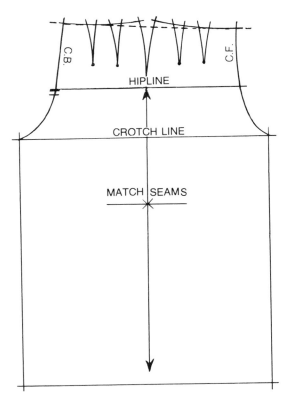

FIGURE 3

To eliminate side seam match side seams of front and back pants from hipline to hemline. Readjust crossmarks at hipline and draw grainline (as illustrated).

SKETCH B

FIGURE 4

If additional fullness is desired for pants with shirred waistline, add additional fullness at side seams of front and back pants continuing line to waistline (broken line).

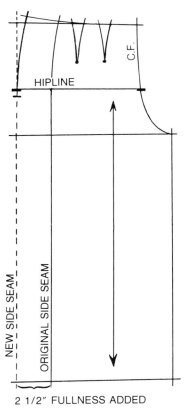

Sketch B
Knickers with Bands

Sketch A Knickers with Cuffs

Knickers are "knee pants" that are cut full and gathered just below the knee into a cuff or buckled strap.

SKETCH A

FIGURE 1

A.   Cut paper approximately 30" × 45" (76.2 × 114.3 cm).

B.   From top edge of paper measure down 10" (25.4 cm). Draw a horizontal line across paper. Label *hipline*.

C.   Use *two-dart front and back pants slopers.* Place slopers on paper matching hiplines. Allow space between side seams for seam allowance.

D.   Outline slopers to crotch line. Dot (as illustrated). Crossmark waistline darts, all crossmarks at hipline and knee line. With awl indicate bottom of darts.

E.   Remove slopers. True all lines crossing all intersections.

F.   Draw a line between dots and crossmarks for crotch line and knee line.

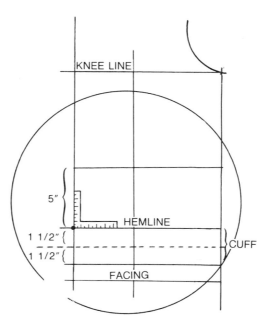

FIGURE 2

A.   Square a line from crotch line to bottom of paper at inner leg seams.

B.   From waistline at side seam measure down length of knickers desired. Dot. Square a line across paper. Label *hemline.* Length should be below knee.

C.   Determine the width of the cuff desired. From hemline measure down twice the width cuff desired. Draw a line parallel to hemline.

D.   From second cuff line measure down 1" (2.5 cm) for facing. Draw a line parallel to cuff line.

E.   Repeat same on back.

F.   To complete pattern allow seams; cut and notch seams.

G.   For waistline variations refer to Pants Waistline Dart Variations.

H.   For waistband refer to Skirt Waistbands.

SKETCH B

To develop the pattern for this sketch follow the same procedure as for sketch A with the following exceptions:

A.   Plan separate fitted cuff in width desired following procedure in Sleeve Cuffs.

B.   Plan placket opening for cuff on side seam.

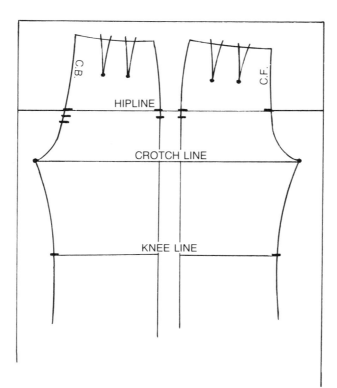

HAREM PANTS
sketch 8

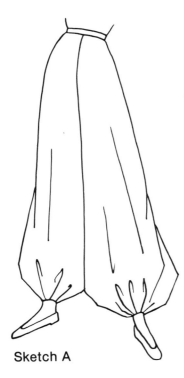

Harem pants are bouffant pants gathered into bands or elastic at the ankles.

Sketch A

Sketch B

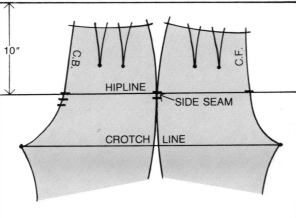

Figure 1.

SKETCH A

FIGURE 1

A. Cut paper approximately 30" × 45" (76.2 × 114.3 cm) for a 41" (104.1 cm) pants length.

B. From top edge of paper measure down 10" (25.4 cm). Draw a horizontal line across paper. Label *hipline.*

C. Use *two-dart front and back pants slopers.* Place slopers on paper matching hiplines and side seams.

D. Outline slopers to crotch line. Dot (as illustrated). Crossmark waistline darts and all crossmarks at hipline. With awl indicate bottom of darts.

FIGURE 2

A. Remove slopers. True all lines crossing all intersections.

B. Draw a line between dots for crotch line.

C. Square a line from crotch line at inner leg seams to bottom of paper.

D. From waistline at side seam measure down length of pants desired. Square a line across paper. Label *hemline.*

E. Draw slash lines parallel to side seams from end of darts to hemline. Number sections (as illustrated).

F. Establish grainline within sections 2 and 5 by squaring lines from crotch line to hemline.

G. Cut away excess paper from draft through side seams separating front and back.

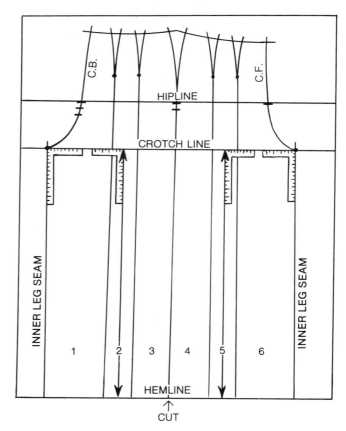

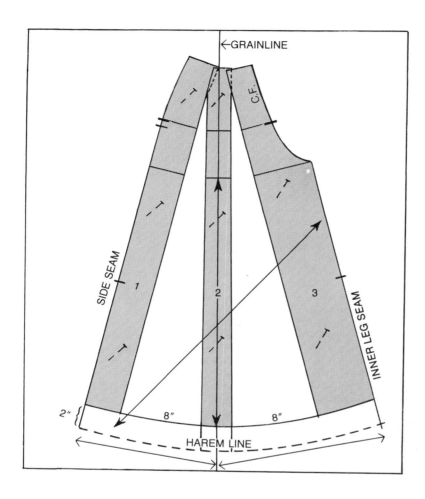

FIGURE 3

A.   Cut another sheet of paper approximately 45″ (114.3 cm) square for a 41″ (104.1 cm) pants length. Cut paper wider and longer depending upon width and puffed effect desired at ankle.

B.   Fold paper in half and crease. Open paper. Draw a line over crease. Label *grainline*.

C.   Cut lines on front section through dartlines nearest center front. Place front section #2 to paper matching grainlines.

D.   For fitted waistline with bottom of darts touching, overlap waistline darts. Spread sections at hemline fullness desired. Pin. Illustrated: 8″ (20.3 cm).

E.   Outline draft. Indicate all crossmarks on hipline. Add crossmark between crotch line and hemline at inner leg and side seam.

F.   Remove sections. True all lines crossing all intersections.

G.   Repeat for back. Crossmark on inner leg and side seams must match front crossmarks. *Note:* Back and front fullness must be the same from grainline to inner leg and side seams for balanced seams. See arrows.

H.   Add to hemline desired amount of puffing (broken line).

I.   Retain grainline in center of pattern. Pants may also be cut on the bias for a more graceful puff.

J.   To complete pattern allow hem, where applicable, and seams; cut and notch seams.

To develop waistband refer to Skirt Waistbands.

SKETCH B

FIGURE 4

A.   If a shirred waistline is desired, spread at waistline (as illustrated.
Note: When preparing paper for spreading waistline for additional fullness, measure down from top of paper 10" (25.4 cm). Dot. Square line from dot across paper. Label *hipline.*

B.   Adjust side seam from hipline to waistline for shirred waistline (broken line).

C.   Repeat for back.

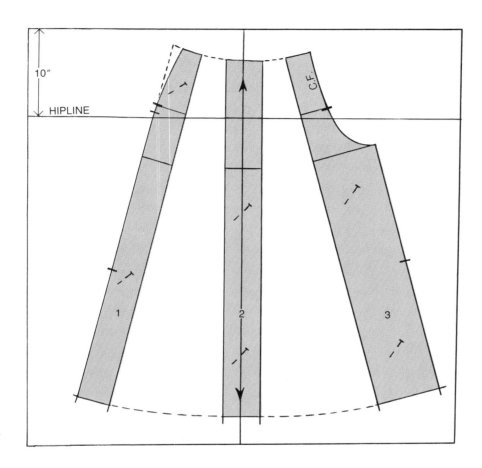

Palazzo pants are long with voluminous flared legs and may be gathered at the waist.

BLOOMERS
sketch 10

Bloomers are thigh-length pants with legs gathered into elastic.

To develop pattern refer to Harem Pants, sketch 8, with the following exception:

Shorten the draft the length desired and add hem for width of elastic desired.

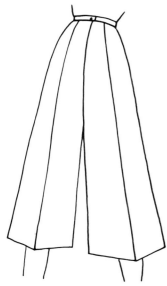

Gauchos are calf-length pants with wide legs.

To develop the pattern for gaucho pants follow the same procedure as for Harem Pants with the following exceptions:

A. Plan only one slash line.

B. Hipline on paper is not necessary as waistline is not spread.

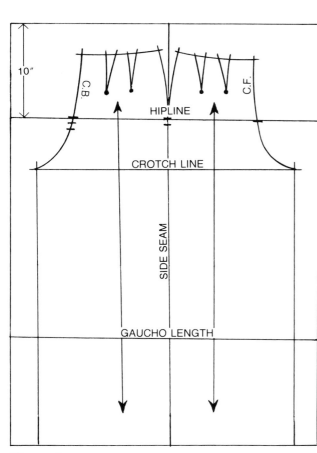

CLOSED DART

C.F.

2"   2"

Figure 2.

10"

C.B.

HIPLINE

C.F.

CROTCH LINE

SIDE SEAM

GAUCHO LENGTH

Figure 1.

C.F.

Finished Pattern

Sketch A

Sketch B

Peg-top pants are wide at the waistline and narrow through the hips to the hemline.

SKETCH A

FIGURE 1

A.   Cut paper approximately 30" × 45" (76.2 × 114.3 cm) for a 41" (104.1 cm) pants length.

B.   From top edge of paper measure down 10" (25.4 cm). Draw a horizontal line across paper. Label *hipline*.

C.   Use *two-dart front and back pants slopers*. Place slopers on paper matching hiplines and side seams.

D.   Outline slopers. Indicate crossmarks at hipline, crotch line and knee line. *Do not* indicate waistline darts.

E.   Remove slopers. True all lines crossing all intersections. Draw lines between crossmarks at hipline, crotch line and knee line.

F.   Establish grainline from waistline to hemline through center of sections by squaring a line from hipline.

G.   Cut excess paper from draft separating front and back.

H.   Cut each draft on grainline from waistline to, but not through, hemline.

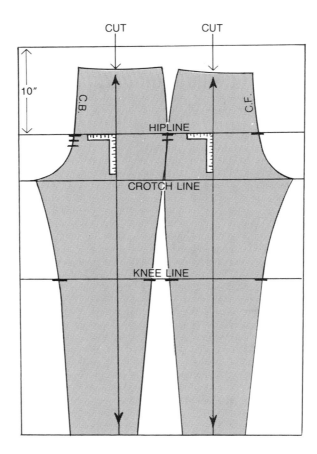

CUT   CUT

10"

C.B.   C.F.

HIPLINE

CROTCH LINE

KNEE LINE

FIGURE 2

A. Cut another sheet of paper approximately 15″ × 45″ (38.1 × 114.3 cm) for a 41″ (114.1 cm) pants length.

B. Fold paper in half lengthwise and crease. Open paper. Draw a line over crease. Label *grainline*.

C. Place front cut section to paper starting at hemline and matching grainlines. Spread waistline amount desired for shirring. Illustrated: 2″ (5.1 cm) on each side of grainline. Pin.

D. Outline draft. Indicate crossmarks at hipline and knee line.

E. Remove draft. True all lines crossing all intersections.

F. Repeat for back.

G. To complete pattern allow hem and seams; cut and notch seams.

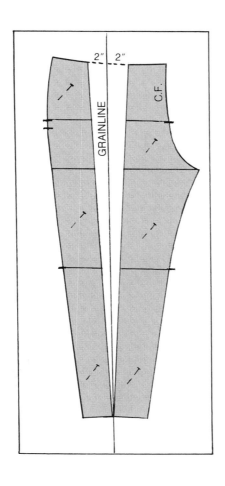

SKETCH B

To introduce more fullness at waistline add another slash line on either side of grainline and spread as desired.

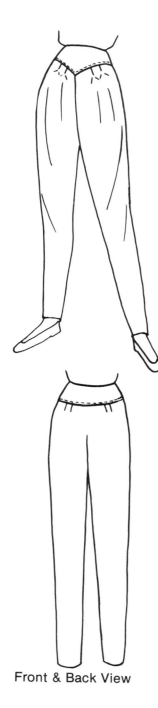

Front & Back View

FIGURE 1

A.   Cut paper approximately 18″ × 45″ (45.7 × 114.3 cm).

B.   Use *two-dart front pants sloper.* Place sloper on paper and outline. Indicate crossmarks at hipline, crotch line and knee line. *Do not* indicate waistline darts. Indicate grainline.

C.   Remove sloper. True all lines crossing all intersections.

D.   To establish position of unpressed pleats:

  1.   From center front measure in 1″ (2.5 cm). Dot.

  2.   Measure depth of dart underlay on sloper. For first pleat measure this amount from first dot. Dot.

  3.   For space between pleats from second dot measure 1″ (2.5 cm). Dot.

  4.   For second pleat measure depth of dart underlay from third dot. Dot.

E.   From waistline/side seam intersection measure down 10″ and 16″ (25.4 and 40.6 cm). Dot.

F.   To establish slash lines draw a line from dots at waistline to dots at side seam. Number sections (as illustrated).

G.   Cut excess paper from draft. Cut on slash lines from waistline to, but not through, side seam.

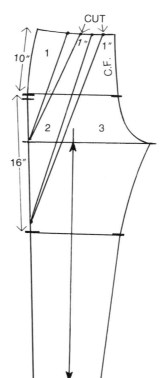

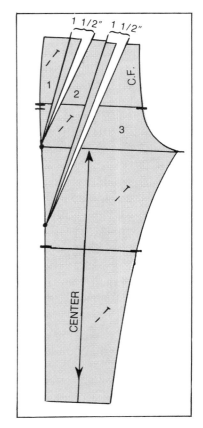

FIGURE 2

A.   Cut another sheet of paper. Pin center front section #3 to paper. Spread section towards side seam until each pleat underlay measures 1½″ (3.8 cm). This includes the depth of the original dart underlay.

B.   Outline draft. Indicate all crossmarks at waistline, hipline, crotch line and knee line. Dot ends of slash lines at side seams.

C.   Remove sections. Pencil in all traced crossmarks. True all lines crossing all intersections.

FIGURE 3

A. Draw dartlines from waistline crossmarks to dots at side seam (as illustrated).

B. Crease dartlines nearest center front.

C. To facilitate folding and closing darts, cut paper to side seam line dots. Close and pin darts (as illustrated).

D. With darts in folded and pinned position:

    1. True waistline.

    2. At center front measure down 4½" (11.4 cm) for hip yoke. Crossmark.

    3. Measure down 1¼" (3.2 cm) at side seam. Crossmark.

    4. Draw a curved line between crossmarks.

    5. Add crossmark on yoke line between darts.

    6. Copy hip yoke area and crossmark.

    7. From yokeline measure down 1" (2.5 cm) to establish pleats. Crossmark parallel to yokeline.

    8. Trace yokeline at dart area to opposite side.

    9. Allow ½" (1.3 cm) seam above yokeline. Cut and notch seams. Indicate grainline at center front.

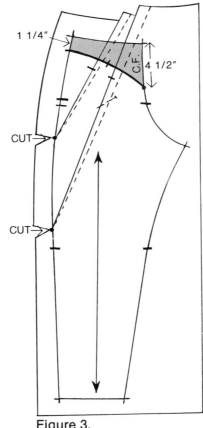

Figure 3.

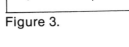

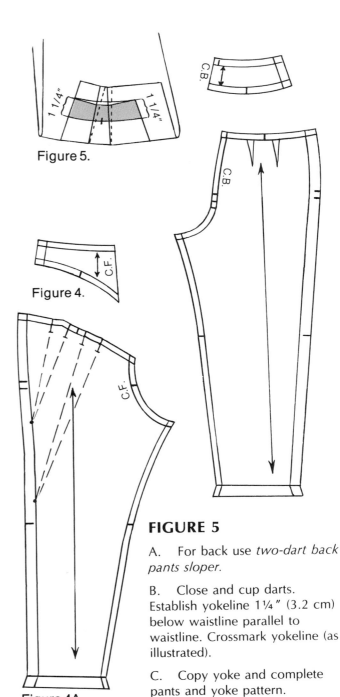

Figure 5.

Figure 4.

Figure 4A.

FIGURES 4 & 4A

A. Open draft. Pencil in traced pleat line. Allow hem and seams to remainder of pants and yoke.

B. Draw grainlines on pants and yoke (as illustrated).

FIGURE 5

A. For back use *two-dart back pants sloper.*

B. Close and cup darts. Establish yokeline 1¼" (3.2 cm) below waistline parallel to waistline. Crossmark yokeline (as illustrated).

C. Copy yoke and complete pants and yoke pattern.

D. Draw grainlines on pants and yoke (as illustrated).

E. To complete pants and yoke patterns, allow hem and seams; cut and notch seams. *Note:* Front and back yokes may be finished with a lining or just a turned back waistband.

SHORTS
sketch 14

Shorts are brief trousers from knee length to any length above knees.

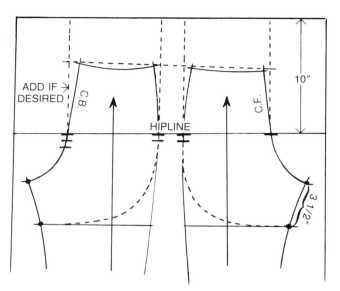

FIGURE 1

A.   Cut paper approximately 25" (63.5 cm) square.

B.   From top edge of paper measure down 10" (25.4 cm). Draw a horizontal line across paper. Label *hipline*.

C.   Use *two-dart front and back pants slopers*. Place slopers on paper matching hiplines. Allow space between side seams for seam allowance.

D.   Outline slopers to crotch line. Dot. Continue to length desired. Illustrated: 3½" (8.9 cm) below crotch line dots. Omit darts. Indicate grainline and all crossmarks at hipline.

E.   Remove slopers. True all lines crossing all intersections. Draw a line between dots for bottom of shorts.

F.   Draw in style line desired for bottom of shorts (curved broken line).

G.   For a shirred waistline, draw a straight line from center front/waistline intersection to center back/waistline intersection (broken line).

H.   From hipline at center front, center back and side seams, square lines up to top edge of paper (broken lines).

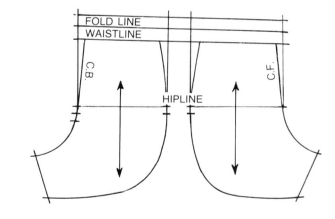

FIGURE 2

A.   For a self-turned elastic casing from straight waistline measure up 1⅛" (2.9 cm) for 1" (2.5 cm) elastic. Draw a line parallel to straight waistline. Label *fold line*.

B.   From fold line measure up 1⅛" (2.9 cm). Draw another line parallel to fold line for self facing.

C.   To complete pattern allow seams; cut and notch seams.

1. To develop draft for these shorts refer to Shorts, sketch 14, Figures 1 and 2 with the exception of the style line at the bottom of the shorts. Allow hem at bottom of shorts as illustrated in Figure 3.

2. The elastic casing becomes the heading above the drawstring at waistline.

3. To develop patch pocket, outline pocket on draft as desired (see illustration). Copy pocket and add facing as illustrated in Figure 2.

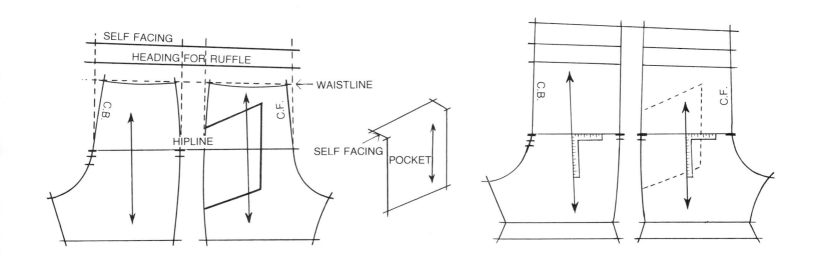

SHORTS
sketch 16

1. To develop draft for these shorts refer to Shorts, sketch 14, Figure 1 with the exception of the style line at the bottom of the shorts.

2. To develop cuff at the bottom of the shorts refer to Short Sleeve with Turned-up Self Cuff.

3. To develop waistband refer to Skirt Waistbands.

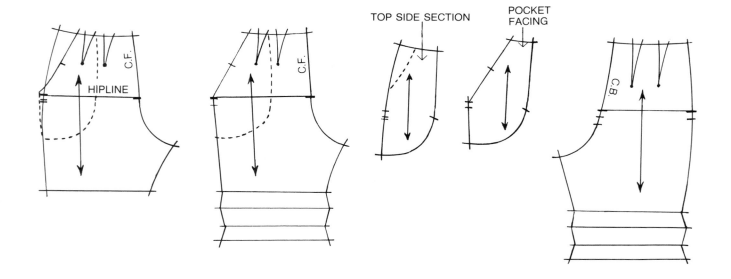

Sketch A

Sketch B

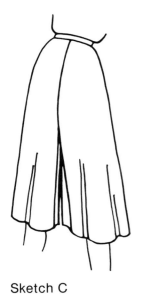

Sketch C

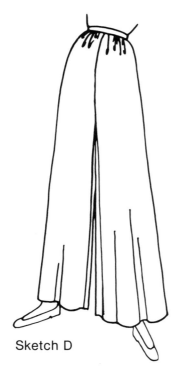

Sketch D

Culottes are a divided skirt. They are actually a combination of a skirt and pants. Culottes may be developed in any of the various skirt lengths and may be used in any garment categories for all occasions.

SKETCHES A & B

FIGURE 1

A.   Use basic *front and back skirt slopers.*

B.   Cut paper approximately 40″ (101.6 cm) square for a 28″ (71.1 cm) culotte length. If pleat is desired at center front and center back, cut paper approximately 10″ (25.4 cm) wider.

C.   Fold paper in half and crease. Open paper. Draw a line over crease. Label *side seam line.*

D.   From top of side seam line measure down 10″ (25.4 cm). Crossmark. Square a line across paper. Label *hipline.*

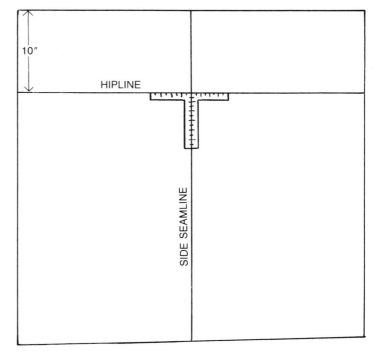

FIGURE 2

A.   Place slopers on paper matching hiplines and side seam lines (for culottes without side seams).
Note: If side seams are desired, place front and back skirt slopers 1″ (2.5 cm) away from side seam for seam allowance.

B.   Outline slopers extending center front and center back full length of paper.

C.   Crossmark waistline darts. With awl indicate bottom of darts.
Note: 1. For *waistline pleats* refer to Pants Waistline Dart Variations. 2. For *shirred waistline,* do not indicate darts.

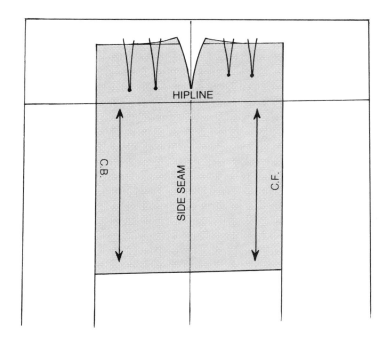

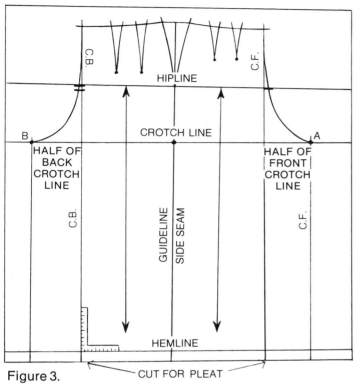

Figure 3.

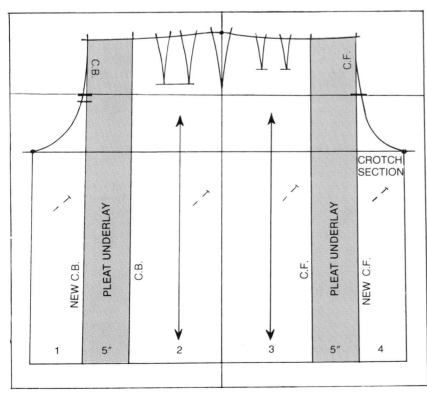

Figure 4.

FIGURES 3 & 4

A.   Remove slopers. True all lines crossing all intersections.

B.   Draw a straight line between front and back waistlines from side seam. Dot side seam/waistline intersection.

C.   From center back waistline measure down desired length of culottes. Square a line parallel to hipline across paper. Label *hemline.*

Note: For sketch B with a straight pleat at center front and center back of culottes, from center front and center back measure 5" (12.7 cm). Draw lines. Label lines: *new center front* and *new center back* (Figure 4). Proceed as for sketch A, Figure 3, using new center front and center back lines.

D.   To establish crotch line from dot at side seam line/waistline intersection measure down crotch depth with an additional 2" (5.1 cm) for ease. Dot. Draw a line parallel to hipline. Label *crotch line.*

Note: 1.   Crotch measurement may be determined from pants sloper or refer to *How to Draft Basic Patterns* for a measurement chart and instructions on how to take individual crotch measurements.

2.   Crotch measurement should include 2" to 3" (5.1 to 7.6 cm) for ease. A lower crotch line is needed as culottes must not fit as tightly as pants, but should hang like a skirt.

E.   To establish crotch width from center front at crotch line measure one-half of front hip measurement. Dot. Label *A.*

F.   From center back at crotch line measure out one half of back hip measurement with an additional 1" (2.5 cm). Dot. Label *B.*

G.   From A and B draw two lines parallel to centers down to hemline.

H.   Curve front crotch from A to a point above hipline (as illustrated). Repeat for back.

I.   Establish grainlines parallel to centers.

J.   To complete pattern allow hem and seams; cut and notch seams.

K.   To develop waistband refer to Skirt Waistbands.

SKETCH C

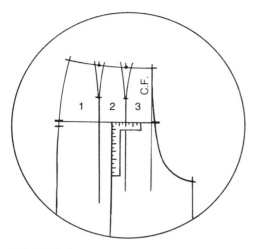

FIGURE 5

A.   Cut away excess paper and cut draft apart at side seam line.

B.   To introduce flares and maintain a fitted waistline and hipline on culottes, draw lines parallel to centers from end of each dart to hemline.

C.   Label sections *1, 2, 3* (as illustrated).

D.   Square a line from hipline through center of section 2.

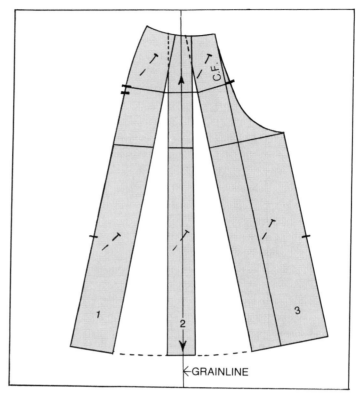

FIGURE 6

A.   Cut another sheet of paper approximately 30" × 45" (76 × 114 cm) for a 41" (104.1 cm) pants length. Cut paper wider and longer depending upon width and length desired.

B.   Fold paper in half and crease. Open paper. Draw a line over crease. Label *grainline*.

C.   Cut slash lines on front section through dartlines nearest center front. Place front section #2 to paper matching grainlines. Pin.

D.   With bottom of darts touching, overlap waistline darts.

Spread sections at hemline fullness desired. Pin. Illustrated: 4" (10.2 cm).

E.   Outline draft. Indicate all crossmarks on hipline. Add crossmark between crotch line and hemline at side seam and inner leg seam.

F.   Remove sections. True all lines crossing all intersections.

G.   Repeat for back. Crossmarks on inner leg and side seams must match front crossmarks.
Note: Back and front fullness must be the same from grainline to inner leg and side seams for balanced seams.

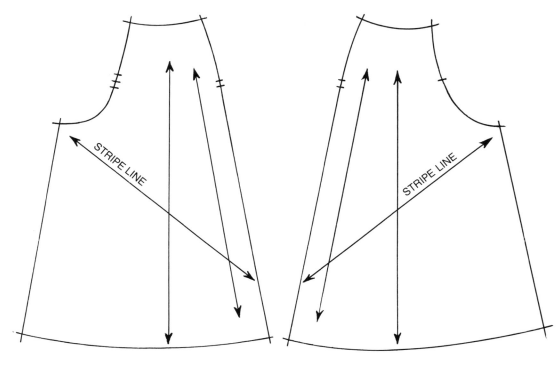

STRIPE LINE

STRIPE LINE

FIGURE 8

If more fullness is desired, spread sections at bottom of darts causing sections to spread at hipline. See illustration.

SKETCH D
FIGURE 9

A. To introduce shirring at waistline spread waistline (as illustrated).   To prepare paper refer to Harem Pants, sketch 8.

B. Establish grainline as desired (Figure 8).

FIGURE 7

A. Grainline variations for a stripe, plaid or checked fabric (as illustrated):
  1. original grainline;
  2. parallel to side seam;
  3. on the diagonal.

B. To complete pattern allow hem and seams; cut and notch seams.

To develop waistband refer to Skirt Waistbands.

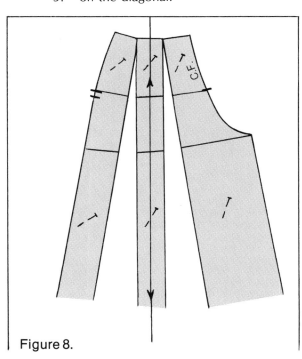

Figure 8.

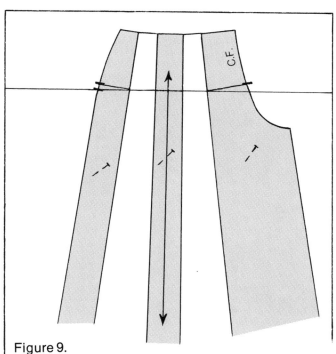

Figure 9.

TAB OPENINGS FOR WAISTS, SKIRTS & SLEEVES
introduction

A tab is a band of fabric used to finish an opening on a garment. It is used on waists, skirts and sleeves in all garment categories.

A waist or dress with a tab opening could be designed with a variety of necklines with or without collars. Three popular collars used with tabs are: (1) a convertible collar, that can be worn open or closed, (2) a collar that extends to the end of the tab and can only be worn open, and (3) a mandarin collar.

The length of the tab has no limit and the end of the tab can be straight, pointed or rounded. The width of a tab varies with the whims of fashion. The most popular tabs measure between 1½" to 3" (3.8 to 7.6 cm) wide.

Tabs may be planned with or without buttons and buttonholes.

Sketch A

Sketch B

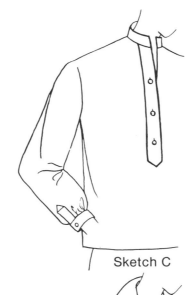

Sketch C

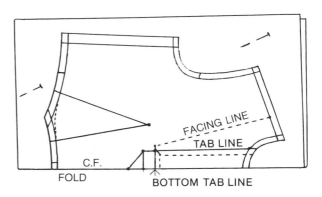

Sketch D

FIGURE 2

A.   Open waist draft. Pencil in traced lines. *Do not* pencil in traced facing line on right side of draft (dotted line).

B.   Add a crossmark at center front neckline.

C.   To develop tab sections cut two sheets of paper approximately 16″ (40.6 cm) square. Pin sheets of paper together.

D.   Place front waist draft to paper (shaded area).

E.   Accurately trace tab lines, neckline, shoulderline, facing line and crossmark at center front neckline. *Do not* trace center front line or seam allowance (broken line).

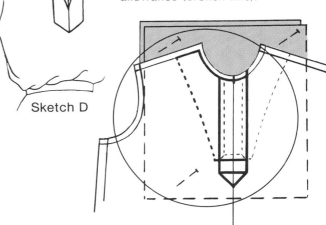

SKETCH A

FIGURE 1

A.   To develop waist for tab cut paper approximately 24″ (61 cm) square.

B.   Fold paper in half and pin.

C.   Use *one-dart front waist sloper.* With fold of paper towards you place center front of sloper to fold of paper. Outline sloper and indicate dart if desired.

D.   Remove sloper. True all lines crossing all intersections. Draw a line on crease. Label *center front.*

E.   From fold at neckline measure in one-half width of tab desired. Dot.

F.   From dot draw a straight line parallel to fold length of tab opening. Dot. Label *tab line.* Established length: 8″ (20.3 cm)

G.   From dot at end of tab line square a line to fold. Label *bottom tab line.*

H.   From tab line measure towards fold ½″ (1.3 cm) for seam allowance (broken line). Repeat at bottom tab line.

I.   To develop tab point measure over 1″ (2.5 cm) from dot at end of tab line. Dot. Square a line to fold. Dot.

J.   From this dot measure down on fold 1″ (2.5 cm) for tab point. Dot. Draw lines for point (as illustrated).

K.   For facing measure in 2″ (5.1 cm) at neckline/shoulderline intersection. Dot.

L.   Draw a slightly curved line from shoulderline to ½″ (1.3 cm) away from dot at bottom of tab line (broken line).

M.   Trace all lines to opposite side.

N.   With paper in pinned position allow seams; cut and notch seams. *Do not* cut broken seamlines at tab opening until tab sections are completed.

473

FIGURE 3

A.   Remove waist draft. Separate tab sections and place facing lines opposite each other. Label *A* (top tab) and *B* (under tab) (as illustrated).

B.   On section A pencil in all traced lines crossing intersections. Recheck lines for accuracy. Label *fold line*.

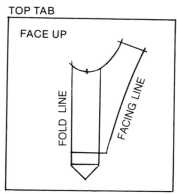

Figure 3.

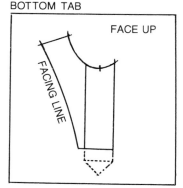

Figure 6.

FIGURE 4

A.   Fold paper under on fold line. Pin.

B.   Adjust neckline at fold by squaring a line to center front (broken line).
Note: This adjustment is necessary when a collar is planned.

C.   Trace adjusted neckline, tab lines, tab point and crossmark at center front neckline to opposite side.

D.   With tab in pinned position add seams (as illustrated). Cut and notch seams. Notch center front at neckline.

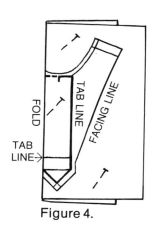

Figure 4.

Figure 7.

FIGURE 5

A.   Open tab. Pencil in traced lines. Add seam on under tab line and cut. Cut away excess paper at facing line.

B.   Draw center front line from notch at neckline to tab point (as illustrated). Label *centerfront* and *face up*.

C.   Notch each end of tab line (stitching line for tab).

FIGURES 6, 7, 8

Repeat same for section B with the following exception: Disregard tab point (dotted lines) and just allow seam (as illustrated).

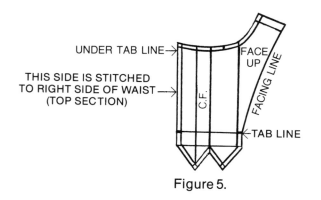

Figure 5.

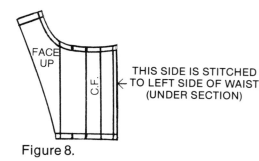

Figure 8.

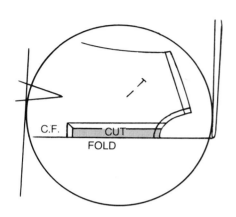

FIGURE 9

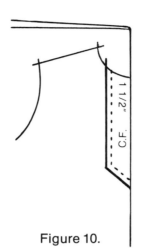

Figure 10.

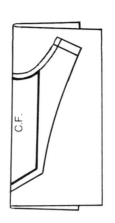

Figure 10A.

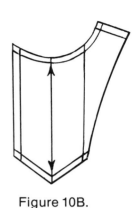

Figure 10B.

To complete front waist refold, pin and cut excess paper from tab seam allowance (shaded area). Open.

SKETCHES B, C, D

Note: As illustrated in sketches B, C, and D any sloper may be used depending upon design of garment. The procedure for developing the tab variations are the same as for sketch A.

Sketch B—illustrates a tab opening within a princess silhouette and a collar planned to end at tab opening. Collar is planned to be worn open. Since both tab sections are the same, one pattern is necessary.

Sketch C—illustrates shoulder dart pivoted to underarm on a torso-length garment with long buttoned tab opening and mandarin collar.

Sketch D—illustrated tab opening meeting at center front (Figure 10, 10A and 10b.)

TAB OPENINGS FOR SLEEVES
sketch 2

DEVELOPING SLEEVE FOR TAB

A sleeve with a tab opening can be developed either on a shirtwaist or bishop sleeve.

FIGURE 1

A. Develop sleeve desired.

B. To obtain line for sleeve opening, match back underarm seam to grainline of sleeve and crease.

C. Open sleeve. At wristline crossmark crease.

D. From crossmark draw a line on crease the desired length of tab. Dot. Illustrated: 4" (10.2 cm). Label *seamline*.

E. From dot square a line towards grainline of sleeve the desired width of tab. Illustrated: 1" (2.5 cm). Dot.

F. From dot square a line down to bottom of sleeve.

G. Draw a line through center and diagonally into corners. Cut.

DEVELOPING SLEEVE TAB

FIGURE 2

A. For top tab with point, cut paper approximately 8" × 16" (20.3 × 40.6 cm).

B. Fold paper in half lengthwise.

C. With fold towards you measure up from fold at each end of paper width of tab desired. Dot. Illustrated: 1" (2.5 cm). Draw line between dots. Label *tab seamline*.

D. From fold square lines to tab seamline length of tab opening established on sleeve. Illustrated: 4" (10.2 cm). Allow space at top for tab point.

E. To develop tab point measure over from top line 2" (5.1 cm). Square a line from fold to tab seamline.

F. Square a line through center of these two lines from fold to tab seamline.

G. Draw tab point as illustrated.

H. Trace tab point and finished tab lines to opposite side.

I. With paper folded allow seams. Cut.

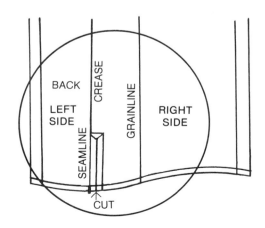

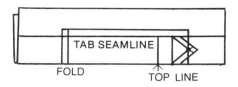

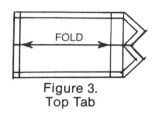

Figure 3.
Top Tab

FIGURE 3

A. Open tab. Pencil in all traced lines.

B. Establish grainline on fold of tab.

FIGURES 4 & 5

To develop the pattern for under side of tab opening, follow the same procedure as for top tab eliminating the tab point. *Note:* The under side of tab is often developed in one-half the width of the top tab.

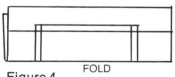

Figure 4.

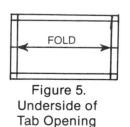

Figure 5.
Underside of
Tab Opening

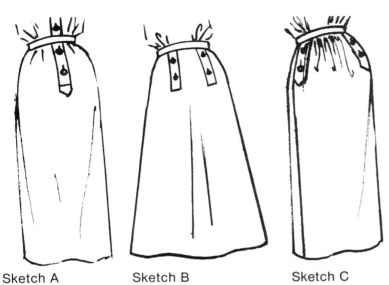

Sketch A   Sketch B   Sketch C

The procedures for developing the skirt tab opening are the same as for the sleeve tab opening only position of the tab differs.

SKETCH A

FIGURE 1

A.   Cut paper approximately 32″ (81.3 cm) square.

B.   Fold paper in half. Pin.

C.   With fold of paper towards you place center front of skirt sloper to fold of paper. Outline sloper and indicate darts if desired.

D.   Remove sloper. True all lines crossing all intersections.

E.   For slight side seam flare add amount desired. Illustrated: 2″ (5.1 cm).

F.   On fold at waistline measure down length of tab opening desired. Dot. Illustrated: 5″ (12.7 cm). Square a line from dot half the width of tab desired. Label *tab line*. Illustrated: 3/4″ (1.9 cm) for 1½″ (3.8) tab.

G.   From tab line measure ½″ (1.3 cm) for seam allowance (broken line).

H.   Trace all lines, crossmarks, darts (if desired) to opposite side.

I.   With paper in pinned position allow hem and seam; cut and notch seams and crossmarks.

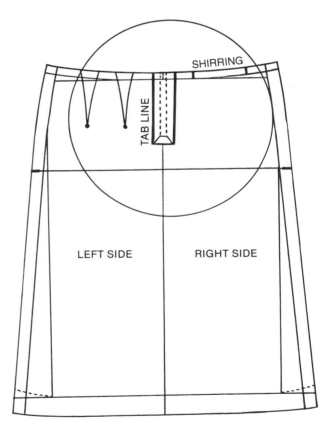

FIGURE 2

Open pattern. Pencil in all traced lines.

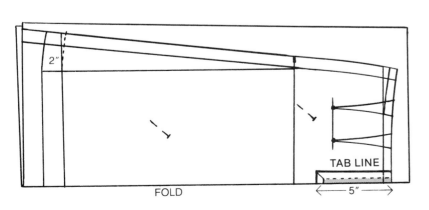

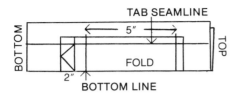

FIGURE 3

A.   For top side of tab point cut paper approximately 8″ x 16″ (20.3 x 40.6 cm).

B.   Fold paper in half lengthwise.

C.   With fold towards you measure up from fold at each end of paper width of tab desired. Dot. Illustrated: 1½″ (3.8 cm). Draw line through dots. Label *tab seamline.*

D.   From fold square lines to tab seamline length of tab opening desired allowing space at bottom for tab point. Illustrated: 5″ (12.7 cm).

E.   To develop tab point measure down from bottom of tab line 2″ (5.1 cm). Dot. Square a line to fold.

F.   From this line measure up half the length for tab point. Illustrated: 1″ (2.5 cm). Square a line parallel to bottom line.

G.   Draw a tab point (as illustrated).

H.   Trace tab point and finished tab lines to opposite side.

I.   With paper folded allow seams. Cut.

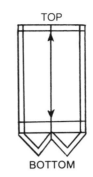

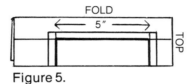

Figure 5.

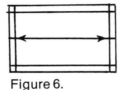

Figure 6.

FIGURE 4

A.   Open tab. Pencil in all traced lines.

B.   Establish grainline on fold of tab.

FIGURES 5 & 6

To develop the pattern for under side of tab opening, follow the same procedure as for top tab eliminating the tab point.

SKETCH B

This sketch illustrates a slightly flared, four-gored skirt with no center seam.

1.   Plan tab at gore seamline area

2.   This tab can also be used to introduce pockets.

SKETCH C

This sketch illustrates a mock tab on a basic skirt using dart fullness for shirring. A mock tab is used when tab is placed on a seam. Tab is just a strip of fabric width and length desired stitched on top of skirt at seam area.

1.   Plan tabs from side seam towards center front.

2.   This tab can also be used to introduce seam pockets.

3.   If more skirt fullness is desired, add amount desired parallel to center front.

A pocket is a pouch formed by a piece of fabric stitched to a garment with top edge open. Pockets play an important role in fashion design as they are both functional and decorative features of a garment. They are applied to all parts of a garment such as on the center front, over the bustline, on front and back hipline, sleeves, pants legs and belts.

Pockets fall into three categories:

1. Surface pocket such as the patch pocket. It can be enhanced with such trimmings as monograms, emblems, insignias, beads, embroidery, rickrack and braid. Patch pockets with flaps may vary in size and shape.

2. A seam pocket is a pocket inserted into a basic or decorative seam of a garment with the pouch on the underside of garment.

3. A combination pocket such as the welt pocket. Welt of the pocket is on the surface side of the garment with the pouch on the underside.

Pockets vary in size, shape and in the number used on one garment. They are used in all garment categories such as sportswear, coats and suits, dressy and evening wear and loungewear.

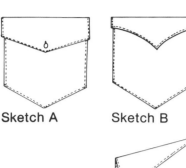

Sketch A

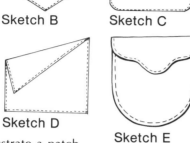

Sketch B

Sketch C

Sketch D

Sketch E

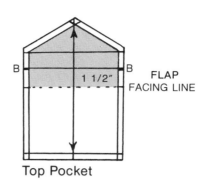

Top Pocket

These sketches illustrate a patch pocket and flap designed in one piece; flap is faced and turned over pocket loosely at flap fold line. Sketches B, C, D and E illustrate different shapes of pocket and flap.

SKETCH A

FIGURES 1 & 1A

A. Cut paper approximately 12″ (30.5 cm) square.

B. Fold paper in half and pin. Square a line from fold half the desired width of pocket. Illustrated: 2½″ (6.4 cm). Dot. Label *A*.

C. From A draw a line parallel to fold the desired length of pocket. Illustrated: 5½″ (14 cm). Crossmark. Label *B*. This crossmark indicates pocket flap fold line.

D. From B measure 1″ (2.5 cm). Dot. Label *C*. From C square a line to fold. Label *D*.

E. For pocket point from D measure 1½″ (3.8 cm). Dot. Draw a line from dot to C.

F. Trace all lines and crossmark B to opposite side.

G. With paper in pinned position allow seams; cut and notch seams. See Figure 1A.

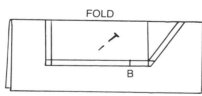

Figure 1.

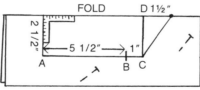

Figure 1A.

FIGURE 2

A. Open paper. Pencil in traced lines.

B. Draw a line between crossmarks B. Establish grainline on fold line.

C. The entire pocket or the flap only may be faced. To establish flap facing line from crossmarks B measure down 1½″ (3.8 cm). Draw a broken line parallel to line B. Label *flap facing line.*

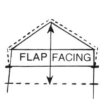

Figure 3.

Figure 3A.

FIGURES 3 & 3A

A. Copy flap (shaded area in Figure 2) without seam allowance.

B. Add ease to both sides of flap facing. Start at fold line and draw line from nothing to 1/16″ (0.2 cm) (broken line).

C. To face entire pocket, copy pocket and flap and add ease (see Figure 3A).
Note: To develop patterns for facings refer to Facings.

D. To complete pattern sections allow seams; cut and notch seams.

SKETCHES B, C, D, E

To complete patterns for these sketches follow same procedure as for sketch A. The difference is in the shape of the pocket and flap.

480

Sketch A

Sketch B

SKETCH A

This sketch illustrates a patch pocket and mock flap; flap is turned over pocket and stitched down onto pocket before pocket is stitched to garment.

FIGURES 1, 2, 2A, 2B

Follow same procedure as for One-piece Patch Pocket & Flap, Figures 1 and 2 with these exceptions:

> 1. If fabric has *no* right or wrong side, flap is turned over on line B towards right side of pocket and stiched down.

> 2. If fabric *has* a right and wrong side, flap and pocket sections are cut separately (Figures 2 and 2A). Wrong side of flap is stitched to the right side of pocket (Figures 2 and 2B).

Note: The mock flap may be applied to any one of the pockets illustrated in sketch 1.

SKETCH B

This sketch illustrates stitching variations.

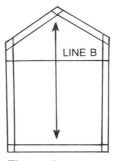

Figure 1.

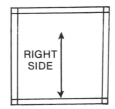

Figure 2.

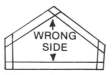

Figure 2A.

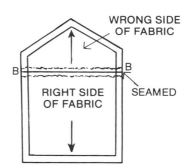

Figure 2B.

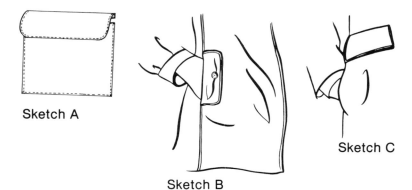

Sketch A

Sketch B

Sketch C

UNLINED POCKET

HEM

TOP FLAP FACING

UNDER FLAP

Finished Pocket Flap & Facing

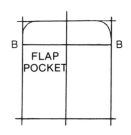

FLAP POCKET

This sketch illustrates a patch pocket and flap designed as two separate pieces. The pocket is stitched to the garment and the flap is stitched slightly above the pocket and turned over to cover the top opening of the pocket.

FIGURE 1

A.   To develop the pattern for this sketch follow the same procedure as for One-piece Patch Pocket & Flap, Figures 1 and 2.

B.   Style flap as illustrated or as desired.

FIGURE 2

A.   Copy patch pocket allowing enough paper on top for self facing of pocket.

B.   Fold paper under on line B. Trace finished lines to opposite side.

C.   Open draft. Pencil in all traced lines. Label *fold line, top pocket* and *under pocket.*

D.   To conceal seam allow ease on top pocket (broken line). Illustrated: $1/16''$ (0.2 cm)

E.   To complete pocket pattern allow seams; cut and notch seams.

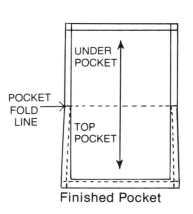

UNDER POCKET

POCKET FOLD LINE

TOP POCKET

Finished Pocket

FIGURE 3

Note: For an unlined pocket add approximately $1\frac{1}{2}''$ (3.8 cm) for a self-turned hem. Additional ease is not necessary on an unlined pocket.

FIGURE 4

A.   Copy flap on two sheets of paper.

B.   Separate flaps and place opposite to each other. Label *top flap facing* and *under flap.*

C.   To conceal seam allow ease on top flap facing. Illustrated: $1/16''$ (0.2 cm).

D.   To complete flap pattern allow seams; cut and notch seams.

SKETCHES B & C

These sketches illustrate the use of the flap in combination with a seam pocket. To develop the seam pocket refer to Seam Pocket.

Pocket flaps may also be stitched on a garment without pocket to give the impression of a pocket on the garment.

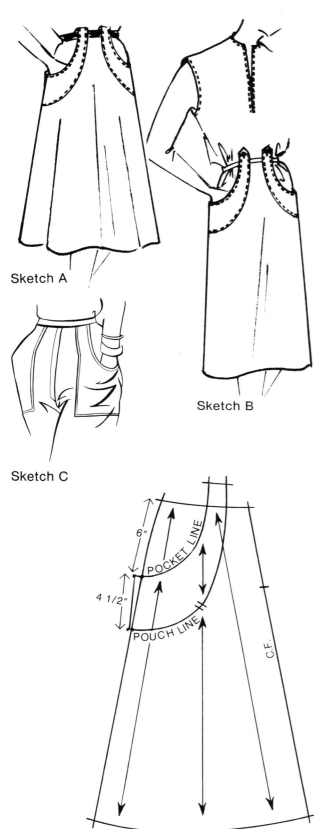

Sketch A

Sketch C

Sketch B

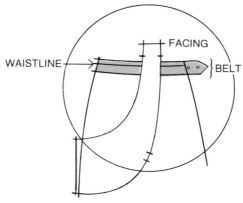

SKETCH A

FIGURE 1

A.   To develop flared skirt refer to Four-Gored Flared Skirt.

B.   On front skirt draft plan pocket line desired. From waistline measure down 6" (15.2 cm). Dot.

C.   For depth of pocket from dot measure down 4½" (11.3 cm). Dot.

D.   Draw shape of pocket desired between these dots extending:

>   1.   Pocket lines above waistline indefinitely;
>
>   2.   Pocket line at side seam ¼" (0.6 cm). Dot. Extend pocket pouch line ⅛" (0.3 cm). Dot. Draw a line between dots.

Note: This ease is allowed so that the finished pocket opening will roll and fit smoothly over the body curve of the skirt. More ease may have to be allowed depending upon the thickness of the fabric used.

E.   Place two crossmarks on pouch line. Establish grainline desired on skirt.
Note: Grainline on pocket and pocket facing must match grainline on skirt.

FIGURE 2

A.   From extended pocket lines at waistline measure up ⅜" (1 cm) for a 1" (2.5 cm) belt. This allows enough space for belt to cover waistline. Crossmark ends of both lines.

B.   From these crossmarks measure up 1" (2.5 cm) for self facing. When self facing is turned under at crossmarks it is stitched to underside of skirt.

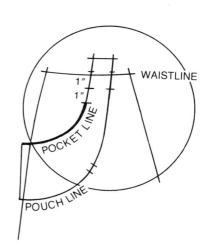

FIGURE 3

A.   On pouch line from waistline measure down 1" (2.5 cm) for end of stitched line of pocket. Opening allowed for belt.

B.   On pocket line from waistline measure down 1" (2.5 cm). Crossmark. From this crossmark measure down 1" (2.5 cm). Crossmark.
Note: The space between crossmarks is stitched to skirt leaving pocket line open to side seam (heavier line).

FIGURE 4

A. Cut two pieces of paper approximately 12″ × 20″ (30.5 × 50.8 cm). Pin together.

B. Pin pocket draft to paper (as illustrated). Trace pocket, all crossmarks and desired grainline to opposite side (heavier lines).

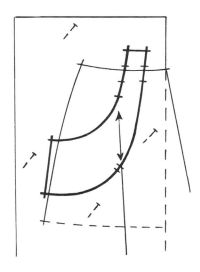

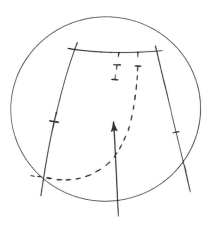

FIGURE 6

This figure shows area on skirt for stitching finished pocket. To complete skirt allow hem and seams; cut and notch seams.

SKETCH B
FIGURE 7

To develop patch pocket for shift dress follow same procedure as for sketch A with this exception:

Add point above belt loop. *Note:* 1. Belt loop may be longer if desired. 2. Shoulder dart may be pivoted into an underarm dart or eliminated by surface seam or yoke details.

SKETCH C

To develop patch pocket for pants follow same procedure as for sketch A.

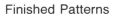
Finished Patterns

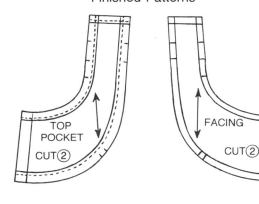

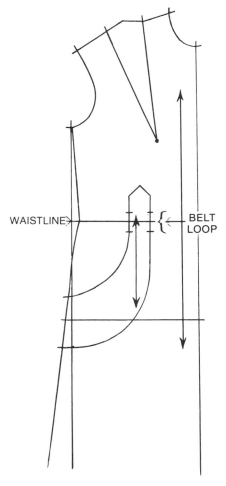

FIGURE 5

A. Remove skirt draft. Separate pocket drafts and place opposite to each other. Label one draft *top pocket* and other draft *facing* (as illustrated). Pencil in traced lines, all crossmarks and grainline.

B. On top pocket add ¹⁄₁₆″ (0.2 cm) ease (broken line). Allow seams; cut and notch seams.

C. On pocket facing allow seams; cut and notch seams.

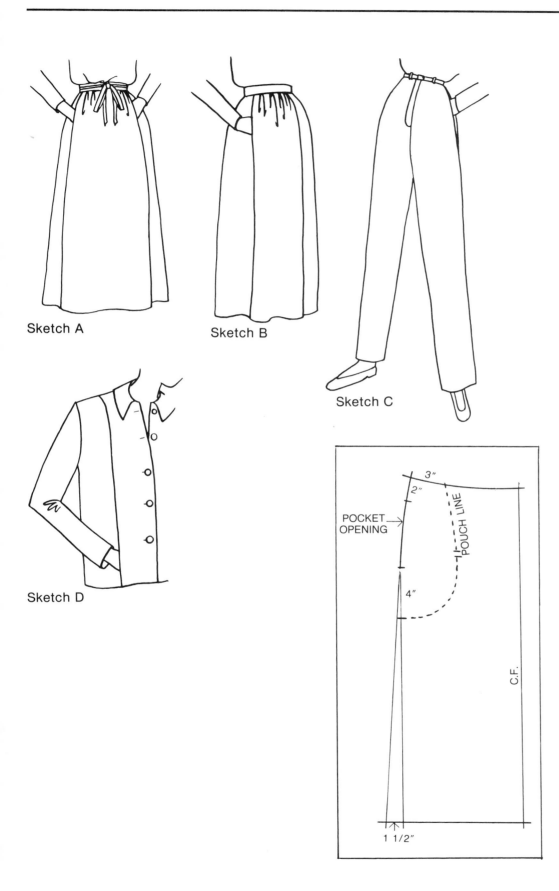

Sketch A

Sketch B

Sketch C

Sketch D

Seam pockets are used in the side seams of all types of garments as well as on surface seams such as gore and princess line seams.

FIGURE 1

A.   Use *two-dart front skirt sloper.*

B.   Cut paper approximately 18″ × 35″ (45.7 × 88.9 cm) for a 28″ (71.1 cm) skirt length.

C.   Place center front of sloper near right-hand side of paper.

D.   Outline sloper eliminating darts. Dart fullness will be absorbed into shirring.

E.   Remove sloper. True all lines crossing all intersections.

F.   Allow desired flare at side seam. Illustrated: 1½″ (3.8 cm). Draw a line from hemline up to widest part of hips.

G.   To plan position of pocket pouch line, from side seam on waistline measure in 3″ (7.6 cm). Crossmark.

H.   From waistline on side seam measure down 1″ to 2″ (2.5 to 5.1 cm). Crossmark.

I.   To plan pocket opening at side seam from crossmark measure down 5″ to 6″ (12.7 to 15.2 cm). Crossmark. To plan pocket pouch line from this crossmark measure down 4½″ (11.4 cm). Crossmark.

J.   Draw a curved line from pouch crossmark on side seam to crossmark on waistline for pocket pouch line (broken line). Place two crossmarks on pouch line ½″ (1.3 cm) apart—these will be used in garment construction.

POCKET OPENING

POUCH LINE

3″

2″

4″

C.F.

1 1/2″

FIGURE 2

A. Fold paper under at side seam. Crease a straight line to hem. *Do not follow hip curve.*

B. Trace pouch line, side seam, waistline to pouch line and all crossmarks to opposite side.

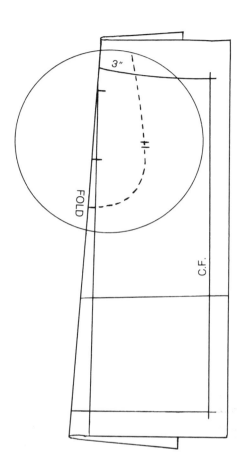

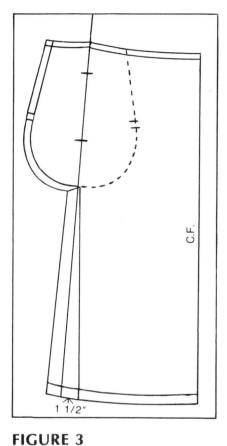

FIGURE 3

Open draft. Pencil in traced lines and crossmarks.

continued

FIGURE 4

A.   To develop back skirt follow same procedure as for front skirt with the following exception:

Place and outline skirt sloper near left-hand side of paper allowing space for skirt pocket pouch.

Note: Do not plan back pocket pouch as it must match front pouch.

B.   To develop back skirt pouch refold front side seam of draft. Match folded seam to back side seam of draft with excess paper extending under front draft. Pin.

C.   Trace pocket pouch and all crossmarks to opposite side.

D.   Remove front draft. Pencil in traced lines and crossmarks.

E.   True and balance front and back side seams and pouch together. Allow seams; cut and notch seams.

F.   Separate drafts. Allow seams to remainder of pattern.

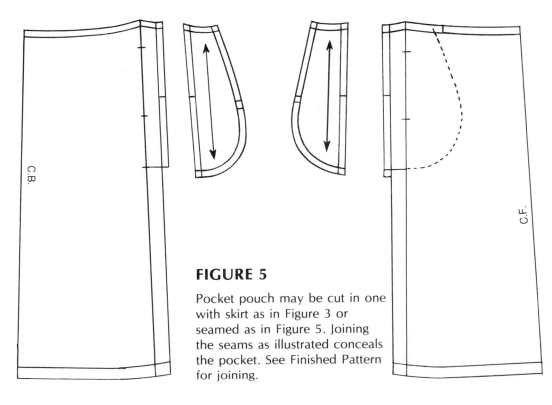

FIGURE 5

Pocket pouch may be cut in one with skirt as in Figure 3 or seamed as in Figure 5. Joining the seams as illustrated conceals the pocket. See Finished Pattern for joining.

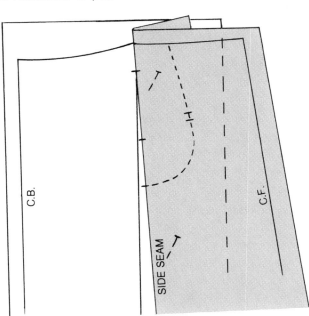

SURFACE-STITCHED SEAM POCKET
sketch 6

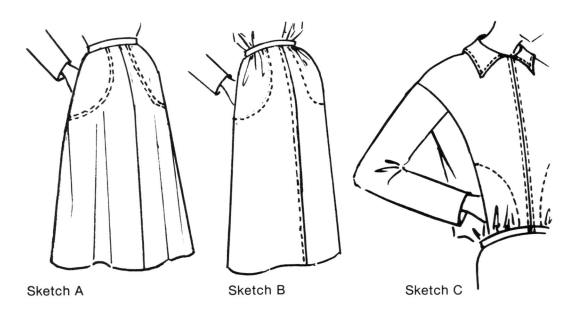

Sketch A   Sketch B   Sketch C

SKETCH A

FIGURE 1

A.   To develop front and back flared skirt refer to Four-Gored Flared Skirt.

B.   For front pocket side seam opening, from waistline measure down 1″ (2.5 cm). Crossmark. For pocket seam opening from crossmark measure down 5″ to 6″ (12.7 to 15.2 cm). Crossmark. For pouch measure down from crossmark 4½″ (11.5 cm). Crossmark.

C.   Draw a curved line from pouch crossmark at side seam to waistline ending at approximately 2″ (5.1 cm) from center front. Label *surface stitched line*.

D.   For self facing at pocket opening add 1½″ (3.8 cm). Draw a straight line ½″ (1.27 cm) below pouch line and allow seam and self hem; cut.

E.   To shape self facing at waistline fold paper under on seamline and trace waistline. Open draft. Pencil in traced line.

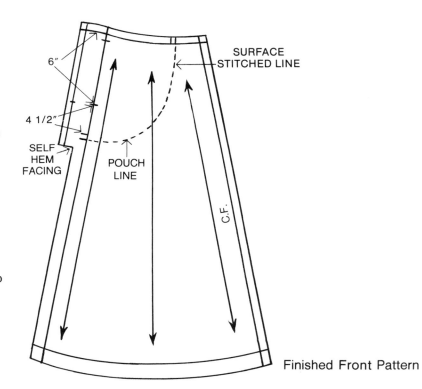

Finished Front Pattern

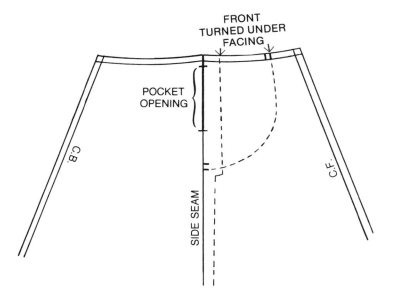

Figure 2.

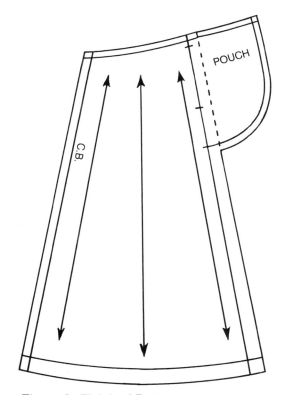

Figure 3. Finished Pattern

FIGURES 2 & 3

A.   To develop back skirt follow same procedure as for front skirt with the following exception:

Place and outline skirt near left-hand side of paper allowing space for pocket pouch

B.   To develop back skirt pouch refold front side seam of draft and match seam to back side seam with excess paper extending under front skirt. Pin.

C.   Trace surface stitched line, waistline and all crossmarks.

D.   Remove front draft. Pencil in traced lines and crossmarks.

E.   To complete pattern true side seams with front and back together. Separate sections. Allow hem and seams to remainder of pattern; cut and notch seams.

F.   Establish grainline as desired (Figures 1 and 3).

SKETCH B

This sketch illustrates basic skirt with shirred waistline and surface-stitched seam pocket.

SKETCH C

This sketch illustrates surface-stitched seam pocket on jacket.

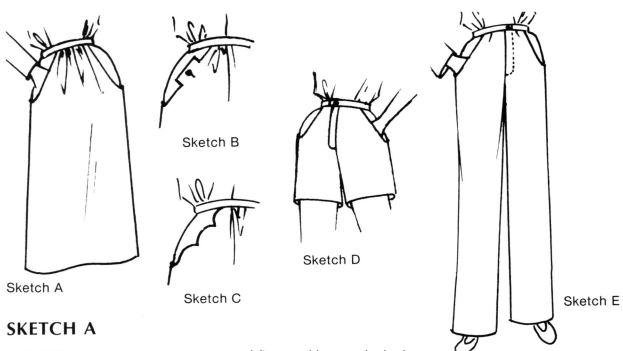

Sketch B

Sketch A

Sketch C

Sketch D

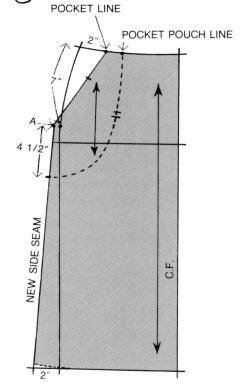

Sketch E

SKETCH A

FIGURE 1

A. Use *two-dart front waist sloper.*

B. Cut paper approximately 18″ × 35″ (45.7 × 88.9 cm) for a 28″ (71.1 cm) skirt length.

C. Place center front of sloper near right-hand edge of paper.

D. Outline sloper eliminating darts. Dart fullness will be absorbed into shirring.

E. Remove sloper. True all lines crossing all intersections.

F. To plan position of pocket line from side seam on waistline measure in 2″ (5.1 cm). Dot. From waistline on side seam measure down 7″ (17.8 cm). Dot.
Note: The pocket line may vary in shape and design as illustrated in the sketches.

G. For pocket ease from 7″ (17.8 cm) dot measure out ¼″ (0.6 cm). Dot. Label *A.*
Note: The ease is allowed so that the finished pocket will roll and fit smoothly over the body curve of the skirt. More ease may have to be added depending upon the thickness of the fabric used.

H. Draw a straight line from A to dot on waistline or shape desired for pocket line.

I. Draw a straight line from dot A to hem allowing for flare desired. Illustrated: 2″ (5.1 cm).

J. From pocket line on waistline measure towards center front 1½″ (3.8 cm). Dot. From pocket line on side seam measure down 4½″ (11.4 cm). Dot. Draw a curved line between these dots for pocket pouch line (broken line).

K. Place one crossmark on pocket line and two crossmarks on pocket pouch line to be used for garment construction.

L. Establish grainline parallel to center front.
Note: Grainline on pocket facing and pocket pouch must match grainline on skirt.

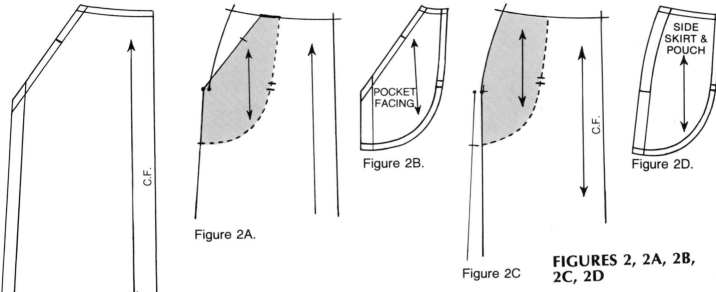

Figure 2

Figure 2A.

Figure 2B.

POCKET FACING

Figure 2C

Figure 2D.

SIDE SKIRT & POUCH

C.F.

FIGURES 2, 2A, 2B, 2C, 2D

A.   To develop pattern for skirt copy pocket line and crossmark, waistline, center front, hemline, new side seam and grainline (shaded area in Figure 1).

B.   To develop pattern for pocket facing copy shaded area in Figure 2A plus crossmarks and grainline. Figure 2B is completed pattern.

C.   To develop pattern for pocket pouch with upper skirt section copy shaded area in Figure 2C plus crossmarks at 7″ (17.8 cm) dot and pouch line and grainline. Figure 2D is completed pattern.

D.   Back skirt may be a basic one- or two-piece skirt with a 2″ (5.1 cm) flare added to side seam to balance with front skirt.

E.   To complete pattern allow hem and seams; cut and notch seams.

SKETCHES B, C, D, E

To develop pattern for these sketches follow same procedure as for sketch A. The only difference is in the shape of the pocket style line.

WELT POCKET
sketch 8

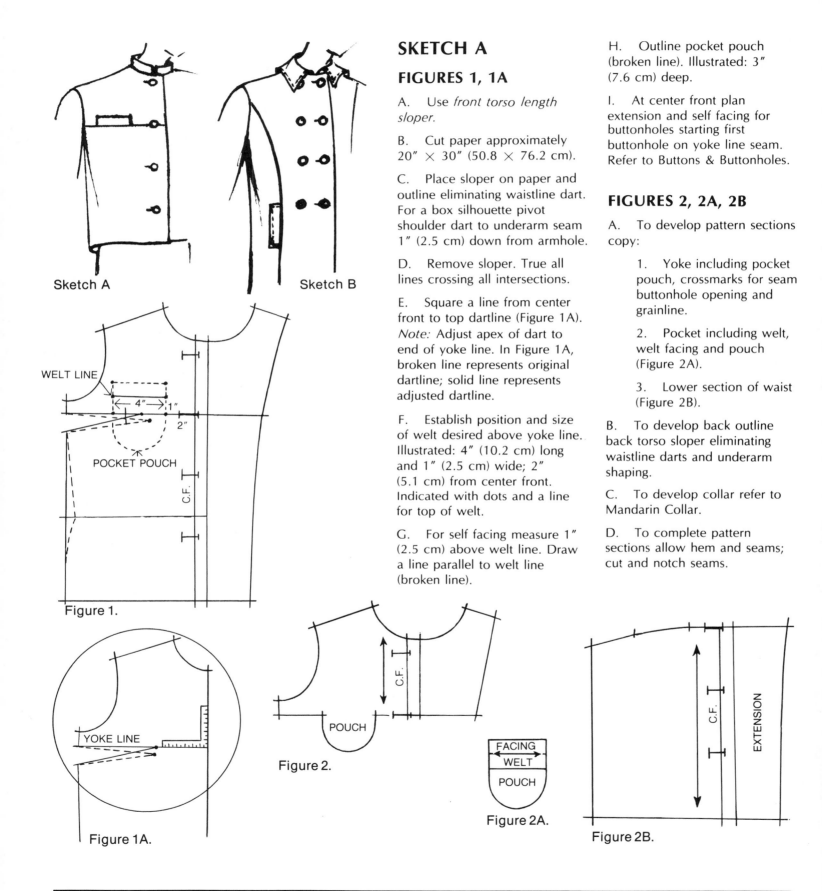

Sketch A

Sketch B

WELT LINE

4" → 1"

2"

POCKET POUCH

C.F.

Figure 1.

YOKE LINE

Figure 1A.

POUCH

C.F.

Figure 2.

FACING
WELT
POUCH

Figure 2A.

C.F.

EXTENSION

Figure 2B.

SKETCH A

FIGURES 1, 1A

A.   Use *front torso length sloper*.

B.   Cut paper approximately 20" × 30" (50.8 × 76.2 cm).

C.   Place sloper on paper and outline eliminating waistline dart. For a box silhouette pivot shoulder dart to underarm seam 1" (2.5 cm) down from armhole.

D.   Remove sloper. True all lines crossing all intersections.

E.   Square a line from center front to top dartline (Figure 1A). *Note:* Adjust apex of dart to end of yoke line. In Figure 1A, broken line represents original dartline; solid line represents adjusted dartline.

F.   Establish position and size of welt desired above yoke line. Illustrated: 4" (10.2 cm) long and 1" (2.5 cm) wide; 2" (5.1 cm) from center front. Indicated with dots and a line for top of welt.

G.   For self facing measure 1" (2.5 cm) above welt line. Draw a line parallel to welt line (broken line).

H.   Outline pocket pouch (broken line). Illustrated: 3" (7.6 cm) deep.

I.   At center front plan extension and self facing for buttonholes starting first buttonhole on yoke line seam. Refer to Buttons & Buttonholes.

FIGURES 2, 2A, 2B

A.   To develop pattern sections copy:

> 1.   Yoke including pocket pouch, crossmarks for seam buttonhole opening and grainline.
>
> 2.   Pocket including welt, welt facing and pouch (Figure 2A).
>
> 3.   Lower section of waist (Figure 2B).

B.   To develop back outline back torso sloper eliminating waistline darts and underarm shaping.

C.   To develop collar refer to Mandarin Collar.

D.   To complete pattern sections allow hem and seams; cut and notch seams.

Front & Back View

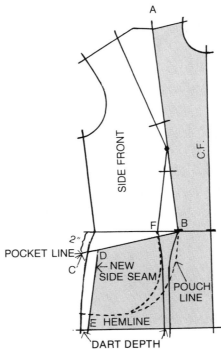

FIGURE 2

A.   To establish pocket line draw a straight line from B to side seam dropping line below waistline amount desired. Label C. Illustrated: 2″ (5.1 cm).

B.   To eliminate dart underlay on pocket section and establish new side seam:

.1.   For pocket ease measure depth of dart at waistline minus ¼″ (0.6 cm) or more depending upon thickness of fabric.

2.   From side seam at C measure in depth of adjusted dart measurement. Dot. Label D.

3.   From side seam at hemline measure in dart depth at hemline. Label E.

4.   Draw a straight line from D to E. Label new side seam.

C.   Draw pocket pouch from B at waistline to E and from F at waistline towards E depth desired (broken curved line).

FIGURE 1

A.   Use two-dart front torso sloper.

B.   Cut paper approximately 16″ × 30″ (40.6 × 76.2 cm).

C.   Outline sloper. Crossmark shoulder dartlines. Indicate waistline dartlines and apex with awl.

D.   Remove sloper. True all lines crossing all intersections.

E.   Dot waistline dartlines and apex. Label shoulder dartline nearest center front A and waistline dartline nearest center front B (as illustrated).

F.   Draw a line between A and B. If line does not cross apex, place a dot on princess line at apex (as illustrated).

G.   Draw lines from dartlines to adjusted apex.

H.   Establish bustline crossmarks at apex and 2″ (5.1 cm) above and below apex.

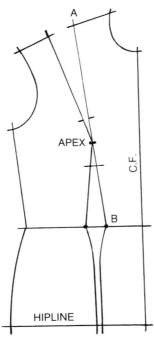

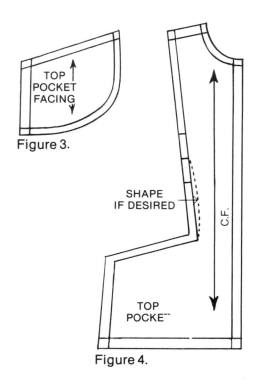

Figure 3.

Figure 4.

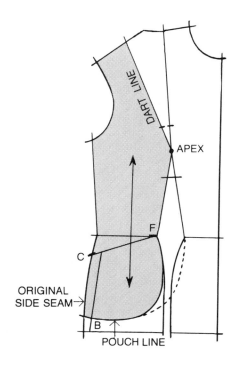

FIGURE 5

A.   On front side section establish grainline parallel to center front.

B.   Copy side front (shaded area) including grainline and crossmarks at C, waistline and bustline.

FIGURE 3

A.   For pocket facing copy pocket pouch starting at B to D, new side seam down to E, pouch line to B.

B.   Before removing pouch draft establish grainline parallel to center front.

FIGURE 4

A.   Copy center front section and crossmarks at apex (shaded area).

B.   Establish grainline parallel to center front.

C.   See dotted line for shaping at midriff area of dart if a more form-fitting garment is desired.

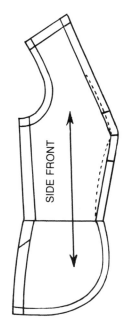

FIGURE 6

A.   See broken line for blending seamline above apex and for shaping midriff area if desired.
Note: Shaping on midriff area must match shaping on center front section.

B.   To develop back waist refer to Princess Line Back Waist.

C.   To complete pattern allow hem and seams; cut and notch seams.

Princess line seams were discussed in the Waist unit of this text. However, princess line seams are also used in designing torso-length or full-length garments without waistlines. Garments may be fitted, semi-fitted or straight and loose.

Princess lines may be used in all types of apparel such as dresses, coats, suits, pants and loungewear.

Based on the information developed for princess line waists the following sketches may also be developed.

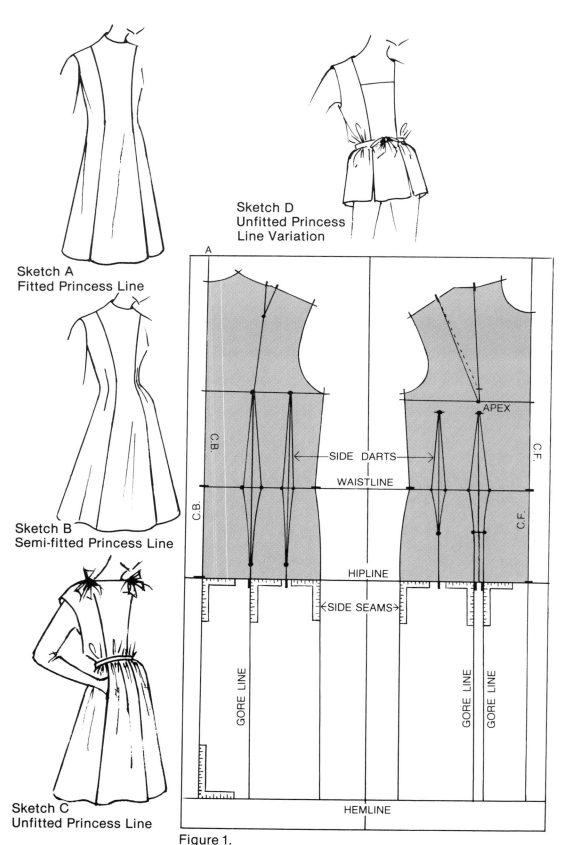

Sketch A
Fitted Princess Line

Sketch B
Semi-fitted Princess Line

Sketch C
Unfitted Princess Line

Sketch D
Unfitted Princess
Line Variation

Figure 1.

SKETCH A

FIGURES 1 & 1A

A.   Cut paper approximately 32" × 50" (81.3 × 127 cm). Cut wider if fuller flares than illustrated are desired.

B.   Draw two parallel lines in from left- and right-hand sides of paper the full length of paper. *Note:* Check parallel lines at top and bottom for accuracy.

C.   Label *center back* and *center front* (as illustrated).

D.   Label top of center back *A.*

E.   Use *front and back torso length slopers.* Measure length of center back from neckline to hipline plus 4" (10.2 cm).

F.   Measure this amount on paper down from A. Crossmark. Square a line across paper. Label *hipline.*

G.   Place slopers on paper matching center front, center back and hipline.
Note: If lines on paper and slopers are drawn accurately, all lines will match.

H.   Outline front sloper. On paper crossmark waistline and dartlines at shoulder and at hipline.

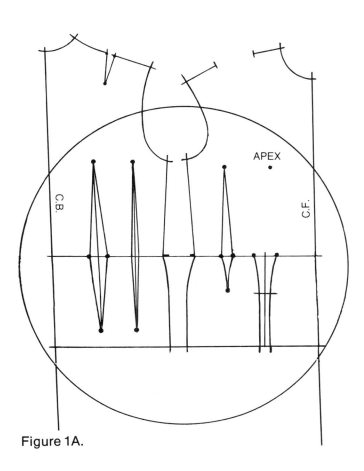

Figure 1A.

I. With awl indicate depth and top and bottom ends of waistline darts and apex.

J. Repeat with back sloper.

K. Remove slopers. True all lines crossing all intersections. Pencil in dots. Draw darts as illustrated in Figure 1A.

L. To develop skirt section:

1. From center back at waistline crossmark measure length of skirt desired. Illustrated 28" (71.1 cm). Square a line to center front. Label *hemline.*

2. Square a line from end of darts near center front and center back down to hemline (as illustrated). Label *gore lines.*

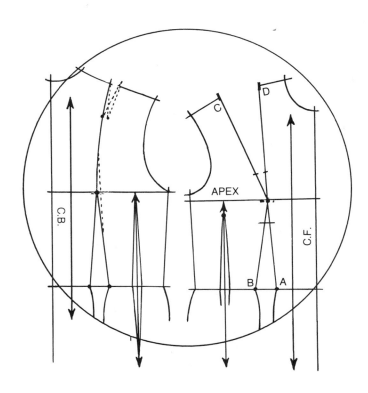

FIGURE 2

A. To develop princess line on front waist section refer to Princess Line Front Waist from Two-Dart Sloper, Sketch 1, Figure 1.

B. To develop princess line on back waist section refer to Princess Waist Line Back.

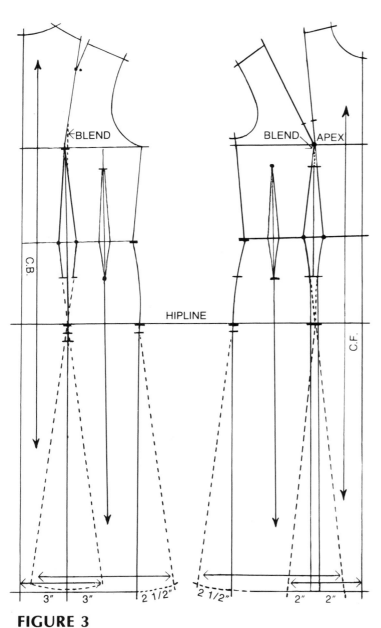

FIGURE 3

To develop skirt flares refer to
Six-Gored Flared Skirt.

FIGURE 4

A.   Copy front sections (as illustrated). Repeat for back section.

B.   To complete patterns true all lines crossing all intersections. *Note:* 1. To true balanced seams add seam allowances and refer to Trueing Vertical Seams for cutting procedure. 2. To true bustline crossmarks for notching refer to Crossmarks & Notches.

C.   Establish grainlines and skirt crossmarks (as illustrated).

D.   Allow hem and seams on remainder of pattern; cut and notch seams.

E.   Plan and copy facing. Refer to Facings.

F.   Develop sleeve desired.

SKETCH B

To achieve a semi-fitted princess line garment, eliminate small side darts.

SKETCHES C & D

To achieve an unfitted princess line garment, eliminate small side darts, reduce size of basic darts and shape of underarm seam.

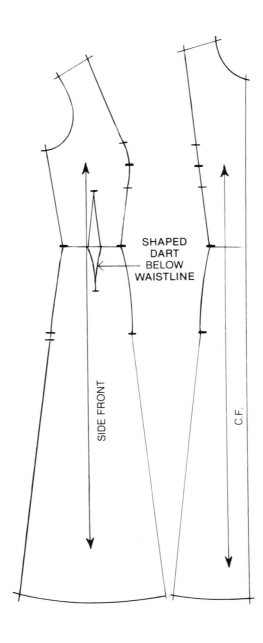

SHAPED DART BELOW WAISTLINE

SIDE FRONT

C.F.

Front & Side View

FIGURE 2

A.   Remove sloper. True all lines crossing all intersections. Draw lines for front and back shoulder darts and side darts.

B.   From crossmarks at hipline (bottom of side darts) draw a line parallel to center back and center front to hemline. Label *gore line*.

C.   Draw stylized princess lines and crossmark at armhole.

D.   To develop skirt flares as desired or illustrated refer to Six-Gored Flared Skirt.

E.   Draw bust dartline to apex. Bust dartline may be at right angles to center front (broken line) or at a slight angle (solid line). Crossmark 2″ (5.1 cm) above and below establish bust dartline and top of back dart.

F.   Establish grainlines parallel to centers. Crossmark waistline. Place one crossmark at front hipline and two crossmarks at back hipline.

FIGURE 1

A.   Cut paper approximately 32″ × 50″ (81.3 × 127 cm). Cut wider if fuller flares than illustrated are desired.

B.   Fold paper in half and crease. Open paper. Draw a line over crease. Label *grainline*.

C.   Use *front and back torso length slopers.* Place slopers on paper matching hiplines, side seams and touching underarm seams to grainline on paper.

D.   Outline slopers with one exception:

Do not outline underarm seam.

E.   On paper crossmark back waistline, shoulder darts and side dartlines at hipline.

F.   With awl indicate apex, depth of front and back side darts at waistline, top and bottom of darts and bottom of back shoulder dart.

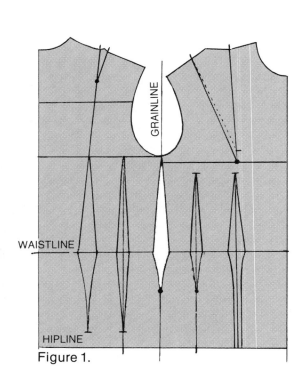

Figure 1.

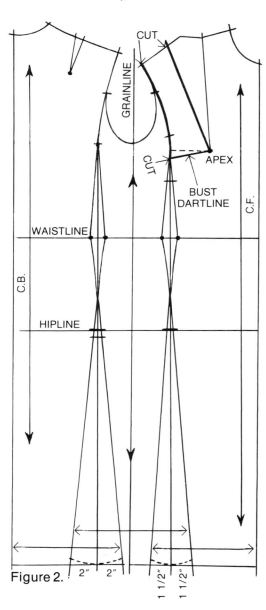

Figure 2.

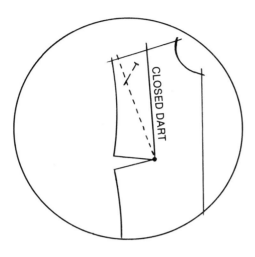

CLOSED DART

FIGURE 4

A.   To complete pattern true all lines crossing all intersections. *Note:* To true balanced seams add seam allowances and refer to Trueing Vertical Seams for cutting procedure.

B.   Allow hem and seams on remainder of pattern; cut and notch seams.

C.   Plan and copy facings. Refer to Facings.

D.   To develop sleeve refer to Short Fitted Sleeve.

FIGURE 3

A.   Copy center front section.

B.   Cut on front bust dartline to apex and shoulder dartlines nearest center to apex. Close shoulder dart and pin.

C.   Pin onto another sheet of paper. Trace all lines and crossmarks to paper.

D.   Copy center back and side sections.

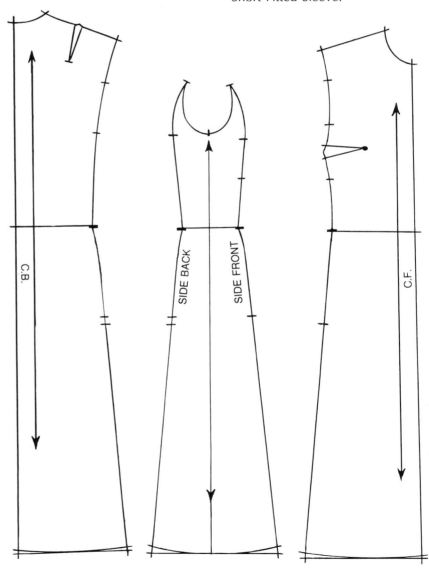

C.B.

SIDE BACK

SIDE FRONT

C.F.

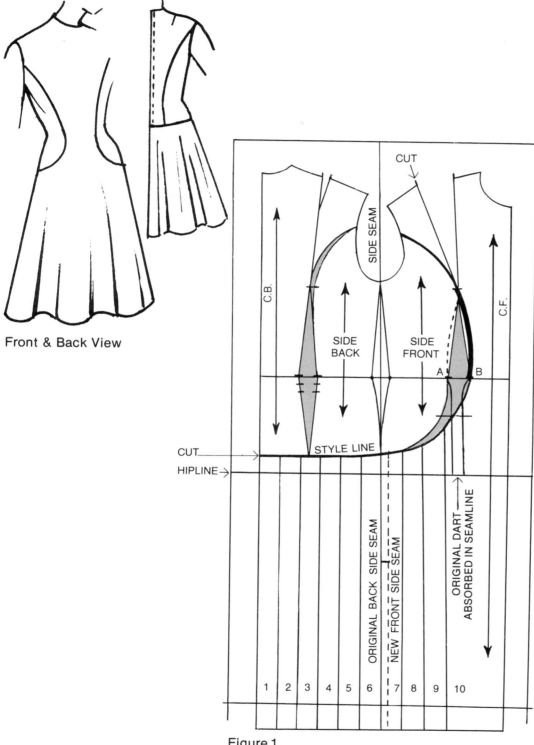

Front & Back View

Figure 1.

CUT

HIPLINE →

C.B.

SIDE SEAM

SIDE BACK

SIDE FRONT

C.F.

CUT

A   B

STYLE LINE

ORIGINAL BACK SIDE SEAM

NEW FRONT SIDE SEAM

ORIGINAL DART ABSORBED IN SEAMLINE

1 2 3 4 5 6 7 8 9 10

FIGURES 1 & 1A

A. Cut paper approximately 32″ × 50″ (81.3 × 127 cm). Cut wider if fuller flares than illustrated are desired.

B. Fold paper in half and crease. Open paper. Draw a line over crease. Label *side seam*.

C. Use *front and back torso length slopers.* Place slopers on paper matching hiplines at side seam on paper and touching underarm seams.

D. Outline slopers eliminating side darts. Indicate darts.

E. Remove slopers. True all lines crossing all intersections. Label center front dart A and B (as illustrated).

F. Establish grainlines parallel to centers.

G. Plan and draw a curved princess line from front armhole to apex (as illustrated).

H. Plan and draw a curved hipline starting at waistline at A and ending 1″ (2.5 cm) above hipline at center back (as illustrated).

I. To curve waistline dartline nearest center front, draw a line parallel to waistline across dartlines at the point where the space between the original dart underlay and the space between the stylized line and dartline nearest underarm seam are equal. See area enlarged in Figure 1A. Label *guideline.*

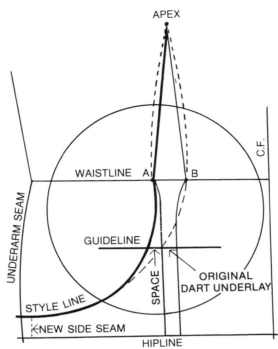

Figure 1A.

J.   From B draw lower section of curved dart crossing guideline intersection and blending line into stylized line.

Note: For a tight fit at midriff area, shape dart (broken line in Figure 1A).

K.   The two front curved hiplines will vary in length due to the shape of the dart. To adjust, measure lengths of the two curved lines from waistline to end of stylized dart towards side seam.

L.   Shorten curved line on skirt to match curved hipline on waist by eliminating the difference at side seam of skirt (broken line).

M.   Plan and draw lines for flared skirt on draft (as illustrated). Number sections.

N.   To develop back waist princess line refer to Princess Line Back Waist with Curved Seam.

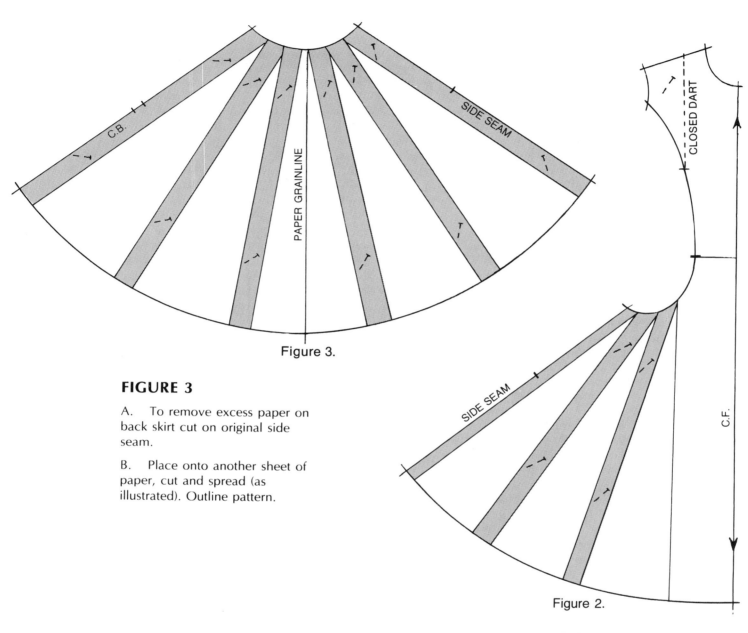

Figure 3.

Figure 2.

FIGURE 3

A.   To remove excess paper on back skirt cut on original side seam.

B.   Place onto another sheet of paper, cut and spread (as illustrated). Outline pattern.

FIGURE 2

A.   Cut draft apart on style line from center back to curved line nearest center front to armhole.

B.   Cut skirt sections apart at new side seam (broken line).

C.   Place onto another sheet of paper; cut and spread (as illustrated). Outline patterns.

FIGURE 4

To establish grainline on skirt back so that side seams will be balanced, place skirt back over skirt front matching side seams. Copy center front line as grainline.

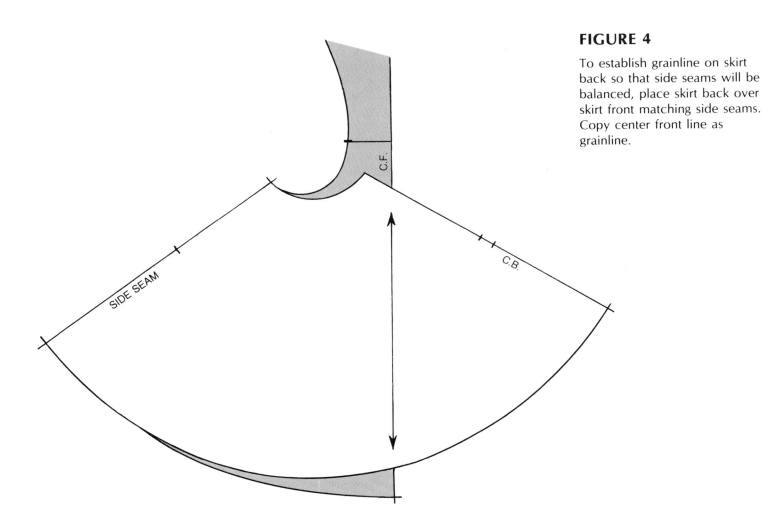

Finished Patterns

A. To complete pattern true all lines crossing all intersections. Allow hem and seams; cut and notch seams.

B. Develop sleeve desired.

C. To develop neck facings refer to Facings.

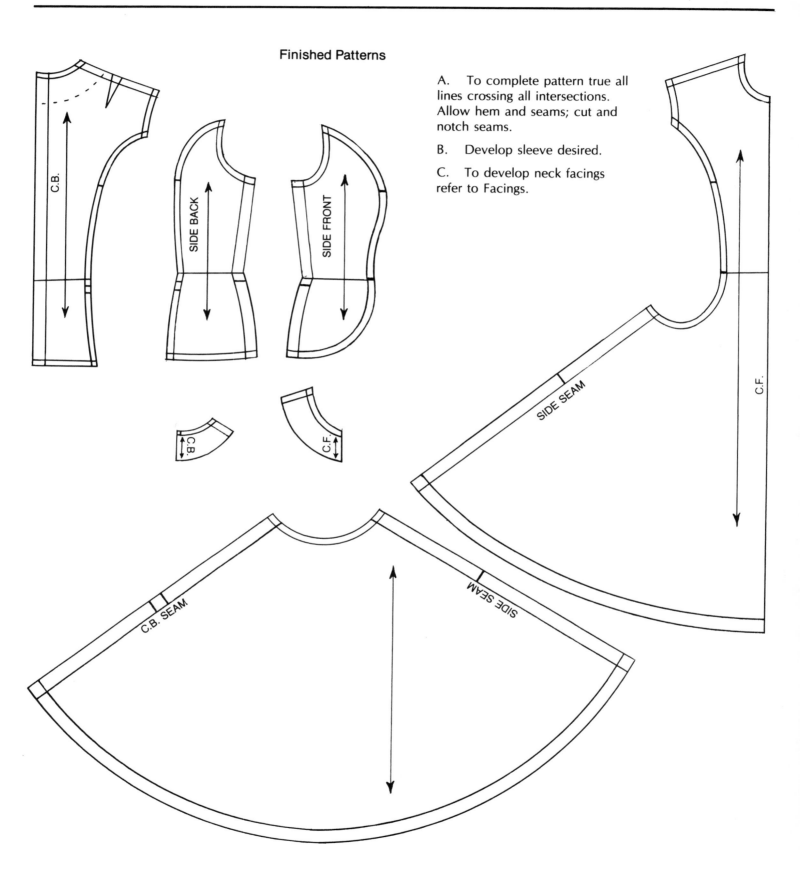

The dartless sloper may be substituted for the darted waist sloper when developing the sketches of loose fitting garments included in this text. The following sketches and instructions are a few examples of such garments.

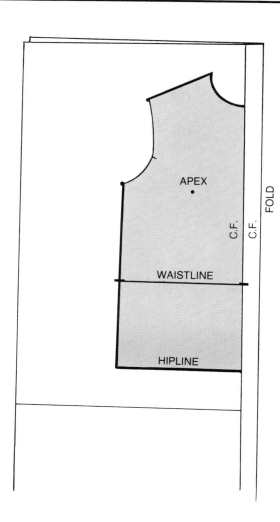

FIGURE 1

A.   Cut paper approximately 40″ × 50″ (101.6 × 127 cm).

B.   Fold paper in half. From fold measure in 1″ (2.5 cm). Draw a line parallel to fold. Label *center front.*

C.   Use *front dartless torso length sloper.* Place sloper on paper matching center fronts. Outline sloper (heavier line). Dot armhole/shoulder and armhole/underarm intersections. Crossmark waistline at underarm seam and center front. Remove sloper. Label *center front* and *hipline.*

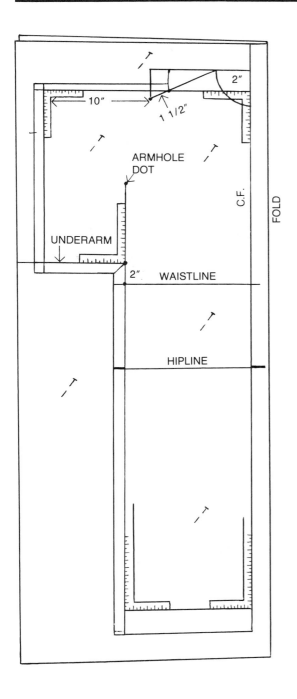

FIGURE 2

A. Draw a line between crossmarks at waistline. Label *waistline*.

B. From center front at waistline measure down desired length of skirt. Illustrated: 28" (71.1 cm). Square a line across paper from center front to side seam and up to hipline.

C. For depth of armhole, from waistline/underarm intersection measure up 2" (5.1 cm). Dot. Square a line from dot to edge of paper.

D. For bateau neckline, from dot at armhole/shoulder intersection measure in 1½" (3.8 cm). Dot.

E. Square a line from center front/neckline intersection through dot to desired length of kimono sleeve. Illustrated: 10" (25.4 cm).

F. Square a line from end of sleeve to underarm (as illustrated).
Note: Due to the design, the casual fit of the garment, the matching of the stripes, check or plaids, the back and front sections are the same with the exception of an opening at center back.

G. Trace all finished lines to opposite side.

H. Allow hem and seams; seam at neckline should be 2" (5.1 cm) to serve as a facing.

I. Pin paper securely to prevent shifting when cutting. Cut excess paper from hem and all seams with one exception. Lift front section at center front and cut on center front line retaining seam at center back.
Note: If front opening is desired, cut on center back retaining seam on center front.

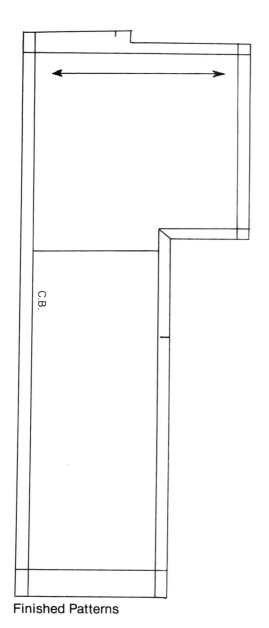

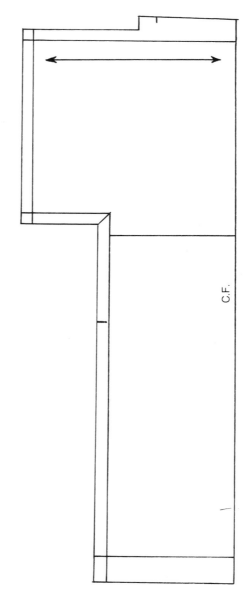

Finished Patterns

FIGURE 3

A.   Turn pinned draft to opposite side. Pencil in all traced lines. Label *center back*. *Note:* If developed accurately, the center back seam allowance should be 1″ (2.5 cm).

B.   Separate front and back sections.

C.   Indicate stripe line (grainline) as illustrated.

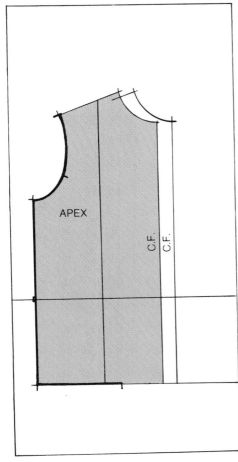

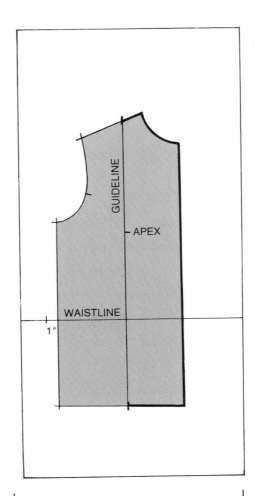

Figure 2.

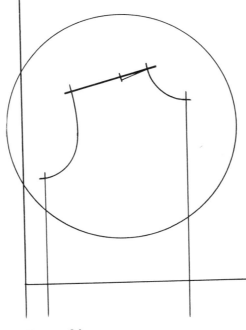

Figure 2A.

FIGURE 1

A. Cut paper approximately 18″ × 40″ (45.7 × 101.6 cm).

B. From bottom edge of paper measure up hip length plus 6″ (15.2 cm). Draw a line parallel to bottom edge of paper. Label *waistline.*

C. Use *front dartless torso length sloper.* Draw a line on sloper parallel to center front from shoulderline to hipline through apex. Label *guideline.*

D. Place sloper on paper matching waistlines allowing margin at center front for extension and collar.

E. Place a crossmark on paper at hipline and shoulderline at each end of guideline.

F. Outline sloper from crossmark at shoulder to neckline, neckline, center front and hipline to crossmark (heavier line).

G. With sloper in position, from waistline at underarm measure out 1″ (2.5 cm). Crossmark.

FIGURES 2 & 2A

A. Move sloper on waistline until underarm seam of sloper touches crossmark at waistline and center front of sloper is parallel to original center front.

B. Outline remainder of sloper (heavier line).

C. Remove sloper. Draw a line connecting shoulderline (enlarged area in Figure 2A).

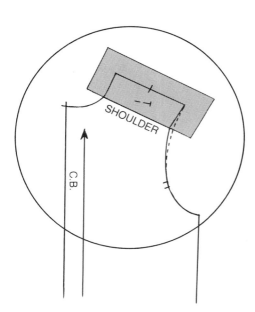

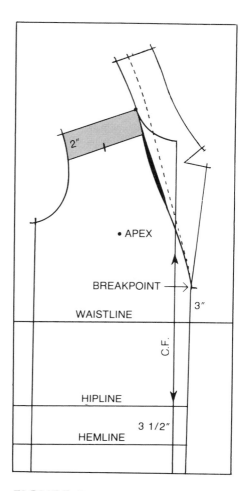

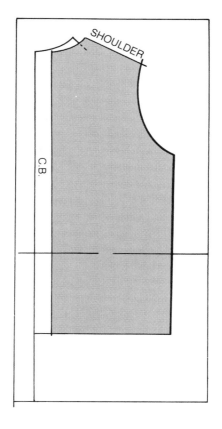

FIGURE 3

A.   Extend lines at center front and underarm seam length of shirt desired. Illustrated: 3½" (8.9 cm) from hipline.

B.   To develop collar refer to revere and shawl collars, in Collar unit.

C.   For a lowered front shoulderline and yoke effect, from shoulderline measure down 2" (5.1 cm). Draw a line parallel to shoulderline (shaded area). Add crossmark for joining (as illustrated).

FIGURE 4

A.   For back, use *back dartless torso length sloper.*

B.   To develop back section follow same procedure as for front. Shift back 1" (2.5 cm).

C.   To adjust back shoulderline, copy front shoulder yoke section and crossmark. See shaded area in Figure 3. Label *shoulder* (as illustrated).

D.   Cut away excess paper only on shoulderline of yoke draft.

FIGURE 4A

A.   Place cut yoke to back matching shoulderlines. Pin or tape together.

B.   Blend at armhole/neckline intersection if necessary (broken line at armhole).

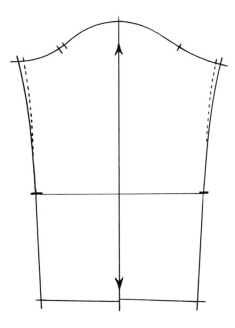

FIGURE 5

A. To develop sleeve, copy straight sleeve sloper.

B. To shorten cap refer to Short Sleeve with Shortened Sleeve Cap.

C. Check armhole of sleeve to armhole of waist. Ease over cap area should not exceed ½" (1.3 cm). If more than ½", decrease at underarm seam and blend (broken line).

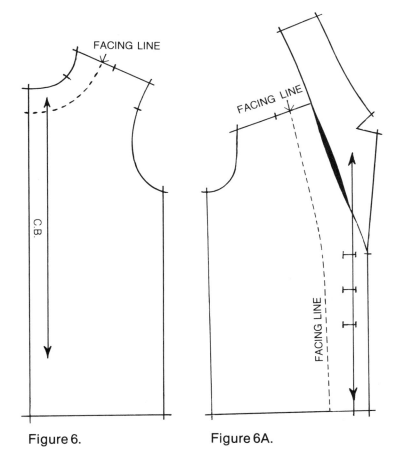

Figure 6.   Figure 6A.

FIGURES 6 & 6A

To complete all pattern sections:

A. To plan buttonholes refer to Buttons & Buttonholes.

B. To plan front and back neck facings refer to Facings.

C. Establish grainlines (as illustrated). Allow hem and seams; cut and notch seams.

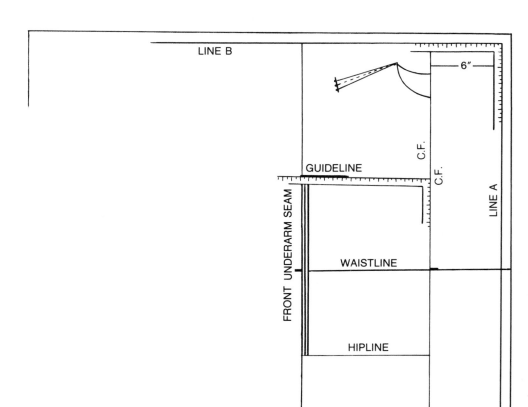

FIGURE 1

A. Cut paper approximately 40″ × 50″ (101.6 × 127 cm).

B. Draw a line near right-hand edge of paper extending line full length of paper. Label *line A*. Square a line from end of line A across top edge of paper. Label *line B*.

C. From line A measure in 6″ (15.2 cm). Draw a line parallel to line A. Label *center front*. Recheck lines for accuracy. Area between center front and line A allows for extension and narrow self facing.

D. Use *front dartless torso length sloper*. Place sloper on paper matching center fronts. Outline sloper omitting armhole. Dot armhole/underarm and armhole/shoulderline intersections and crossmark waistline at center front and at underarm seam. Remove sloper. True lines. Draw in waistline extending line to line A.

E. With L square on center front extending to armhole/underarm seam dot, draw a short guideline from dot (heavier line).

F. Place back sloper over draft matching centers and neckline/shoulderline intersections.

G. Outline neckline, shoulder and underarm. Dot end of shoulder and underarm.

H. To balance shoulderline for matching stripes, plaids and checks, place a dot in center between two shoulderlines. Draw a new shoulderline from dot to shoulder/neckline intersections.
Note: If shoulders do not match (as illustrated), refer to Two-piece Kimono Sleeve Sloper with Gusset and Waistline Darts for Stripes, Plaids and checks, Figure 7 and 7C, to adjust.

I. To balance underarm seams for matching, place a dot between two underarm seams. Draw a new underarm seam from dot down to hipline. *Note:* If a fuller look is desired, underarm seam need not be balanced. Use front underarm seam and continue line up to top edge of paper for sleeve joining and extend line down full length of paper for side seam (see Figure 2).

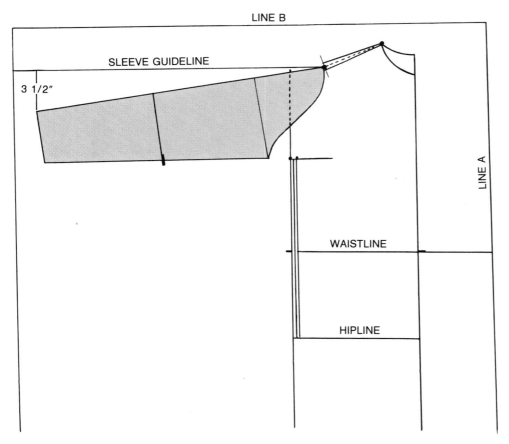

LINE B

SLEEVE GUIDELINE

3 1/2"

LINE A

WAISTLINE

HIPLINE

FIGURE 2

A.   To develop sleeve draw a line parallel to line B from adjusted shoulderline dot. Label *sleeve guideline.*

B.   Use *basic sleeve sloper.* Fold sloper in half. Place sleeve cap of folded sloper to shoulderline dot. Pivot sloper from this point to height desired. Illustrated: 3½″ (8.9 cm) below sleeve guideline at wristline.

C.   Outline sleeve sloper omitting armhole. Crossmark elbow on paper. Remove sloper. True overarm seam and wristline, crossing intersections. Blend shoulder if necessary.

FIGURE 3

A.   For depth of armhole from original armhole/underarm seam dot measure down 2½" (6.4 cm). Dot.

B.   For width at wrist from wristline/underarm seam intersection measure down 1" (2.5 cm). Draw a new underarm seamline (as illustrated).

C.   For length of garment from center front at waistline measure down length desired. Dot. Illustrated: 28" (71.1 cm). Square a line from dot to side seam.

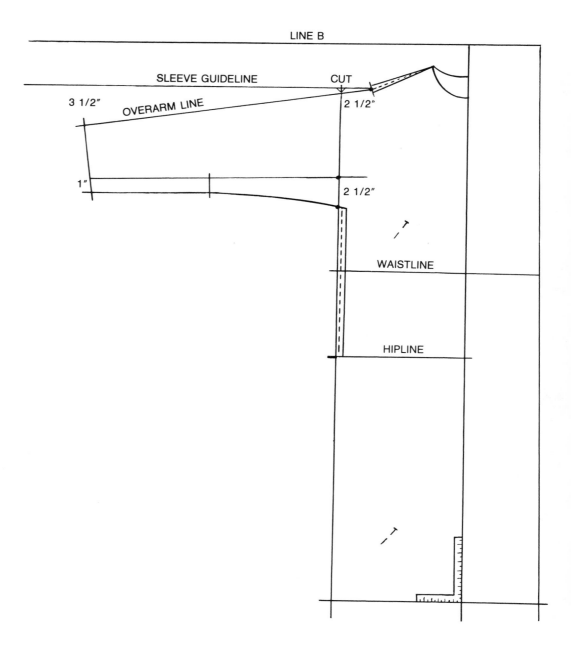

DRESS DEVELOPED FROM DARTLESS SLOPER
sketch 3 continued   FOR STRIPES, PLAIDS, CHECKS

ORIGINAL ARMHOLE

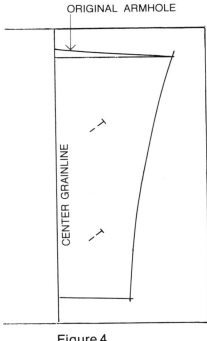

Figure 4.

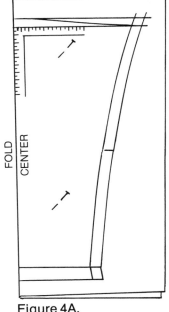

Figure 4A.

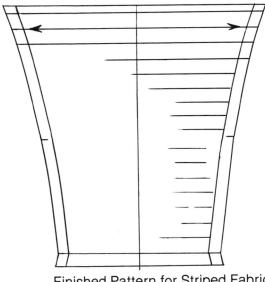

Finished Pattern for Striped Fabric

FIGURES 4 & 4A

A.   To complete sleeve cut another sheet of paper approximately 27" (68.6 cm) square. Draw a line through center of paper. Label *center grainline.*

B.   Match center grainline on paper to overarm line of sleeve. Pin. Copy sleeve and crossmark elbow.

C.   Remove sleeve. Fold paper under on center grainline. Pin. True all lines crossing all intersections.

D.   To establish stripe line square a line from fold through armhole/underarm seam intersection. Allow hem at wristline and seams. Cut and notch seams. Trace all lines to opposite side.
Note: If plain fabric is used, retain original armhole.

E.   Open sleeve. Pencil in all traced lines.

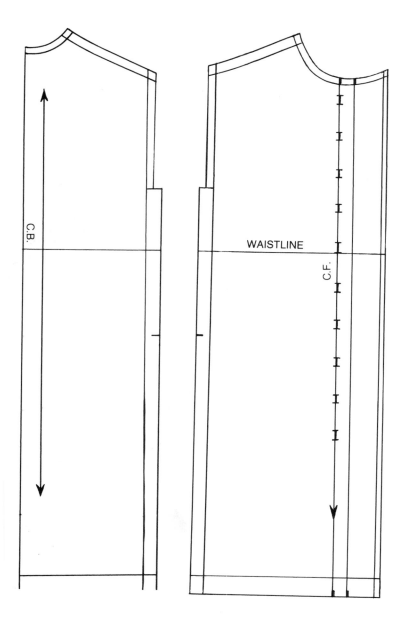

FIGURE 5

A.   To complete back and front, pin draft (Figure 3) securely to another sheet of paper.
Note: Back and front are the same except for necklines and center front opening.

B.   Trace center line, hemline, underarm seam up to shoulderline to opposite side. Trace shoulderline and back neckline.

C.   Allow hem and seams except at necklines and centers. Cut and notch seams.

D.   Turn pinned draft to opposite side and true all lines. Label *center back.*

E.   Separate front and back sections. Add seam to back neckline. Cut away excess paper from neckline and center back.

F.   To plan buttonholes refer to Buttons & Buttonholes.

G.   To plan front and back neck facings refer to Facings. With facing folded on extension line add seam to neckline. Cut and notch seam.

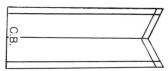

FIGURE 6

To develop collar refer to One-Piece Mandarin Collar.